Hybrid HTML Design

A Multi-Browser HTML Reference

Kevin Ready

Janine Warner

New Riders

New Riders Publishing, Indianapolis, Indiana

HYBRID HTML DESIGN

By Kevin Ready and Janine Warner

Published by:

New Riders Publishing
201 West 103rd Street
Indianapolis, IN 46290 USA

Copyright © 1996 by New Riders Publishing

Printed in the United States of America 1 2 3 4 5 6 7 8 9 0

Library of Congress Cataloging-in-Publication Data

CIP data available upon request

WARNING AND DISCLAIMER

Publisher	*Don Fowley*
Publishing Manager	*Jim LeValley*
Marketing Manager	*Mary Foote*
Managing Editor	*Carla Hall*

Product Development Specialist
Sean Angus

Project Editor
Sarah Kearns

Technical Editor
Rich Evers

Associate Marketing Manager
Tamara Apple

Acquisitions Coordinator
Tracy Turgeson

Publisher's Assistant
Karen Opal

Cover Designer
Karen Ruggles

Cover Production
Aren Howell

Production Manager
Kelly Dobbs

Production Team Supervisor
Laurie Casey

Production Analysts
Jason Hand
Bobbi Satterfield

Production Team
Dan Caparo
Kim Cofer
Terrie Deemer
Tricia Flodder
Christine Tyner
Karen Walsh

Indexer
Carol Sheehan

ABOUT THE AUTHORS

Kevin Ready is a freelance multimedia consultant. He has taught HTML and multimedia, as well as desktop publishing and office software products, for the past five years. In addition to teaching, Kevin has designed internal and public Web sites for companies such as VISA International, @Home, and others. Prior to Web development, he freelanced for many Fortune 500 companies, including Price Waterhouse, Levi's, and others, developing custom solutions using many standard office software products. He is presently the Webmaster of PDT at "http://www.onthemap.com," as well as one of the founders of Browser by Design at "http://www.browserbydesign.com." Kevin has degrees in French and International Relations, a background in music, and speaks several European languages.

Janine Warner is a freelance writer, teacher, and Internet consultant living in Northern California. After working for more than eight years as a reporter and editor at several California newspapers, she discovered the Internet and the World Wide Web in late 1994. Drawing on her background in journalism, she has contributed to more than a dozen Web sites, often coordinating teams of graphic designers, programmers, editors, and HTML authors. Her client list can be found at "http://www.janine.com/clients." A featured writer for *Publish Magazine,* Janine's stories and reviews focus on the World Wide Web and HTML authoring tools. She earned a degree in Journalism and Spanish at the University of Massachusetts, Amherst, and maintains her view that information has the power to change lives and make the world a better place. Janine is a founder of Browser by Design.

Both authors are contributing 10 percent of their share of the book's net profits to organizations providing hardware, software, and training to children and adults in inner city areas. If you are interested in contributing products or services, or know an organization that could benefit from this service, please direct your browser to "http://www.browserbydesign.com/," and pass the news to a colleague.

TRADEMARK ACKNOWLEDGMENTS

DEDICATION

This book is dedicated to all of the frustrated HTML designers looking for a practical and comprehensive HTML resource, one that is up-to-date with all the latest breaking news and developments on the Web. We believe this will prove to be the book you've been waiting for—the one that has all the answers.

ACKNOWLEDGMENTS

As Janine and I began to put together the acknowledgments list, we knew it would be difficult to include everyone to the extent that they inspired us, or became involved with this project. We were fortunate to have broad support from almost everyone that understood what we were covering in the book. Tips here, tricks there—seems like everyone threw in a little bit to expand our book's content!

For all of you folks who had to put up with our 3 a.m. phone calls, or our excuses for not having time to spend with you (usually after we woke you up), thank you for your extreme patience and charitable acts of kindness. For our clients who have seen our participation atrophy in recent months, this book is for you, and we hope you feel, as we do, that it merited the time to break away from our other projects.

Both Janine and I would like to express our strongest acknowledgments for the New Riders staff for believing in us, for believing in the strength of the book, for letting us do our own desktop publishing, and for giving us color pages! Sean Angus, in particular, was a great help in editing and inspiring the content of this book. Sarah Kearns and Rich Evers each helped keep our prose reined in. Tracy Turgeson was the first person I spoke with at New Riders, and remained diligent throughout the project. A special thanks to another New Riders' author, Lynda Weinman, for her valuable advice and guidance and her much-needed book, *Designing Web Graphics*.

Thanks in advance to those individuals at New Riders and Macmillan who we will continue to work with in the immediate future, including Mary Foote, Marty Roan, and Michelle McCracken. Thanks to Susan Skipper of Prentice Hall for believing the book should be translated into Spanish. For all the other folks behind the scenes, including Don Fowley, Jim LeValley, Carla Hall, and anyone who we have not mentioned, thank you each for your participation in this project. Without your involvement, this book would not have been possible.

Many of the illustrations in the book and on the Web site were designed by Phillip Sanchez, assisted by Caren Sanchez. Phil is an excellent artist, and he was, in fact, the student mentioned on the first page of the introduction. Special thanks go to Sonia Quintero for her keen editing eye and the fresh perspective of a new HTML student. Mutual thanks are also expressed to many of the individuals and companies listed in our respective acknowledgments.

KEVIN'S ACKNOWLEDGMENTS

This book is dedicated to Guy and Brenda Ready, as testament to the will to live and the persistence to never quit in the face of adversity. This book is presented as an example that your kind acts and selfless dedication to others outlived the time you had here on Earth. For Christopher Laxson, this book is dedicated in the hopes that this may inspire you to pursue your own dreams, whatever they may be.

Among the many people who have given their energy, time, and support to me over the years, I must thank Riley and Dalton Greene, Karyn and Tom Greene, and David Ready for their ongoing patience and understanding. Having a family that can be as supportive as you means more to me than I can put into words. I would also like to express my sincerest gratitude, respect, and appreciation to María Terésa López García for her unconditional love and support over the past four years. She has just completed a doctoral dissertation in Madrid, and has consistently inspired me in the many years that we have known each other.

This book would not have materialized if not for Steven Warren, who hired me as a multimedia instructor and supported the development of Web curriculum; John Gehlken, who first put the idea of writing a book into my head; Janine Warner, who, in addition to being the book's co-author, provided the initial impetus to get the book proposal together; and to my students who supported my decision to take a hiatus from teaching to dedicate myself to this book.

Of the many individuals who have helped me from different companies, I would like to thank Jeffrey Menz, John Garris, Federico Romano, and the rest of the gang at Oracle; Yves Piguet, the designer of GifBuilder and Clip2Gif; Park Espenschade and Emil Varona, whom I met at Visa International; John Goecke from @Home; Bryan Byun from Netscape; Bob Monzell from Quark; Martin Marshall from Communications Week; and, not least of all, Professors Devere Pentony, Ray Miller, and Phillip King of San Francisco State University for providing me inspiration through their boundless dedication and commitment to the art of teaching.

JANINE'S ACKNOWLEDGMENTS

First, I must thank my co-author, Kevin Ready, for conceiving this book and for refusing to settle for the limitations of the browsers that view our work. I thank him for his vision and persistence, for his success in finding ways to make Web sites attractive to all our viewers, and for pushing so hard to get it all done so quickly.

I want to thank my mother, Malinda McCain, for showing me that I could accomplish anything I chose to do and for supporting me in every project I've undertaken. I thank her for being the best copy editor I've ever known and for making every deadline, even when it meant e-mailing her edits back before dawn on the west coast.

Thanks to my father, Robin Warner, for his confidence and encouragement, and to Helen Welford and Janice Webster for being such wonderful partners to my parents and great friends to me. To David Mitchell for being my mentor, for giving me my first job as a reporter at the Pulitzer Prize-winning *Point Reyes Light Newspaper*, and for letting me build a Web site for him as my first project on the Net. And thanks to my many other Web site clients: The Oracle Review, Arts and Healing Network, MicroDesign Resources, Coastal Lodging, Investor's Edge, and all of the gang at Aslan.

Thanks to Sonia Quintero for being such a great business partner and such a wonderful friend, for all her assistance with the book, for being a fabulous cook, and for helping me keep up with my Spanish. To Víctor Reyes for encouraging me to take care of myself, to Fran Reyes for staying up late to gather software for the CD-ROM, and to Ken Milburn for his insightful comments and wise perspective.

A special thanks to Jeanette Borzo and the other editors at *Publish Magazine,* who taught me so much about writing software reviews. To my journalism professors at the University of Massachusetts, Amherst, for teaching me to do thorough research and to appreciate the power of news and information. To my favorite alumni friends, María Sacchetti and Sharon Wilke, for never letting me abandon my passion for writing.

And a final, heartfelt thank you from all those who know them to Grumpy, Blacky, and Gypsy (Kevin's cats) for not completely destroying the project as they trampled across the keyboards or shed cat hairs in the print—and, lest we forget, the occasional moments they pay us attention to keep our minds off the more mundane aspects of existence.

CONTENTS AT A GLANCE

Introduction xix

Chapter 1: The Browsers 1

Chapter 2: HTML Authoring Tools 29

Chapter 3: HTML 2 87

Chapter 4: HTML 3 123

Chapter 5: Browser-Specific Design 163

Chapter 6: The Art of Hybrid HTML Design 227

Chapter 7: Rich Media File Formats 277

Chapter 8: Server Side Issues .319

Chapter 9: On the Horizon 347

Introduction to the Appendices 355

Appendix A: HTML Tag and Attribute Support 357

Appendix B: HTML Editors 365

Appendix C: Special Characters 367

Appendix D: MIME Types 369

Appendix E: Online Resources 371

Index 389

TABLE OF CONTENTS

Introduction xix

Chronology xx
The World Wide Web xxi
    HTML xxi
    Sample HTML Document .xxiii
Web Sites and Webmasters xxiv
    Word Processors xxiv
    Desktop Publishers xxiv
    Database and Computer Programmers xxv
    Graphic Artists xxv
The Layout of the Book xxvi
New Riders Publishing xxvii

Chapter 1: The Browsers 1

Introduction to Browsers 2
    Designing for Multiple Browsers 3
Netscape Navigator 2.0 4
Internet Explorer 2.0 6
Oracle PowerBrowser 1.0 8
HotJava Alpha 1.0 10
NCSA Mosaic 2.0 12
CompuServe Spry Mosaic .04.10.9.20 14
America Online 2.5 16
Prodigy 2.0d 18
Cyberdog Beta Release 2 20
PointCast Network PCN Browser 22
Other Browsers 24
    Accent Multilingual Mosaic .24
    Alis Multilingual Browser 25
    The Lynx Browser 25
    GNN Works 26
    Virtual Places 26
    Opera Browser 27
    WebExplorer 27
Summary 28

Chapter 2: HTML Authoring Tools 29

HTML Editors and Converters 30
Word Processors 32
Special Characters 32
Advanced Word Processing Features 35
   Macro and Template Usage 35
   Search and Replace 35
   Spell Check and Thesaurus 35
   Mail Merge 36
Converters and Assistants for Word Processors 37
   HTML Transit 37
   Internet Assistant for Microsoft Word 38
   Cyberleaf 38
   Web Publisher 39
   ANT_HTML 39
   WebAuthor 40
   WordPerfect Internet Publisher 40
   2 HTML 40
Spreadsheets 41
   Advanced Spreadsheet Functions 42
      Macro and Other Programming 42
      Application Design 42
Excel Converters 43
   XL2HTML.XLS 43
   Excel to HTML Converter Macro 43
   Excel to HTML Conversion Utility 44
Databases 45
Choosing a Database Solution 47
Database and Middleware Applications 48
   Illustra 48
   dbWeb 49
   Oracle WebServer 2.0 50
   Cold Fusion 51
   4W Publisher 52
      HTMakeL Database Merge 52
HTML Text Editors 53
   HTML Assistant Pro 2 V2.0 54
   HotDog V2.0 56
   World Wide Web Weaver V1.1.1 58
   Aardvark Pro V2.0.4 60
   BBEdit V3.5 62
   HTMLed Pro V1.1 64
   Arachnid V0.5 65

Other HTML Text Editors . . . .*.66*
    Webber V1.1 . . . .*.66*
    WebEdit V1.2 . . . .*.66*
    HTML Easy! Pro V1.3 . . . .*.66*
HTML WYSIWYG Editors . . . .*.67*
    FrontPage V1.0a . . . .*.68*
    PageMill V1.0 . . . .*.70*
    SiteMill V1.0 . . . .*.72*
    Navigator Gold V1.0b2 . . . .*.74*
    GNNPress V1.1 . . . .*.76*
    HotMetal Pro V2.0 . . . .*.78*
Desktop Publishing Converters . . . .*.80*
    BeyondPress V1.0 . . . .*.80*
    HexWeb XT V1.1 . . . .*.83*
    Collect HTML V1.3.2 . . . .*.83*
    PageMaker . . . .*.84*
        Other PageMaker Converters Include: . . . .*.84*
    FrameMaker Conversion Programs . . . .*.85*
        WebWorks Light and Pro . . . .*.85*
        WebMaker 2 . . . .*.85*
        Other FrameMaker Converters . . . .*.85*
Summary . . . .*.86*

Chapter 3: HTML 2 . . . .*.87*

Document Elements . . . .*.88*
    <HTML> . . . .*.88*
    <HEAD> . . . .*.88*
    <BODY> . . . .*.88*
    <!..comment.> . . . .*.88*
Head Elements . . . .*.89*
    <BASE> . . . .*.89*
    <LINK> . . . .*.89*
    <ISINDEX> . . . .*.89*
    <TITLE> . . . .*.89*
Body Elements . . . .*.91*
    Text Formats . . . .*.91*
        <H1, H2, H3...H6> . . . .*.91*
        <STRONG> . . . .*.91*
        <EM> . . . .*.91*
        <B> . . . .*.91*
        <I> . . . .*.91*
        <PRE> . . . .*.91*
        <S> . . . .*.91*

<U> *91*
<ADDRESS> *92*
<BLOCKQUOTE> *92*
<CITE> *92*
<CODE> *92*
<KBD> *92*
<PLAINTEXT> *92*
<SAMP> *92*
<STRIKE> *92*
<TT> *92*
<VAR> *92*
<XMP> *92*
Which Text Format is Most Appropriate? *93*
Listing Tags *99*
The List Item Tag *99*
<li> *99*
Ordered Lists *99*
<OL> *99*
Unordered Lists *99*
<UL> *99*
Definition Lists *100*
<DL> *100*
<DT> *100*
<DD> *100*
Directory Lists *100*
<DIRECTORY> *100*
<DIR> *100*
<MENU> *100*
Which List is Most Appropriate? *101*
Spacing Tags *107*
*
* *107*
<P> *107*
Image Tag *108*
<IMG> *108*
Anchor Tag *109*
<A> *109*
Horizontal Rule Tag *109*
<HR> *110*
Form Tags *111*
<FORM> *111*
<INPUT> *111*
Form Input Types *112*
<TEXTAREA> *113*
<SELECT> *113*

<OPTION> 114
    Design Considerations 120
Summary 122

Chapter 4: HTML 3 123

Head Elements 124
    <LINK> 124
    <META> 125
Body Elements 127
    The Body Tag 127
        <HR> 129
        <P> 129
    The Image Tag 130
    Listing Tags 131
        <UL> 131
        <OL> 131
        <li> 131
        <LH> 131
Using HTML 2 Tags with HTML 3 Attributes 132
    Effectively Integrating HTML 3 Attributes for HTML 2 Browsers 139
Table Tags 140
    Approaching Table Design 140
        <TABLE> 141
        <CAPTION> 141
        <TR> 141
        <TD> 142
        <TH> 142
        Steps to Ensure Effective Display of Tables 154
Font and Text Formatting Tags 155
    <FONT> 155
    <SUB> 155
    <SUP> 155
    <BIG> 155
    <SMALL> 155
Other HTML 3 Tags 156
    <CENTER> 156
    <DIV> 156
    <MAP> 156
    <AREA> 156
Integrating HTML 2 and HTML 3 Tags 157
Summary 162

Chapter 5: Browser-Specific Design 163

Navigator 2.0 . . . . *164*
   Extensions to HTML 2 and HTML 3 . . . . *165*
      <BASEFONT> *165*
      <BLINK> *165*
      <IMG> *165*
      <NOBR> *165*
      <WBR> *165*
      <TITLE> *166*
      <BODY> *166*
      The Embed Tags *168*
      <EMBED> *168*
      <NOEMBED> *168*
      Embed Tag Usage *169*
   Frames *170*
      <FRAMESET> *170*
      <NOFRAMES> *170*
      <FRAME> *171*
      Targets Revisited *174*
      Frame Tag Usage *175*
   JavaScript *179*
      <SCRIPT> *179*
      <! - -//> *179*
      Event Handlers *180*
      Statements *181*
         Functions *182*
         Objects *183*
         Properties *183*
         Methods *184*
         JavaScript Usage *184*
   Java *189*
      <APPLET> *189*
      <PARAM> *189*
   Navigator 3 and Beyond *190*
      Public Key Cryptography *191*
      <CERTIFICATE> *192*
      <PAYORDER> *192*
   Navigator 2.0 Summary *193*
   Internet Explorer 2.0 . . . . *194*
      Internet Explorer Tags *195*
      <MARQUEE> *195*
      <BGSOUND> *196*

Internet Explorer HTML Attributes 196
        <AREA> 196
        <HR> 196
        <BODY> 197
        <FONT> 197
        Image Tag Attributes 198
        Table Tag Attributes 199
        Explorer Tag Usage 200
    Explorer 3.0 206
        <FRAME> 206
        <OBJECT> 206
        <SCRIPT> 207
    Summary of Internet Explorer 2.0 212
    Oracle PowerBrowser 1.0 213
        Network Loadable Objects 214
        Network Loadable Object Attributes 215
        Layout Frame Tags 216
            <LAYOUTFRAME> 217
            <LAYOUTFRAMERESET> 217
        NLO and Layout Frame Tag Usage 217
        Oracle Basic 222
    Summary of Oracle PowerBrowser 1.0 225
    Summary 226

Chapter 6: The Art of Hybrid HTML Design 227

    Introduction 228
    Non-Recognition of HTML Tags 229
        Browser-Specific Tags 229
    Non-Recognition of HTML 3 Tags 238
        Table Tags 239
        Special Characters 240
        Hybrid HTML 3 Tag Design 240
    Summary of Non-Recognition Design Strategy 248
    Partial Recognition of HTML Tags 249
        Attributes 249
    Partial Recognition: Attributes 250
    Partial Recognition: File Types 253
    Partial Recognition: Observations 254
    Summary of Partial Recognition Design Strategy 262
    Hardware and Platform Incompatibilities 263
    Advanced Table Design Using Hybrid HTML 264

Advanced Frame Design Using Hybrid HTML 271
Summary 276

Chapter 7: Rich Media File Formats 277

Image Files 278
    Digital Color 278
    RGB, CMYK, and Hexadecimal Color Systems 279
Color Palettes 281
    Special Color Names 282
    Image File Formats 283
    Image Compression 286
Image Maps versus Adjacent Images 287
Tips for Image File Usage 289
Audio File Formats 290
    MIDI File Format 292
Tips for Audio File Usage 293
Video and Animation 294
    Video and Animation Alternatives 295
    Animated GIFs 295
    Other Animation Devices 295
    VRML 296
        Other File Formats 296
Helper Applications 297
    Graphics 297
    JPEGView 297
    LView Pro 297
    Imagenation Viewer 298
    GifBuilder, Clip2Gif 298
    Audio 298
    GoldWave 298
    RealAudio Player 298
    Video 298
    Sparkle 298
    MPLAYER.EXE 298
    AviLxp AVI Movie Viewer 299
    MPEG2PLY.EXE 299
    Virtual Worlds 299
    Fountain 299
    Webspace Navigator 299
    CyberGate 299
    QuickTime VR 299
    PhotoSphere Viewer 299

Utilities . . . . *.300*
Eudora . . . . *.300*
PKZip . . . . *.300*
Stuffit . . . . *.300*
WinZip . . . . *.300*
Plug-ins . . . . *.301*
Acrobat Amber Reader . . . . *.302*
QuickTime . . . . *.302*
OpenScape . . . . *.302*
FIGleaf Inline . . . . *.303*
VR Scout . . . . *.303*
CMX Viewer . . . . *.303*
Timbuktu Plug-in . . . . *.304*
FutureSplash . . . . *.304*
Emblaze . . . . *.304*
Astound Web Player . . . . *.304*
ViewMovie . . . . *.304*
ichat Plug-in . . . . *.305*
Lightning Strike . . . . *.305*
Word Viewer Plug-in . . . . *.305*
VRealm . . . . *.305*
InterCAP InLine . . . . *.306*
MovieStar Plug-in . . . . *.306*
PreVU . . . . *.306*
Crescendo . . . . *.306*
CoolFusion . . . . *.307*
Fractal Viewer . . . . *.307*
Shockwave for Director . . . . *.307*
Shockwave for Freehand . . . . *.307*
Play3D . . . . *.308*
Chemscape Chime . . . . *.308*
mBED Software . . . . *.308*
Carbon Copy . . . . *.308*
Talker 2.0 . . . . *.308*
OLE Control Plug-in . . . . *.309*
Live3D . . . . *.309*
RealAudio . . . . *.309*
MediaViewer . . . . *.310*
HistoryTree . . . . *.310*
DWG/DXF Plug-in . . . . *.310*
Koan Plug-in . . . . *.310*
ASAP WebShow . . . . *.311*
EarthTime . . . . *.312*

Wavelet Image Plug-in 312
ViewDirector Plug-in 312
Sizzler 312
Envoy 313
Formula One/Net 313
VDOLive 313
WIRL Interactive 3D Plug-in 314
ToolVox for the Web 314
Wayfarer Plug-in 314
Tips on Using Plug-ins and Helper Applications 315
Distributed Applications 316
Java 316
Visual Basic 317
Distributed Application Usage 317
Summary 318

Chapter 8: Server Side Issues 319

Running Your Own Server vs. Using a Service Provider 320
Domain Names and Moving a Web Site 320
Commercial Internet Service Providers 321
Selecting a Service Provider 324
Mirroring a Web Site 324
Web Site Organization and Relative Links 325
Setting Relative Links 326
Examples of Relative Links 326
Web Site Organization and Cross-Platform Issues 327
Putting a Web Site Online: FTP Software 328
Fetch 3.0 330
WS_FTP 332
Snatcher 334
Common Gateway Interface (CGI) Scripts 336
CGI Scripts: How They Work 337
Diagram of a Simple CGI Script in Action 337
CGI Scripts 338
Using an Image Map Script 339
Using a Basic Forms Script 342
A Basic Form 343
E-Mail Response with Data 343
The Configuration File 344
Template Files 344
Web Statistics and Determining Your Audience 345
Summary 346

Chapter 9: On the Horizon 347
The Evolution of HTML 348
New HTML Design Strategies 350
Demographics: Browsers and Bandwidth 351
Summary 353

Introduction to the Appendices 355

Appendix A: HTML Tag and Attribute Support 357

Appendix B: HTML Editors 365
HTML Text Editors 365
HTML WSIWYG Editors 366

Appendix C: Special Characters 367

Appendix D: MIME Types 369

Appendix E: Online Resources 371
Browsers 371
Browser Resources 372
HTML 373
JavaScript 375
Java 376
Graphics 378
Audio 379
Video 380
VRML 381
Internet Service Providers 382
Server Scripts 383
Image Maps 386
Search Engines 387

Index 389

INTRODUCTION

This book is intended for anyone designing pages for the World Wide Web and company networks, or Intranets. Hybrid HTML design is a method that will ensure your pages are optimized for browsers such as Netscape Navigator and Internet Explorer, while being acceptable in less-sophisticated browsers, such as America Online and Air Mosaic. Throughout this book, you will be shown how to make your Web pages come alive with animations, frames, plug-ins, and other newly available technologies. You will also learn how to maintain the integrity of your Web page display in all browsers.

Hybrid HTML Design is a long overdue reference for Web publishers. This book graphically describes what you can expect from HTML tags and file formats in many of today's most popular browsers. It will help you to avoid developing duplicate Web sites by showing you new techniques for building tables and other advanced features. The book will assist you in selecting the most appropriate software for converting your existing files to HTML. It also will help you choose the best way to make your pages rich with multimedia effects.

In addition to HTML, a familiarity with file types, server issues, and new functionalities made possible with browser extensions has become more and more important. This book will help you become adept in all of these areas. The CD-ROM and appendices complement the chapters, and are excellent resources for HTML and Web-specific file creation and display.

Following the methods described within will enable you to take advantage of the latest HTML tags, while not sacrificing your browser audience. This book is dedicated to providing answers to the most pressing concerns facing HTML developers today, including hybrid design, HTML editor choice, and file format issues.

CHRONOLOGY

This book was inspired by a confluence of events in the fall of 1995. As instructors of a Macintosh-based multimedia program, Steven Warren, Craig Barnes, and I raced to include Web design as a core component of our program's curriculum. During the previous year, we had been teaching interactive program development using Director, Photoshop, SoundEdit 16, and a number of other multimedia programs. The lure of the Internet inspired the three of us to quickly learn HTML and the way of the Web.

After several weeks of teaching HTML using BBEdit Lite and Navigator 1.1 on the Macintosh, I was confronted by a student who demanded to know why the pages that were so well-designed in class looked so horrible in the browser provided with America Online. Rather surprised by his complaints, I did what any instructor would, and told him that I would investigate. And investigate I did! Not only did I test with America Online's browser, but I also downloaded other browsers to test pages designed in class. Realizing that not all browsers are created equal was a discovery as large as the spherical nature of the Earth.

At about that same time, Janine Warner, the co-author of this book, was also beginning to immerse herself in the world of HTML. After designing several Web sites, she was commissioned to write an article on HTML editors for *Publish Magazine*. After meeting in November and having some lengthy talks about large gaps in existing HTML books, the idea for this book was formed.

Believing our idea to be too hot a concept to shop around, we decided to send the proposal to a single publisher. We researched the market for quite some time before approaching New Riders with the idea. The publisher was selected due to its impressive, cutting-edge library of Web resources. We knew that we would need to be typing up until the moment the book was pressed, and we could not afford to jeopardize the timing of the book's release.

In ten packed weeks of surfing, typing, and testing every imaginable combination of tags and attributes on different browsers and operating systems, this book was produced. It was forged in coffee and fatigue. Four hours of sleep per night was considered a scandalous luxury. The moment a final period was inserted in a chapter, it became a comma due to a new development. But enough of the fun stuff. Let's talk about what's inside.

THE WORLD WIDE WEB

After 25 years of existence with little fanfare or notoriety, the Internet has exploded in the past three years due in large part to the arrival of the World Wide Web. The Web's relationship to the Internet is similar to the relationship of Windows to DOS. In the case of Microsoft Windows versions 3.1 and earlier, the graphical interface is an interpretation of code that the DOS operating system recognizes. The DOS environment is hidden from the user once Windows is started.

In the case of the Web, the interface is interpreted by a browser. A *browser* is a program that interprets HTML code, and displays the information graphically. Once you are connected to the Internet using a dial-up account or online service, the World Wide Web supports a series of protocols that enable display of HTML documents, file transfer, e-mail, and other functions. While you are browsing the Web, like in Windows, the system that supports the graphical interface is hidden.

HTML

HyperText Markup Language, or HTML, is the language used to design Web pages, files that display on your monitor as you surf the Internet. It is a very simple language, one that resembles word processing, or traditional page layout markup. Being a relatively easy language to learn, and enabling anyone to design graphic interfaces, HTML has gained widespread acceptance.

Originally, HTML was an open language intended to be supported by all Internet browsers. Using a minimal amount of text, considerable control over the monitor's display was possible. This was due to protocols being agreed upon and standards being accepted. As the Web evolved and some browser manufacturers provided non-standard HTML code for their products, a diversification of design methods began to proliferate.

As a result of innovations spearheaded by Netscape, HTML has suddenly become a more complex, dialectic language. At one time, the Web page was designed with little consideration for how it appeared in other browsers. You could have any flavor you liked, as long as you liked vanilla. Netscape changed all that with its introduction of tables and other sophisticated formatting. Since then, Microsoft, Oracle, and others have followed Netscape's lead, and have begun to introduce their own HTML dialects. We also found that even when two browsers recognize the same HTML formats, they often display Web pages differently.

During the course of our research, Janine and I studied how other designers dealt with the diversity in browser displays and found that few people had learned to design pages that used advanced features without compromising their audience. Instead, some designers choose to limit formatting tags to those defined in the HTML 2 specifications. HTML 2 is considered to be the lowest common denominator in Web design (HTML 1 had a short shelf life, predating most browsers). If you only use HTML 2 formatting tags, you can expect your page to be consistent in all browsers. As your pages become more sophisticated in their display—with images, embedded objects, and tables—you will be using HTML and file formats that are not recognized by all browsers.

In an effort to get around this problem, many HTML designers have resorted to maintaining parallel sites, one designed with advanced features for browsers like Netscape, and the other limited to basic HTML 2 for all others. That means every day, week, or month that the site is updated, two pages are made in the place of one. Other HTML designers have taken an elitist approach to the art and disregard viewers who are not using the designer's favorite browser. As a result, CompuServe and Prodigy subscribers often arrive to see "Best viewed in Netscape," with little consideration for their garbled view of the information.

In March 1996, CompuServe and America Online both pledged to offer Internet Explorer and Netscape Navigator to their subscribers. CompuServe launched a new dial-up service called Wow!, which uses Explorer as its primary browser. There are still, however, a large number of America Online and CompuServe subscribers that continue to use the older browsers.

The techniques described in this book show you how to create HTML documents that are optimized for the latest browsers, yet still look good in the older versions. One of the earliest and most valuable discoveries we made was that unrecognized HTML tags are generally ignored by browsers. We also discovered that by combining supported and unsupported tags, browser displays varied considerably. Through trial and error, we began to develop design techniques for creating Web pages to be viewed differently, yet acceptably, in all the browsers we tested.

Before we go on, let's do away with assumptions and introduce the minimal HTML document. This can be made with any text editor, including Notepad, SimpleText, and TeachText. Personally, I use a word processor due to my familiarity with it, while Janine prefers to use a combination of HTML authoring tools. The program that you use to create an HTML document will not affect the page display—only the HTML tags and their interpretation by the browser affect page display.

For all the smoke and mirrors, the Web uses nothing more than unformatted text as its principal file type. If you type what you see below with any text editing program, save it as a plain text file (*.TXT file format), and name it with a .HTM or .HTML extension, you can open the document with any Web browser. It's that simple.

SAMPLE HTML DOCUMENT

```
<HTML>
<HEAD>
<TITLE>A Small HTML Document</TITLE>
</HEAD>

<BODY>
<H1>The HTML Document</H1>
In this very small document, you can see the formatting symbols that define the
HTML document, define the HEAD and BODY sections, and give the page a title, a
level 1 heading, a paragraph mark, and some body text.

The characters that surround the tags can be typed using the SHIFT key with the
comma and the SHIFT key with the period.
<P>
Most tags have accompanying closing tags, made with the forward slash character
to the right of the period on the keyboard. Spacing is optional within HTML
documents. The browser will only insert a paragraph return when it reads a
paragraph tag. Enter space as you require for organizing your document, knowing
that it will not affect your page display.

</BODY>
</HTML>
```

A tag refers to an element of HTML syntax contained between "<" and ">" characters. In this example, there are six tags present: <HTML>; <HEAD>; <TITLE>; <BODY>; <H1>; and <P>. Most tags have closing tags, formed by inserting the "/" character between the "<" and the tag name (e.g., </HTML>). A tag's contents refer to the information between the opening tag and the closing tag. The contents of the <H1> tag in the example are "The HTML Document." The contents of the <HTML> tags begin with <HEAD> and end with </BODY>. This book will introduce you to all of the HTML formatting tags presently available.

WEB SITES AND WEBMASTERS

Over the course of the past three years, *Web sites* and *Webmasters* have crawled into the vernacular. Since the introduction of the Mosaic browser, several industries have been formed around this new phenomenon. "Check out our home page at..." or "my e-mail address is..." have become commonplace sayings in the world of 1996. When was the last time you watched a newscast that did not let you know about their online counterpart?

As professionals in an industry without history, Webmasters and Web page designers come from any and all walks of life. Nobody has a B.S. in HTML. Nobody has to show credentials to design a beautiful, often-visited Web site. Many of us have found ourselves in roles as a result of the evolution of our job descriptions. Who are we? What road did we take to get here? Many of us have experience in one or more of the following program groups. The present work that you do will very likely influence the manner in which you create HTML documents.

WORD PROCESSORS

If you have worked with any word processor, such as Lotus Ami Pro, Microsoft Word, WordPerfect, or others, HTML will be easy for you to pick up. If you are accustomed to using *Reveal Codes* or *Show*, then the use of HTML formatting will come easily after accepting the design constraints of the language.

In approaching HTML design, you come with knowledge of Search and Replace functions, spell checking, thesaurus usage, and features like Macros and Mail Merge, which are unavailable in most HTML editors. You will have all the skills you need to quickly design Web pages once you understand the formatting tags of HTML. For users of older word processing programs like DOS WordPerfect 5.1 and earlier, the opening and closing formatting tags will be quite familiar.

DESKTOP PUBLISHERS

One thing that will drive you crazy in the new world of HTML is the relative lack of control you have over your page layout. Screen displays will be affected by different browsers, different monitors, and different operating systems. Once you overcome the initial frustration, HTML is not difficult to learn. There are translators available to help you, but you will have to manicure the HTML to make them hybrid pages and readable in all browsers.

Most of the conversion programs support style sheets and convert them into HTML equivalents, but all of them will require additional edits. It is likely that you will have to do the cleaning up in a text editor or word processor. As the language evolves and more sophisticated tools become available, you can expect to have a less painful migration to HTML. This book will help you fine-tune your pages.

DATABASE AND COMPUTER PROGRAMMERS

The arrival of HTML has probably affected you as much as anyone else at most companies. Suddenly, everyone in the world wants you to write a query or CGI script for their Web pages. Like never before, people from different departments come to you with questions and suggestions on HTML design. Although MIS functions are concerned primarily with information, other departments will begin to insist on aesthetic considerations in your HTML output. You can expect users to become increasingly sophisticated in their demands. This book will help you resolve issues that they bring up, as well as to anticipate those not yet discovered.

Your involvement with HTML may consist primarily of designing templates, writing SQL queries, or programming CGI scripts. Distributed applications, such as Java and Visual Basic, are discussed in Chapter 7, but you will want to get additional books on these topics. *Hybrid HTML Design* answers all of your HTML questions, as well as the questions of all those users that keep hovering around your cubicle. You will probably want to buy a second copy of this book just for loaning to those overly inquisitive types.

GRAPHIC ARTISTS

For graphic artists, HTML is one further extension from reality in design. Computer graphics, by description, are not tangible, and require manipulation in a non-physical environment. The first extension, working with virtual tools such as magic wands and paint buckets, is generally taken for granted. The second extension takes place when you cannot see what you are intending to produce, such as a 3D rendering. You set up the lights, cameras, objects, and textures, and then render— hoping for the best!

With HTML, you are forced into another extension from physical realities. Even if you use WYSIWYG editors, you will not see how your document appears in multiple browsers. This book will help you feel more comfortable in this medium that is so distant from traditional design. Chapter 7, in particular, will answer a lot of questions that you may have regarding image and color issues.

THE LAYOUT OF THE BOOK

Hybrid HTML Design is divided into three general topics. The first one discusses the programs used to view, create, and edit Web pages. The second deals with HTML tags, the focus of this book. The third covers issues beyond HTML that affect Web page design. The book concludes with appendices showing browser and editor comparisons, special characters, MIME types, and online resources.

In the first chapter, the browsers are introduced. The browsers listed are by no means exhaustive, but are intended to be a representative sample. Older versions of America Online and CompuServe software are included, due to the large number of their subscribers that will continue using the older browsers. Chapter 2 introduces many of the most popular HTML editors available, as well as converters and middleware available for common off-the-shelf software.

Chapters 3 through 6 lead you through HTML tags in a logical progression. Chapter 3 introduces HTML 2, the lowest common denominator in browser design. Chapter 4 discusses the HTML 3 tags. Chapter 5 examines browser-specific tags, including frames, plug-ins, and other new innovations. Chapter 6 reinforces the hybrid HTML design advocated throughout the book by confronting the various issues that can negatively affect your Web page display.

Chapter 7 introduces the many file types and plug-ins that will help your Web pages come alive. These include image, audio, video, and other file types that are not supported in all browsers. Chapter 8 examines server issues, such as naming conventions, how to transfer files, and how to select a service provider. Finally, Chapter 9 discusses the direction in which the Web is going. Issues regarding bandwidth, demographics, and other areas that affect the sophistication and size of your intended audience are reviewed.

Since we began this book, the Web has shifted, flexed, twisted, and turned. America Online and CompuServe now offer Navigator and Explorer for surfing the Internet. Explorer 3 and Navigator 3 have arrived in beta versions. Browsers have become more sophisticated; plug-ins and functionality have multiplied. Using hybrid design methods will become even more important as HTML continues to diversify. This book will provide you with the skills you need to proactively respond to the challenges presented to you by the Web's evolution.

NEW RIDERS PUBLISHING

The staff of New Riders Publishing is committed to bringing you the very best in computer reference material. Each New Riders book is the result of months of work by authors and staff who research and refine the information contained within its covers.

As part of this commitment to you, the NRP reader, New Riders invites your input. Please let us know if you enjoy this book, if you have trouble with the information and examples presented, or if you have a suggestion for the next edition.

Please note, though: New Riders staff cannot serve as a technical resource for hybrid HTML design or for questions about software- or hardware-related problems. Please refer to the book's Web site at "http://www.browserbydesign.com/" or to the applications' Help systems.

If you have a question or comment about any New Riders book, there are several ways to contact New Riders Publishing. We will respond to as many readers as we can. Your name, address, or phone number will never become part of a mailing list or be used for any purpose other than to help us continue to bring you the best books possible.

You can write us at the following address:

> New Riders Publishing
>
> Attn: Publisher
>
> 201 W. 103rd Street
>
> Indianapolis, IN 46290

If you prefer, you can fax New Riders Publishing at (317) 581-4670.

You can also send electronic mail to New Riders at the following Internet address:

`sangus@newriders.mcp.com`

NRP is an imprint of Macmillan Computer Publishing. To obtain a catalog or information, or to purchase any Macmillan Computer Publishing book, call (800) 428-5331.

Thank you for selecting *Hybrid HTML Design*!

THE BROWSERS

Browsers are the programs used to view documents on the World Wide Web. Today there are literally hundreds of browsers in the market. This chapter introduces some of the most significant browsers available. These form a representative cross sample of existing browsers. When designing for the Internet or Intranet, knowing your browser audience should influence your HTML choice.

This book is intended to develop HTML skills that will enable you to anticipate your Web page display in all browsers. In this chapter, hybrid HTML was used to create the screen images. Using hybrid development techniques, you can ensure acceptable viewing in all browsers, with optimized viewing in those browsers that have advanced features, such as frames and animation.

When using the browsers to view the page in this chapter, you will find that some of them support animation and that images actually move in the HTML document. This cannot be conveyed on the printed page, but can be seen by directing your browser to view the document in Chapter 1 from the CD-ROM.

INTRODUCTION TO BROWSERS

Before the World Wide Web (the Web) was introduced, online services were limited in their display to text or to proprietary browsers by companies such as America Online, CompuServe, and Prodigy. These companies provided online services that used a common interface to display information. News, sports, chat rooms, and other services were made available by the "Big Three."

The Web brought a great denominator to online service providers. Proprietary online information services, based on an hourly usage charge, became dramatically less popular as Internet Service Providers began to offer unlimited access to the Internet at a fixed price. The availability of the Mosaic browser and cheap Internet access together led to a revolution now shepherded by Netscape, Microsoft, and others. Each of the Big Three online services now offer, or are planning to offer, unlimited access to compete with dial-up services.

Web browsers, as contrasted to the displays of the proprietary online services, interpret HyperText Markup Language (HTML) formatting for their screen contents. America Online and CompuServe, on the other hand, have traditionally provided most of their information content in a form that only their software can interpret. The Big Three now provide their own Web browsers in addition to their proprietary platform for recognizing HTML documents. These function like any other browsers used to access the Web.

The delivery of small text documents (which is all that HTML documents really are) over the Internet, which are then compiled, or interpreted, at the desktop computer, has allowed for transmission of screen elements that would otherwise be slow and unmanageable to transfer—the smaller the amount of information, the quicker it transfers to your computer monitor.

The way that browsers interpret HTML differs greatly, as you will see in the following pages. In this chapter, one document was used to generate all of the pages displayed. In the framed documents in Navigator and PowerBrowser, other HTML pages are contained in the frame windows. They are, however, referenced, like the images, in the single Web page. The formatting tags that will be introduced in Chapters 3 through 5 have been used here to graphically demonstrate the power and diversity that a single HTML document can have. This HTML page was intentionally designed to show the differences among browsers. Using techniques described in this book, the pages could have been made to look uniform.

DESIGNING FOR MULTIPLE BROWSERS

When designing for multiple browsers, many designers stick to the formatting tags defined in the HTML 2 specifications. As noted in the introduction, if you use only HTML 2 formatting tags, you can expect your page display to be consistent in all browsers. Many companies do this and do not attract many repeat visitors.

Other companies maintain duplicate sites: one to support Netscape, Explorer, or other advanced browsers; and the other to support basic HTML 2 formatting. This solution requires an ongoing commitment to substantial additional man-hours, and increases the likelihood of inconsistencies in your Web site information.

Finally, there are companies intending to make information available to all visitors that publish Web pages many browsers cannot interpret. These companies put too high a price on the cost of their HTML design. Sophisticated pages are great, but losing a large percentage of your potential browser audience is unacceptable. It is, above all, the information content that brings people to your Web site.

In this chapter, the screen displays will be described so that the effects of HTML in multiple browsers can be understood. The HTML source code that defines the pages will be reviewed in Chapter 6. The intention of the authors was to create a page that could accentuate the variation in HTML interpretation by making it different, yet acceptable, in all possible browser displays. In application, it is highly unusual to find such a combination of tags in a single HTML document.

Among the formatting and file types used on the page are tables, frames, and animated GIFs. These will be introduced in Chapters 4, 5, and 7, respectively. It is often the case that Webmasters use each of these design methods without taking into consideration the visitors to their site that use other browsers. In *Hybrid HTML Design*, you will learn how to provide alternative content in a single Web page to satisfy visitors with other browsers.

The bar beneath the browser display on each of the pages illustrates the tags and files that it supports. From left to right, these are: forms; JPEG; transparent GIFs; animated GIFs; fonts; special characters and entities; image maps; the CENTER tag; tables; plug-ins; scripting languages; frames; and Java. The levels of support are green, for total support; blue, for partial support; yellow, for planned support; and red, for no support. The version numbers of the browsers tested in this chapter are provided. In Appendix A, Navigator 3.0 and Explorer 3.0 are also included.

NETSCAPE NAVIGATOR 2.0

Netscape has been the early leader in the design and function of its browser products. In the display on the facing page, Navigator's appearance reflects its support of frames, background images, and tables. The split-screen effect is caused by frames, which are described in Chapter 5. In the top frame, the image is aligned right, and the text flows in the opposite margin. Navigator is the only browser reviewed in this chapter that supports animated GIF files (see Chapter 7). In the bottom frame, the images are centered within a table. The background image is a brick formation that repeats across the page.

Navigator 2.0 supports the majority of HTML 2 and HTML 3 formatting standards. Navigator's own standards are often imitated by other browser manufacturers. Frames, for example, had been developed in the fall of 1995 for the Navigator 2.0 beta product. By the end of the year, Oracle's browser and @Home's browser were developed to recognize the FRAMESET definition.

On the opposite page is the Navigator interface. From the top, you can see the Title Bar, the Menu Bar, the Toolbar, the Location Bar, and the Directory Buttons. The Title and Menu Bars are always visible, whereas the latter three are optionally displayed by the viewer. The Toolbar has buttons that will lead you to the previously displayed page, the following page, or the home page (which you set in the General Preferences under the Options menu); that will reload the page, load images on the page, or open a page; and that print the page, search the current document, or stop the page from loading.

The Location bar displays the Uniform Resource Locator (URL) of the displayed page. Beneath the Location Bar are the Directory Buttons. These link to pages on Netscape's site that are titled What's New, What's Cool, Handbook, Net Search, Net Directory, and Software. To the right of the Location Bar and Directory Buttons is the Netscape logo. The logo animates while loading new pages. Among the features that distinguish Navigator are its integration of e-mail, newsgroups, and other services, frames, progressive loading of JPEG images, support for client-side image maps, and other advanced formatting.

Using the Options menu, you can set your browser's home page, font choice, color, and other aesthetic, security, network, news, and mail preferences. The Bookmarks menu enables the user to reference pages for future usage. The Go menu lists the most recently visited documents.

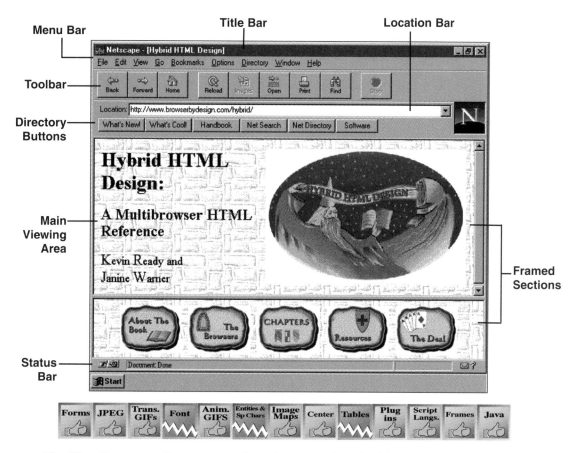

The View Document Source menu item is extremely valuable to developers. Selecting this option displays the HTML code that describes the page in the application set in the general preferences. Nothing will help you more in writing HTML than to see how others have done it. Always treat the code skeptically. The rules of syntax in this book will help you to check the HTML of others.

As a designer, it is important to remember that many viewers will have the Toolbar, Location Bar, and Directory Buttons displayed, which limits the amount of space in the Main Viewing Area. A good rule of thumb to follow in designing for 640×480 monitors is that only 300 pixels of vertical height can be taken for granted. The latest version of the Navigator browser is available for Unix, all Windows platforms, and the Macintosh OS. It can be downloaded from the following:

http://home.netscape.com/

INTERNET EXPLORER 2.0

Microsoft's Windows 95 operating system ships with the Internet Explorer browser. The screen is very different from Navigator's, due primarily to the fact that Explorer does not support frames. Explorer 3.0, introduced in Chapter 5, will support frames. As seen here, the browser's display reflects Explorer's support of tables, as well as its own formatting tags. Tables are introduced in Chapter 4, and Internet Explorer's own tags will be presented in Chapter 5. The checkerboard patterns were created by embedding tables and using background colors of table cells. The page elements are center aligned and distributed according to the table definition.

With a relatively late start, Microsoft has quickly caught up with Netscape aesthetically by recognizing almost all of the HTML 2 and HTML 3 tags, and demographically by reaching millions of Windows 95 users without an independent marketing effort. In addition to supporting the standard HTML tags, Microsoft has been launching many of its own formatting standards. Unlike Netscape, Internet Explorer is able to take full advantage of a single operating system's functions. This includes being able to specify font selection, and accessing Windows dynamic link libraries (DLLs) and other controls that would be unobtainable in a cross-platform browser.

The Explorer interface features the Title Bar, the Menu Bar, the Toolbar, the Address Bar, the Main Viewing Area, the Scroll Bars, and the Status Bar. The areas are the same as Navigator's, except for the Location Bar, which is named the Address Bar; and the Directory Buttons, which do not exist. The Toolbar in Explorer enables viewers to open a document, go to the home page (set by the View Options menu item) and a search page (also set by the View Options menu item), view news-groups, go backward and forward, stop loading the document, reload the document, open and edit the Favorites list, increase and decrease the font size, and cut, copy, and paste information.

The Favorites menu is Explorer's hotlist. Regularly visited sites can be added here by the user. The View menu has selections to go backward and forward; display the Toolbar, Address Bar, and Status Bar; change the font size; stop loading and reload the document; view the HTML source; view newsgroup listings; and set color, font, and other preferences. In other words, the View menu serves just about all your needs, taking over the functions of several menu lists from Navigator. The View Source option will display the HTML behind the active page.

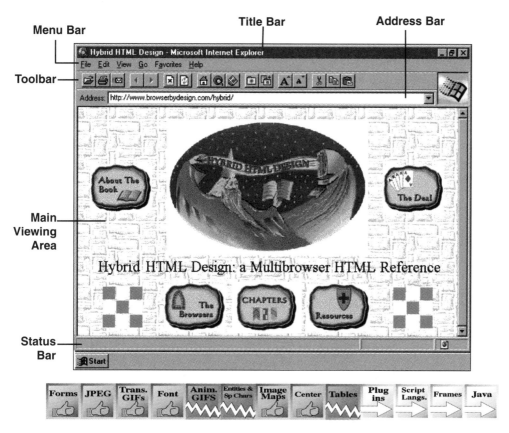

The screen elements of Internet Explorer take up less vertical space than those of Navigator. It is still wise to stick to a 300 pixel-high display for design purposes. If you are designing an HTML document that has images or contiguous areas more than 300 pixels in height, be aware that viewers may need to hide their toolbars, locations, and other screen elements from their display to see the element as intended. Most browsers enable you to hide Toolbars and Location Bars from view.

The latest version of the Explorer browser is available for all Windows versions and the Macintosh OS. It can be downloaded from the following:

```
http://www.microsoft.com/
```

ORACLE POWERBROWSER 1.0

In late 1995, Oracle launched the beta version of PowerBrowser. The display on the opposite page demonstrates that Oracle quickly adopted Netscape's frame feature. PowerBrowser's own tags were used to reverse the order of the picture and text in the top frame. The brower recognized everything that Navigator did, including the animated GIF file. It has been designed to recognize most of its competitors' tags, in addition to its own. The browser also has a unique Personal Server that is a powerful HTML development tool.

The browser contains a Menu Bar, Title Bar, Toolbar, and URL bar. The Toolbar enables you to go backward and forward; reload the page, load the home page, save the page, and stop loading; search the page and the Internet; display the Bookmarks and History window; and open a new browser, server, or NLO window.

The Bookmarks and History window, to the left of the Main Viewing Area, resemble frames. These are displayed through selecting the Bookmarks and History item in the View menu or from the Toolbar. It is also possible to display the Bookmarks and History across the top by selecting Horizontal Panes from the View menu. The browser defaults to the Vertical Pane, as displayed on the following page. At the bottom of the page is a Frame Status Bar, in addition to a Browser Status Bar.

From the File menu, the viewer can open a Personal Browser, Personal Server, or NLO Window (see Chapter 5 for descriptions on all of these); send e-mail; open a URL or local file; save the page as HTML or plain text; and print the page. The Edit menu features a copy function and two search functions: one on the page and one using an Internet search engine. From the View menu, the Toolbar, URL Bar, Frame Status Bar, Browser Status Bar, Large Buttons, and the Bookmarks and History frames can be selected or deselected; the panes can be set horizontally or vertically; and the page can be viewed in HTML form or as unformatted text.

The Navigate menu links to the pages preceding and following the current page, to the home page, and to the parent page. It also provides selections to reload or to stop loading the page, and to clear the history. The Bookmarks menu enables you to import, save, add to, and edit bookmarks; and to organize them into folders. The Options menu is used for setting user preferences, for debugging Oracle Basic, for encryption settings, for logging on and off, and for changing your password. The Window and Help menus are standard in function.

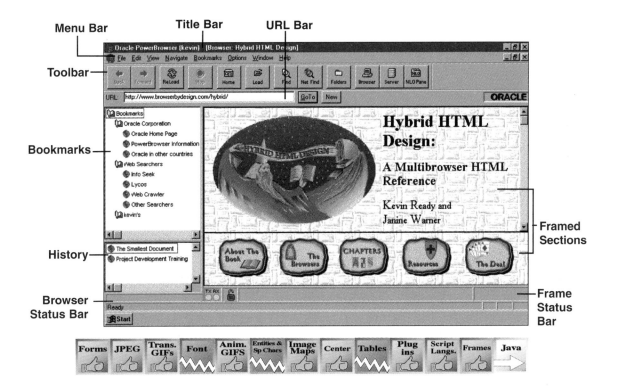

When designing pages for view in this browser, you need to consider that the Main Viewing Area provides little more than 300 pixels by 400 pixels if the Bookmarks and History frames are visible. The page divisions are moveable. In other words, the user can slide the dividing bars between frames up or down and left or right to make the screen areas larger or smaller.

When designing pages specifically for a browser that has optional display areas, you may want to alert visitors to deselect toolbars or other screen elements. This can be particularly useful if you are designing for an Intranet. It is often the case that users are not familiar with options like this that could improve the way the Web page is displayed.

The latest version of Oracle PowerBrowser is available for Windows NT and Windows 95. It can be downloaded from the following:

```
http://www.oracle.com/
```

HOTJAVA ALPHA 1.0

The display of the HotJava browser reveals its relative weakness in supporting traditional HTML. The table and frames features are not supported, although it does recognize the center tag. If it did not recognize the center tag, the screen elements would be aligned left. As of this writing, the HotJava browser is still in Alpha release, and its features are not as compelling as they have been reputed. With all the attention being given to the Java programming language, and the promise of advanced support by Sun's own browser, it is quite possible that this browser could become quite important in the near future.

Sun Microsystem's HotJava browser is designed to take full advantage of the Java programming language. Other browsers, such as Navigator and Explorer, have stated that they will support Java, but it is probable that higher Java functions will be possible using the HotJava browser than those of Sun's competitors.

The HotJava interface is rather sparse. The File menu has the Reload and View Source options. This is a less common place to find these functions in the Menu Bar. The standard File menu selections like Open and Print are also available here. The Options menu enables viewers to set font, color, security, and other preferences. The Navigate menu provides links to the following, previous, and home pages, as well as to the program's navigation history and hotlist.

The Goto menu acts more like a hotlist in its usage than the hotlist selection in the Navigate menu. This is because you do not have to go through the extra step of selecting the page from a dialog box. Instead, you select the page from the Goto menu itself. The Help menu links to much of HotJava's online documentation.

Beneath the Main Viewing Area in the browser is a Control Panel with five buttons. The first three lead to the previous page, the following page, and the home page; the last two reload and stop loading the page. At the bottom of the browser window is a Status Bar.

HotJava has one of the largest Main Viewing Areas of the browsers seen here. Not much more than 150 pixels are taken up by the Menu Bar, Location Bar, Control Panel, and Status Bar combined. Other browsers, however, generally enable viewers to hide the navigation buttons and Location Bar. In HotJava, the screen elements are fixed on the screen and cannot be hidden.

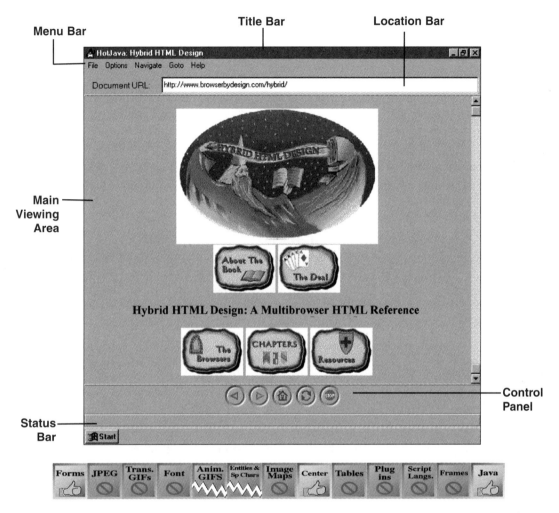

As with the other browsers reviewed here, HotJava will probably undergo considerable reconstruction in its interface design in the months and years ahead. If you are designing with this browser in mind, make sure that you have the most recent version available.

The latest version of the HotJava browser is available for Sun, Windows NT, and Windows 95. It can be downloaded from the following:

```
http://java.sun.com/
```

NCSA MOSAIC 2.0

The browser display of Mosaic is enabled through its treatment of the table and center tags. With the exception of the checkerboard area, the page looks the same as the one displayed by Explorer. The display of earlier versions of Navigator also appears like this. Each of the images is positioned within table cells in a grid fashion. Chapter 4 introduces tables; Chapter 6 describes their use in this page.

Developers at the National Center for Supercomputing Applications (NCSA) were the first to create a World Wide Web browser. One of those developers, Marc Andreessen, left NCSA to form Netscape with James Clark, former CEO of Silicon Graphics. Mosaic was the first widely used browser.

Mosaic is rather sophisticated in its displaying of HTML. It recognizes some HTML 3 formatting, but not all of it. The screen elements from the top are the Title Bar, Menu Bar, Toolbar, Location Bar, Main Viewing Area, and Status Bar. From the File menu, selections for newsgroups, e-mail, and document source are available, as well as the standard File selections. Collaborate is a unique menu item that is used for individuals to host or join a collaboration session with others.

The Options menu enables viewers to select or deselect the Toolbar, Status Bar, and Location Bar. There is also a Presentation Mode selection that uses the entire monitor display as the Main Viewing Area. In Presentation Mode, no menus, toolbars, or status bars are displayed. The Preferences option provides a great deal of control over the browser's appearance and functionality.

The Navigate menu links to the preceding page, the following page, and the home page, as well as reloads the current page. The session history can be selected here, as well as the hotlists for editing. The hotlist items are selectable under the Hotlist menu. The Help menu is quite complete. A large number of point-and-click examples are available, as well as an indexed reference.

There are six groups of buttons available: open and save a document; print and print preview; copy and paste; go backward, forward, reload, go home, and stop loading; find and add to hotlist; read newsgroups, send e-mail, and help.

When designing for Mosaic, it is nice to have the full monitor screen available for display. In this regard, the browser makes a good presentation vehicle. As with other browsers, if you want more of the screen to be available for display, it is important that you notify your viewers to adjust their browsers.

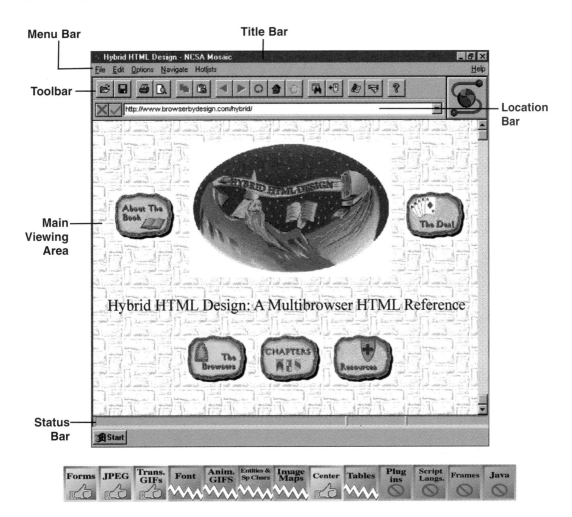

Mosaic was the first widely used browser on the Internet. Many other browsers use its publicly available source code as a building block for more sophisticated browsers. It remains to be seen whether or not this browser will have staying power after the challenges posed by Netscape and Microsoft, among others.

The latest version of the NCSA Mosaic browser is available for Unix, all Windows versions, and the Macintosh OS. It can be downloaded from the following:

```
http://www.ncsa.uiuc.edu/SDG/Software/Mosaic/
```

CompuServe Spry Mosaic .04.10.9.20

Believe it or not, Spry Mosaic actually has a version number—.04.10.9.20! It would be nice for the company to eventually come up with a numbering system for the layperson. This latest release of the Spry browser is made available as the default browser to subscribers to Wow!, CompuServe's new online dial-up service. Unlike earlier versions, Spry now supports tables, the center tag, and others. In the browser display, you can even see that it supports the background colors in the table.

CompuServe, America Online, and Prodigy offered online services to subscribers several years prior to the World Wide Web's introduction. These companies provide various informative, educational, and entertaining pages, as well as chat rooms and other services. Until recently, CompuServe did not support its users with a very sophisticated browser. The present version is a definite improvement and can be used independently of the CompuServe and SPRYNET online services.

The File menu contains the Hotlist editing function and the Web Page Source function. From the Edit menu, a Find option searches the present document, whereas the Search Internet option enables viewers to conduct a search of active sites on the Web. The View menu lets the viewer select or deselect the Toolbar and Web Page Bar for display. It also has a Load to Disk Mode option, which saves documents without displaying them; an Auto Load Images option; and a Kiosk Mode option, which uses the full monitor screen for display. Finally, an Options menu item enables the viewer to set display, font, and home and search page information.

The Navigate menu enables you to go backward and forward; to reload and stop loading the document; to go to the home page; to view the present history; and to add the Web page to the Personal Favorites Hotlist menu. The Tools menu enables viewers to connect to other CompuServe services, such as mail, news, and their Information Manager; to import an NCSA hotlist; and to establish Internet services, file type, proxy, and miscellaneous options. The Search the Web menu is new to this version and leads to three places: a "Spry meets Yahoo" page, Yahoo, and InfoSeek. The first of these virtually duplicates the Yahoo interface and will be known here as the Spryhoo page. The second and third are well-known search engines.

The Toolbar features a Search button, which leads to the Spryhoo page; a Hotlists button, which allows for the display of additional menus; an Add to Present Hotlist button; backward, forward, reload, and home buttons; a stop loading button; and mail and news buttons.

Menu Bar   Title Bar   Web Page Bar

Toolbar

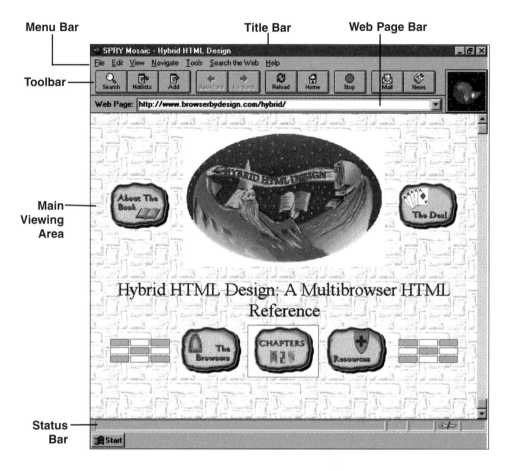

Main
Viewing
Area

Status
Bar

The latest version of the CompuServe software is available for IBM's OS/2, all Windows versions, and the Macintosh OS. The SPRYNET software is presently only available for all Windows versions. They can be downloaded from the following:

http://www.compuserve.com/

and

http://www.sprynet.com/

America Online 2.5

In the browser display on the facing page, all the screen elements are aligned left. This version of their browser does not support frames, tables, the center tag, or the animated GIF. As it appears here, this is the lowest common denominator in your HTML design. Realizing that some browsers will not recognize any of your formatting should persuade you to develop hybrid design techniques.

Like CompuServe, America Online offered proprietary information services for several years prior to the introduction of the World Wide Web. As the Big Three online service providers began offering Internet access to their clients, their browsers often presented the greatest challenge to HTML developers. Recently, however, all three have moved to offer greater Web functionality to their subscribers. America Online has gone so far as to offer both Netscape Navigator and Internet Explorer in its upcoming releases. They will still be developing their own browser, which should be released during the summer of 1996.

The discussion here concerns the America Online browser for Windows, version 2.5. The functionality of the Macintosh version differs slightly, and has been upgraded to version 2.6 already. In the Windows version, the menu items available to the company's browser are all used for America Online's proprietary information services. The exception to this is the File Open option, which can be used to open local HTML files, viewed with their browser. The icons in the Toolbar are also used with the company's proprietary services. The only exceptions are the Print and Open icons, and the Add to Favorite Places icon.

In the browser Window, a second group of icons, Web Controls, give the viewer navigation, hotlist, and preference controls. The icons enable you to go backward, reload, or go forward; access a hotlist feature called Favorite Places; set Web preferences, such as home page, graphics loading, and helper applications; go to the home page; go to a help page on America Online's Web site; and stop loading the current document.

When using browser statistics to guide your Web site design, be aware that browsers like America Online's and CompuServe's are notoriously undercounted. This has to do partly with the software that is used to recognize the browser, which fails to recognize those of the Big Three, and partly to the fact that many of the sites that monitor browser statistics are made for developers and are skewed toward Navigator and Explorer. Many of your visitors will use America Online's browser.

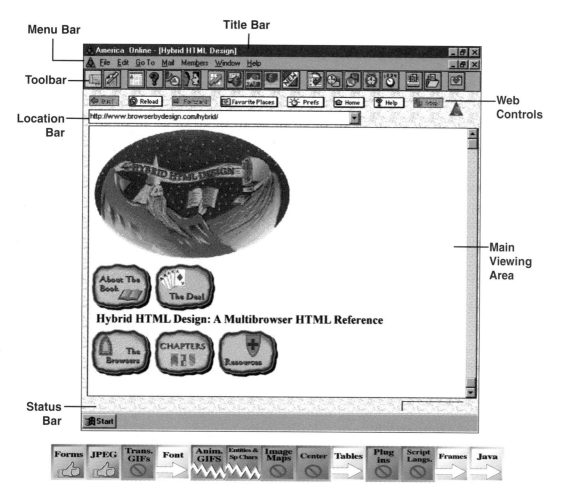

The company recently has formed several high-profile partnerships with companies such as Netscape, Microsoft, Apple, and AT&T. As a result of these developments, testing your pages in their latest browser versions is likely to become increasingly important. Check the America Online site regularly for the latest beta version. The latest-released version of America Online software is available for all Windows versions and the Macintosh OS. It can be downloaded from the following:

```
http://www.aol.com/
```

PRODIGY 2.0D

Prodigy, the last of the Big Three proprietary information service providers, has been the quickest to integrate advanced HTML formatting in its browser display. On the opposite page, the table and center tags are recognized, and the background image is supported, like Explorer and Mosaic. Neither frames nor background table colors are supported.

The File menu enables viewers to open local documents, save the current document to disk, view the document's HTML source, and print and exit. The Edit menu only supports the Copy function. The Options menu enables you to specify how images are loaded; customize color and link usage; set your history preferences; determine the font selection; and with the advanced setup, specify Helper applications, stage setup, and document setup.

With the Navigate menu, you can go to a URL location; edit or select from hotlists; access the global history; go to the home page, previous page, or following page; reload or reload from host (as opposed to cached documents); and send e-mail. The Help menu provides additional help for information specific to the browser part of Prodigy's services.

The Toolbar has icons that stop the page from loading; that lead to the previous or following pages; that lead to the home page; that open editable hotlists; that save or print the document; and that reload the document. There is also a checkbox that determines whether or not images are automatically loaded.

Although the Toolbar is not very tall, the gain in browser display size is offset by the fixed position of the Title and Location Bars. These bars cannot be hidden and reduce the vertical height of the main viewing area to approximately 300 pixels on a 640×480 monitor display.

Prodigy, like America Online and CompuServe, finds itself in a challenging and evolving time in its history. The company has been developing its HTML content substantially to attract subscribers. Like its two traditional competitors, Prodigy needs to convince its clients that the proprietary services it offers in addition to its browser product are worth the premium paid for access to its online services.

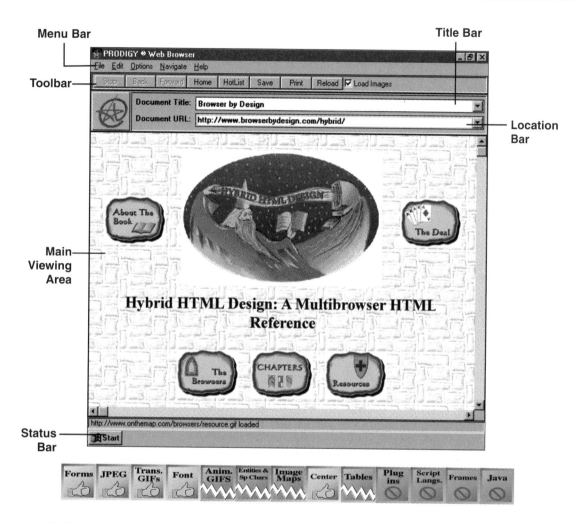

In the last few months, IBM and Sears, the two main investors in Prodigy, have been selling their interests in the company. Prodigy will face increasing competition, such as CompuServe and America Online, in the immediate future. Unlike the latter two, Prodigy has yet to make any big partnership announcements (in fact, the divestiture is more like the announcement of a divorce). The latest version of Prodigy software is available for all Windows versions and the Macintosh OS. They can be downloaded from the following:

```
http://www.prodigy.com/
```

CYBERDOG BETA RELEASE 2

In the display on the opposite page, Cyberdog supports the table and center tag formats, as well as the background image. Apple's new suite of Internet tools, code named Cyberdog, includes a Web browser, with e-mail, newsreader, and FTP capabilities. Apple created Cyberdog to demonstrate OpenDoc, a new cross-platform component architecture designed to work in Windows, Mac OS, OS/2, and Unix. Still in beta at the time of this writing, Cyberdog provides a simple browser ready for the addition of any new OpenDoc components.

The Web browser, which Apple calls Internet Explorer, has an almost bare interface. The Toolbar displays only three options—forward and back arrows and an arrow that displays cached pages. The File menu has selections for the typical New, Open, and Close options; an option to save a copy as OpenDoc and Internet Reference file formats; document information; and print options.

In the Edit menu, the standard Cut, Copy, Paste, Select All, Undo, and Redo are available. There are also Get Info, Preferences, and Find menu options. The first provides the URL of the current document, the second is used to set various user preferences, and the third is a search function for the active document. The Cyberdog menu has a Connect to... option for selecting an FTP, Gopher, Mail, or News server. It also provides a history window, a window to display the default notebook (Cyberdog's hotlist), and an option for adding a page to the notebook.

The Navigate menu has options for going forward and backward, accessing security information, displaying the Controls and Location Bar, refreshing the page, and stopping the page from loading. The Mail/News menu has several options for accessing mail servers and newsgroups. Finally, the Web menu has a single option: Show Source HTML, which enables you to view the code behind the active page.

There is no stop button, but anywhere you see a "running dog" icon, you can cancel a download by clicking on it. Apple is inviting developers and users to build on the interface, adding icons and other options based on OpenDoc standards. One unique innovation of Cyberdog is the capability to create Cybericons that represent URLs. A few simple art tools are built-in for design.

Cyberdog is the first application designed specifically to take advantage of the new technology known as OpenDoc. OpenDoc components are based on industry standards set by Component Integration Laboratories, an association of companies including Apple, Adobe Systems, IBM, Lotus, Novell, and Oracle.

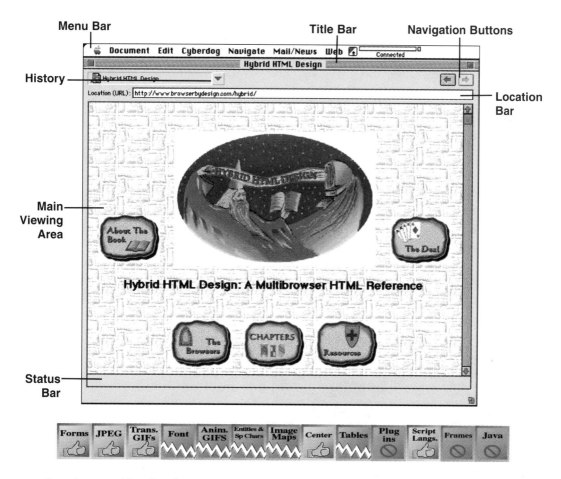

OpenDoc enables developers to create small, modular applications that work together. Mini-applications will be called by individual file types within documents. The Cyberdog beta 2 release requires a power Macintosh with at least 12 megabytes of RAM, OpenDoc version 1.0, and Mac TCP. The beta version can be downloaded from the following:

```
http://cyberdog.apple.com/
```

POINTCAST NETWORK PCN BROWSER

As displayed on the opposite page, the PCN browser supports the center alignment and table formatting tags, and the background GIF. Launched on February 13, 1996, PointCast Inc. provides a free, personalized news and information service. Their browser combines proprietary, yet freely available, content in a customized display with a sophisticated Internet browser.

The program has no standard menus, but it does have two groups of buttons: one used for navigation; the other for updating and customizing the interface. The following figure illustrates the function and structure of the browser interface. With the primary controls, subject categories are selected that determine the folders of documents that appear in the secondary controls screen.

Selecting the document from the secondary controls displays it below. The cursor becomes a magnifying glass when you drag the mouse across the displayed document, which, when selected, expands to fill the entire screen. Clicking on the top-right frame activates the Internet site of the displayed company.

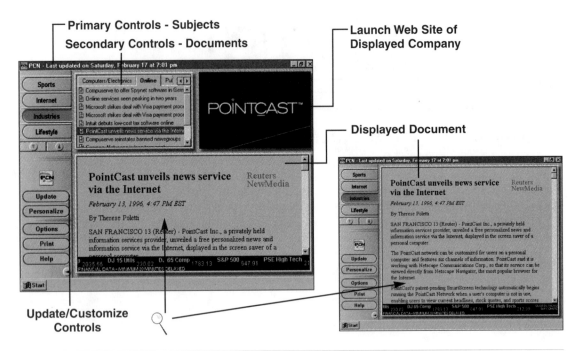

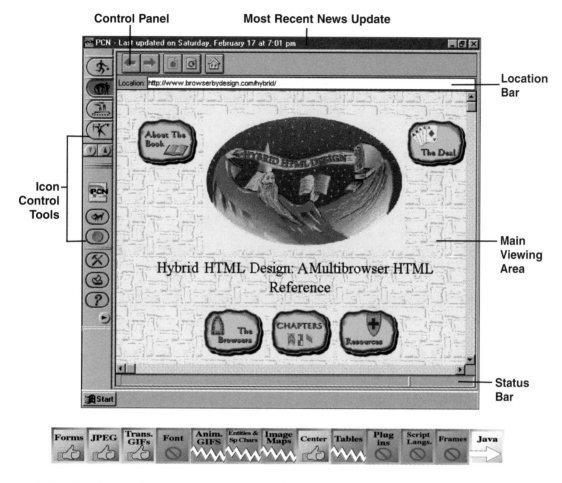

PointCast is introducing a plug-in within the next few months, which will provide many of its features directly into the Navigator interface. Its browser currently handles HTML relatively well, although its navigation tools are sparse. The browser Control Panel has five buttons: go to the previous or following page, stop loading the page, reload the page, and go to the home page.

The PCN browser is available for Windows NT and Windows 95. It can be downloaded from the following:

```
http://www.pointcast.com/
```

OTHER BROWSERS

There are hundreds of Web browsers for the Internet and Intranets worldwide, not to mention the large number of browsers using Standard Generalized Markup Language, or SGML. HTML is a subset of SGML, although it has recently developed independently of the former parent. In addition to the SGML and HTML browsers, there are also VRML, OOGL, and others for viewing additional file formats. The VRML browsers are examined in Chapter 7. An extensive list of online resources, including VRML, are listed in Appendix E.

The following browsers are introduced as a representative sample of what's available on the Web. Specialized browsers are becoming increasingly popular as software developers work to incorporate virtual reality, real-time chat capabilities, and greater levels of security for Internet commerce. A few browsers have been developed for the Amiga computer—this is more common in countries outside the U.S., such as Mexico and Britain. Another category of browsers supports foreign languages, such as Japanese and Hebrew, which require special character sets.

ACCENT MULTILINGUAL MOSAIC

Supporting more than 30 languages, Accent's Multilingual Mosaic features a myriad of special characters and enables viewers to select menu options in their preferred language. Accent can be used in Japanese, Russian, Arabic, Turkish, Greek, and Hebrew, as well as many Western and Eastern European languages.

Most browsers only allow the display of languages already supported by a viewer's operating system because other languages require installing special fonts. Accent's Viewer works in any language version of Windows, including Windows 95. Accent is now a development partner with Netscape and plans to create a plug-in version that will work with Netscape Navigator 2.0. Accent's multilingual Internet programs include a browser, an HTML authoring tool, and an e-mail reader. The e-mail browser supports GIFs, HTML 2, and some HTML 3 including tables. Users can browse in multiple windows simultaneously.

The Multilingual Mosaic browser is available for all Windows versions. It can be downloaded from the following:

```
http://www.accentsoft.com/
```

ALIS MULTILINGUAL BROWSER

The Alis Multilingual Browser enables viewers to switch between French, Italian, German, Spanish, Russian, and English. Menus, messages, and online help are displayed in the language selected. Alis states that it supports more than 75 languages, with plans to add more.

This browser also has built-in access to international content, changing links to reflect the language of choice. The "What's New" button, for example, provides a list of hot spots in the language to which the browser is set. While the "Quoi de Neuf" button is set, for example, the program displays a list of French Web sites. You can also set the browser to favor the display of languages in the order you prefer.

The Multilingual Mosaic browser is available for all Windows versions. It can be downloaded from the following:

```
http://www.alis.com/P_NET/P_MCP/P_MCP.EN.HTML
```

THE LYNX BROWSER

Lynx is most commonly used in universities, libraries, freenets, and other public institutions. One of the first browsers created for the Web, Lynx was designed to reach as wide an audience as possible. Unfortunately, that lead to its biggest limitation—it doesn't support graphics. Because it is limited to Unix commands, Lynx offers only a text-based interface. Most universities have now upgraded their systems to support Netscape, but many public institutions are still limited to Lynx.

The Lynx Options Menu can be accessed by pressing the "o" key. Options include a bookmark file, FTP sort criteria, searching type, character set, VI keys, e(M)acs keys, and keypad options such as arrows or numbered links. This browser offers novice, intermediate, and advanced options. In the novice mode, two lines of help are displayed at the bottom of the screen. The advanced mode displays the URL of the currently selected link. Lynx was developed at the University of Kansas, building on an early version of the Common Code Library developed by the CERN World Wide Web Project.

The Lynx browser is available for Unix and VMS. It can be downloaded from the following:

```
http://kuhttp.cc.ukans.edu/about_lynx/about_lynx.html
```

GNN WORKS

Global Network Navigator, or GNN, provides a Web browser in conjunction with its information services. The browser can be used independently of the GNN services. The company claims that the browser supports HTML 3 and Netscape extensions, although testing has revealed this to be only partially true. Although America Online acquired GNN in 1995, the new parent has not shown how GNN fits in with its overall Internet strategy.

The GNN Works browser is available for Windows. It can be downloaded from the following:

```
http://www.gnn.com/
```

VIRTUAL PLACES

America Online acquired Ubique, formerly called Ubique Sesame, early in 1996. Virtual Places introduces an innovative approach to social surfing on the Web, enabling viewers from remote locations to communicate with each other in real time as they view the same Web site. Small icons representing the portraits of other viewers are overlaid on Web pages so that users viewing the same site can see each other's images.

Virtual Places' integrated audio capability is promised to enable users to have voice conversations, but all participants must be connected to the Internet's MBone. Text chat is also available and requires no special connectivity.

This program's features include the ability for a group to travel together from one virtual Web site to another, led by one user who navigates. A guided tour can also be used to give live multimedia presentations to remote audiences. Current platforms supported are Sun Sparcstation running SunOS 4.1.3, Sun Sparcstation running Solaris 2.3, Hewlett-Packard workstations running HP-UX 9.X, and Silicon Graphics Indy (SGI) running IRIX 5.2.

The Virtual Places browser extension can be downloaded from the following:

```
http://www.ubique.com/
```

Opera Browser

Created by Opera Software, this browser enables the use of multiple windows and the capability to navigate using keyboard commands. Opera supports HTML 2, as well as HTML 3 tags such as tables. Context-sensitive menus are activated by the right-mouse click. These menus can be used to navigate, copy graphics, and change typefaces. The program keeps a history and cache for all active windows.

Opera loads documents and graphics at the same time and automatically saves documents for retrieval. The user can control the size of the archive, and how often new versions should be retrieved. Users can set load image options for each browser window independently, and can load images one at a time or by page. Opera was developed in Norway, and is available in both English and Norwegian.

The Opera browser is available for Windows. It can be downloaded from the following:

```
http://www.fou.telenor.no/opera/opera_en.html
```

WebExplorer

IBM's Secure WebExplorer browser provides unique security features to facilitate online purchases. The program uses encryption to scramble data before it's sent and verifies the identity of those receiving secure data by authentication. To help ensure secure electronic purchases, WebExplorer provides browser-side support to servers with Internet security protocols.

WebExplorer employs the Secure Sockets Layer (SSL) and Secure Hypertext Transfer Protocol (S-HTTP) to ensure compatibility with security protocols on almost any Web server. From the Secure WebExplorer, users can obtain the security information on a current document, change key passwords, and configure security alerts. A graphic representation of a document's security level is also provided.

WebExplorer supports HTML 2 tags and some HTML 3 (such as centered text), HR attributes, and tables. Link, text, and background colors are also supported, as well as background gifs.

IBM's Secure WebExplorer browser is available for OS/2 Warp. It can be downloaded from the following:

```
http://www.ibm.com/Internet/
```

SUMMARY

As you have now seen, browsers can be dramatically different in their display of HTML code. If this fact is still new to you, it may be hard to believe that every one of the preceding images was created by the same HTML document. The code behind the pages will be introduced in Chapter 6.

Without careful testing and design, the use of advanced HTML can lead to pages so garbled, they are unreadable in many browsers. The general rule is that HTML tags that are not recognized by a browser are ignored. In some cases, however, that may mean the information within those tags is not displayed at all. In other cases, such as an HTML table with multiple text columns, content may be bunched together in a way that changes its order and spacing, making it difficult to decipher. In the rest of the book, you'll learn to create your own HTML documents with these differences in mind. As you learn how HTML tags and attributes are displayed in each of the main browsers, you'll be able to capitalize on those differences and design your pages in a manner that avoids common obstacles.

Testing your Web pages in more than one browser is the best way to ensure that your documents look good with multiple browsers. Using the formats described in this book will help isolate possible display inconsistencies, but there really is no substitute for testing. Generally, you should test on the latest versions, as well as older versions, of your anticipated browser audiences. Remember, just because you have the latest version of Netscape or America Online's software doesn't mean the Nielsen family in Peoria does.

Although browsers have gone through many updates since their introduction, there are still a considerable amount of Web users that have never upgraded the Navigator 1.1 that came with their Internet start-up kit. The older browsers were not presented here, but the design tips within apply especially to them—Navigator 1.2 versions and earlier still account for approximately half of all Web browsers.

Now that you have been introduced to the diversity of browsers in the market, you can begin to understand the potential problems of designing Web pages that are optimized for all of them. The next step is to start thinking about how to build HTML pages, and to decide which programs may be best suited to your projects. In the following chapter, a range of applications that can be used to develop Web pages will be presented.

HTML Authoring Tools

Any text editor can be used to create HTML. At its heart, every page on the Web is unformatted text, so why not use SimpleText or Notepad to create HTML documents? You can, and sometimes that may be the most efficient way to make quick corrections or whip up a page. For the most part, however, Web development demands more than a simple text editor. As HTML becomes more complex and Web sites get bigger, developers need better tools.

In determining the best program, consider the software you are already familiar with. If you've been doing word processing for years, you may find that the advanced functions of Microsoft Word give you all you need. If you work in Quark, you may be delighted to find a conversion Xtension called BeyondPress. And if you do a variety of things on the Web, you may want to use several programs in combination. There are many ways to develop HTML—some approaches call for specialized tools, others may work best by tailoring programs you already have. In this chapter, you'll see a review of the hottest new HTML editors and converters, as well as tips on how best to use your word processor and other software.

HTML EDITORS AND CONVERTERS

Software companies are racing to create tools that support the latest developments on the Web. Searching Yahoo and many other sites on the Internet, you'll find more than 60 programs that claim to create HTML. This plethora of software is due to a few unique facets of Web design. First, many HTML developers come from a programming background, and many of them decided to write their own authoring tools. Second, the Web provides the most accessible system of software distribution ever created. Most of these programs can be downloaded for a free trial or demo. With more than 60 programs to choose from, however, it can be hard to determine which ones are worth the space on your hard drive.

In the race to market, the first wave of HTML editors and converters was so limited that some programmers said they just got in their way and went back to SimpleText or Notepad to write the code by hand. If you've been disappointed by the HTML software you've found so far, don't give up just yet. As these programs make it through beta testing, some are becoming useful tools. HTML text editors can make good assistants, providing lists of HTML tags in toolbars and palettes. Most insert tags on either side of selected text, making it easy to mark up pages and ensuring that you won't have typos in your code. WYSIWYG editors take the HTML out of development with drag-and-drop linking options and graphic displays. Conversion programs automate the process of moving content from traditional desktop publishing programs into HTML. Xtensions for programs such as Quark and FrameMaker map style sheets to HTML tags and let you tailor and preview conversion settings. Many designers are learning to use these programs in combination—for example, running a newsletter designed in Quark through a converter, and then opening it in an HTML editor for final revisions. None of these programs do everything you want yet, but they can save you hours of tedium by automating repetitive tasks.

HTML is uniquely universal, and a wide variety of software can be used to create Web pages. Unfortunately, none of these programs address the problems of designing for multiple browsers, which you will learn about in the rest of this book. Work-arounds and hybrid HTML designs will have to be built in manually in all the applications you'll find for Web design.

Creating Web sites often requires converting content from traditional desktop programs into HTML. Many of these programs can be used individually or in conjunction with other software to create Web pages. This chapter presents HTML editing tools in the following order:

1. Word processors
2. Spreadsheet programs
3. Database programs
4. HTML text editors
5. WYSIWYG editors
6. Conversion programs
    a. QuarkXPress
    b. PageMaker
    c. FrameMaker

In this new and emerging market, you'll find a plethora of programs that can be used as HTML authoring tools. None has emerged as the clear winner yet, so your decision on which tool to use should be based on your comfort with the interface and any unique features you find especially useful. Each HTML project may warrant a different approach, and you should look for the program that best fits the task at hand.

In the following pages, you'll find descriptions of some 40 programs that can be applied to Web design. You'll learn their most useful features and most annoying bugs, and view samples of interface design. You'll also learn some tips for making the best use of the software you choose. As each program is reviewed, careful attention will be given to HTML support, the capability to tailor features, and the most useful options for creating HTML.

Recognizing opportunities to automate your work and integrate the software programs you use will make your work faster and more efficient. You will learn in this chapter that the best approach often requires more than one program. Many of the programs described in this chapter can be found on the accompanying CD-ROM or can be downloaded for a free trial or demonstration version.

WORD PROCESSORS

Word processors are highly tailorable and have many functions that still aren't included in some HTML editors, such as mail merge, spell check, and the capability of creating macros to automate repetitive tasks. Spell check, for example, can be tailored to HTML development simply by adding HTML tags to the custom dictionary to check typos in your code. Using search and replace for special functions, such as replacing paragraph marks, is an easy way to insert <P> tags and set breaks in the text. This can also be used to add attributes to the same tag throughout a document by searching for the tag and replacing it with the attribute added to the tag.

SPECIAL CHARACTERS

One of the first problems you may find with content designed for print is the use of "special characters." Graphics designers cringe when they don't see smart quotes (the curly ones) in a document. But browsers can't read smart quotes and turn them into "different" characters. The examples on the following pages demonstrate what Netscape Navigator and Internet Explorer display when viewing common special characters. There are HTML tags for entities and special characters (such as accents, the copyright (©), registration (®), and other symbols). Special characters are a common problem on the Web because browsers are inconsistent in their support. Whether you should remove or replace them with the HTML code depends on which browsers you want your pages to work in. (See Chapter 6 and Appendix C for more information and a complete list of HTML special character tags.)

HTML Developer Tip #1

Don't overlook your word processor as an HTML development tool. Some projects can be automated using macros in a program such as Microsoft Word. Mail merge and search and replace functions can also be used to generate HTML code.

```
<HTML>
<HEAD><TITLE>Special Characters</TITLE></HEAD>
<BODY>

<CENTER><H1>Special Characters</H1>

<H2>This document demonstrates how Netscape Navigator 2.0 and Internet
➥Explorer<BR>
display common special characters</CENTER></H2>
<P><BR>

<STRONG>Smart quotes</STRONG><br>
Created in word processor: " "
<BR>HTML tags: &#179; &#178;
<BR>Straight quotes: " "
<P>

<STRONG>Apostrophe</STRONG><BR>
Created in word processor: '
<BR>HTML tag: &#185;
<P>

The long dash created in word processor:          —
<BR>(no HTML tag)
<P>

<STRONG>Accents</STRONG><br>
Created in word processor: A - á - E - é - I - í - O - ó - U - ú
<BR>HTML tags: A - &aacute; - E - &eacute; - I - &iacute; - O - &oacute; - U -
➥&uacute;
<P>

<STRONG>Other characters:</STRONG><BR>
Created in word processor: ® - Registered - Copyright - ©
<BR>HTML tags: &reg; - &copy;

</BODY></HTML>
```

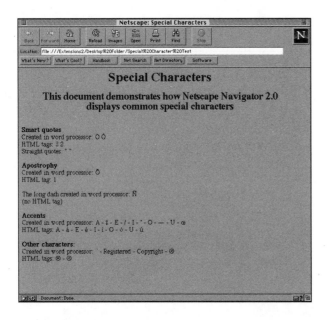

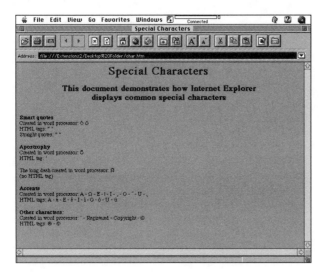

In the examples on the left, you see how Netscape's Navigator and Microsoft's Internet Explorer display the characters in the HTML code on the previous page. Browsers usually ignore tags they can't read. In the case of special character tags, however, the browser will display the HTML code as text. A browser that doesn't support the copyright tag, for example, would display "©" instead of the © symbol.

The simplest and most universal way to fix special character tags is to replace each character with an ASCII equivalent. For example, search for all of the copyright symbols (©) and replace them with the word "Copyright." A GIF can also be used. Some HTML editors replace special characters with HTML tags. If you want an ASCII or graphic alternative, you may be better off in a word processor where a simple macro can be used to replace them with the alternatives you prefer.

ADVANCED WORD PROCESSING FEATURES

MACRO AND TEMPLATE USAGE

Most word processors give users the ability to record macros, a series of keystrokes and mouse movements sequentially entered and recorded to perform common tasks. Whether or not you have an HTML extension to your word processor, if the program you use supports macros, you may be able to design your own special key functions. You could assign, for instance, the SHIFT and F12 keys to enter <HEAD> and </HEAD> around highlighted text.

While macros are used to perform regularly executed tasks, templates are used to provide structure to page design. For example, all HTML documents begin with <HTML>, end with </HTML>, and have <BODY> and <HEAD> sections. A document template could have all of these body elements already in place for the beginning of a new Web page. Used together, macros and templates can enable word processors to automate many aspects of Web page development.

SEARCH AND REPLACE

Although many HTML editors are now equipped with search and replace functions, few are as full-featured as those of your word processor. If you need to replace smart quotes, strip out paragraph marks, insert formatting tags, or do any other insert or replace function, you may be better off in a sophisticated word processor.

Integrating search and replace with macro usage can further leverage your word processor's power as an HTML editor. If you know you will be performing certain tasks regularly, such as processing large numbers of documents that have similar search and replace needs, recording a macro to automate the task may be the most efficient approach.

SPELL CHECK AND THESAURUS

Although many HTML editors provide spell check, you may find better dictionaries in word processors. Because you can add words to the dictionary in most word processors, you will want to add all of the HTML tags you use. Some word processors even have grammar checks and thesauri with synonyms, antonyms, and homonyms—features you will not find in any of the HTML authoring tools currently on the market.

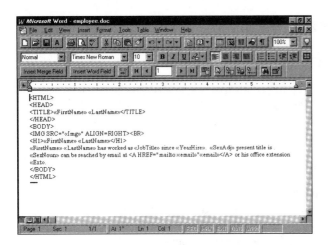

MAIL MERGE

If you need to generate pages that will have identical page layout, but with information that can be supported using form fields, you may be able to take advantage of your word processor's mail merge function. In place of the more expensive database solution, using a word processor's mail merge function can enable you to quickly design HTML pages using fields in the place of the information that will change for each individual document.

The preceding example illustrates the two documents needed to create a series of HTML documents. The one on the left is the primary document that contains the page layout for all the documents to be generated. The one on the right is the source document that contains the data that will be placed in the fields in the generated documents. The table headings correspond with the form field names in the screen on the left.

When using the mail merge feature to generate HTML documents, you will generally have to manicure the output by separating each section into an individual HTML page. You will also have to remember to save the generated documents as plain text files. Again, macros can be written in the word processing program to automate these tasks. Using the mail merge feature of your word processor enables you to create and arrange a series of pages quickly, without having to be familiar with database applications to generate them.

Converters and Assistants for Word Processors

In addition to the features built into most word processors, there are many word processing conversion programs, macros, and assistants available on the Web. Some simply remove special characters and convert basic formatting, such as paragraph tags, bold, and center. More sophisticated conversion programs can handle hundreds of pages at a time, create index pages with links, and even convert graphics to GIFs and JPEGs. In the following pages, you'll learn about a few of the most popular programs available for word processors.

HTML Transit

Windows

HTML Transit supports HTML 2 and 3 and some Netscape and Microsoft extensions. This is a powerful conversion program capable of turning hundreds of pages into HTML documents complete with automatically generated menus linking every page. The program includes a variety of premade graphic files such as common icons, background tiles, and headings that can be built in as the conversion is set up.

In addition to converting Rich Text Format (RTF) and ASCII text, HTML Transit imports native formats from Microsoft Word (DOS and Windows), WordPerfect (DOS and Windows), Lotus Ami Pro, FrameMaker, and Interleaf. The 18 most common graphics formats can be converted into JPEG or GIF, and image conversion can be set globally or one graphic at a time.

Matching Word style sheets to HTML tags makes it possible to convert many elements at once. If you don't use style sheets in Word, the program automatically assigns them to all elements that are the same in the document. Style sheet mapping can be tailored to each job or recorded as a template to automate future conversions. This program is most useful to developers who are converting large documents and use consistent styles.

> **InfoAccess**, $495. (800) 344-9737, (206) 747-3203; Fax: (206) 641-9367
> http://www.infoaccess.com/

INTERNET ASSISTANT FOR MICROSOFT WORD

Windows (Macintosh version in beta)

This extension plugs in to MS Word and can be disabled when not in use. Internet Assistant is a simple Word converter that inserts HTML code corresponding to basic Word formatting, such as alignment and paragraph breaks. Only one page can be converted at a time. The program can also be used as a limited HTML editor to add code. HTML tags can be changed or added through the view source option, but there is no graphic conversion. The plug-in also allows Word to act as a limited browser on the Web and display inline images.

> **Microsoft Corp.**, Free to Microsoft Word owners.
> http://microsoft.com/

CYBERLEAF

Unix (Windows NT version in beta)

Cyberleaf uses the Rich Text Format (RTF) to create hyperlinked documents from MS Word, WordPerfect, Interleaf, FrameMaker, and ASCII formats to HTML. The program simultaneously converts graphics to GIF or PostScript, and can automatically reduce graphics to thumbnail-size images. Interleaf and FrameMaker hyperlinks are converted to HTML. The program also converts tables to GIFs, PostScript, or HTML 3 table markup.

Cyberleaf preserves footnotes automatically, adding HTML hyperlinks to corresponding information. During the conversion process, Cyberleaf analyzes the styles contained in the original documents and automatically matches those styles to equivalent HTML styles. You can also modify default style matching through a point-and-click interface and refine and save the parameters for future conversions. When documents are deleted or revised, Cyberleaf automatically reapplies previously defined styles and hyperlinks to the updated site, and identifies any broken links.

> **Interleaf**, Price not available. (800) 955-5323
> http://www.ileaf.com/

Web Publisher

Windows

Web Publisher converts Microsoft Word, WordPerfect, Lotus Ami Pro, and FrameMaker into HTML pages. During conversion, the program turns images into GIFs and creates a table of contents with links to headings. The program supports HTML 2 and some 3, including basic tables. It interprets style information to build corresponding code.

Web Publisher can also be used to convert PowerPoint presentations, turning up to 20 slides into a linked collection of HTML and GIF files. Each slide becomes an HTML page. Buttons beneath each slide facilitate navigation to the next or previous slide. An outline page is also created, with each heading hyperlinked to the proper slide.

> **SkiSoft**, Free trial, no price available. (617) 863-1876; Fax: (617) 861-0086
> http://www.skisoft.com/skisoft/

ANT_HTML

Windows, Macintosh

ANT_HTML is a shareware conversion program for MS Word. HTML tags can be inserted into any new or previously prepared Word document or any ASCII text file. In addition to HTML 2, options include some Netscape extensions and a special toolbar that can be customized to hold any tags or combinations. With a click of the tool, the tags you've chosen will surround any selected text. ANT_HTML enables authors to enter any and all tags and combinations of tags. The ANT is designed to enable HTML authors to experiment with whatever unconventional tag sequences they choose. The full version of the program includes a Special Characters tool, a Form tool, and options to remove markup from the document or selected text.

> **Created by Jill Swift**, $39.00. jswift@mail.infohwy.com
> http://mcia.com/ant/

WEBAUTHOR

Windows

WebAuthor converts MS Word documents into HTML, maintaining tables of contents, annotations, footnotes, endnotes, and revisions, and creating links between them and their respective places in the document. The converter supports common Netscape and HTML 3, including tables, backgrounds, and center. Toolbars make basic HTML formatting readily available. WebAuthor is bundled with WebImage— an image map editor and image converter. This program enables you to make simple buttons and backgrounds, as well as set the coordinates for image maps. The package includes sample backgrounds, clip art, and Quarterdeck Mosaic.

> **Quarterdeck**, (800) 683-6696, (310) 309-3700; Fax: (310) 309-4217
> www.quarterdeck.com

WORDPERFECT INTERNET PUBLISHER

Windows

Internet Publisher works as an extension with WordPerfect to automatically convert WordPerfect documents into HTML. Toolbar options include hypertext links, graphics, and bulleted lists. A template can be used to create new pages, and basic style mapping is supported.

> **Novell**, Free to owners of WordPerfect 6.1 for Windows. (800) 451-5151
> http://wp.novell.com

2 HTML

Macintosh

A Microsoft Word 6.0 macro for the Macintosh is designed to strip out smart quotes and other special characters, and convert basic formatting such as bold and center to HTML. Point sizes can be mapped to HTML header sizes, and ordered lists can be automatically converted.

> **Group Cortex**, $5. mcrae@cortex.net
> http://www.cortex.net/

Spreadsheets

More than any of the other program types reviewed here, spreadsheet applications are seen as auxiliary in HTML design. The fact that large amounts of information that companies would like to publish are in spreadsheet format has resulted in the arrival of many freeware and shareware conversion utilities ready to integrate your spreadsheet data into HTML format.

For those who have experience with formulas and scripting in spreadsheet applications, it should not be difficult to come up with your own custom solutions to problems as they are presented to you. As you learn HTML, and especially as you explore the usage of tables, opportunities to automate your workload will become more apparent.

The insertion of data into HTML documents is usually done in a manner to preserve the appearance from the spreadsheet program. It is generally desirable for the rows and columns to maintain their integrity and distribution. Many times you can do this simply by cutting and pasting between your spreadsheet and word processing program.

To copy the data, highlight the information you want to bring into the Web page, choose a Paste Special option from the Edit menu of your word processor, and insert the data in a manner that you can manage it. Next, you will generally want to remove the data from the table cells and have it formatted for display. If you need to, you can temporarily insert paragraphs or other formatting that you can remove later with a search and replace function in the word processor.

Many of the functions in spreadsheets can be applied to the treatment of data needed to be processed into HTML format. Suppose that once a month, a list of client balances and properties is generated from your company's database and fed into your spreadsheet. Suppose also that the format of the HTML page demands that the character count for a table cell needs to be 20 or less. Using the (LEFT(CELL REF)) function of most spreadsheet programs will concatenate the client name to the length necessary for HTML display.

ADVANCED SPREADSHEET FUNCTIONS

MACRO AND OTHER PROGRAMMING

Even more than with word processing programs, spreadsheet applications provide their users with incredible opportunities to automate their workload. Custom dialog boxes, formulas, and event-driven scripts efficiently and effectively enable users to input data that could be generated into HTML documents.

If your spreadsheet program is integrated with other software components, you may even be able to extend the programming to affect other applications. The only limits to your usage of a spreadsheet program's functionality are your imagination and the power of the programming language.

APPLICATION DESIGN

Taking programming a step further, application design involves the creation of an interface used to enter and/or retrieve information. Behind the interface may lie a spreadsheet or database source, which may be added to or accessed following whatever security structure is in place. If used for creating HTML, there may be some custom dialog boxes with input boxes, checkboxes, and buttons with which viewers may enter data.

An important thing to remember in building applications to support HTML creation is that all final documents must be in plain text format. Not all spreadsheet applications can export in plain text, so some additional scripting and intermediary applications may be required.

Most of the HTML translating tools listed in this section are macros created in the programs they are intended to support. It is not difficult to create your own macros with a custom interface to let anyone enter or access data. For those who want to use existing converters, following are some currently available conversion tools.

EXCEL CONVERTERS

XL2HTML.XLS

Windows 3.x, 95, Macintosh

XL2HTML.XLS is a Visual Basic Macro for Microsoft Excel 5.0 and Excel 7.0 for Windows 95. It enables users to specify a range of cells to be converted, and then automatically generates a new file with the data in HTML table format. The program converts bold, italic, and underline formatting used in the spreadsheet. A variation on XL2HTML.XLS called CAL2HTML.XLS can be used to make monthly calendars. It enables you to edit a calendar in Excel and then output the data as HTML with tables.

> **Created by Jordan Evans**, Freeware. jordan.evans@gsfc.nasa.gov
> http://www710.nasa.gov/704/dgd/xl2html.html/

EXCEL TO HTML CONVERTER MACRO

Windows, Macintosh

This is an Excel 4.0 macro that will convert part or all of an Excel spreadsheet to an HTML table. The program can generate a complete document or just one table. It retains cell formatting (bold, italic, underline, strikethrough), can use the first row of the spreadsheet as table headers, can reduce font size by 1, and can set cellpadding and custom border sizes. To use the program, select the area of the spreadsheet you want to convert, run the macro, and fill out the dialog box that appears.

> **Created by Scott Blanksteen and Phil Wade**, Freeware.
> http://www.nar.com/people/sib/excel-to-html.html/

EXCEL TO HTML CONVERSION UTILITY

Macintosh

Excel to HTML can be used to convert an Excel 5.0 spreadsheet into an HTML-formatted table. The program was written in AppleScript and requires that AppleScript be installed on the machine. The original table must be in Excel format, and Excel 5.0 must be installed. To run the program, double-click on the icon and follow the instructions in the dialog box. You can also drag an Excel file onto the Excel-to-HTML icon. This program converts bold and italic text and horizontal alignment (left, center, right). Some features may be customized, including border size, width, cellpadding, and table captions. Because this conversion utility does not alter the values of the cells, you can include URLs in the original Excel spreadsheet and they will work in the HTML table. This method can also be used to insert images.

Created by R. Trenthem, Freeware. trenthem@rhodes.edu
http://www.rhodes.edu/software/readme.html/

HTML Developer Tip #2

When using spreadsheet programs, you will almost always be involved in the creation of only a part of a document. Often, copying and pasting between your spreadsheet and word processing software will be the best way to insert data into HTML documents. If you see yourself doing the same type of copying and pasting repeatedly, see how you can use the macro language of your word processor or your spreadsheet program to automate the task. Finding these opportunities will greatly increase your productivity in Web page design.

DATABASES

Database-generated Web sites combine the ultimate in automating updates and creating dynamic HTML pages. This is one of the most powerful developments on the Web because it allows the creation of HTML pages on the fly. Through their capability to design Web pages in response to queries and SQL commands, databases have quickly assumed a preeminent role in HTML production.

Many Web sites have developed custom systems to generate HTML documents that match viewer interests to content. Such sites often require users to complete a survey and use a password to gain full access to the site. The survey information is stored and called by the password to inform the script to create the HTML document for that user. On an efficient system, the entire process can be completed in seconds, and most users are unaware that they are viewing a custom page.

Other sites use databases to maintain portfolios for individual users, such as a system that tracks stocks for each user. Continually updating stock quotes and other dynamic information is also best handled by a database system. Many sites require the creation of a large number of pages that are very similar to each other. A product catalog can be set up, for example, using indexes or menus that list all the products and generate an individual page for each item requested.

Advanced technologies in object-based databases make it possible to store multimedia file types to support complex HTML pages. These high-end databases can be used to organize text, graphics, sound, and video files. Sophisticated search mechanisms can scan graphics for textures and recognizable images. A few have been designed specifically for development on the World Wide Web. Even with the commercial programs designed to create database-generated Web sites, the process usually requires advanced database management skills or programming in a language such as C++.

In response to the growth of the database as an HTML development tool, an increasing number of companies are developing middleware programs to provide the intermediary functions needed to draw information out of a database and generate an HTML page.

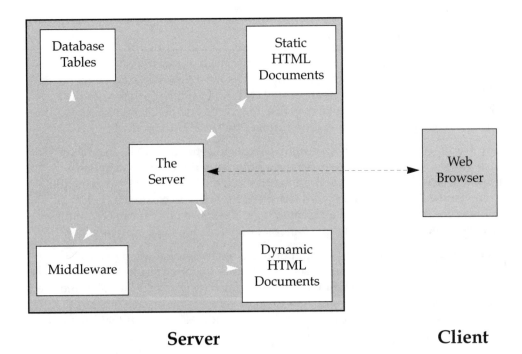

Server   **Client**

The diagram above depicts the relationship between the client browser, the server, and the database. When the client browser asks the server for a document, it is generally routed one of two ways—either the browser requests a static HTML document that has a directory address on the server, or the browser requests the server to look up information that requires the execution of a query. The server directs the query request to the program or script that the HTML form targets. This is generally done by a middleware program or CGI script that uses information from the client to generate a new HTML document from the database based on the information received from the client. In some cases, the program will use an existing template; in others, the program creates documents completely on the fly.

Choosing a Database Solution

There are several ways to integrate database access through a Web site. Factors to consider when choosing a product are the Web server platform, type of project, and security concerns, as well as time and cost. If you are using a Windows NT-based Web server, the majority of products will access information through Open Database Connectivity (ODBC). ODBC is a "translator" that allows a single product to communicate with multiple databases. Most NT Web products will provide Microsoft's drivers (e.g., MS Access, Excel, and SQL Server).

Drivers for other Relational Database Management Systems (RDBMS), such as Oracle, Informix, DB2, or Sybase, must be purchased from third-party vendors. The driver's cost varies and can range from $450 to several thousand dollars for a site license. Unix versions of the ODBC drivers are also available. Vendors include:

Openlink	http://www.openlink.co.uk/
Visigenics	http://www.visigenic.com/
Intersolve	http://www.intersolv.com/dbgate.htm/

The process of accessing a database through HTML occurs in the following manner. The document (HTML) is posted to the Web server and calls a "stub" program through the Common Gateway Interface (CGI). The stub is provided by the software manufacturer or purchased from a third-party manufacturer. The stub extracts information from the form, then connects to the database through ODBC. Once connected, the stub converts the HTML information into Structured Query Language (SQL) and performs the action (insert, query, update, or delete). If the action returns data, the stub converts the information to HTML and returns to the server, which serves the data back to the browser. In the diagram on the left, the stub would be the middleware program in the bottom left corner.

When evaluating products, it is important to keep in mind the requirements that will make a product valuable to you. Some products have great GUI tools that make implementation a snap, while others require manual HTML coding but provide greater functionality. Expected traffic will also influence the solution you choose. In the end, you may find that you really do need more than one database and middleware software program to meet all your needs. There are many database and middleware programs on the market. The programs described in the following pages offer a representative sample of what you can expect in this increasingly popular approach to Web development.

DATABASE AND MIDDLEWARE APPLICATIONS

ILLUSTRA

Illustra embeds Object-Oriented (OO) capabilities in a relational model, providing the industry's first Relational Database Management System (RDBMS) that efficiently handles alphanumeric characters, text, video, images, and documents within a single repository. Illustra Server is an RDBMS that supports data access via standard SQL, security controls, server-enforced data integrity, transactions, recovery, and scalability. Illustra also gives relational developers the ability to do rapid development with low maintenance through encapsulation, inheritance, polymorphism, and direct data access through object IDs. Illustra also supports a rich rule system that enables a developer to specify an action to be taken before, after, or instead of the user-requested action. It supports alerters, a mechanism for informing external programs about events within the database.

DataBlades, a feature unique to Illustra, enable you to plug intelligence into your DBMS for your specific kinds of data. When fitted with a DataBlade, the Illustra system "understands" your data types, so that it can deliver fully optimized query and storage for nontraditional data. DataBlades represent a new approach to supporting rich data, well beyond simple BLOB support. A DataBlade is a snap-in module that adds expertise and intelligence to the DBMS, extending the system with the key functionality required for native support of specific data types. Just as a general-purpose utility knife can be extended to perform different cutting jobs by inserting special-purpose blades, so the Illustra server can be extended to manage new data types by snapping in the required DataBlade. The Illustra server combined with DataBlade modules supercharges the relational model, extending the SQL query language to efficiently process rich data. It provides content-based queries, optimized query plans, and high-performance storage and retrieval tailored to the individual data type.

Informix and Illustra merged in late 1995 and plan to create a combined product in mid-1996.

Illustra Information Technologies, Inc.
http://www.illustra.com/

DBWEB

Windows NT

dbWeb provides database connectivity for HTTP Web servers running under Microsoft Windows NT. Using dbWeb, you can provide real-time access to Open Database Connectivity (ODBC) data sources through Web browsers such as Netscape and Internet Explorer. dbWeb provides full insert/update/delete capabilities, as well as Query-by-Example record selection for dynamic SQL and stored procedures. Records are returned in tabular, detail, or custom forms and can optionally contain "SmartLinks" that allow hypertext-style navigation within a data source.

dbWeb is a high-performance CGI-compliant application implemented as a 32-bit multi-threaded Windows NT service. Administrative tools for managing database schemas, forms, and data sources are included. dbWeb uses 32-bit ODBC to provide access to a wide variety of database products, such as Microsoft SQL Server, Microsoft Access, Sybase, and Oracle. The HTTP servers supported are Alibaba, EMWAC HTTPS, Purveyor, WebSite, Netscape Communications/Commerce Server, and Microsoft Internet Information Server.

The program's greatest strength is its capability to quickly generate HTML pages with no scripting required by the user. dbWeb has a unique repository database that stores all the information that dbWeb needs to dynamically create HTML forms for your database. Graphical administration tools to set up and maintain the repository are included. Knowledge of HTML and CGI programming is not required.

The Schema Wizard creates Query-by-Example, Tabular, and Freeform displays from your database. dbWeb is compatible with Microsoft Back Office, integrating key components such as SQL Server, the Internet Information Server, and Systems Management Server. dbWeb Service works with Microsoft Windows NT 3.5.1 Server or Workstation. dbWeb Administrator works with Microsoft Windows 3.x, Windows 95, and Microsoft Windows NT 3.5.1 Server or Workstation. Data Sources work on Windows NT, Unix, VMS, OS/2, and more.

> **Aspect Software Engineering**, $495. (808) 539-3785
> http://www.aspectse.com/products/dbweb/

ORACLE WEBSERVER 2.0

Oracle WebServer 2.0 integrates database management software with Web server software. The combination provides a scalable platform for building secure, dynamic Web sites and applications for use over corporate Intranets, as well as the Internet. The program integrates high performance, advanced security, and native database connectivity into a single server solution. WebServer also provides Java capabilities on the server, so users are no longer limited to creating small "applets" that run in Web browsers.

Oracle database features include a sophisticated, scalable, multi-platform RDBMS. Development of forms is done through PL/SQL, Oracle's proprietary, stored procedure language. Because the code is stored in the database, replication of applications is fairly straightforward. Oracle is positioned as a "one-stop-shop" where you can get the database, Web server, and Web browser from a single vendor. Oracle appears to be devoting significant resources to the product and plans to introduce an integrated text search engine and Web "agents" by Fall, 1996.

If you have large data requirements (millions of rows) or plan to be replicating corporate information into a data warehouse-type environment, Oracle is worth considering. If you already have Oracle installed, Web Station can give you many new avenues of distributing information through your enterprise.

Oracle WebServer 2.0 offers an open, extensible architecture. Web Request Broker ensures interoperability of applications written in different languages and residing on different Web servers. As a result, users are able to write their own back-end services and plug them into the system. Web Request Broker facilitates the exchange of components implemented in relevant industry standards. Web Request Broker supports Java, PL/SQL, and C/C++, and provides an open Application Programming Interface (API) for building server objects to extend WebServer's capabilities. Unlike simple protocol programming interfaces at the HTTP level, the Web Request Broker API is a true application programming interface for building robust, secure, and manageable applications.

> **Oracle**, $2,495. (415) 506-7000
> http://www.oracle.com/

COLD FUSION

Windows NT, 95

Cold Fusion is a Web Application Development (WAD) platform for Windows NT and Windows 95. Cold Fusion can be used to create a wide variety of applications that integrate relational databases with the Web. As part of Cold Fusion 1.5, Allaire is releasing a Database Component Framework (DCF) for Java. This framework enables Cold Fusion developers to integrate database-driven Java components into their Web applications. The framework also provides Java programmers with a standard set of classes for applets to retrieve and insert data into databases.

Contrasted with dbWeb, Cold Fusion takes longer to set up the initial HTML document (they are not actually generated on the fly), but you have much greater control over the appearance of the generated pages. Cold Fusion can be used to create almost any type of application. It requires a bit more familiarity with SQL and rudimentary programming tasks; however, this is offset by the product's customization features.

More complicated applications include online customer feedback, order entry and registration, bulletin-board style conferencing, technical support, interactive training, and information publishing. Advanced applications include internal client/server systems and Web-based groupware. Developing applications with Cold Fusion does not require coding in a traditional programming language, such as perl, C/C++, Visual Basic, or Java. Instead, developers build applications by combining standard HTML with database commands stored in templates.

> **Allaire**, $495. (612) 831-1808
> http://www.allaire.com/

HTML Developer Tip #3

As more and more Internet database tools become available, companies looking for ways to make their information accessible over local and wide area networks are increasingly finding that their solutions lie in multiple, integrated programs. Some manufacturers, such as Oracle and Microsoft, offer complete turn-key solutions to meet a company's Internet server needs. Influencing your choice will be the operating system that houses your company data, the server that hosts the Web pages, and the amount of control you want to have over HTML design.

4W PUBLISHER

Windows NT, 3.1, 95

4W Publisher is a database tool for developing and storing Web pages. The current version generates static Web pages that can be stored on any Web server. The program lets you create reusable "page components" that are fragments of HTML pages. These components can be utilized in any page (index or document). Each document in the database can specify a different page template, enabling you to create groups of documents that have a particular background, header, and footer.

After you've created your documents, 4W Publisher will automatically index them for you and create a home page listing all of the documents in the database and sorting by any keyword. Indexes use the header, navigation, and footer page components to define the resulting HTML page, but also use style sheets to define the body of the page. The program functions in much the same way as the report designer utility of many popular database packages. 4W Publisher supports embedded variables (such as %%[Description]). Any field in a document can be referenced in the document body, page components, or indices. 4W Publisher includes "helper" dialog boxes that enable you to add HTML markup tags and %% variables to your database records. 4W Publisher uses MS Access to store its information, but it expects to see all data, such as pages and templates, in the tables it knows about.

> **Information Analytics**, $250. (402) 476-6222; Fax: (402) 476-3359
> http://www.4w.com/4wpublisher/

HTMakeL DATABASE MERGE

Windows NT, 95

HTMakeL Database Merge is a shareware program that takes an ASCII or ANSI text file and merges data from an ODBC data source into a new ASCII or ANSI text file. It can be used to merge the data into pre-designed HTML pages. HTMakeL does not come with any ODBC files, so you must have your own. This is a low-cost shareware program with limited features that was created in C++.

> **MacMunnis**, $25.
> http://miso.wwa.com/~mmunnis/htmakel.html

HTML TEXT EDITORS

HTML text editors let you work directly with the code. As with any text editor, you can always type HTML tags and text directly onto the page. In addition, these editors provide easy access to HTML tags. At the click of a toolbar or palette, code is inserted on either side of selected text. Some also feature table editors, form builders, and image conversion.

The best HTML editors support HTML 2 and 3, as well as Microsoft and Netscape extensions. Many will also let you add other HTML tags and combinations of tags to toolbars and palettes. Creating combinations can automate common, repetitive tasks. For example, assign a palette option that includes <H1> and <CENTER> for all your headlines. Another common feature is a preview button that will launch any browser available.

There are dozens of HTML editors on the market, making it tough to find the one that may be best for you. None of them do everything you are likely to want, and some are better tailored to one task than another. For now, a combination of these tools may be the best option. Because most can be downloaded for a free trial, it's easy to test the ones that interest you and keep an eye out for upgrades. (Trial versions of some of these programs are included on the CD-ROM.)

HTML Developer Tip #4

HTML code editors can be useful assistants. Because you can type in the code manually, these editors offer the ultimate in flexibility. Many provide comprehensive lists of HTML tags that can be quickly and easily placed on either side of highlighted text. They are also handy for cleaning up the work of HTML converters.

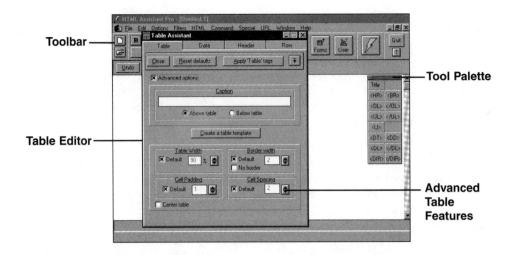

HTML ASSISTANT PRO 2 V2.0

HTML Assistant Pro 2 is one of the few editors with advanced HTML table options. A table builder features collspan, rowspan, and cellpadding. A template can also be created by simply setting the total number of rows and columns. A toolbar includes HTML 2 and HTML 3, and can be tailored to include your own tags and combinations.

Many of the features offered in HTML Assistant Pro 2 are split into two levels, as you can see in the table editor above. The first level handles the basic HTML tags; selecting Advanced options reveals a list of attributes that can be inserted into the code. A preview option lets you view documents in any browser without leaving the editor.

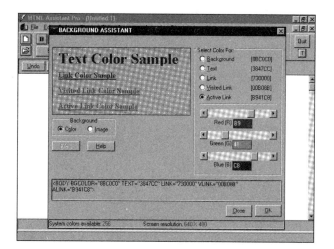

HTML ASSISTANT PRO 2

Windows

Supports
- HTML 2; some HTML 3
- Some Netscape extensions
- Can add HTML tags

Features
- Table builder
- Sets color code

Bookmark files from browsers such as Netscape and Mosaic can be retrieved in HTML Pro and used to set external links. Local files can be linked through a browse option, and URLs and file names can be typed in directly. This text editor has another feature that is becoming increasingly common—you can strip all of the HTML tags out of a document.

The Background Assistant shown above finds the hexadecimal color code to set background, link, and text colors. After you select the color, the code can be inserted directly into the <body> tag. Background images are also supported. In Windows 95, this program supports the right mouse button. It also features spell check, electronic help files, and a manual. An Automatic Page Creator further automates the development of HTML pages.

> **Brooklyn North Software Works**, $99.95. (800) 349-1422, (902) 493-6080
> http://fox.nstn.ca/~harawitz/

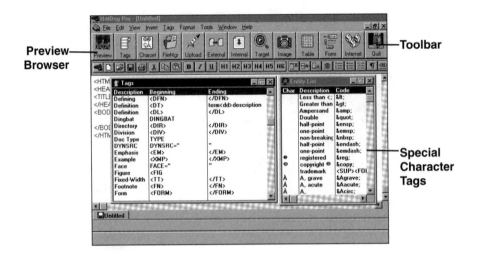

Preview–Browser

Toolbar

Special Character Tags

HOTDOG V2.0

HotDog is one of the few editors to support Microsoft extensions such as DYNSRC and MARQUEE. Custom tags can be added and the toolbar can be customized to support any code. Large, colorful buttons give this program a user-friendly interface, and handy pull-down menus clearly explain options.

A help menu outlines the differences between HTML 2.0 and the Microsoft and Netscape extensions, a rare feature in an editor. Other help functions explain the basics of HTML development, making this an especially useful program for those new to HTML design. A simple site manager maintains a list of local files. To set internal links, simply highlight the text you want to be 'hot' and select the file manager to see the documents and folders available. To finish the link, select the file, and HotDog inserts the appropriate path in the text.

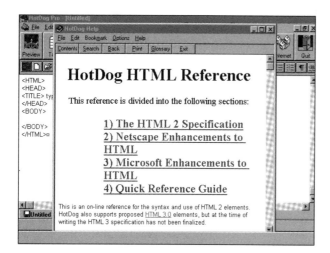

HOTDOG

Windows

Supports

- HTML 2; some HTML 3
- Some Netscape extensions
- Some Microsoft extensions
- Can add HTML tags

Features

- Colorful interface
- Built-in FTP capability

HotDog has a limited table menu. Such attributes as collspan and rowspan have to be added manually. Another pop-up menu can be used to create basic HTML forms. A comprehensive list of special character tags is provided, as well as many other HTML tags, all in easy-to-access windows.

A preview button can be set to view documents in any HTML browser, and the page is automatically refreshed each time the preview option is selected. Other options assist with setting links to graphics or other files. A built-in file transfer protocol program bundled with HotDog makes this a well-rounded development tool. Files can be loaded to a remote server from within HotDog.

Sausage Software, $99.95. Fax number in Australia: 613-98-16-3922
http://www.sausage.com/

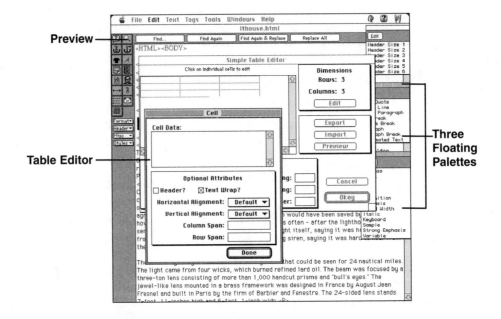

WORLD WIDE WEB WEAVER V1.1.1

Providing a menu bar, toolbar, and three floating palettes, Web Weaver offers many options for selecting and inserting HTML tags. The palettes can be placed anywhere on the screen and easily edited to host any tag or combination. A Preview button lets you view your work in any browser and can be set to handle more than one browser—a great feature for testing hybrid HTML designs.

The table builder shown above assists in creating HTML tables and supports cellspacing and cellpadding. Data can be added to each cell independently. A link option lets you set links to local files and also facilitates external links. The program automatically determines the height and width of GIFs when you set image links, and features border, alignment, and hyperlink options.

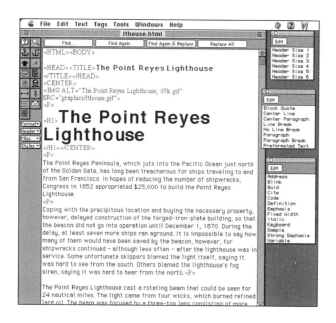

WWW WEAVER
Macintosh

Supports

- HTML 2; some HTML 3
- Some Netscape extensions
- Can add HTML tags

Features

- Color codes tags
- Table editor
- Browser preview
- Floating palettes
- Hexadecimal color finder

Most HTML editors will place open and close HTML tags on either side of selected text. Web Weaver takes this a step further, letting you set preferences about how it handles selected text. The option "keep text and tags highlighted" makes it easy to place a second tag set after the first. Web Weaver color-codes all HTML tags to help distinguish them from text. The program formats the content as well, reflecting how it will appear in a browser. As you can see in the image above, text that has been assigned an <H1> tag is displayed in a larger font size than other text in the code. A body tag editor lets you assign the background, link, and text color with the hexadecimal code and offers the advanced option of finding hexadecimal colors. The program also supports background images.

Included in the HTML tag set is a long list of special character tags that can be set manually or automatically and can be used to convert smart quotes, accents, and other special characters throughout a document.

Created by Robert Best, $50. (315) 265-0930
http://www.northnet.org/best/

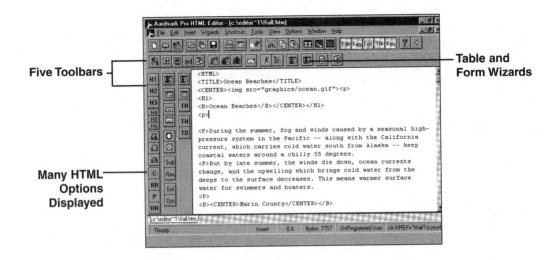

Five Toolbars

Table and Form Wizards

Many HTML Options Displayed

AARDVARK PRO V2.0.4

Aardvark Pro combines many popular features to create an HTML text editor with five toolbars and many options. The toolbars can be turned on or off and new tags can be added. Aardvark includes a URL Library that tracks all your HTML documents and facilitates linking. A Project Manager enables you to graphically view your entire site, and the program handles files up to 16 MB in size.

HTML Wizards help you define complex tags such as tables and forms. Both options are easily accessible from the toolbar and can be tailored for each task. Choose from the predefined macros to automate projects or create your own. The Color Chooser lets you find hexadecimal color codes from a spectrum and insert them into the body tag. Aardvark comes with many sample documents to choose from as well.

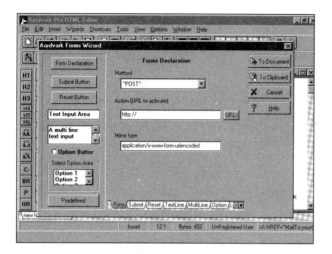

AARDVARK PRO

Windows

Supports
- HTML 2; some HTML 3
- Some Netscape extensions
- Can add HTML tags

Features
- Five toolbars
- Wizards, macros, and templates

Image options are limited; you cannot import graphics or browse for a file name. Graphics options from the menu will insert the image source tag, including attributes, but you have to add the file name, path, and attribute values manually.

Smart tabs let you automatically indent source code, and a built-in preview option lets you view your pages in any browser. A number of templates are included in the program. A built-in Notepad provides a handy place to store regularly used text. Predefined commands provide access to commonly used phrases or paragraphs, such as "Last Updated on June 4, 1996." Throughout the program's features, Aardvark lets you define and create your own options.

> **Aardvark Pro**, $89. Australia.
> http://www.ozemail.com.au/~kread/aardvark.html/

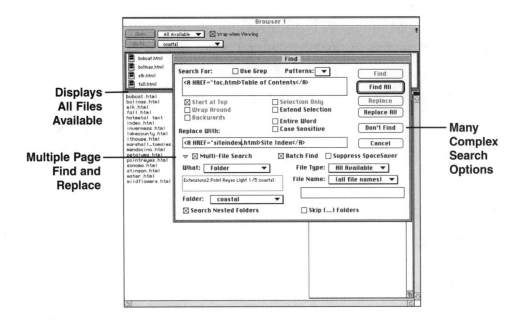

Displays All Files Available

Multiple Page Find and Replace

Many Complex Search Options

BBEDIT V3.5

BBEdit, by Bare Bones Software, supports HTML 2, some HTML 3, and a few Netscape extensions. The CD-ROM version includes a developer's kit that has led to the development of extensions by other programmers, adding many options to this text editor. This openness to other programmers may help BBEdit out-feature some of the competition.

One of its most outstanding features is the capability to handle multiple-document find and replace functions, which is invaluable if you are working on a large Web site. Featuring complex search functions (such as grep), this program can make global changes quickly. Unlike many HTML editors that limit file sizes, BBEdit enables
you to work with files as large as your available memory can handle (there's a theoretical 2 GB maximum). The program includes an integrated HTML-aware spelling checker, as well as support for external spell-checking systems via the Apple Event Word Services Suite.

BBEDIT

Macintosh

Supports
• HTML 2; some HTML 3
• Some Netscape extensions
• Can add HTML tags

Features
• Developer's kit
• Many extensions
• Multiple-page
  find and replace

A floating tool palette makes HTML code easily accessible, and Macintosh drag-and-drop features enable placement of markup tags, image files, and anchors. The program supports forms and tables and provides HTML syntax checking. HTML pages can be viewed with any available Web browser and can be integrated with other Internet tools such as FTP clients and newsreaders via the Internet Configuration System.

Repetitive tasks can be automated using Frontier, AppleScript, and other OSA-compliant scripting systems. An optional feature lets you automatically back up files when saving. The program's HTML syntax checker boasts the capability to correct HTML, even if it was created in another editor. In its most recent upgrade, BBEdit features a new "PageMill Cleaner" to correct the HTML output of Adobe PageMill.

Bare Bones Software, $119. (508) 651-3561
http://www.tiac.net/biz/bbsw/

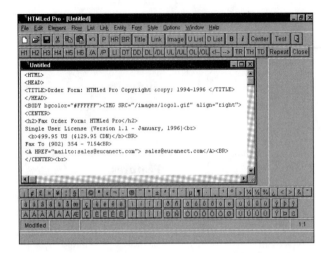

HTMLED PRO V1.1

Windows

Five toolbars line the top and bottom of HTMLed Pro, making an impressive list of HTML tags accessible. Toolbars can be turned off one at a time, and 10 buttons are provided for customizing or adding other tags. Markup code, text, and entities are displayed in different colors to make the HTML easier to distinguish. The origin of each HTML tag is displayed in the status bar when using the menu so that you can distinguish HTML 3 from Netscape extensions. Table and form editors are included, as are a few simple templates. Users can define and record their own templates as well. If you're in Windows 95, you'll find a fully configurable right-mouse button menu. Undo and redo are supported, as well as spell check. Special characters can be automatically converted from RTF format.

> **Internet Software Technologies**, $99.95. Australia.
> http://www.ist.ca/

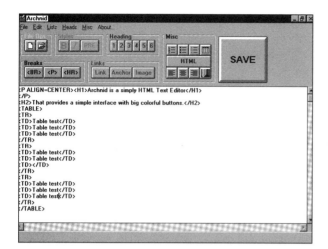

ARACHNID

Windows, Macintosh

Supports
- HTML 2; some HTML 3
- Can add HTML tags

Features
- Colorful toolbar
- Easy interface

ARACHNID V0.5

Large colorful buttons make common tags easily accessible from the toolbar, but there is no way to add your own—they are limited to HTML 2 and a few HTML 3 options. A built-in color manager will let you select hexadecimal colors and insert them as the background color. Images can be imported and linked within the editor. A site management tool creates a basic map of project files, but cannot be used to alter or correct links. Search and replace operations work on multiple pages and can be used to make global changes. The preview option can be set to work with any browser, and a simple table editor can be used to create tables but does not support any of the table attributes.

> **Second Look Computing**, Freeware.
> http://sec-look.uiowa.edu/

OTHER HTML TEXT EDITORS

WEBBER V1.1

Windows

This is an HTML editor with an SGML-compliant parser. It supports drag-and-drop editing and multilevel undo and redo. The full-featured help system includes descriptions of HTML 2 tags and attributes. Additional options facilitate creating anchors, forms, images, and tables. Registered versions include some HTML 3 tags and Netscape extensions.

> **Cerebral Systems Development Corp.**, $30.
> http://www.csdcorp.com/webber.htm/

WEBEDIT V1.2

Windows

WebEdit includes support for HTML 2, plus some HTML 3 and Netscape extensions. The unregistered version doesn't have all the toolbars, but the demo is fully functional. The toolbars are intelligently arranged with each icon representing a different class of tools, making common HTML tags easily accessible. One of the strengths of this program is its support of foreign languages. WebEdit is available in English and German, and is soon to be released in Japanese, Italian, and Swedish.

> **Nesbitt Software**, $79.95.
> http://www.nesbitt.com/

HTML EASY! PRO V1.3

Windows

An HTML text Editor, HTML Easy! Pro supports HTML 2, HTML 3, and some Netscape extensions. The program is available in English and Chinese.

> **Basic Concept Studio**, Price not available. Taiwan.
> Canada mirror site: http://www.trytel.com

HTML WYSIWYG EDITORS

What You See is rarely What You Get with HTML authoring tools because they can't reflect the display of all the browsers that may visit your pages. One of the biggest limitations of WYSIWYG editors is that they provide their own graphic view, but offer no preview option to test your work in other browsers. As you'll learn in this book, the display provided by a WYSIWYG editor such as PageMill may look very different from the display you'll see in Netscape Navigator or other browsers.

As a general rule, the better the WYSIWYG interface, the fewer HTML tags the program supports. Most of these programs are limited to HTML 2 tags. If you want to add unsupported tags, you'll almost always have to use a text editor. Some of these WYSIWYG programs have attracted large audiences with the promise of easy Web page creation without the HTML. For those interested in advanced design and control, however, these programs still have little to offer. Some of these editors do show promise, and in the future you can expect more Web development tools with good graphic interfaces and advanced HTML support. In the meantime, these programs make it possible for novices to create basic pages and offer the more advanced HTML author a few useful features, such as importing and converting graphics, drag-and-drop link functions, and form and table builders. If you like the graphic interface, you could start in one of these programs and use a text editor to add advanced code later.

HTML Developer Tip #5

There are many new HTML authoring tools on the market, but they are as inconsistent in their support of HTML tags as the browsers that display their creations. When selecting an HTML authoring tool, make sure it supports the tags you want. Better yet, some programs let you add your own tags. In each program presented, HTML support and the capability to tailor functions will be carefully reviewed.

Toolbar —

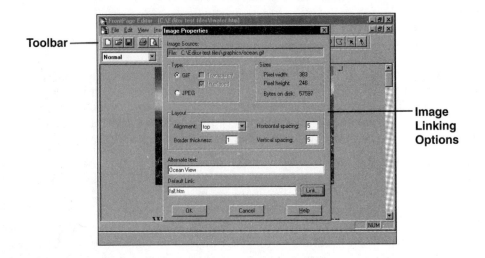

— Image
Linking
Options

FRONTPAGE V1.0A

FrontPage provides a WYSIWYG interface, making it easy to create simple pages. Bundling an HTML editor with software to run a Web server, CGI scripts, and a site manager for organizing links makes this a powerful tool with a high-end price tag. The HTML editor provides a graphic interface, but no preview option to check your work in other browsers. And it's limited in HTML tags—you can't create tables, and you can't add your own HTML.

A "view generated source" option lets you see the HTML code, but you can't add or change anything in the viewer. Graphics can be imported into the WYSIWYG environment through the Image Properties window shown above. The program does not convert images and you cannot resize images within FrontPage. Height and width are automatically inserted in the image tag when the image is linked through the Image Properties option.

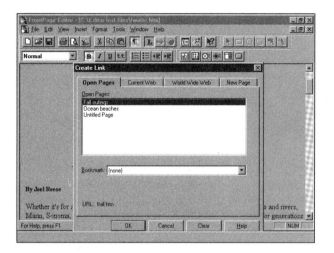

FRONTPAGE

Windows (Macintosh beta)

Supports
• HTML 2; some HTML 3

Features
• WYSIWYG
• Bundled with server software
• Includes CGI scripts

A toolbar option facilitates creating image maps. A site manager, included in the package, can be used to change or correct links globally and displays an entire site in a graphic window. FrontPage also checks for broken links. Links can be inserted by using the window shown above. Select the words or graphic you want linked, and a pop-up window lets you browse any open pages, browse any page in the site you are working on, or type any URL to set the target.

CGI scripts bundled with FrontPage include WebBots for setting up threaded discussion groups and search functions. Originally from Vermeer, Microsoft bought FrontPage in January, 1996 and plans to continue development of the program. (An upgrade was in the works at the time of this writing that promised to support tables.)

> **Microsoft**, $695. (800) 426-9400 or (206) 882-8080
> http://microsoft.com/

Toolbar 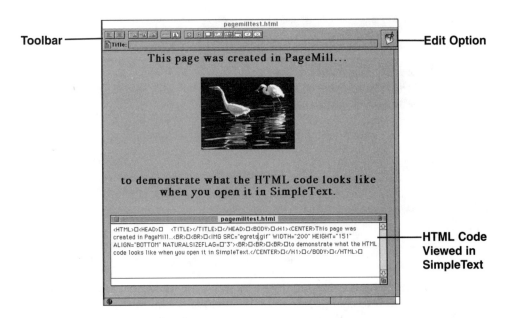 **Edit Option**

HTML Code Viewed in SimpleText

PageMill V1.0

Adobe's PageMill provides a graphic interface ready for the most novice developers. PageMill was the first WYSIWYG editor for the Mac, but it's limited to HTML 2 and a few HTML 3 tags, so you can't build complicated pages. Code that PageMill doesn't understand, it displays in the WYSIWYG environment as red text. On the following page, the program couldn't read the table tags, so the HTML is displayed and the formatting is ignored. Adobe claims this option means you can add any tags you want, but adding tags this way clutters the interface and interferes with the alignment of other items on the page.

PageMill automatically inserts the height and width in the image tag when you import a graphic and sets the path to the link. In addition to converting PICT files into GIFs, a built-in image editor can interlace GIFs and make any one color transparent. PageMill will also let you import JPEGs, but you have to create them in another program such as Photoshop.

PAGEMILL

Macintosh

Supports
- HTML 2
- Very little HTML 3

Features
- WYSIWYG
- Displays graphics
- Image conversion
- Transparency
- Interlacing

PageMill's biggest limitation isn't obvious until you look at the raw HTML behind each document. PageMill doesn't put enough space in the code, making it hard to read in a text editor. On the previous page, you see a document created in PageMill's WYSIWYG editing environment. Superimposed over the bottom of the screen is the HTML code as it appeared when opened in SimpleText.

You may also notice that Adobe has added its own code to the HTML mix. If you look closely at the source code, you'll find "Naturalsizeflag=3" in the image tag. If you've never seen that HTML addition, you're not alone. Adobe created it so that PageMill could keep track of graphics and determine if you've replaced an inline image with a new version. This addition, combined with the spacing problems, make it difficult to work with the raw HTML code in a text editor. PageMill provides its own browse mode, but does not provide a way to preview your work in other browsers.

> **Adobe**, $99. (415) 961-4400 or (800) 833-6687
> http://www.adobe.com/

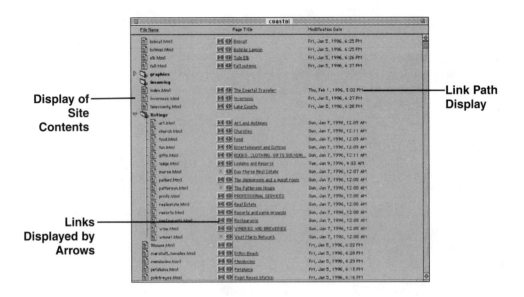

Display of Site Contents

Links Displayed by Arrows

Link Path Display

SITEMILL V1.0

Adobe's SiteMill provides a Web site management system where links can be verified, organized, and changed in a graphic interface. PageMill is bundled with SiteMill and the package is sold as an upgrade, but no improvements have been made to the HTML editor since its initial release. SiteMill can be used as a stand-alone program to check the links on existing Web sites, even if they were created in a program other than PageMill.

To view the links in any Web site, simply select Load Site from the Site option in the menu bar. SiteMill displays all the folders and files in the site, verifying every link as it loads. It's fast, too—a 700-page Web site took less than a minute to analyze and load. The first thing SiteMill displays is an Errors window reporting broken links. If you have changed the name of a file without correcting the name in the link tag, for example, SiteMill will report it as an error. Functional links are represented by two sets of arrows on the left of each HTML file name. Selecting the left arrows displays the pages that link to the document; the right arrows display outgoing links. A red "X" indicates that a file is not linked anywhere.

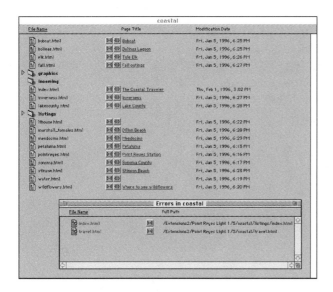

SITEMILL

Macintosh

Supports

• Link management
• Checks local URLs

Features

• WYSIWYG
• Global corrections
• Drag-and-drop linking
• PageMill is bundled with SiteMill

To correct broken links in SiteMill's drag-and-drop environment, you can drag the icon to its representation in the Error window and SiteMill will automatically correct it. You can also move a file to the location indicated in the link tag or correct the file name within SiteMill. Double clicking on any file name opens the page in PageMill where the link can also be re-created.

SiteMill's biggest limitation when checking Web sites created in other programs is that it can't identify case differences (such as ARTIST.GIF linked as artist.gif). This can be a problem because on a Macintosh system, links with case differences will work, but if you send your site to a Unix server (which are case-sensitive), your links will be broken when the site goes online. SiteMill does, however, maintain case in links created in PageMill and in changes made within SiteMill.

To alter a functional link, simply move or rename the file within SiteMill's graphic display, and it will alter all related links in the HTML code. You cannot change the name of an existing folder if it contains files, but you can create new folders and change the names of empty folders.

> **Adobe**, $595. (415) 961-4400 or (800) 833-6687
> http://www.adobe.com

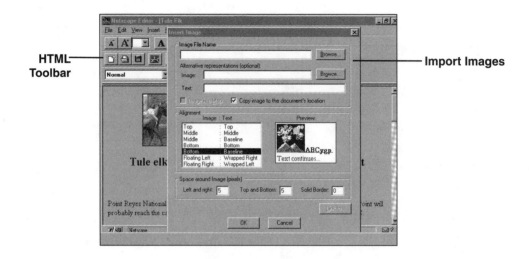

HTML Toolbar — labeled on the left

Import Images — labeled on the right

NAVIGATOR GOLD V1.0B2

A familiar interface greets the user—it looks just like Netscape's browser—but the first beta release of Navigator Gold is a limited editor unable to create many of the features supported by the Navigator 2.0 browser. The biggest limitation of this program is that it does not support tables and has no forms editor. Graphic files can be imported into the WYSIWYG editing environment, but there are no conversion capabilities and it doesn't set interlacing or transparency. When graphics are imported, a pop-up window enables you to insert vspace, hspace, alignment, and the alt tag in the HTML code.

A toolbar has been added to the Netscape interface, featuring a few basic HTML functions such as bold, italic, and alignment. Font size, one of Netscape's extensions, can be adjusted by using the plus and minus options in the toolbar. To use the list of header tags, however, you have to open Paragraph under the Format option in the main menu. The toolbar can be redesigned, but there is no way to add new or custom HTML tags to the limited set of options.

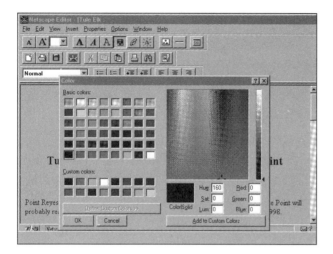

NAVIGATOR GOLD

Windows, Macintosh

Supports
- HTML 2; very little 3
- Some Netscape extensions

Features
- WYSIWYG
- Image insertion
- Color code window

The Browse button in the middle of the toolbar lets you switch between the editor and Netscape's browser, but you can't set it to work with other browsers. You can view the source from within Navigator Gold, but unlike the browser that displays source in a text editor, Navigator Gold displays it in a window where it can't be altered. To change the HTML code manually, you will have to leave this program and use a text editor. If you open a document that includes unsupported tags in Navigator Gold, it will display like a limited browser, ignoring any HTML it can't interpret. Although the alpha version for the Macintosh didn't support table tags, it did display an animated GIF created in GifBuilder.

The toolbar includes some icons found in word processing programs, such as cut and paste options, but there is no spell checker. Only the alpha version of the Macintosh and beta version of the Windows programs were available as of this writing. Updates can be found through Netscape's Web site.

> **Netscape**, Price not yet available. (415) 528-2555
> http://home.netscape.com/

Toolbar —

Supports
Tables and
Attributes

GNNPRESS V1.1

One of the most feature-packed graphical editors on the market is GNNPress by America Online's Global Network Navigator (GNN). This program was formerly NaviPress by NaviSoft. Combining HTML 2, HTML 3, and Netscape extensions puts GNNPress ahead of many other WYSIWYG programs—and it's available for Macintosh and Windows. In GNNPress, you can easily switch between a graphic editing environment and the raw code where you can add your own HTML. Changes made in the HTML code can be saved and are reflected in the WYSIWYG view. The program also doubles as a Web browser, but it does not offer a preview option for other browsers.

GNNPress features a table editor that supports attributes and facilitates the creation of complex tables. The program's support of table tags is a bit ironic, considering that AOL owns GNNPress and, as of this writing, AOL's browser still couldn't read tables. A form builder makes it possible to create guestbooks and other forms in a graphical environment.

GNNPRESS

Macintosh, Windows

Supports

• HTML 2; some 3
• Some Netscape extensions

Features

• WYSIWYG
• Can make changes to HTML code directly
• Table builder
• Drag-and-drop linking
• Imports graphics

Images can be imported in GIF or JPEG format. Once in the editor, graphics can be moved around in a drag-and-drop environment and aligned. Graphical and other links can be set with assistance from the program—simply highlight the text, find the file you want linked using the browser option, and the path is automatically inserted.

GNNPress builds in FTP capability and directs it at GNNServer, an AOL Web hosting service. GNNServer customers will receive technical support for GNNPress; others may use the program free with no technical support offered. The program can be used to create Web sites for any server.

Global Network Navigator, Free. (800) 819-6112
http://www.gnnhost.com/

Toolbars —

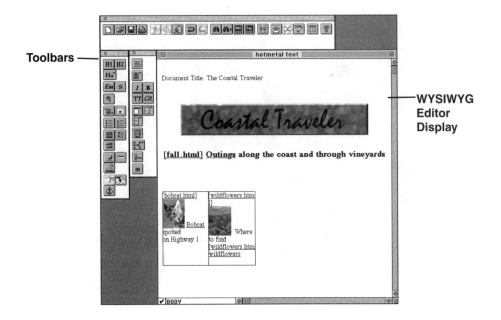

— WYSIWYG
Editor
Display

HotMetal Pro V2.0

HotMetal Pro supports HTML 2, as well as many HTML 3, Microsoft, and Netscape extensions. An unusual interface lets you switch between a WYSIWYG environment and an option that lets you see the tags, but won't let you change them. The tags can be deleted individually if they are on, but they can't be typed in directly and you can't add attributes once they are in place.

HotMetal Pro provides a table editor, but it doesn't support attributes such as border size, cellpadding, or cellspacing. The table shown above was created in another program and should have no border and more space in each cell. HotMetal Pro, like most browsers, simply ignores the tags it doesn't understand.

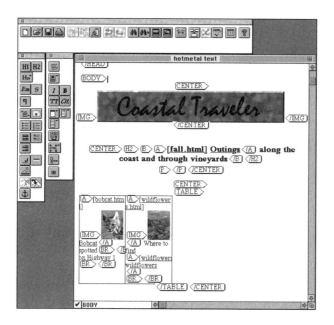

HotMetal Pro

Macintosh, Windows

Supports

- HTML 2; some HTML 3
- Some Netscape extensions
- Some Microsoft extensions

Features

- WYSIWYG
- Drag-and-drop linking
- Table builder
- Word Processor conversion

The program offers an error-checking option, but if you use advanced features, you'll confuse it. It also misses errors that HotMetal Pro built in, such as an </LI> tag, which doesn't exist in HTML, but is inserted at the end of every list item with an <LI> tag because the close </LI> tag is part of the SGML standard. Another SGML tag, the close break tag </BR>, is shown in the editor, but removed when the page is saved as HTML.

One of the best features of this program is that it provides multiple levels of undo and redo, something more of these editors should offer. Supporting 30 actions in Smart Undo, HotMetal Pro can take away your changes one tag at a time. HotMetal Pro is also a conversion program capable of turning most word processing files into HTML code.

> **SoftQuad Corporation**, $195. (416) 239-4801
> http://www.sq.com/

DESKTOP PUBLISHING CONVERTERS

Quark, PageMaker, FrameMaker

Many developers argue that the Web is so different from print, you should throw away your desktop publishing documents and start over. But that's not always practical, especially if you have large documents to put on the Web. Creating hyperlinks requires a different approach to design than linear publications, but it is possible to accommodate such differences in the conversion process. Sidebars, linked text boxes, and graphics pose the biggest challenge.

The best conversion programs break documents into elements, letting you arrange individual text boxes and graphics on separate pages. Style sheet mapping allows for global changes and—once developed—settings can be saved to automate future conversions of the same documents. In many conversion programs, links can be set by selecting the text in the original document, and then setting the target location in the same document or typing in any URL. Unfortunately, most converters are limited to HTML 2, with only a few HTML 3 options or browser-specific extensions. These programs are great for setting up the initial conversion and automating the most repetitive tasks, but more sophisticated layout and style options have to be added in a text editor or other program.

BEYONDPRESS V1.0

QuarkXPress for Macintosh

Atrobyte's BeyondPress Xtension plugs neatly into QuarkXPress 3.3 and lets you tailor how the page will look when exported to HTML. A preview option displays the output in any browser, and the export function creates a new HTML file, leaving your original document unaltered. Although the program only provides HTML 2, any styles or combinations of tags can be added to the master list.

BeyondPress adds a palette called the Content Manager, which lists all of the elements of the document separately. Any element, such as a linked text block, headline, or graphic, can be renamed within the content manager, and the order and arrangement can be changed by dragging icons around the palette.

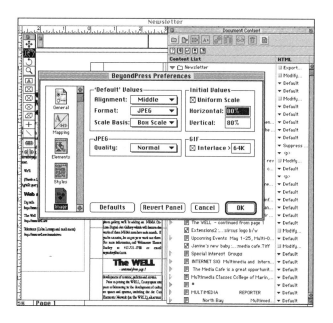

BEYONDPRESS

Macintosh

Supports
- HTML 2; some 3
- Some Netscape extensions

Features
- Style sheet mapping
- Converts large files
- Creates multiple pages
- Point-and-click linking

To create hyperlinks, highlight the text you want "hot" in the XPress file, and then select the destination within the same document or type in any URL. Some converters have trouble organizing graphics and sidebars. BeyondPress lets you group elements in separate folders and makes each folder its own HTML page. This provides great flexibility, enabling you to break a large document into many linked pages.

Style sheets are mapped to HTML tags in the preferences window. This works best if you use consistent styles in XPress, because it lets you assign many elements at once. You can also match elements individually, match multiple HTML tags to any style, and suppress any elements you don't want to display (such as page numbers) from your original document. BeyondPress will convert graphics into GIFs or JPEGs. Image options include scaling image size, interlacing, and transparency. Settings can be applied to all of the images or on an image-by-image basis.

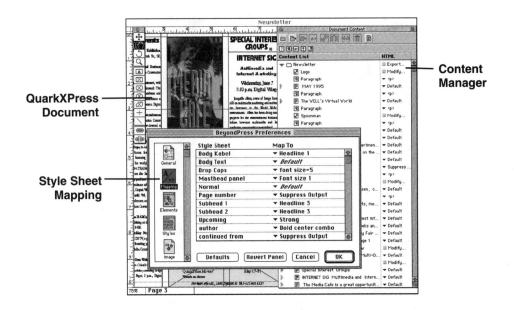

QuarkXPress Document

Style Sheet Mapping

Content Manager

Sections of text can also be converted into images to preserve color and typography, but if you're concerned about keeping the best image quality with the smallest file size, you'll have better control in a program such as Photoshop than in any converter. BeyondPress automatically converts bold, italic, and alignment to corresponding HTML. The problem is, the alignment option can't be turned off. Thus, all of the justified text in an XPress document will automatically be assigned <P align=justified>. Alignment was one of the first additions in the proposed HTML 3 specifications, and center, right, and left alignment are now widely supported by many browsers. Align justified is not commonly supported by browsers, however, so you might not even notice this unless you look at the raw code after conversion. Justified text is not generally recommended on the Web because you can't control the width of the viewer's screen.

Astrobyte, $595. (303) 534-6344
http://www.astrobyte.com/

HEXWEB XT V1.1

HexWeb XT, by HexMac International, takes a different approach to converting Quark documents. Instead of mapping style sheets, this extension matches point size to header options and automatically converts bold and italic. To organize pages and links, HexWeb takes a point-and-click approach. Select each element in the XPress document in the order you want them to appear in the HTML document, and HexWeb does the conversion in that order. HexWeb also converts graphics into JPEG files or GIFs and supports interlacing. In the latest upgrade, HexWeb even handles one of the newest features on the Web—frames, a Netscape extension that lets you break a page into multiple windows. HexWeb XTND adds features for HTML conversion from Claris Works, MacWrite Pro, and Nisus Writer.

> **HexMac International**, $349. Available from Xchange. (800) 788-7557
> http://www.hexmac.de/

COLLECT HTML V1.3.2

This Quark converter is better suited to posting single articles than translating multiple page documents, but it's handy for quick and simple conversions. Styles can be matched to HTML tags. The extension converts graphics to GIF or JPEG and can create an image of an entire Quark page, any text section, or picture box. Links can be set to local or remote URLs on selected text from within Quark. All links are stored within the Quark document for subsequent linking.

> **Markzware**, $149. (800) 300-3532 or (714) 241-3877
> http://www.logic.be/

HTML Developer Tip #6

HTML support in conversion programs is less important than in HTML editors. Even converters that are limited to HTML 2 can automate the most repetitive tasks of HTML conversion and save you hours of tedium. A text editor can always be used later to refine the conversion and add tags or attributes.

PAGEMAKER

Adobe built an HTML converter into the 6.0 upgrade of PageMaker. This shows great foresight by Adobe, but after looking at what's available for FrameMaker and Quark, you may be disappointed by the limitations of Adobe's HTML Author. Adobe recommends you design your original PageMaker document with HTML limitations in mind, and warns it has trouble with complicated formatting. The manual explains what can't be done on the Web, but the program doesn't help compensate for those limits. The style options offer only the most common HTML 2 tags, and you can't add your own. Worse, the conversion program looks at your PageMaker document as pages, not individual elements, so you have no control over the arrangement of sidebars or continuations.

Trying to convert anything as complicated as a multi-page newsletter with sidebars and continuations is futile using this new addition to PageMaker. The program first presents a warning list of all the elements that don't conform to HTML (such as multiple columns of text). The Help File then states it will translate the document anyway. Unfortunately, if you have continuations or other complex formatting, it will not retain its links in the converted version and will break linked elements into different places in the resulting HTML document. There is no support for graphic conversion unless your images are already GIFs. If you start with a simple linear document with only one column on each page, the plug-in will put the essential HTML code in your document. But if you're starting with a complicated PageMaker file, you're probably better off using an HTML editor to build your Web pages.

> **Adobe**, bundled with PageMaker 6.0. (415) 961-4400 or (800) 833-6687
> http://www.adobe.com/Apps/PageMaker/

OTHER PAGEMAKER CONVERTERS INCLUDE:

> **Websucker,** (Mac, Windows, Unix) by Multimedia Systems, Freeware.
> http://www.iii.net/users/mcohen/websucker.html/

> **PM2html,** (Windows) by EDCO Services, Inc., $49. (813) 962-7800
> http://www.w3.org/hypertext/WWW/Tools/PM2html.html/

FRAMEMAKER CONVERSION PROGRAMS

WEBWORKS LIGHT AND PRO

If you use FrameMaker, you'll find WebWorks Light bundled on its own disk in the 5.0 upgrade. WebWorks Light features style mapping to a basic list of HTML 2 tags. Unfortunately, it's a short list, and you can't add your own HTML tags. The upgrade, WebWorks Publisher, provides many advanced features, such as graphic conversion, more style sheet mapping options, and better control over output. It also supports image conversion to GIF and JPEG. This sophisticated conversion tool is capable of handling multiple pages and complex designs. The light version is handy for simple projects, but if you're doing serious HTML conversion, you'll want the upgrade right away.

> **Quadralay Corporation**, $895. Macintosh and Windows.
> $1,295 for Unix. (512) 305-0240
> http://www.quadralay.com/

WEBMAKER 2

Harlequin's WebMaker 2 provides style templates to help automate conversion and will let you tailor functions and create automatic hyperlinks. It generates an index page automatically and links can be set throughout the document. This program supports image conversion to GIF and JPEG.

> **Harlequin Ltd.**, $99. (617) 374-2400
> http://www.harlequin.com/

OTHER FRAMEMAKER CONVERTERS

There are other converters that work with FrameMaker, but be aware that many of these will only support the Maker Interchange Format (MIF)—Frame's equivalent of the universal Rich Text Format you would find in a word processor. These programs often claim to translate many kinds of documents, but if they only read MIF, they won't give you as much control when you set up the conversion. Some of these programs are included in the "Word Processors" section at the beginning of this chapter.

SUMMARY

HTML development is a new and evolving field. Unlike other professions—such as desktop publishing, where Quark, FrameMaker, and PageMaker rule—there are still no clear leaders in the area of HTML editors or converters. As HTML continues to change and browsers remain inconsistent in their support of HTML, it will be tough for anyone to create the ultimate HTML authoring tool. There are many similar programs, distinguished only by subtle differences in code options and interface. Once you've found an application that supports the tags you want, take note of additional assistants such as graphic conversion, table and form builders, and toolbar options. With more than 60 programs to choose from, selecting the right tool can be a challenge. The information in this chapter should help narrow your search for the best program for your project, but the ultimate decision on which program to use should be based on your personal taste and the needs of your unique project.

Most of these applications can be downloaded as trial versions (usually good for 30 days) and many are included in the CD-ROM bundled with this book. Such availability makes it easy to collect a few programs and experiment with their options before purchasing them. Online help and longer descriptions of all of these programs are available at the Web sites noted in this chapter.

Test these programs with real projects to make sure they will work on large files and in complicated conversion situations. Make sure to save backup copies before using a new editor or converter, however, as some are unpredictable and can make annoying changes to your code. Ultimately, finding the best tool is a subjective process, and you may want a combination of programs available for different jobs. In the previous pages, each program's greater features and biggest limitations were outlined to make it easier for you to find the best tool for your project.

HTML 2

In this chapter, the HTML 2 formatting tags are displayed in the browsers introduced in the first chapter. The standards referred to as HTML 2 and 3 have been in constant evolution. The World Wide Web Consortium, or W3C, continued to amend the standards long after they had been established. The inclusion of tags here is restricted to those that have been the most widely accepted and implemented. A complete list of HTML tags is provided in Appendix A.

The majority of the HTML 2 formatting tags are supported by all the browsers covered in this book. If you intend to design pages that are identical in all browsers, although the layout may be bland, stick to the tags in this chapter. All screen elements will be left aligned, no background colors or tables are included, and images are the only non-text media types that can be embedded in the Web page.

HTML 2 tags are a subset of the tags available to HTML 3 browsers. When HTML 3 tags and attributes are used, considerable divergence can be seen in the browsers' display. For those wanting to focus on HTML 3 or browser-specific design, future chapters assume that you are familiar with the tags and attributes introduced in this chapter.

Document Elements

Following are the elements that initiate and divide the HTML document. All other tags are contained between these tags and their corresponding closing tags. Closing tags are formed by inserting the "/" character between the "<" character and the tag name (e.g., <HEAD> and </HEAD>). The descriptions that follow refer to the information between the opening and closing tags. Attributes, as specified in HTML 2, are provided where appropriate.

<HTML>	Data formatted to be interpreted using the HTML browser. No attributes.
<HEAD>	General information about the page intended for host computer usage, and header and/or title bar areas of the browser. Only supports one visible tag: the <TITLE> tag. No attributes.
<BODY>	Information to be displayed in the main viewing area of the browser. According to HTML 2 standards, this tag has no attributes. Most browsers today do support <BODY> attributes, but these will be explored in the following chapter.
<! ..comment.>	The exclamation point alerts the browser that this is a comment field. This can be used anywhere in the document and alerts the browser to ignore all text between the "<! " and ">". No attributes and no accompanying closing tag. Comments that affect the entire document are generally included in the <HEAD> section.

The document elements will always appear in the following order:

```
<HTML>
<HEAD></HEAD>
<BODY></BODY>
</HTML>
```

All head elements are contained within the opening and closing <HEAD> tags, and all body elements are contained within the opening and closing <BODY> tags.

HEAD ELEMENTS

Following are the elements contained between the <HEAD> and </HEAD> tags. The <BASE> tag helps the HTML designer considerably when working with some files that are already uploaded to a Web site. Using this tag, you can reference a URL that the document treats as its home folder. For instance, if you were developing a page that you intended to reside at "http://www.onthemap.com", and there were images already uploaded to the host computer, you could test your page locally by including the following in the document's <HEAD> section:

```
<BASE HREF="http://www.onthemap.com/">
```

<BASE>
: Provides the base URL for relative referencing within the HTML document. Default is the folder or directory that contains the HTML document. Sole attribute is HREF, which contains the relevant URL.

<LINK>
: Contains information linking HTML document with other documents or entities. Has one required and three optional attributes, as follows:

   HREF
   : The URL of the document that has a relationship with the present document. Only required attribute for <LINK>.

   TITLE
   : The title of the related document.

   REL
   : The nature of the relationship between present document and the URL specified by the HREF attribute. Possibilities are "next," "previous," "parent," and "made."

   REV
   : Same as REL, except generally in the reverse direction. See example on the following page.

<ISINDEX>
: Indicates that a searchable index is available for the document on the server. No attributes.

<TITLE>
: Contains the title of the HTML document. No attributes.

Head elements are useful for organizing and indexing purposes. With the exception of the <TITLE> tag, the HTML tags in the head are not visible at the browser level. The inclusion of most <HEAD> tags is to aid search and index functions for host computers. Designers would include these elements as directed by those responsible for hosting the HTML document.

The head element is generally the preferred section of the HTML document for including comments and other non-viewed items. The comment tag begins with the exclamation point (!), and will not appear in the browser view of the HTML document.

```
<HEAD>

<! - - Only the title and the body text will be visible. The BASE tag indicates
which directory will be used as the base reference; the two LINK tags that follow
indicate that Chapter 2 is associated with Chapters 1 and 3. Spaces and paragraphs
are included for clarity.>

<BASE HREF="http://www.onthemap.com/evolindx.htm">
<LINK HREF="http://www.onthemap.com/evolve1.htm" REV="previous" TITLE="Chapter 1">
<LINK HREF="http://www.onthemap.com/evolve3.htm" REL="next" TITLE="Chapter 3">
<TITLE>Chapter 2</TITLE>
</HEAD>
<BODY>

This is a very small document.

<! It is a good idea to include comments close to the material you are commenting
on. They can be anywhere in the document, but are often best located in the head
element. If your comment refers to the entire page, keep it in the head. If it
concerns a specific item in the page, place it near the specific item.>

</BODY>
</HTML>
```

BODY ELEMENTS

Body elements describe the view that will appear in the main browser window. These include text formatting tags, listing tags, spacing tags, image tags, anchor and horizontal rule tags, and form tags. They also include tables, which will be introduced in the following chapter.

TEXT FORMATS

Text formats are grouped into physical and logical styles. In HTML 2, the standard tags available to all browsers are the following:

<H1, H2, H3...H6>	Heading styles 1 through 6. The formatting will be determined by the individual browser.
<STRONG>	The <STRONG> tag is usually interpreted as **Bold**. It is the preferred "logical tag" alternative to the <B> tag.
<EM>	The Emphasis tag is usually interpreted as *Italic*. It is the preferred "logical tag" alternative to the <I> tag.
<B>	The **Bold** tag. This tag is the *physical* alternative to <STRONG>. Bolds text.
<I>	The *Italicize* tag. This tag is the physical alternative to <EM>. Italicizes text.
<PRE>	The `Preformatted` tag. This tag distributes all characters and punctuation evenly (fixed-width), allowing for columnar page design in browsers that do not support tables.
<S>	The ~~Strikeout~~ tag. This tag puts a line through the text. Not often recognized. The <STRIKE> tag is more supported.
<U>	The <u>Underline</u> tag. This tag is supported by many browsers that support the minimum HTML 2 markup, but is not supported by Netscape. It still should be considered an HTML 2 tag due to its chronological appearance and acceptance. Underlines text.

In addition to the standard tags on the preceding page, there is also a considerable number of less-used tags in HTML 2, some of which are included for historical accuracy. These are the following:

<ADDRESS>	Usually appears at the end of the page and is italicized. Almost always commands its own paragraph. Used as a signature by the document creator or publisher on a page.
<BLOCKQUOTE>	Usually indents section. Intended for material quoted from another source.
<CITE>	Usually forces italicized font, sometimes fixed-width. Intended for titles of others' works.
<CODE>	Usually fixed-width font. Designates computer code.
<KBD>	Usually fixed-width. This is intended to indicate that the text is to be entered with a keyboard.
<PLAINTEXT>	The <PLAINTEXT> tag. Text contained within this tag is not rendered. This a unique tag. Its syntax is:

```
<PLAINTEXT><BOLD>This will not be bold.</BOLD></PLAINTEXT>
```

All of the characters between the opening and closing tags will appear in the browser window as fixed-width text. They will not be rendered.

<SAMP>	The sample tag. Another fixed-width font tag. <SAMP> is used to demarcate sample areas.
<STRIKE>	The ~~Strikeout~~ tag. Puts a line through the middle of text. Not widely supported.
<TT>	Typewriter text. Can be fixed-width, bold, or other. One of the least predictable tags.
<VAR>	Usually italic. This font is intended to indicate that the highlighted text is treated as a variable.
<XMP>	Example. This tag is usually rendered as a fixed-width font, and generally commands its own paragraph.

WHICH TEXT FORMAT IS MOST APPROPRIATE?

It is often recommended that you use logical instead of physical styles. By using <EM> instead of <I>, for instance, you give the user the benefit of selecting the text formating that he or she chooses. If someone had a problem distinguishing italicized text, he or she may want to set the emphasized text to underline, or a larger font size. Another suggestion is to identify and avoid tags that are dissimilar in various browsers. If you stick to the tags on page 91 (with the exception of <U>), you can be quite sure how your text will appear in most browsers. The formats on the preceding page, on the other hand, are not supported equally in all browsers. Including them in your HTML design can lead to unanticipated text display.

The <PLAINTEXT> tag is not very safe to include. Many browsers do not recognize this tag, so all HTML following the opening tag is unrendered. If you want to display raw HTML code in your Web page, it is recommended that you either use the special characters from Appendix C to describe the tag symbols (< and >), or that you use an image of the HTML you want to display.

One consideration often overlooked is that viewers may change the default browser preferences so that <H6>, for instance, is larger than <H1>. Browsers that support HTML 3.0 <FONT> tags enable designers to be more exact in their font selection. The order that the tags are opened and closed should not overlap. Consider the following examples:

```
<H1>This is a header</H1>
<FONT size=7><STRONG>This is a header</STRONG></FONT>
<FONT size=7><STRONG>This is a header</FONT></STRONG>
```

The three techniques tend to produce the same results, but the second and third choices enable the HTML programmer to override the preferences that the viewer has established for the browser. This is only possible for those browsers that support the <FONT> tag, which is introduced in the following chapter.

Notice the order in which the <FONT> and <STRONG> tags were opened and closed in the second example. If a tag is opened while another tag is still open, the second tag should be closed before the original open tag is closed. Although some tags may not be affected by being overlapped with other tags, it is an excellent work habit to acquire. In this case, the display will not be different in most browsers. In other cases, functionality on the page might be disabled through overlapping tags.

Following is an HTML document viewed in many of the browsers reviewed in Chapter 1. Notice the similarities and differences between the tag displays, particularly those that remain constant, and those that are less predictable.

```
<HTML>

<HEAD>
<TITLE>Text Format</TITLE>
</HEAD>

<BODY>

<H1>Header 1</H1>
<H2>Header 2</H2>
<H3>Header 3</H3>
<H4>Header 4</H4>
<H5>Header 5</H5>
<H6>Header 6</H6>
<STRONG>Strong</STRONG>, <EM>EM (Emphasis)</EM>, <B>B (Bold)</B>, <I>I
(Italic)</I>, <U>U (Underline)</U>, <S>S (Strike)</S><P>
And here are <CITE>CITE </CITE>,
<CODE>CODE</CODE>,
<KBD>KBD</KBD>,
<SAMP>SAMP</SAMP>,
<TT>TT</TT>,
<STRIKE>STRIKE</STRIKE>, and
<VAR>VAR</VAR>.
<ADDRESS>Address is usually italicized.</ADDRESS>
<PRE>And finally PRE</PRE>

<BLOCKQUOTE>This is a blockquote section. There are usually indents from the right
and left hand margins. This is not always true.</BLOCKQUOTE>

</BODY>

</HTML>
```

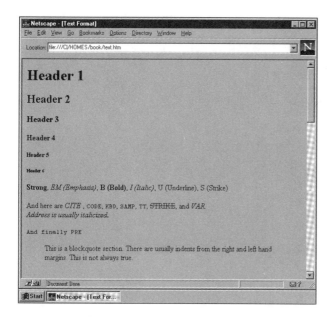

Netscape Navigator 2.0 supports most of the HTML 2 text formatting tags. Exceptions to this are the <S> and <U> tags. <CITE>, <VAR>, and <ADDRESS> are italicized, whereas most of the other less-used tags from page 92 are fixed-width. The exception is <BLOCKQUOTE>, which is indented from both the left and right margins. <ADDRESS> and <PRE> command their own paragraphs.

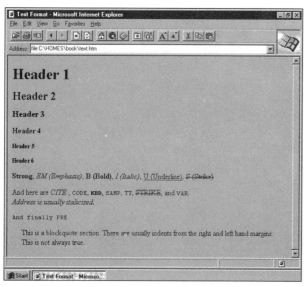

Internet Explorer recognizes all of the HTML 2 text formatting tags, including the <U> and <S> tags. <CITE> and <ADDRESS> are italicized, <KBD> is a bold fixed-width font, and the other less-used tags, including <VAR>, are fixed-width. <BLOCKQUOTE> is indented from the left and right margins, and <ADDRESS> and <PRE> command their own paragraphs.

Oracle's PowerBrowser recognizes all of the HTML 2 tags except <S> and <STRIKE>. It italicizes the <CITE> and <VAR> tags, as well as the <ADDRESS> tag, which is given its own paragraph. Unique to the browser, it gives the <SAMP> tag its own paragraph, as it does to the <PRE> tag. <BLOCKQUOTE> is indented from the right and left side.

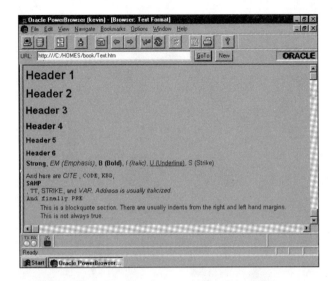

The HotJava browser supports all of the HTML 2 text formatting tags except the <S>, <U>, and <KBD> tags. <CITE>, <VAR>, and <ADDRESS> are italicized. <ADDRESS> and <PRE> command their own paragraphs. <BLOCKQUOTE> is indented from both sides.

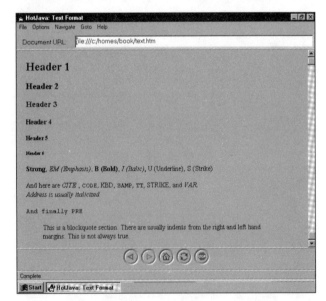

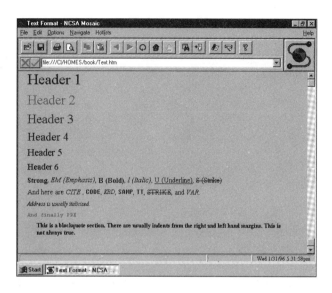

NCSA Mosaic recognizes all of the HTML 2 text formatting tags. All the <H1> through <H6> tags are colored differently, as is the <PRE> tag. But do you want your <PRE> text to be colored? <CITE>, <KBD>, <VAR>, and <ADDRESS> are italicized, while the <CODE>, <SAMP>, and <TT> tags are narrow fixed-width fonts. <BLOCKQUOTE> is indented from both sides and bolded. <PRE> and <ADDRESS> command their own paragraphs.

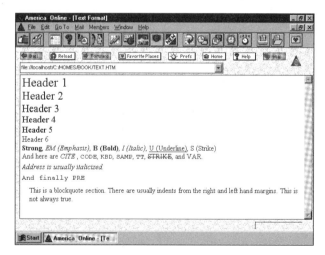

America Online 2.5 supports all HTML 2 tags except the <S> tag. As viewed on the left, the browser has very tight leading in the header tags. A <BR> or <P> tag may be used to force a space beneath header tags. <CODE>, <VAR>, and <ADDRESS> are italicized, <BLOCKQUOTE> is indented only from the left, and the rest of the less-used tags are treated as fixed-width. <PRE> and <ADDRESS> command their own paragraphs.

At the time of this writing, this version of Spry Mosaic was most widely used by CompuServe members. Of the tags listed in this section, <CITE>, <CODE>, <KBD>, <SAMP>, <STRIKE>, and <TT> are not recognized. This means that to include all of the CompuServe subscribers in your design planning, avoid the use of these tags and stick to <PRE> for fixed-width spacing. <PRE> and <ADDRESS> command their own paragraphs.

Prodigy recognizes all of the basic text formatting tags except the <S> and <STRIKE> tags. <CITE> and <ADDRESS> are italicized, <BLOCKQUOTE> is indented from the left margin only, and the rest of the less-used tags are defaulted to fixed-width text. Again, the <PRE> and <ADDRESS> tags command their own paragraphs.

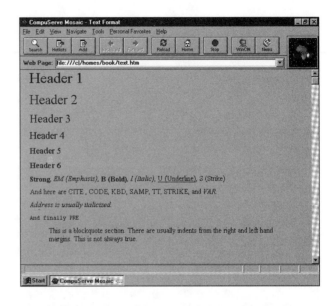

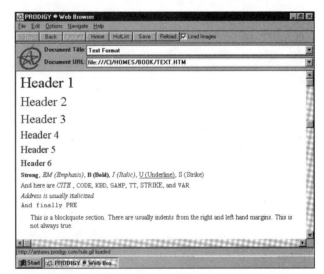

LISTING TAGS

There are several groups of listing tags in HTML 2.0—ordered lists, unordered lists, definition lists, and directory lists. Sometimes definition tags are not treated as listing tags, due to the fact that they do not use the <li> tag for line items. This section does not want to challenge this from an aesthetic viewpoint. It is the authors' intention to speak of the function of the tags within the document.

THE LIST ITEM TAG

<li>   This is the tag contained within <OL>, <UL>, <MENU>, <DIRECTORY>, and <DIR> tags. It does NOT have an accompanying closing tag. The <li> tag indicates an individual list item. No attributes.

ORDERED LISTS

<OL>   The ordered list tag displays the <li> tags that follow as numbered list items in the browser. The first <li> tag beneath the <OL> tag will be 1, the second <li> tag will be 2, and so on. The COMPACT attribute is supported in some browsers, which indents the list less from the left margin.

UNORDERED LISTS

<UL>   The unordered list tag displays the <li> tags that follow as bulleted list items in the browser. All the first level <li> tags contained within the <UL> and </UL> tags will be bulleted. The COMPACT attribute, which indents the list less from the left margin, is supported in some browsers.

DEFINITION LISTS

Definition lists enable HTML designers to create hierarchical lists, such as glossaries and indices. These tags can be nested, which give a tier-like structure to your Web page contents. Using a combination of embedded definition lists with other lists, such as the <UL> or <OL> tags, can give visually appealing and informative layout to your pages. The definition tags are the following:

<DL>   The Definition List tag. Contains <DT> and <DD> tags. The COMPACT attribute is supported in some browsers.

<DT>   The Definition Term. In the definition list hierarchy, this tag precedes the <DD> tag, and is occasionally slightly indented from the left margin. No attributes and no closing tag.

<DD>   The Definition Description. This tag places text slightly more indented on the page than the definition term. The <DD> tag, like the <DT> tag, generally does NOT have bullets preceding it. No attributes and no closing tag.

DIRECTORY LISTS

Directory lists are intended for smaller, more compact lists. These are not supported in as many browsers as the other lists, nor are they rendered as more compact lists. It is usually the case that directory lists are treated like the unordered list, with or without bullets. The tags are as follows:

<DIRECTORY>   The Directory Tag is used for very small names. The list is sometimes broken into two or more columns. The <li> tags often have bullets and are slightly indented. No attributes.

<DIR>   Same as <DIRECTORY>.

<MENU>   More condensed than <UL>. The <li> tags usually appear with a smaller bullet. No attributes.

Which List is Most Appropriate?

Listing tag selection is primarily a question of style, although the choice is strongly influenced by the nature and content of the information you want to organize.

Ordered lists work well for documents that have a linear nature to them, such as recipe steps or chapters. If your list is of objects that have no hierarchical or ordinal relationship, such as a list of Web sites related to a topic, but not to each other, then an unordered list might be the most appropriate. The unordered list almost always has a bullet on the left side.

If you want to list a series of books and a brief description of their contents, you may find a definition list the best choice. Stylistically, using <DL>, <DT>, and <DD> tags in the place of other nested list formats is generally preferred. This rule will, of course, be influenced by the appearance you want to give to the Web page in question.

The choice of <MENU>, <DIRECTORY>, and <DIR> is not as typical in HTML as the ordered, unordered, and definition listing tags. This can be attributed to several considerations. These tags are among the least predictable for the various browser formats. Sometimes they are single column; sometimes multicolumn; sometimes fixed-width; sometimes indistinguishable. If you want to give a predictable list of items in a multicolumn format, you might want to consider the <PRE> tag. The <TABLE> tags help you pass this dilemma, but they are not included in HTML 2.

One solution to unpredictable or undesired bullet formats is substituting your own bullet using the <IMG> tag. This would be done by creating a bullet (or finding one somewhere), converting it to GIF or JPEG format, and including it as an inline image. To make an indented line with a custom bullet, the inline image could be placed as the first character in a <DD> tag or an <li> tag, taking the place of the default bullet in the <UL> tag. The <IMG> tag is examined later this chapter.

In the example that follows, the listing tags are viewed in several browsers. Additional attributes for the listing tags are introduced in Chapter 4. As more and more browsers move to support tables, reviewed in the following chapter, your options for organizing information on-screen will expand. Using listing tags and tables together can give your Web pages structure, integrity, and function. Communicating to your audience can be greatly enhanced by taking advantage of formatting devices such as lists and tables, which visually organize your content.

```
<HTML>

<! This is a display of various listing tags in HTML 2.0>

<HEAD>
<TITLE>Listing Tags</TITLE>
</HEAD>

<BODY>

<H1>Listing Tags</H1>
Here is a list of the listing tags.<P>
<OL>
<li>This is the first OL.
<li>This is the second OL.
</OL><P>
<UL>
<li>This is the first UL.
<li>This is the second UL.
</UL><P>
<DL>
<DT>This is a DT tag within a DL list.
<DD>This is the DD tag accompanying the DT tag.
<DT>This is another DT tag within the DL list.
<DD>This is the DD tag accompanying the second DT tag.
<DD>This is a second DD tag beneath the second DT tag.
</DL><P>
The DIRECTORY tag is not always recognized. The format is not very predictable.<P>
<DIRECTORY>
<li>Directory 1
<li>Directory 2
<li>Directory 3
<li>Directory 4
</DIRECTORY><P>

The DIR tag is not always recognized. The format is not very predictable.<P>

<DIR>
<li>Dir 1
<li>Dir 2
<li>Dir 3
<li>Dir 4
</DIR><P>
```

```
The MENU tag is not always recognized. The format is not very predictable.<P>

<MENU>
<li>Menu 1
<li>Menu 2
<li>Menu 3
<li>Menu 4
</MENU><P>

</BODY>

</HTML>
```

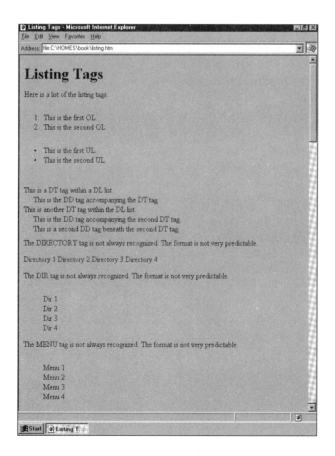

Almost all of the listing tags display in the Internet Explorer except the <DIRECTORY> tag, which is not recognized. The <OL> tags are numbered and indented, and the <UL> tags are bulleted and indented. The <DT> tag is not treated differently from normal text. The <DD> tag is indented, and the <MENU> and <DIR> tags are also indented. The lack of bullets in the less-used listing tags is not typical in the browsers reviewed here. It is generally not recommended to use the less-used listing tags for this reason.

Navigator 2.0 indents the ordered and unordered lists slightly. The <DD> tag is indented approximately twice as far as the <UL> tag. The <DIRECTORY>, <DIR>, and <MENU> tags are all recognized and bulleted. The <DIR> tag and <MENU> tag are indented. Even though Navigator and other browsers may display bullets with certain listing tags, you should avoid using the ones that are less supported. If you want a bullet, use a <UL> tag; if not, use a <DD> within a <DL> or <BLOCKQUOTE>.

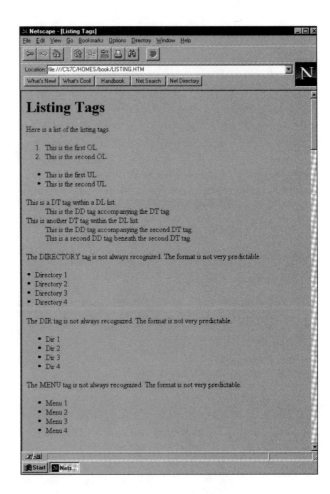

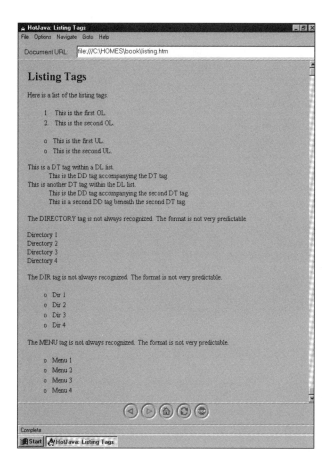

In HotJava, the small bullets accompanying the <UL>, <DIR>, and <MENU> tags look like a lowercase "o" with their baseline raised. The <DIRECTORY> tag is recognized and appears as an unbulleted list. The <DT> and <DD> tags are displayed as in the other browsers, as are the ordered and unordered lists. In all these examples, a custom-made bullet postioned as an inline image avoids including the undesirable bullets in the browser's listing tags. In HotJava, this is more apparent.

America Online's browser recognizes all of the listing tags. The ordered and unordered lists are both mildly indented to the same position as the <DT> tag. Unlike the other browsers here, the AOL browser indents the <DT> tags, indenting further the <DD> tags within the <DL> set. The <DIRECTORY> tag is bulleted and flush against the left margin. The <DIR> and <MENU> tags are indented to the same level as the <DD> tags.

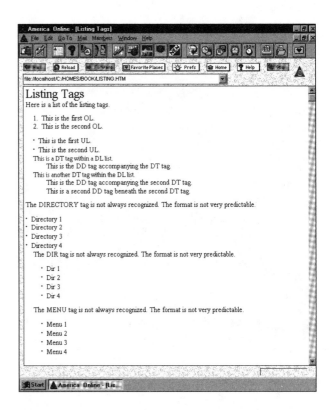

SPACING TAGS

The spacing tags <BR> and <P> can only be used one at a time in an HTML document. Although some browsers may support multiple instances of these tags, that is generally not the case. If it works in one browser, that does not mean it will work in the next one.

                    The line break tag. This ends a line. The first text following will
                        not have a space above it. No attributes.

<P>   The paragraph tag. This ends a line, but this tag also adds some
                        white space between the lines. No attributes.

The space character is also limited to one at a time in HTML. That means that even if you do enter two spaces after a period, only one will appear. As time goes by, you can expect to see more browsers supporting multiple space elements in HTML. Presently, Navigator and other browsers do support multiple space elements.

The spacing tags should be used to make your Web pages more aesthetically appealing. Experiment with them in various combinations to see what works best for your specific usage. You may find, for instance, that the <DT> and <DD> tags do not space their contents in a way to quickly recognize their association. Alternating the insertion of the <BR> and <P> tags can give the definition list more visual structure. Consider the following:

```
<DL>
<DT>First Author Name<BR>
<DD>Description of first author's book<P>
<DT>Second Author Name<BR>
<DD>Description of second author's book<P>
</DL>
```

This example would force additional space between the author and title definitions, making the grouped pairs more prominently associated on the page.

IMAGE TAG

<IMG>   The image tag contains all of the information it needs within the
                         tag itself, and it has no closing tag. Its contents describe an
                         image to be displayed in the browser. The image is referenced
                         by the SRC attribute. Along with many of the other tags, this
                         tag has had attributes added to it in HTML 3.

SRC		The URL address of the image.
ALT		The text that will appear in text-only browsers in place of the image. Also appears in some browsers before the image loads into memory.
	ALIGN	Some support top, bottom, and center; some support left, right, and middle; others support both. Not always predictable. Generally better to use horizontal alignment.
	ISMAP	Indicates that the image functions as an image map. Requires server programming. Works in conjunction with the <A> tag to link to the map file.

The image tag can be used to insert custom bullets, logos, or other graphic elements not described by HTML. The ALT attribute is frequently overlooked by programmers. This is an unwise practice to adopt. Many Web surfers have blocked images from loading so that they can access information more quickly. If you use the ALT attribute, the browser will display its text equivalent. Consider the following:

```
<IMG SRC="images/green_cone.gif" ALT="Green Cone">
```

If the browser does not display images, the viewer will see the text "Green Cone." If you intend the viewer to navigate by clicking on an image, this attribute becomes even more important to include in the tag description.

Anchor Tag

HTML, or *HyperText Markup Language*, derives its name from its use of "hyperlinks" between documents. Hypertext refers to the text that is formatted to respond to a mouse-click by opening another HTML document. Similarly, hypermedia refers to media that is formatted in such a manner that selecting the object will lead to another document. The tag that enables this in HTML is the anchor tag.

<A>   The anchor tag contains the text or graphic object that is referenced to or by another HTML anchor tag or document. In HTML 2, the tag has the following attributes:

HREF	The location to which the anchored text or graphic object takes you when selected.
NAME	The name of the anchor. Use this to provide a link for other documents to access this location.
REL	Similar to its use in the <LINK> tag in the <HEAD> section. It references another document with which it has a relationship. Possible values are "next," "previous," "parent," and "made."
REV	Same as REL, except generally in the reverse direction.
TITLE	Title of the URL to which the HREF attribute links. This attribute, like REL, REV, and NAME, is generally optional. NAME, however, is needed when the anchor is linked from another anchor in the document or other document.

The following HTML is required for creating links within a Web page. The first line is used at the location in the document to which you want to link; the second one creates a link to the first line; and the third example links to a named location in another Web page.

```
<A NAME="LinkName"><H1>LinkName<./H1></A>
<A HREF="#LinkName">LinkName</A>
<A HREF="otherdoc.htm#LinkName">LinkName</A>
```

HORIZONTAL RULE TAG

The horizontal rule tag is unique and has no closing tag. The tag inserts a horizontal line across the page. Unlike spacing tags, this tag can be used repetitively.

<HR>   This tag places a horizontal line across the browser screen. In HTML 2, this tag has no attributes.

HTML Developer Tip #1

When creating references using the anchor tag, it is generally a good idea to use *relative* references. Relative references, as opposed to *absolute* references, define pages in relation to the page that called them. Absolute references specify an exact document residing on a specific computer in a unique directory location. In the case of relative referencing, if an HTML document is residing in the same folder as one you would like to link it to, the most appropriate HTML would be:

```
<A HREF="otherdoc.htm">Other Document</A>
```

as opposed to:

```
<A HREF="http://www.domainname.com/folder/otherdoc.htm">
Other Document</A>
```

When you are linking to a page that does not share any of the directory structure with the document initiating the link, relative referencing is not an option. In that case, the absolute address must be used. The same rule applies when you are using named locations within documents, such as:

```
<A HREF="otherdoc.htm#LinkName">Other Document</A>
```

Form Tags

Forms enable viewers to enter or access information. Although forms are considered within the HTML 2 tag definitions, not all browsers support them. The HTML designer provides one side of the programming necessary to process forms. The other side, the Common Gateway Interface (CGI) script, is written in a language such as perl, C, or another program that processes the fields returned by the viewer and interacts with the computer containing the data that the form refers to. This is discussed in Chapter 8. See Appendix E for online resources for CGI scripting and other server issues. The HTML 2 form tags are as follows:

<FORM>   Contains all form tags. The <FORM> tag can contain other HTML, such as listing tags and tables, which enable the designer to create interesting form interfaces. The tag has the following attributes:

    ACTION   Targets the URL of the CGI script that processes the form field data.

    METHOD   Describes the manner that the form field data will be processed. Possible values are GET or POST.

<INPUT>   A form field that enables the viewer to enter data in a manner determined by the type attribute. In HTML 2, this tag has the following attributes:

    TYPE   Determines how form field is processed and appears on browsers. Possible values are TEXT, PASSWORD, HIDDEN, RADIO, CHECKBOX, SUBMIT, RESET, and IMAGE.

    NAME   Names the input tag. In the case of radio buttons, NAME is shared by all input tags in a group. Used for processing by the host computer.

    VALUE   Defines a value for the input tag entry.

    SIZE   Width of TEXT or PASSWORD type <INPUT> tag, as measured in number of text characters.

    MAXLENGTH   Number of characters permitted in TEXT or PASSWORD type INPUT field.

    SRC   File source of IMAGE type <INPUT> tag.

FORM INPUT TYPES

Following are the possible TYPE definitions for the <INPUT> tag. One particular difference to be aware of is the RADIO type of button, contrasted with the CHECKBOX type. RADIO allows only one selection at a time, usually of exclusive, nonoverlapping categories. With the CHECKBOX, you can list multiple options. Its selections are generally nonexclusive, and it is expected that more than one option will, at least on occasion, be chosen.

TEXT	Text input area. Uses NAME, VALUE, SIZE, and MAXLENGTH attributes.
PASSWORD	Password entry. Uses NAME, VALUE, SIZE, and MAXLENGTH attributes. Usually obscured by asterisks or other characters for browser view.
HIDDEN	Not visible at browser level. Used in form processing by the computer serving the HTML documents. Uses NAME and VALUE attributes.
RADIO	Radio button. Allows only one selection of options sharing same name. Uses NAME and VALUE attributes.
CHECKBOX	Checkbox selection. Allows multiple selection of options, each having a unique name. Uses NAME and VALUE attributes. VALUE is passed on to the computer only if the checkbox is selected.
IMAGE	Image type. This type supports selection by clicking on an image specified by the SRC attribute. Uses NAME, VALUE, and SRC attributes.
SUBMIT	The submit button sends the form field data back to the computer used to process the information. The VALUE attribute is used to change the visible name on the button to something other than SUBMIT.
RESET	The reset button resets all the form field data already entered to its original VALUE attribute.

Beyond the individual input types, there are several other devices used for inputting information within the HTML 2 specifications. These tags are as follows:

<TEXTAREA>   Unlike the <INPUT> tag, this tag supports multiple lines. Although defined within the HTML 2 specifications, this tag is not supported by all browsers. Many of those that do recognize the tag do not support the WRAP attribute, which forces the text input to wrap in the entry box. Many others require viewers to enter a carriage return to be inserted for a line to wrap within the text area box. The <TEXTAREA> tag has the following attributes:

NAME   Names the <TEXTAREA>. Used for processing by the host computer.

ROWS   Height of <TEXTAREA>, as measured in number of lines of text. Does not control the amount of text able to be entered.

COLS   Width of <TEXTAREA>, as measured in number of text characters. Does not control the amount of text able to be entered.

WRAP   This attribute is not supported as widely as the other three. It forces text entry to scroll in the input box.

<SELECT>   Defines an option group. Contains <OPTION> tags. Some browsers do not support all of its attributes, which are the following:

NAME   Names the <SELECT> option group. Used for processing by the host computer.

SIZE   Height of <SELECT> entry box as measured in lines of text. List will scroll as necessary. Oracle's browser interprets this attribute as width of the selection group in characters.

MULTIPLE This attribute enables you to select more than one option from a <SELECT> option group.

<OPTION>   Defines a single selection within an option group. There is no
                 closing option tag. Has the following attributes:

        NAME   Names the selection. Does not determine the value as
                     read by the server.

        VALUE   Associates the selection as a value for the variable named
                     by the <SELECT> tag as read by the server.

        SELECTED   As the form page is first accessed, this attribute
                     highlights the option selection. Can only be used once
                     in an option group, unless the MULTIPLE attribute is
                     contained in the <SELECT> tag.

Most browsers are able to recognize forms these days. In addition to supporting
forms, many companies and individuals are demanding security in form processing.
Netscape and Microsoft are both developing their own security protocols that are
optimized when using both the server and client product. Security issues should not
affect your HTML design too much, although Navigator 3 will be adding tags
specifically for such uses.

The differences between browser displays of forms are relatively minimal. On the
following pages, the form elements will be viewed in several browsers. The HTML
behind the pages is as follows:

```
<HTML>

<HEAD>
<TITLE>The Form Page</TITLE>
</HEAD>

<BODY>
<H1>Form Elements</H1>

<FORM METHOD=POST ACTION="/cgi-bin/">
```

```
We will start with a simple text box: <BR>

Name: <INPUT TYPE="text" SIZE=45 MAXLENGTH=10><P>
An option group:<BR>
Gender:
<INPUT TYPE="radio" NAME="Sex" VALUE="Male">Male
<INPUT TYPE="radio" NAME="Sex" VALUE="Female">Female
<INPUT TYPE="radio" NAME="Sex" VALUE="Other"> Other
<P>

A checkbox group:<BR>

Music:
<INPUT TYPE="checkbox" NAME="Rock"> Rock
<INPUT TYPE="checkbox" NAME="Country"> Country
<INPUT TYPE="checkbox" NAME="Soul"> Soul
<P>

Submit and Reset buttons with send and cancel selection as values.<BR>

<INPUT TYPE="SUBMIT" VALUE="Send Selection">
<INPUT TYPE="RESET" VALUE="Cancel Selection">
<P>

Option group.<BR>

<SELECT name="list" width=300>
<OPTION VALUE="First">First
<OPTION VALUE="Second">Second
<OPTION SELECTED VALUE="Third">Third
</SELECT>
<P>

Option group with multiple selections.<BR>

<SELECT name="list" size="3" MULTIPLE width=300>
<OPTION VALUE="First">First
<OPTION VALUE="Second">Second
<OPTION SELECTED VALUE="Third">Third
</SELECT>
<P>

And finally, a text area:<BR>

<! If you insert text between the TEXTAREA tags, it will be visible in the text
box when the document is loaded.>

<TEXTAREA ROWS=10 COLS=50 WRAP></TEXTAREA>

</FORM>
</BODY>
</HTML>
```

Netscape Navigator recognizes all the form tags and displays them with three-dimensional metaphors. The use of sunken and raised elements on the screen is a regularly used metaphor in software design. The table tags from the following chapter also use this effect. Navigator adheres to all the HTML 2 form tag attributes. Notice the size of the multiple selection box and the size of the <TEXTAREA>. In the former, the number of entries visible in the select group defaults to the number of items in the list. In the latter, ROWS=10 means that there are 10 rows available for character display, and COLS=50 means that up to 50 characters across will be visible in the browser. Navigator is one of several browsers that supports the WRAP attribute.

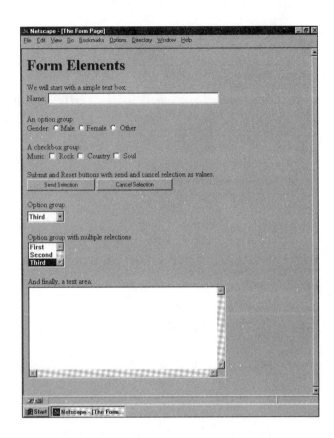

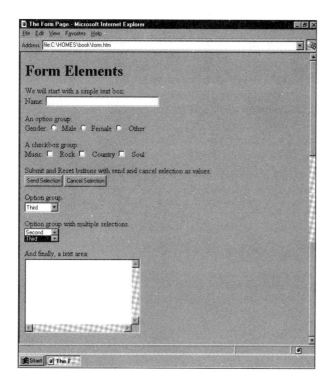

Internet Explorer treats form tags basically the same way as Navigator, except for the <OPTION> tag with the MULTIPLE attribute and the <TEXTAREA> tag. The WRAP attribute is not supported by Explorer. The viewer still has to enter a return to force the text to wrap in the box. You might want to enter instructions for this on the Web page where the data is entered. Explorer does not recognize the COLS attribute in a standard manner, although setting different values will increase and decrease the size of the box on the page. The best thing to do is experiment. A strange feature of the browser is the way it subtracts 1 from the number given in SIZE for MULTIPLE <OPTION> tags. In this example, SIZE was set to 3 and only two values are visible. If no value is given, the default SIZE is 3.

HotJava adheres very closely to Navigator's treatment of form tags. The <TEXTAREA> is a bit larger (56 characters as opposed to 50) than it should be. The WRAP attribute is not supported. HotJava recognizes the SIZE attribute of the <OPTION> tag, but does not recognize the MAXLENGTH attribute in the <INPUT> tag with the TYPE="text" attribute. HotJava also supports the SELECTED attribute in the <OPTION> tag. This is generally supported by browsers, but it's probably a good idea to make your default selection the top value in the list. For those browsers that do not support the SELECTED attribute, the default is the first <OPTION>.

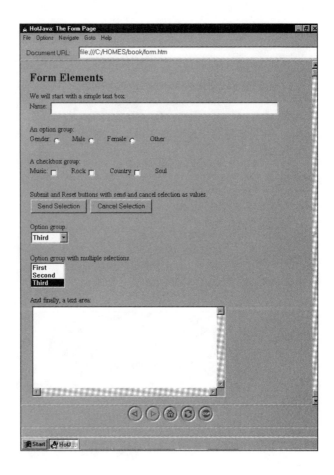

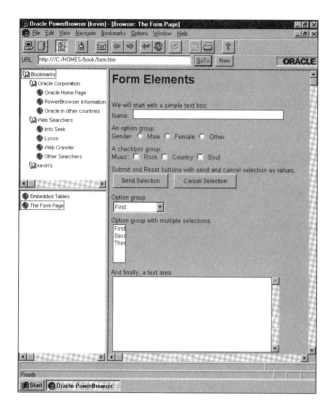

The first developer's release of the Oracle PowerBrowser had problems with HTML 2 form tag recognition. It recognized the SIZE attribute in the INPUT tags whose TYPE="text", but not the MAXLENGTH attribute. It did not recognize the SELECTED attribute in the <OPTION> tag. It interpreted the SIZE attribute of <OPTION> tags with the MULTIPLE attribute as the width of the option box as measured in characters (corrected in DR2). The default height of the <OPTION> tag with MULTIPLE selected is five entries. You can scroll down the list, but a scroll bar never appears on the page. The <TEXTAREA> was displayed with 13 rows, instead of the 10 given in the ROWS attribute. The COLS was also slightly off, and the WRAP attribute was not recognized. Oracle is sure to refine its treatment of form tags by the time PowerBrowser ships commercially.

Design Considerations

Now that you have seen how forms appear in various browsers, it's time to consider the elements in page and form design that will influence your layout choices. Forms have few differences in their browser displays and, for the most part, the same factors that guide you in HTML design apply to form design, as well. In general, form elements should be effectively integrated with other HTML tags. For instance:

Integrating Form Tags with Other HTML Tags

```
<FORM>
<H1>Survey of Browser Choice</H1>
<DL>
<DT>Favorite Browser
<DD><INPUT TYPE="radio" NAME="Favorite">Netscape
<DD><INPUT TYPE="radio" NAME="Favorite">Internet Explorer
<DD><INPUT TYPE="radio" NAME="Favorite">Mosaic
</DL>
Which browsers do you use regularly?<P>

<! The TABLE, TR, TD, and CENTER tags will be looked at in Chapter 3.>

<CENTER>
<TABLE WIDTH=50%>
<TR><TD valign=middle>
<IMG ALIGN=RIGHT SRC="../chap2/netscape.gif">
<INPUT TYPE="checkbox" NAME="netscape">Netscape<P>
<IMG ALIGN=RIGHT SRC="../chap2/xplorer.gif">
<INPUT TYPE="checkbox" NAME="xplorer">Internet Explorer<P>
<IMG ALIGN=RIGHT SRC="../chap2/mosaic.gif">
<INPUT TYPE="checkbox" NAME="mosaic">Mosaic<P>
</TD></TR>
</TABLE>
</CENTER>
</FORM>
```

In the example, you see that the <DL> definition list tag has been used to give a specific layout to the form elements. In the first case, the selections are all indented using the <DD> tag's feature of subordination. In the case of the <TABLE> tags, an image is placed to the left of each of the possible selections, followed by a checkbox, followed by the name of the selected option, as shown here:

Favorite Browser

- Netscape
- Internet Explorer
- Mosaic

Which browsers do you use regularly?

- Netscape
- Internet Explorer
- Mosaic

It is a good idea to begin experimenting with various mixings of HTML tags. Not all will work together, and will work even less if your tags become staggered. Remember that tags are opened and closed in a hierarchical fashion. If the <FORM> tag is introduced, and then a <DL> definition list is included within it, you must close the definition list </DL> before closing the form </FORM>. Following basic HTML guidelines with the <FORM> tags integrated as any other body element will greatly enhance the aesthetic appearance of your forms.

The HTML behind forms only provides a portion of the functionality needed to process user input. The other part is provided by software residing on a host computer. This can be a database, middleware, CGI script, C program, or other software that responds to user input by posting (updating) or getting (retrieving) information. As a designer, you might want to become familiar with your server's software for form processing. If they have something like Cold Fusion, you can supply them an HTML document that they may use as a template. If they are using something like dbWeb, you may save yourself some time by finding out how much information they need to generate dynamic HTML documents (see Chapter 2).

SUMMARY

This chapter has introduced the nuts and bolts of HTML design. From this starting point, hybrid design evolves. You have seen that most of the browsers featured here supported most of the tags included in HTML 2. There have been some instances in which browsers either did not support individual tags, or in which they appeared differently.

As a general rule, and particularly when desiring pages to appear consistent in multiple browsers, you should avoid the less-used tag groups, such as the directory lists and various fixed-width tags. These are the least predictable tags and generally duplicate functions that you can get out of the more standard tags. If you want to see a fixed-width font, use <PRE> and not <CODE> or <KBD>; if you want to use an italicized font, use <I> and not <VAR> or <SAMP>.

Remember to defer to your visitor's own preferences regarding emphasized text. In other words, use the logical tags like <STRONG> and <EM>, rather than <B> or <I>, if your purpose is to bring attention to text. Your visitor might have set preferences that would be ignored by the physical tag, but would be supported by its logical counterpart.

Make effective use of spacing with the <BR> and <P> tags interspersed with listing, heading, and other tags. HTML does not enable you to manipulate the leading or other typographic elements, so you really need to get creative if you plan to make your page appear as nice as the many business letters you have authored. Testing the pages on multiple browsers is essential if you are designing for mass consumption. This is explored more in the following chapters as you learn to integrate advanced HTML formatting with the tags introduced in this chapter.

At this point, you should feel that you have command of the basic HTML 2 tags, and familiarity with their appearance in the browsers listed in Chapter 1. If you stick with these tags, and do not include any of the tags or attributes described in the other chapters of this book, your pages should be supported in all browsers. In the next chapter, your HTML vocabulary will expand to include tags that are not displayed in all browsers.

HTML 3

This chapter introduces the extensions to the HTML 2 formatting tags. The fact that HTML is an evolving language makes it difficult to state precisely where HTML 1, 2, and 3 standards begin and end. Some browsers support advanced tags from HTML 3, but cannot support more basic ones from HTML 1 or 2. There are also some tags that are widely supported, yet are not included in the HTML 3 specifications.

The tags reviewed here are the following: the new <HEAD> tags and attributes; attributes for the <BODY>, <IMG>, <HR>, spacing, and listing tags; the <TABLE> tag group; the <FONT> tag; new text formatting tags; the <CENTER> and <DIV> tags; and client-side image map tags.

Many of the HTML 3 tags are unstable and not advisable to include in documents intended for mass viewing. Some conflict with HTML 2 browser tags, while others are indistinguishable. For this reason, only those tags that are able to be displayed in the most advanced browsers on the market today are referenced. Additional proposed tags for HTML 3 can be found in Appendix A.

HEAD ELEMENTS

Head elements are used primarily for referencing and search functions, and, with the exception of the TITLE tag, are not displayed in the browser. Most of the higher functions anticipated for HTML 3 head elements have not yet been supported in even the most sophisticated browsers currently on the market. Tags such as STYLE, RANGE, and NEXTID are not discussed for that reason. These and other HTML 3 tags and attributes are listed in Appendix A. Extensions to HTML 2 include the following:

<LINK>   The link tag provides information about a relationship between
                    the current document and a document associated with the HREF
                    attribute. The type of relationship is specified by the REL attribute
                    with the following syntax:

```
<LINK REL=relationship HREF="somewhere.html">
```

The types of relationships specified in HTML 3 include:

Copyright	Copyright statement
Glossary	Glossary
Help	Help document
Home	Home page or top of hierarchy
Index	Index
TOC	Table of contents
Up	Hierarchical parent of present document

The function referred to as "client-pull" is performed by the <META> tag that is contained within the <HEAD> tag. The screen display is reloaded with no server interaction by using the HTTP-EQUIV="Refresh" attribute. The tag uses the following syntax:

```
<META HTTP-EQUIV="Refresh" CONTENT="2;URL=http://www.browserbydesign.com">
```

The number following the CONTENT attribute refers to the number of seconds that pass until the second page is called. The URL is the document that is called after the number of seconds specified pass. This can be used in a series of pages for added effect. You can do this by including a <META> tag in the document referred to by the URL attribute that opens another page in response, and so on.

<META>   This tag is used to embed information not defined by other
                HTML elements. The use of this tag would be determined by,
                and in conjuction with, client-server specific uses. An example of
                this would be identifying information for the server to be
                included in an HTTP response header. It has three attributes:

                NAME   Names property such as author, publication date, city,
                            and so on. If absent, the name defaults to the value of
                            the HTTP-EQUIV attribute.

                CONTENT   Value given to the property defined by the name
                            attribute.

                HTTP-EQUIV This binds the META tag to an HTTP response header.
                            If the semantics (i.e., syntax) of the HTTP response
                            header are known, the contents can be ordered for
                            processing by the server. Some values, such as
                            "Refresh," allow for the code to be locally processed.
                            Refresh may be used to reload a page that is likely to
                            change frequently, or to link to additional pages.

The other HEAD elements were introduced in the previous chapter. On the
following page, you see how the HTML 3 head elements are used to give structure
and reference to a page within a series of pages. Notice that the REL attribute
establishes the relationship type between the current document and the one
referenced.

HTML Developer Tip #1

Head elements are generally included for referencing by servers, search
programs, and browsers. Search engines, such as Alta Vista or Yahoo, often
look to <META> tag contents for their search requirements. For free Web
publicity, start including <META> tags in the <HEAD> section of your
documents with the following syntax:

```
<META NAME="Subject" CONTENT="Real Estate">
```

The <META> tag can be used more than once in the <HEAD> section. This
simple device is one of the most overlooked forms of free Web advertising.

Only the TITLE tag is displayed in the browser. The new tags of HTML 3 give much more referencing functionality to designers. These will be used principally in conjunction with programs residing on the host computer that serve the HTML documents. An example of a rather fully documented HEAD section is as follows:

```
<HTML>
<HEAD>
<META HTTP-EQUIV="Refresh" CONTENT="180;URL=reminder.htm">
<META NAME="Book Publishing Date" CONTENT="July 4 1996" HTTP-EQUIV=PubDate>
<META NAME="Book Publishing City" CONTENT="New York City" HTTP-EQUIV=PubCity>
<LINK REL=Up HREF="../zen_and_art_of_html.html">
<LINK REL=Parent HREF="../zen_and_art_of_html.html">
<! -- Parent is included for HTML 2 browsers. It is replaced by the Up attribute.>
<LINK REL=Next HREF="chapter3.html">
<LINK REL=Previous HREF="chapter1.html">
<LINK REL=TOC HREF="Contents.html">
<LINK REL=Glossary HREF="Glossary.html">
<LINK REL=Index HREF="Index.html">
<LINK REL=Made HREF="../../queryBookArchive.html">
<LINK REL=Copyright HREF="../Copyright.html">
<LINK REL=Home HREF="../../WildNewInternetBooks.html">
<TITLE>Zen and the Art of HTML: Chapter 2</TITLE>
</HEAD>

<BODY>
Zen....  zen..... zen...
</BODY>
</HTML>
```

The inclusion or exclusion of HEAD elements will generally be directed by the server or Web administrator. As an HTML designer, it is important to be aware of what type of information might be requested by individuals or devices accessing documents. In the example here, after 180 seconds, the document "reminder.htm" will be called and replace the document.

BODY ELEMENTS

THE BODY TAG

The <BODY> tag has had significant additions in its list of attributes. As with the <FONT> tag, presented later in this chapter, the <BODY> tag uses attributes that refer to the hexadecimal color coding system. The system is described on the following page. The attributes available for the <BODY> tag in HTML 3 are as follows:

BGCOLOR   This establishes the color of the background to the page according to the hexadecimal color coding system.

BACKGROUND   This attribute specifies an image to be used as a background in the document. The image will be wrapped in a pattern if smaller than the screen display.

TEXT   This establishes the color of the foreground text to the page using the hexadecimal color coding system.

LINK   This establishes the color of hyperlinked text that links to a page that has not yet been visited.

VLINK   This establishes the color of hyperlinked text that links to a page that has already been visited.

ALINK   This establishes the color of hyperlinked text while it is actively selected.

If you assume control of one or more of the <BODY> attributes, it is a good idea to take control of all of them. Suppose a visitor has her default background set to black and her default text to white. If you set the background color to white and take it for granted that the text will be black, this visitor will not be able to view your page. Using the following HTML describes all of the colors necessary to prevent conflicts:

```
<BODY BGCOLOR=FFFFFF TEXT=000000 LINK=0000FF VLINK=FF00FF ALINK=FF0000>
```

The Hexadecimal Color Coding System

The hexadecimal color coding system uses a base 16 reference. Using base 16 (which has sixteen digits, as opposed to the ten digits in the commonly used base 10 system), 256 values for Red, Green, and Blue are possible using two digits for each color. Base 16 numbers and their corresponding base 10 equivalents are as follows:

```
0 1 2 3 4 5 6 7 8 9 A  B  C  D  E  F  10 11 12 13 14 15 16 17 18 19  1A  1B 1C 1D 1E  1F  20
0 1 2 3 4 5 6 7 8 9 10 11 12 13 14 15 16  17 18 19 20 21 22 23 24 25  26  27 28  29 30  31  32
```

The A takes the place of 10; the B takes the place of 11; the C takes the place of 12; the D takes the place of 13; the E takes the place of the 14; and the F takes the place of the 15. 16 is represented by 10; 17 by 11; 18 by 12, and so on. To take command of the color in this new medium, you need to become familiar with both the hexadecimal numbering sytem and the RGB method of manipulating colors. If you have used Photoshop or another program that uses an RGB color-based system, you have probably had some experience in combining the Red, Green, and Blue colors to create blends. This is the same way that the hexadecimal color coding works. The six characters that describe the color are interpreted as follows:

RED   GREEN   BLUE

XX   XX   XX

The first two digits give a value for the Red, the second two for the Green, and the third for the Blue. The range in hexadecimal is 00 to FF; or 0 to 255. Cyan is the opposite of Red; Magenta is the opposite of Green; Yellow is the opposite of Blue. If you need more Yellow in a color, decrease the number given to the Blue component. Graphic designers will be using the colors in hexadecimal just as they would with Photoshop. The only problem might be doing some math conversions. There are a lot of programs out there that will do it for you. Chapter 7 and resources listed in Appendix E will address these and other color issues, including how to make the transition from CMYK to hexadecimal.

Many of the body elements have been extended in functionality in HTML 3. Specifically, the <HR>, <BR>, <P>, <IMG>, and listing tags have additional attributes that can be assigned to them. Extensions to the HTML 2 tags include the following:

<HR>   The <HR> tag has had several attributes that allow for more stylish division of the HTML page. The tag has five additional attributes in HTML 3:

SIZE   Sets the height of the horizontal rule measured in pixels. Can also be set in percentage with less predictable results.

WIDTH   Sets the width of the horizontal rule in pixels or percentage of screen display.

NOSHADE   Darkens the horizontal rule. Fills in the sunken feature in some browsers.

CLEAR   This is used to force the line breakdown until either one margin is clear, both margins are clear, or a minimum specified space is clear. This new attribute works in conjunction with the ALIGN attribute of the <IMG> tag. Using the ALIGN attribute, an inline image is anchored to the left or right margin so that the text can wrap in the free space on the opposite side. If you set both the IMG ALIGN attribute and the CLEAR attribute to the same side, you will force the next line of text to be inserted at the first line beneath the image.

ALIGN   This aligns the horizontal rule relative to the page. The possible values are RIGHT, LEFT, and CENTER. Generally used in conjunction with the WIDTH attribute.

</P>   This tag ends the section described by the <P> tag. If not used, the ALIGN attribute of the <P> tag generally ends at the next <P> tag, and reverts to left alignment.

The <BR> and <P> tags share the CLEAR attribute with the <HR> tag. The <P> tag also uses the ALIGN attribute. The <H1...H6> header tags also recognize the ALIGN attribute. The same guidelines in their usage apply. HTML 3 defines ALIGN and CLEAR for many text formats, although not many are supported by browsers.

THE IMAGE TAG

The image tag will be looked at in depth in Chapter 7. Understanding the way that graphic images are processed by the computer will help you when you begin including images. For instance, the JPEG file format is now broadly supported by browsers, although you shall see what happens when a browser does not recognize the format. For the moment, attention is directed to HTML syntax and the <IMG> tag's new attributes:

HEIGHT	Sets the height of the image measured in pixels. Can also be set in percentage with less predictable results.
WIDTH	Sets the width of the horizontal rule in pixels or percentage of the width of the screen display.
UNITS	Specifies unit of measurement for HEIGHT and WIDTH attributes. The possible values are "en" or "pixels." The default is pixels, while "en" refers to half the point size of the default font. This is not supported in all browsers, so using pixel measurements will be a lot safer from a design perspective.
ALIGN	Some browsers support top, middle, and bottom for values; most support left and right. For vertical alignment, this represents how the text to the left or right of the image is aligned with it; for horizontal alignment, this represents an anchored image as opposed to an inline image. The text will then wrap in the free space aligned with the opposite margin. For example, when the image is aligned right, the text will wrap in the vertical space on the left side of the image. Without this attribute, only one line of text would display in the vertical space opposite the image, with the rest of the text wrapping beneath it.
BORDER	Gives a border to the picture. Generally uses the color assigned to the font at that point in the document. That means that the border will be the color of linked text, the <FONT> tag, or the default text color.
HSPACE	Sets the horizontal distance between the image and other screen elements, as measured in pixels or percentage of image width.
VSPACE	Sets the vertical distance between the image and other screen elements, as measured in pixels or percentage of image height.
USEMAP	Used in conjunction with the <MAP> tag to function as a client-side image map. No server programming is required when using this attribute. See the <MAP> tag later this chapter.

Listing Tags

The listing tag groups are all able to take advantage of the <LH> list header tag. It is still advisable to stick to the <UL>, <OL>, and <DL> listing tags, <PRE> text formatting, or <TABLE> tags for consistency in browser display. Following are the HTML 3 extensions to the listing tag groups:

<UL>
: The DINGBAT, CLEAR, SRC, and PLAIN attributes are not covered here, due to their lack of support in current browsers. See Appendix A for their definitions.

> TYPE
> : Determines the appearance of bullet. Possible values are "square," "circle," and "disc." The default is disc, while square and circle produce mixed results in different browsers. When used with the <UL> tag, this affects the entire list.

<OL>
: The ordered list has been expanded to include control over the numbering method. The CLEAR, CONTINUE, and SEQNUM attributes are included in Appendix A.

> TYPE
> : Determines the numbering method of the list items. Possible values are *1, A, a, I,* and *i.* When used with the <OL> tag, this affects the entire list.

> START
> : Determines the number at which the <OL> group begins its numbering.

<li>
: The list item tag now includes the following attributes.

> TYPE
> : Determines bullet type or numbering method for individual list item. Possible values are all those available to the <OL> and <UL> tags.

> VALUE
> : Gives a numeric value for <OL> lists.

<LH>
: The list header tag can be used with any of the listing tags. Unlike the <li> tag, it is recommended that you use a closing </LH> tag. Not all browsers require it, but it is too early to tell how browser manufacturers intend to support the tag. This generally does NOT affect the typeface of the font, so remember to use the <STRONG> tag, <FONT> tag, or other method of bringing attention to the <LH> tag contents. No attributes.

USING HTML 2 TAGS WITH HTML 3 ATTRIBUTES

When designing pages with HTML 3 attributes, the first thing that you must consider is your demographic audience. If you expect to make the documents available for all audiences using the World Wide Web, you should build in backward compatibility for HTML 2 browsers. This means that when using the attributes of HTML 3, you are prepared to have the tags displayed alternatively if the browser does not support the new tags and/or their attributes. This is especially true of the <LH> tag and the ALIGN and CLEAR attributes of HTML 3 tags. In using the <LH> tag, for example, you should generally include any formatting tags you want to use (such as <STRONG> or <EM>), as well as a <BR> tag following the </LH> tag to ensure that the contents of the <LH> tag do not end up on the same line as the <li> tag beneath it. Consider the following example of hybrid HTML. The comments will explain the tag choice and the anticipated display.

```
<HTML>
<HEAD>
<TITLE>HTML 2 in Evolution</TITLE>
</HEAD>

<BODY BACKGROUND="bground.jpg" BGCOLOR=FFFFFF TEXT=000000 LINK=0000FF VLINK=00FF00
ALINK=FF0000>

<! Even though the BACKGROUND attribute will display on top of the BGCOLOR
attribute, thus negating the latter's effect on the page, some browsers that support
the BGCOLOR tag do not support the BACKGROUND tag. Including both avoids the
default background appearing in those browsers that do not support the BACKGROUND
tag.>

<H1>Testing HTML 3 Tags</H1>
<P ALIGN=center>
This is a test of the ALIGN attribute of the P tag. This text should be centered. A
background image should be visible on the page.<P>
```

```
<IMG SRC="html3.jpg" ALIGN=RIGHT HSPACE=10 VSPACE=10 HEIGHT=153 WIDTH=285>
```

Here we will begin to look at how HTML 3 tags can work (or not work) in HTML 2 browsers. To begin with, this text should be to the left of the picture
This line was intended to be displayed on the line following the image. The BR tags recognize the CLEAR attribute more often than the HR tags.

```
<HR NOSHADE SIZE=5 WIDTH=50% >
<HR ALIGN=right NOSHADE SIZE=10 WIDTH=50% >
<HR ALIGN=left NOSHADE SIZE=15 WIDTH=50% >
```

The top horizontal rule above should be 5 pixels high, darkened, span 50% of the page, and be center aligned. The second should be right aligned, darkened, and 10 pixels high. The bottom one left aligned, darkened, and 15 pixels high.

```
<P>
<IMG SRC="html3.jpg" ALIGN=LEFT HSPACE=10 VSPACE=10 HEIGHT=153 WIDTH=285>
This time we will align the image to the left hand margin.<BR>
This should be another line on the right of the image.
<HR WIDTH=75% SIZE=3 CLEAR=LEFT>
```

The Horizontal Rule should be beneath the image. It is likely that this is not the case.

```
<BR CLEAR=LEFT>
```
If the text is now against the left margin, it means that the browser recognized the CLEAR attribute with the BR tag, but not with the HR tag. Now let us look at the listing tags.

```
<! The TYPE attribute in the UL tag gives the default bullet to the list. Using
the TYPE attribute with the li tag only affects that list item. As you will see,
combinations of these tags produce unpredictable results.>
```

```
<UL TYPE="square">
<LH><STRONG>List Title</STRONG></LH>
<li>Square
<li TYPE="circle">Circle
<li>Square
<li TYPE="disc">Default (disc)
</UL>
```

```
<P ALIGN=right>
Now we will test an ordered list. This text should be aligned right.
<P>
```

```
<! The TYPE attribute in the OL tag gives the default numbering method to the list.
Using the TYPE attribute with the li tag only affects that list item.>

<OL TYPE=A>
<li>Uppercase
<li>Uppercase
<li TYPE=1>Numeric
<li TYPE=a>Lowercase
<li TYPE=I>Uppercase Roman
<li TYPE=i>Lowercase Roman
</OL>
<P>
One more list with no TYPE attribute in the OL tag.
<OL>
<li TYPE=a>Lowercase
<li TYPE=I>Uppercase Roman
<li TYPE=i>Lowercase Roman
</OL>
<P>

</BODY>
</HTML>
```

As you shall see in the pages that follow, even those browsers that claim to deliver full HTML 3 compatibility will fail many of the tests of these most standardized HTML 3 tags. If you include the proposed HTML 3 tags included in Appendix A, you find that many browser manufacturers are reluctant to invest the resources to support many promising formatting devices.

There are few HTML programmers who would not love to have control over font choice (which is possible with Internet Explorer), leading, and other typographic parameters. In Chapters 5 and 7, you will see how to have more control over page layout through the use of plug-ins, embedded objects, and helper applications. In the meantime, you can maximize your use of HTML 3 tags without leaving your pages unattractive in HTML 2 browsers.

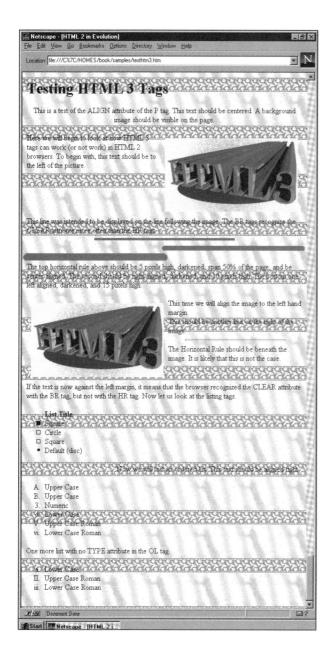

Even Navigator has trouble with some of the HTML 3 attributes to the HTML 2 tags. From the top, you see that Navigator recognizes the BACKGROUND attribute in the <BODY> tag. It also recognizes the ALIGN attribute of the <P> and <HR> tags, as well as all the <IMG> tag attributes and JPEG file format. The CLEAR attribute of the <BR> tag is recognized, but not that of the <HR> tag. Notice how the horizontal rule to the right of the second image should have been placed beneath the image using the CLEAR=LEFT attribute. Instead, the browser waited until the <BR CLEAR=LEFT> was interpreted to force the line to the left margin. The <UL> tags worked reasonably well. The <OL> tags were strongly supported. Notice that you would probably not use the combination of TYPE attributes present in the <UL>, <OL>, and <LI> tags. They are included here solely for design considerations.

Internet Explorer does well in HTML 3 recognition. The browser recognizes all the <IMG> tag attributes, the JPEG file format, and the ALIGN attributes of the <P> and <HR> tags, as well as the CLEAR attribute for the <BR> tag. As with Navigator, Explorer does not recognize the CLEAR attribute of the <HR> tag. It also does not recognize any of the <UL> or <li> attributes. It does, however, recognize the <OL> TYPE attribute. One shortcoming of Explorer is the capability of the <P> tag to recognize ALIGN=center, but not ALIGN=right. In the example here, all of the <HR> attributes are supported, yet the text between the <UL> and <OL> groups is aligned to the left margin instead of the right. Later in this chapter, you'll get around this by having the text you need right aligned contained within a <TD> tag. The <TD>, or table data, tag can be right aligned in almost all browsers that recognize tables.

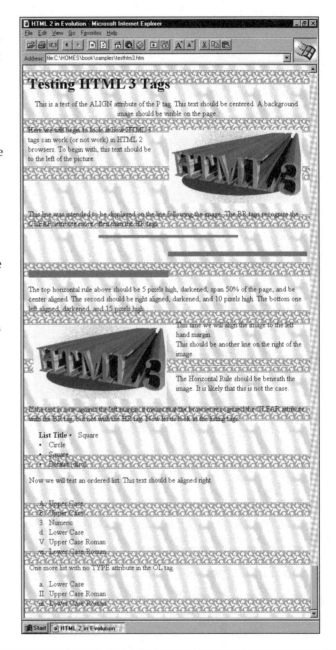

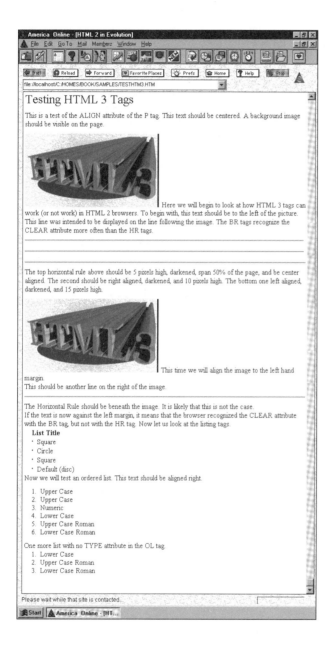

America Online presents a good example of what needs to be considered when using HTML 3 attributes with HTML 2 tags. The text is not aligned, and the BGCOLOR and BACKGROUND tags are not recognized (the default color of the browser is white). None of the <IMG>, <HR>, <BR>, <P>, <UL>, <OL>, or <li> tag attributes are recognized. The <LH> tag is also ignored. On the positive side, the JPEG file format is recognized. America Online is expected to release an upgraded version of their browser this spring.

Sun's HotJava browser fared even worse than America Online in recognizing HTML 3 tags. From the top of the page, you see that the BACKGROUND and BGCOLOR attributes are not supported. The ALIGN attribute of the <P> tag is not supported, yet the ALIGN, WIDTH, and SIZE attributes of the <HR> tag are recognized. The HEIGHT and WIDTH attributes of the <IMG> tag are recognized, but not the ALIGN, VSPACE, or HSPACE attributes. Finally, the listing tag treatment is also disappointing. None of the HTML 3 attributes for the <UL>, <OL>, or <li> tags are supported, and the <LH> tag is not recognized. The browser was still in Alpha release for its review here, and it is likely that Sun will soon remedy many of these short-comings in its browser design.

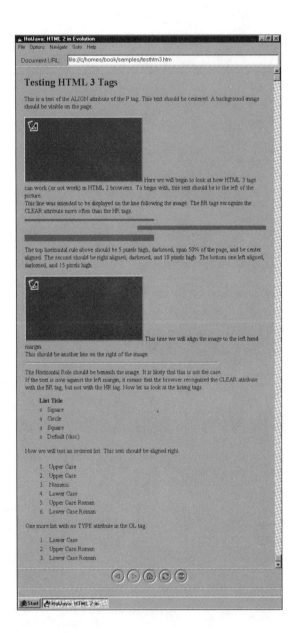

EFFECTIVELY INTEGRATING HTML 3 ATTRIBUTES FOR HTML 2 BROWSERS

As you have seen in the last several pages, after you start moving to the more complex tags of HTML 3, the anticipated display in the browser window begins to diverge. The differences between the Navigator and America Online displays, for instance, should persuade any HTML developer to consider adopting a hybrid approach to page design. You already considered the inclusion of both BACKGROUND and BGCOLOR attributes even though they cancel each other out when both recognized, with the BACKGROUND attribute existing on top of the BGCOLOR attribute. Image treatment will be looked at in depth in Chapter 7.

Using a <BR> tag before the text you want to appear to the right or left of an image will force the text beneath the image in browsers that do not support the ALIGN attribute of the <IMG> tag. The <P> tag will do the same thing, though it generally depresses the aligned text by one full line. This allows the text to be contiguous and to not share the same line as the image itself.

Few browsers support the CLEAR attribute of the <HR> tag. Using the CLEAR attribute of the <BR> tag immediately before the <HR> tag will ensure that the horizontal rule is displayed where intended.

Listing tag attributes should be thought of as ornamental. In other words, it's nice if a browser supports them, but you cannot expect that to be the case. If you really want to have a *1. A. I. a. i.* hierarchical structure, you may want to consider using nested <DL> tags with the actual numbering method typed in as characters. *Nested tags* refer to tags being contained within other tags. When a tag set is contained within another tag set, the effects on the display of the nested tag's contents is generally compounded by the two tags. This can result in nested numbered lists, nested definition lists, nested bulleted lists, and so forth.

The next group of tags are specific to HTML 3. Unlike the tags that were presented in the first section, the tags in this section are often completely unrecognized by browsers. This means that when you design your pages, you should consider how your page would look if none of the HTML 3 tags were present. This is how it will look in many browsers.

TABLE TAGS

Tables are probably the single greatest development in the HTML 3.0 specifications—at least from a design perspective. Tables enable you to divide a page into logical sections that you can align independently of each other. An important thing to consider as you develop documents with tables is that not all browsers support them. Attention will be focused on design techniques that will ensure acceptable display in all browsers. This approach will be explored in more depth in Chapter 5.

More time is given to table tag discussion than other tags for two primary reasons:

1. Tables give you more control over your HTML page layout than any other tags (with the exception of frames, introduced in the next chapter).

2. Tables need to be created with care to ensure acceptable viewing in browsers that do not support their formats.

APPROACHING TABLE DESIGN

A logical approach to table design is to divide a page you want to replicate in HTML into rectangular areas on the page. The areas can span more than one row or column, but they have to be rectangular. You determine the logical breaks in your document by considering how their appearance, including alignment and relationship to other page elements, would look in a perfect world using any desktop publishing or word processing program.

A business letter, for instance, may require an independently formatted area to allow a right-justified logo or text item. A company report may require several columned areas, indented from the rest of the page. An online resume, with photo, may require complex nested tables to subdivide the document in the manner that you feel optimizes the display of your calling card to the world—or you may want nothing more than a page with a margin on one side, both sides, or mixed throughout a document.

Tables give you control over your page not possible with HTML 2 tags. You can use relative or absolute layout control. In other words, you can set your table cells using exact pixel values or using relative percentages. If you use relative percentages, your table will resize to accommodate all monitors. Using exact pixel values preserves your table's layout regardless of the monitor on which it is viewed.

Before we discuss the creation of tables, let's first consider the table tags. The HTML 3.0 table tags and attributes are as follows:

<TABLE>   Contains all table tags. Has the following attributes.

BORDER	Defines outer border width around and between <TD> tags. The border is the attribute that makes a table appear three-dimensional. The border attibute is measured in pixels.
CELLPADDING	Distance between the text or graphic object within a table cell and the inner cell border. This attribute is also measured in pixels.
CELLSPACING	Distance between the borders of the cell and borders of other cells or the outside edge of the table. This attribute is also measured in pixels.
WIDTH	Width of table given in exact number of pixels or percentage of browser width.

<CAPTION>   The caption tag is used to give a title to the table. Has the following attribute:

ALIGN	Possible values are top and bottom. This affects the location of the table caption in relation to the table.

<TR>   The table row tag contains a single row of table cells. Unlike the <TD> and <TH> tags, the <TR> tag always defines one row at a time. Has the following attributes:

ALIGN	Possible values are left, right, and center. The attribute affects the table cells' alignment with respect to the table row.
VALIGN	Possible values are top, bottom, and middle. This attribute affects the table cells' alignment with respect to the table row.

<TD>   The table definition tag contains cell data. Defaults to left-aligned, plain text. Has the following attributes:

ALIGN   Possible values are left, right, and center. The attribute affects the alignment of table cell contents with respect to the table cell.

VALIGN   Possible values are top, bottom, and middle. The attribute affects the alignment of table cell contents with respect to the table cell.

WIDTH   Width of table cell given in exact number of pixels or percentage of table width.

COLSPAN   Number of columns that the table cell spans.

ROWSPAN   Number of rows that the table cell spans.

<TH>   The table header tag is similar to the table definition tag. The primary difference is that this tag defaults to center align and bold. The table header is generally used, as the name indicates, as a header for table definition cells. Has the following attributes:

ALIGN   Possible values are left, right, and center. The attribute affects the alignment of table cell contents with respect to the table cell.

VALIGN   Possible values are top, bottom, and middle. The attribute affects the alignment of table cell contents with respect to the table cell.

WIDTH   Width of table cell given in exact number of pixels or percentage of table width.

COLSPAN   Number of columns that the table cell spans.

ROWSPAN   Number of rows that the table cell spans.

Now that you have been introduced to the table tags, let's consider how to "map out" a page. The use of tables can be viewed in one of two contexts: the table is used, as in a word processor, to present data in a gridlike fashion; or the table is used to provide overall document layout to enable multiple alignments and treatment of text and graphics objects on the page.

The use of tables to format HTML pages solely for layout purposes has not been given enough attention until now. A simple addition such as page margins, for instance, is not possible using other HTML tags. In conjunction with the <CENTER> tag that you shall explore later in this chapter, the <TABLE> tag in the following example establishes a margin on both sides of the document equaling five percent of the browser width on either side of the tabled data.

```
<HTML>

<HEAD>
<TITLE>A Table Example</TITLE>
</HEAD>

<BODY>
<CENTER>
<TABLE WIDTH=90%>
<TR>
<TD>

This table's width is equal to ninety percent of the page, leaving ten percent of
the page to be distributed between the two margins.

<! This solution is often less than optimal in browsers that recognize the CENTER
tag, but not the TABLE tags. Chapter 6 introduces a more complex table that uses
another method for creating margins. The method here works fine on browsers that
support tables.>

</TD>
</TR>
</TABLE>
</BODY>

</HTML>
```

A basic rule to remember is that you design tables *from top to bottom and from left to right*. You complete your rows one at a time across the page, regardless of whether or not a single cell stretches across multiple columns or rows. The example below shows how you would approach the design of a rather awkward-looking table. The table is three rows by three columns. The first row has two cells, the second row has two cells, and the third row has one cell. The HTML is as follows:

```
<TABLE>
<TR><TD COLSPAN=2>Row 1<BR>Cell 1</TD><TD ROWSPAN=2>Row 1<BR>Cell 2</TD></TR>

<TR><TD ROWSPAN=2>Row 2<BR>Cell 1</TD><TD>Row 2<BR>Cell 2</TD></TR>

<TR><TD COLSPAN=2>Row 3<BR>Cell 1</TD></TR>
</TABLE>
```

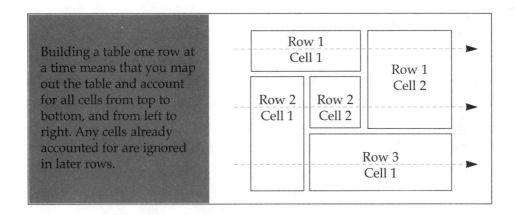

In most browsers that support tables, the <TD> table definition tags are able to contain tables themselves. Mosaic, on the other hand, does not support embedded, or nested, tables. In the following example, you shall see how Navigator, Internet Explorer, Mosaic, and CompuServe interpret embedded tables. The HTML behind the document appears on the facing page.

```
<HTML>

<HEAD>
<TITLE>Embedded Tables</TITLE>
</HEAD>

<BODY BGCOLOR=FFFFFF>
<H1>Embedded Tables</H1>
<CENTER>
<TABLE WIDTH=90% BORDER=10 CELLPADDING=2 CELLSPACING=5>
<TR>
<TD WIDTH=50%>
<FONT SIZE=1>On the right is a table inside a table.</FONT>
</TD>
<TD WIDTH=50%>
<TABLE BORDER=2 CELLPADDING=5 CELLSPACING=10>
<TR>
<TD>
<FONT SIZE=1>This is the top cell of a table inside a table.</FONT>
</TD>
</TR>
<TR>
<TD>
<FONT SIZE=1>This is the bottom cell of a table inside a table.</FONT>
</TD>
</TR>
</TABLE>
</TD>
</TR>
</TABLE>
</CENTER>

</BODY>

</HTML>
```

Netscape continues to provide the most sophisticated handling of tables. Not only does it support embedded tables, but it also recognizes the attributes that give the cell spacing effects, and table cell widths. When width and other areas of possible conflict in table design arise, the results are not always what the designer intended.

Internet Explorer supports table tags as well. The browser does, however, ignore the BORDER, WIDTH, CELLPADDING, and CELLSPACING attributes of the <TABLE> tag. Also, the WIDTH attribute of the <TD> tag is generally ignored. Notice in both Navigator and Explorer that the browser will make a judgement call regarding <TD> width. If you test out table design with impossible width combinations, you will see that both browsers defer to their own choice of display to accommodate conflicting <TD> tag definitions.

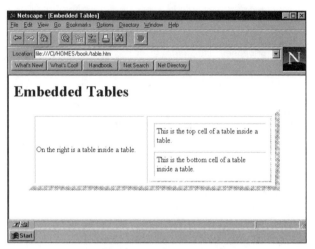

Netscape Navigator 2.0

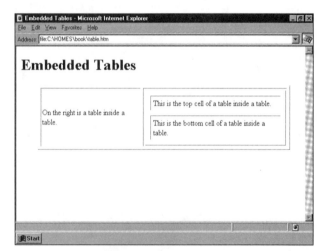

Internet Explorer 2.0

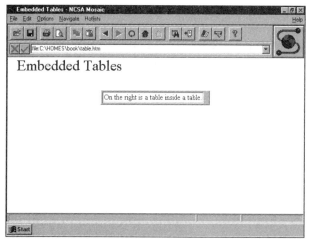

NCSA Mosaic 2.0

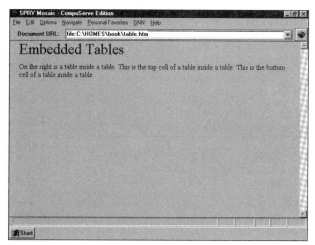

CompuServe

NCSA Mosaic presents a real challenge to developers. Although not as widely used as it once was, the fact that the browser does not support embedded tables might make the HTML designer consider a way to write around such limitations. The browser does not recognize any of the <TABLE>, <TR>, or <TD> tag attributes tested here.

An early version of the CompuServe browser shown here did not recognize any of the table tags. Notice here that no <BR> tags were inserted to force a return after each line of text, although they could have been if the page design demanded it. The fact that there are browsers such as Mosaic that recognize tables, but not tables within tables, poses a real challenge to developers. Fortunately, there are relatively few browsers that fall into this category.

Mapping out a document helps to see how to use tables both for overall page layout and for the presentation of tabled data. There is no single best way for working with tables. There are, however, opportunities to protect your HTML document's display in browsers that do not support tables. Consider the following document:

Our Logo
Our Company
101 Anystreet
Anytown, US 99999

John Doe
Clients, Inc.
123 A Streeet
Baltimore, MD

January 1, 1996

This is to inform you that we will be conducting all future business via our Web site. Regard our estimates of rollout time frame:

February 28	ISP located. Domain name registration completed.
March 31	All HTML design approved.
April 15	All graphic elements acquired.
May 1	All content acquired.
June 3	Web site up and running.

From that point, we will no longer recognize the kill-the-tree approach to interoffice transactions. If you have any questions, e-mail us.

Frederick P. Witherspoon IV
President
Witherspoon@witherspooniv.com

There are several ways to divide the page into tables, and even more if you consider using nested tables. The shaded area of the page below illustrates a logical division of the page. The first shaded section needs independent formatting to be right aligned; the second section is obviously different from the indented section that follows; the third section has its own substructure; and the fourth section returns to the formatting of the second section.

One simple device that can be used in table design is ending the cell contents of a <TD> or <TH> tag with a <BR> or <P> tag. This forces a line break to occur before the contents of the next table cell in a browser that does not recognize the table tags. Care has been taken to avoid embedding tables in this example. It would have been very natural to have made this a 1 column by 4 row table with a nested table in the third cell.

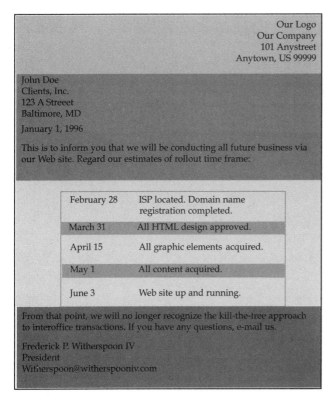

However, the page is grouped into three tables: 1 column by 2 rows; 2 columns by 5 rows; and 1 column by 1 row.

The use of <BR> and <P> tags within the tables helps to maintain the structure of the tabled information. The dates have been bolded to offset them from the milestone information.

```
<HTML>
<HEAD>
<TITLE>The Business Letter Using Tables</TITLE>
</HEAD>

<BODY bgcolor=ffffff text=000000>
<CENTER>

<TABLE width=90%><TR>

<TD align=right>
Our Logo<BR>
Our Company<BR>
101 Anystreet<BR>
Anytown, US 99999<P>
</TD></TR>

<TR><TD>
John Doe<BR>
Clients, Inc.<BR>
123 A Street<BR>
Baltimore, MD<P>
January 1, 1996<P>
This is to inform you that we will be conducting all future business via our
Web site. Regard our estimates of rollout time frame:<BR>
</TD></TR></TABLE>

<P>
<TABLE width=60% border=2 cellspacing=2 cellpadding=2>
<TR>
<TD><STRONG>February 26</STRONG><BR></TD>
<TD>ISP located. Domain name registration completed.<BR></TD>
</TR>

<TR>
<TD><STRONG>March 31</STRONG><BR></TD>
<TD>All HTML design approved.<BR></TD>
</TR>
```

```
<TR>
<TD><STRONG>April 15</STRONG><BR></TD>
<TD>All graphic elements acquired.<BR></TD>
</TR>

<TR>
<TD><STRONG>May 1</STRONG><BR></TD>
<TD>All content acquired.<BR></TD>
</TR>

<TR>
<TD><STRONG>June 3</STRONG><BR></TD>
<TD>Web site up and running.<BR></TD>
</TR>
</TABLE><P>

<TABLE width=90%><TR>
<TD>

From that point, we will no longer recognize the kill-the-tree approach to
interoffice transactions. If you have any questions, e-mail us.<P>

Frederick P. Witherspoon IV<BR>
President<BR>
Witherspoon@witherspooniv.com
</TD>
</TR>
</TABLE>

</CENTER>
</BODY>
</HTML>
```

On the following pages, you will view the document using a browser that supports tables, and another that does not. The efficient use of tables, and the integration of hybrid HTML design methods, will greatly improve the stability and display of your HTML documents.

The document in Netscape looks almost exactly as you planned. Notice how the <BR> tags did not increase the spacing within the <TD> tags. If you would have used <P> tags, on the other hand, a space would have been forced beneath the <TD> content.

The fact that you used three tables is unseen to the viewer. Your margins are as you planned and the table is efficiently presented in the middle of the page.

Internet Explorer, PowerBrowser, and Mosaic look virtually identical to Netscape. The data in the middle of the page was 60 percent of the page width, and the top and bottom sections spanned 90 percent of the page width. Avoiding embedded tables ensured the consistency of the page display for the three browsers.

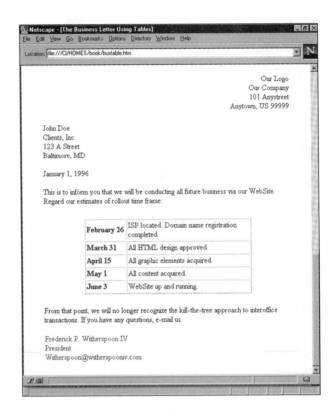

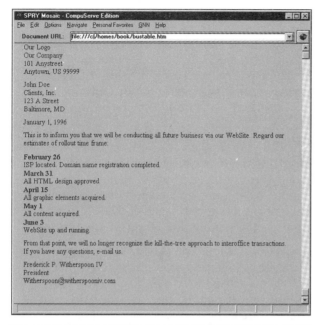

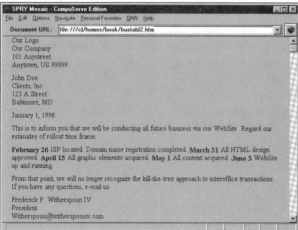

In CompuServe's early browser, which is representative of America Online's and many others, you see all the table data as left-aligned text. Remember from the previous chapter that any tags that are not recognized by the browser are ignored. In this case all the <TABLE>, <TD>, <TR>, and <CENTER> tags were ignored.

A comparison of the top screen with the one beneath it demonstrates what easily occurs when not designing pages with multiple browsers in mind. The bottom page includes no <BR> tags in the <TD> cells of the second <TABLE>. All of the schedule information comes out as a long, uninterrupted stream of text.

STEPS TO ENSURE EFFECTIVE DISPLAY OF TABLES

There are three rules of thumb that should be used in designing tables. The first rule is that if it has to be seen by all people in all browsers with the same horizontal distribution, then the <PRE> tag may be the one to use. This is not the best scenario for those who really appreciate the layout control that tables provide. This does guarantee, however, that the page will be virtually identical from one browser to the next.

The second rule of thumb is to include <BR> tags at the end of cell contents. As seen in the previous example, the use of the <BR> tag forces cell contents to the following line. This is usually preferable to having words or images butted up next to each other. The exception to this could be if you have designed a control panel using several images of the same height that you want to group together. The appearance may be optimized using a table, but is acceptable as a group of icons butted together.

The third rule of thumb, and arguably the most important, is that you use more than one browser to test the display of your pages. Almost all browsers enable you to open your files locally for testing purposes. Some, such as Air Mosaic, only recognize images that share the directory path of the browser application. (This can drive you nuts looking for errors in your code.) There are a considerable number of browsers available as shareware over the Internet.

Tables are increasingly supported in browsers today. Using the <BR> and <P> tags together to visually group your information will optimize your page display in browsers not supporting tables, while maintaining the table outline you desire for more sophisticated browsers.

FONT AND TEXT FORMATTING TAGS

The <FONT> tag is new to HTML 3, although Netscape has used it for quite some time in their Navigator browser. Along with the other text formatting tags, the <FONT> tag greatly extends the control that HTML programmers have over page elements.

<FONT>   Used to control the display of text in the browser window. Can contain most other tags (exceptions are tables—you must specify font attributes within the table cell). The HTML 3 attributes are as follows:

        SIZE   This attribute is a number from 1 to 7 that gives the font a larger or smaller size. The default is 3. Can also be expressed as a relative value (e.g., SIZE=–1 or SIZE=+2).

        COLOR   A new addition to HTML 3. This attribute sets the color of the font using hexadecimal code. The hexadecimal coloring system was introduced earlier this chapter.

<SUB>   Denotes subscript text. Uses a font size one less than the current font size. Its baseline is one x-height space beneath the baseline of the text that surrounds it. Has no attributes.

<SUP>   Denotes superscript text. Uses a font size one greater than the current font size. Its baseline is one x-height space above the baseline of the text that surrounds it. Has no attributes.

<BIG>   Increases the font size to the next size larger. Will not exceed the largest font size (7). Has no attributes.

<SMALL>   Decreases the font size to the next size smaller. Will not be less than the smallest font size (1). Has no attributes.

OTHER HTML 3 TAGS

In addition to the new attributes for HTML 2 tags and the TABLE, FONT, and new text formatting tags, the <CENTER>, <DIV>, and client-side image map tags are the last of the significant HTML 3 tags. Definitions for all the proposed HTML 3 specifications are included in Appendix A.

<CENTER>   Center aligns text. Used in conjunction with the WIDTH attribute of the <TABLE> tag, creates equal margins on both sides of the tabled data. Main drawback in its usage is that some browsers recognize the <CENTER> tag, but do not recognize table tags. This results in all the text within the table being center aligned, as opposed to the table itself being center aligned. Within the table cells, the data is independently aligned. No attributes.

<DIV>   Used to treat a section individually from the rest of the document. Has the following attributes:

ALIGN   Aligns text within section. Possible values are left, right, center, and justify.

CLEAR   Begins the division at the next clear point along the specified margin. Possible values are left, right, and all.

<MAP>   Used in conjunction with the USEMAP attribute of the <IMG> tag, this tag allows image maps to be written into the HTML page. Has one attribute, as follows:

NAME   Name given to map to use as reference for USEMAP attribute of <IMG> tag.

<AREA>   Contained within the <MAP> tag, this tag defines the hot spots of the image whose USEMAP attribute calls the <MAP> by referring to its name. Has the following attributes:

SHAPE   RECT is the only accepted value in most browsers. Defines hotspot of image for linking. Needs COORDS attribute.

COORDS   In conjunction with SHAPE attribute, defines the hotspot on image for linking. Order is left, top, right, and bottom for RECT.

HREF   Specifies destination of hotspot.

NOHREF   Indicates not to link the defined area.

INTEGRATING HTML 2 AND HTML 3 TAGS

The integration of HTML 2 and HTML 3 tags requires the designer to consider that not all browsers will recognize the advanced tags and attributes. Consider the following example:

```
<HTML>
<HEAD>
<TITLE>HTML 3 in an HTML 2 World </TITLE>
<BODY BGCOLOR=FFFF7F TEXT=000080 LINK=FF0000 VLINK=0000FF ALINK=00FF00>

! By looking at the number choice in BGCOLOR (i.e., FF for Red, FF for Green, and
7F for Blue), we can expect a Yellow off-white color. This is because FF, the
maximum value for each color, in all three values makes White. Less Blue equals
more Yellow. Pure Yellow is FFFF00. Midway between White and Yellow is FFFF7F.>

MAP NAME="thismap">
<AREA SHAPE="RECT" COORDS="5, 5, 100, 40" HREF="testhtm3.htm">
<AREA SHAPE="RECT" COORDS="195, 5, 285, 40" HREF="products.htm">
<AREA SHAPE="RECT" COORDS="5, 45, 100, 75" HREF="support.htm">
<AREA SHAPE="RECT" COORDS="195, 45, 285, 75" HREF="about.htm">
<AREA SHAPE="RECT" COORDS="110, 5, 185, 80" HREF="spiro.htm">
</MAP>
<! The map can go anywhere in the document.>
<H1>Integrating HTML 2 and HTML 3 Tags</H1>
<IMG SRC="HTML3.GIF" HEIGHT=153 WIDTH=285 ALIGN=LEFT HSPACE=10 VSPACE=10>
<BR CLEAR=RIGHT>

As we integrate HTML 2 and HTML 3 tags, we need to consider the most likely
places for problems to occur. One of the most typical is for people to overlook
the usefulness of BR tags. Placement of the BR tag can affect the appearance of
the page differently in different browsers.

<BR CLEAR=LEFT>

<FONT SIZE=+1>T</FONT>his is a
<FONT SIZE=+1>V</FONT>ery
<FONT SIZE=+1>T</FONT>ypical
<FONT SIZE=+1>D</FONT>evice.

The use of the larger font size for the first letter in a word is a commonly used
ornamentation.<P>
```

```
<CENTER>
<TABLE WIDTH=80% BORDER=2 CELLSPACING=2>
<TR><TH>Item 1</TH><TD>Green<BR></TD></TR>
<TR><TH>Item 2<BR></TH><TD>Blue<BR></TD></TR>
<TR><TD ALIGN=center><STRONG>Item 3</STRONG></TD><TD>Red<BR></TD></TR>
<TR><TD><STRONG>Item 4</STRONG><BR></TD>
<TD>Grey<BR></TD></TR>
</TABLE>
</CENTER>
```

The table displays the difference between using TH or TD and STRONG combinations, and between using BR tags and not using BR tags. The ALIGN=center attribute in the TD tag gives the TD text the same appearance as the TH text.<P>

E=MC². H₂O. Is this really <BIG>bigger</BIG> or <SMALL>smaller</SMALL>?

When using special text formats, you have to be ready to lose the formatting feature in less-sophisticated browsers. This is also the case with image maps. Including a server-side image map as well as a client-side map will help; however, many browsers do not even recognize the server-side image map.<P>

This image map will work regardless: <P>

```
<CENTER>
<A HREF="filename.map">
<IMG SRC="spiro.gif" USEMAP="#thismap" ISMAP BORDER=0 ALT="Spiro" WIDTH=293
HEIGHT=148 ></A>

</CENTER>
<P>
```

The image above should be recognized as an image map.

```
</BODY>
</HTML>
```

As you shall see in the browser displays that follow, the recognition of some tags and not others will pose a serious challenge to the hybrid designer. Some browsers recognize the <CENTER> tag, but not the <TABLE> tags; some recognize the <FONT> tags, but not other text formatting tags.

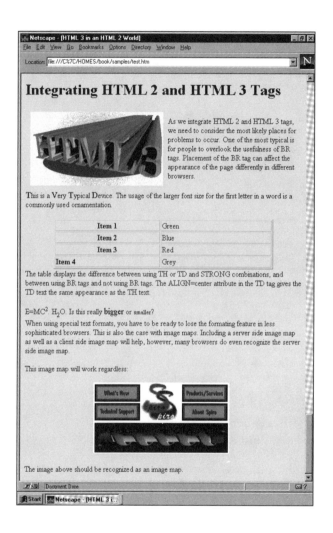

Navigator recognized all of the tags that were tested in this example. Something can be learned from comparing the appearance of the table cells with the HTML code behind them. Notice how the first three item numbers appear the same. The first line uses a <TH> tag, the second adds a <BR> tag, and the third one uses a <TD> tag in conjunction with the ALIGN attribute and the <STRONG> tag. All three produce the same result, but you may choose to use a <TD> tag in conjunction with the <STRONG> tag if you want to ensure that browsers that do not interpret tables can still visually organize the data on the page. All of the text formatting tags were recognized, as well as the client-side image map.

America Online's browser certainly appreciates the hybrid approach to the HTML design. Because the ALIGN attribute of the <IMG> tag was not recognized, the <BR> tag forced the next line beneath the image. None of the text formatting tags were supported. Now you can see how those table tags look in a browser that does not support them. Notice how Item 4 stands out the most clearly as having a relationship with the term beneath it. If a <P> tag would have been placed after the word "Red" within the <TD> above it, the line would become even more prominent. Alternating <BR> and <P> tags is an excellent way to group information on the page. See the previous chapter for more discussion on the use of spacing tags. The image maps were not supported at the client-side or server-side.

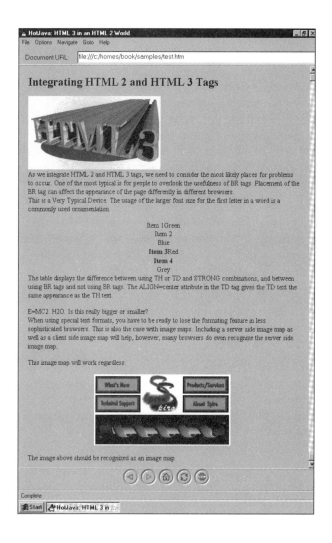

HotJava's display typifies the quandry that designers find themselves in when a browser supports some tags, but not others. The ALIGN attribute of the <IMG> tag is not supported, nor is the BGCOLOR. The text formatting tags are not recognized, nor are the table tags. The <CENTER> tag is recognized, which obviously works against the design you had been building here. Fortunately, most browsers are moving to support tables, and those that do not are not likely to support the <CENTER> tag. Neither the server-side nor the client-side image map was recognized.

SUMMARY

The further you move from the HTML 2 formatting tags to include new tags from HTML 3 and browser-specific tags, care needs to be taken to ensure effective display in all browsers. The first half of this chapter focused on new attributes for the HTML 2 tags. In the second half of the chapter, tags that are not recognized by earlier browsers were introduced. Unrecognized tags are generally ignored, but as seen in the case of Mosaic, some browsers ignore the contents of the tags. In most cases, the text between the opening and closing tag is treated as plain text, but in Mosaic's case, the text between the embedded table tags was not even displayed. Fortunately, this is the exception to the rule.

To appreciate the need for hybrid table design, use an older browser to visit sites that use tables. Many of these, including Netscape's, Macromedia's, and others, have been quite unattractive in browsers that do not support tables. If the information on your site is the reason people visit, rather than for the design or the experience, you will definitely want to remedy any display conflicts caused by tables.

The JPEG file format and client-side image maps are not supported in all browsers. In Chapter 7, you will see how to design around image maps by having interconnected images, instead of one image supported by an image map.

When using the <FONT> and text formatting tags, you must be prepared for the tags to be ignored by less-sophisticated browsers. This is also true of the listing tags with HTML 3 attributes. If you really need to see a specific numbering method, type the number as you want to see it. If you really need to use a specific font, use an image of the text you want to display. Knowing when to rely on the browser for support and when to take control are important.

One thing made clear in this chapter is that it is possible to design HTML documents that can take advantage of advanced formatting, yet can still be acceptably displayed in browsers that do not recognize certain tags. Anticipating likely problem areas can help programmers avoid possible tag conflicts. These skills will be developed in Chapter 6, when you will be introduced to designing hybrid HTML. The next chapter looks at specific HTML formats for individual browsers.

Browser-Specific Design

At this point, the focus is brought to those tags intended for display in a single browser. Other browser manufacturers may recognize these browser-specific tags, but their common characteristic here is that they are not part of the HTML 2 or HTML 3 formatting tags. The Internet in general, and the World Wide Web in particular, has seen a tremendous growth in the embrace of standards and open systems.

It has lately been the case, however, that companies such as Netscape, Microsoft, Oracle, and others have sought to extend the functionality of HTML by integrating their own formats with those introduced by Mosaic. Adding to the complexity are differences between the same products on different operating systems. As these browser-specific tags evolve in closed environments, subject to licensing and other prohibitive measures, HTML design begins to stratify. This chapter introduces tags unique to individual browsers, and is of particular value to those designing for a company network or for those desiring to maximize a single browser's functionality.

NAVIGATOR 2.0

The most recent version of Netscape's flagship product supports a large number of its own tags. Since Marc Andreessen, a co-developer of NCSA Mosaic, left to form Netscape with Silicon Graphics CEO James Clark, the company has been at the forefront of HTML development. Many of the HTML 3 formatting tag proposals were originally created by Netscape. The Netscape extensions to be looked at here are the following:

1. Embedded Objects	Documents displayed through the use of plug-ins allow various media to appear in the HTML page. The <EMBED> tag is used for this function.
2. Frames	The <FRAME> tag is used to display more than one HTML page in the main viewing area of the browser.
3. JavaScript	JavaScript is a language developed by Netscape and Sun Microsystems to handle low-level and middle-level functions. Uses the <SCRIPT> tag.
4. Java	Java is the cross-platform full-feature programming language developed by Sun Microsystems. Uses the <APPLET> tag.

Each of these features considerably extends the functionality of the HTML display. Embedded objects, or plug-ins, allow documents created in other file formats to be displayed within the HTML page. Frames allow independent control of multiple HTML documents within the main viewing area of the browser. JavaScript and Java extend Navigator's functionality by delivering scripts and applications through the transfer of uncompiled code that is interpreted locally. Before turning to these new tags, the additional attributes that Navigator has made available to existing HTML tags will be reviewed.

EXTENSIONS TO HTML 2 AND HTML 3

Some of Navigator's features are only available in individual operating systems, which are noted below. Netscape extensions to HTML 2 and 3 include the following tags and attributes:

<BASEFONT>   Determines base font size. Has one attribute, as follows:

                      SIZE   Possible values are 1 through 7. Default is set to 3.

<BLINK>   Alternates the display of the contained text from visible to invisible, creating a blinking effect.

<IMG>   File format issues will be addressed in Chapter 7. Many of Netscape's attributes have been included in the HTML 3 specifications. The following is not among them:

                      LOWSRC   Allows for the loading of a low resolution image prior to the higher resolution image supported by the SRC attribute. This allows the low resolution image and text to be loaded before the larger image files.

<NOBR>   Forces the text within the opening and closing tags to remain unbroken on the page. This can make the text extend beyond the view of the page, requiring the viewer to scroll to see information.

<WBR>   Allows a line break to occur within the <NOBR> and </NOBR> tags.

HTML Developer Tip #1

When using the Netscape extensions, remember that not all browsers can understand these tags. For that reason, it is advisable to set your basefont size in the <BODY> section using the <FONT> tag. Many more browsers recognize the <FONT> tag than the <BASEFONT> tag. If other font sizes are required in the body, the font size will return to the size of the original <FONT> tag after the nested font tags have been closed.

The following features are only available on the Macintosh versions of Navigator:

<TITLE>	This tag can be scrolled in the Title Bar of the Macintosh version of the browser. This is achieved by using a series of <TITLE> tags in the <HEAD> section of the HTML document. These will all be displayed before any of the <BODY> elements are displayed in the main viewing area of the browser.
<BODY>	Like the <TITLE> tag, the BGCOLOR attribute of the <BODY> tag can be introduced in a series for older Macintosh versions. Navigator 2 no longer supports this function, but version 1.1 and 1.2 do. To make this effect happen in Navigator 2, you would need to use JavaScript and change the BGCOLOR property of the document object (see later in this chapter). Use of multiple BGCOLOR attributes in versions 1.1 and 1.2 on the Macintosh results in the background color changing rapidly in a series, and before the <BODY> elements are loaded.

The example on the following page will make the word "TEST" scroll across the Title Bar, surrounded by periods. Then the word "TEST" will load as the name in the Title Bar, while the background color changes from black to dark green to cyan, then finally white. Then "Body Text" will appear in the main viewing area, after which the document is done loading.

When designing this type of effect, you must realize that your Windows audience only recognizes the final <TITLE> and final <BODY> tags. This type of "bell and whistle" can be fun, but its potential audience is relatively small. If you know that many or most of your viewers use the Macintosh OS, it may be nice as an occasional feature. Using JavaScript could give you a cross-platform solution.

In the case of the <BLINK> tag, the multiple <TITLE> and <BODY> tags, and the <META HTTP-EQUIV="Refresh"> tag, one must be cautious of distracting and overburdening the viewer with unnecessary effects. Sometimes the use of such features can complement a Web site's design; however, that is not always the case.

```
<HTML>

<HEAD>

<TITLE>.....T</TITLE>
<TITLE>....TE</TITLE>
<TITLE>...TES</TITLE>
<TITLE>..TEST</TITLE>
<TITLE>.TEST.</TITLE>
<TITLE>TEST..</TITLE>
<TITLE>EST...</TITLE>
<TITLE>ST....</TITLE>
<TITLE>T.....</TITLE>
<TITLE>......</TITLE>
<TITLE>TEST</TITLE>

</HEAD>

<BODY

BGCOLOR=000000
BGCOLOR=002200
BGCOLOR=004400
BGCOLOR=006620
BGCOLOR=008840
BGCOLOR=00AA60
BGCOLOR=00CC80
BGCOLOR=00EES0
BGCOLOR=20FFC0
BGCOLOR=40FFE0
BGCOLOR=60FFFF
BGCOLOR=80FFFF
BGCOLOR=A0FFFF
BGCOLOR=C0FFFF
BGCOLOR=FFFFFF>

Body Text

</BODY>
</HTML>
```

THE EMBED TAGS

The <EMBED> and <NOEMBED> tags are known collectively as the embed tags. Using these tags as described here, the HTML programmer can design the document for Navigator and other browsers simultaneously.

<EMBED>   Embeds an object in the HTML document. This is used in conjunction with helper applications and plug-ins, software extensions to the browser. If you want to insert a Macromedia Director document, you use the <EMBED> tag, which accesses the Shockwave plug-in to display the Director document. The file type is determined by the suffix of the file name. Embedded objects may use the following attributes, although many have unique attributes of their own. No corresponding closing tag.

ALIGN	Determines alignment of embedded object. Possible values are left, right, and center.
BORDER	Border width of embedded object in pixels.
HEIGHT	Height of embedded object in pixels.
PLUGINSPAGE	Provides URL of the page to download plug-in.
SRC	URL of the document that will be displayed in the <EMBED> tag location.
WIDTH	Width of embedded object in pixels

<NOEMBED>   Contains content to display in browsers that do not support embed tags. Has no attributes. Used with <EMBED> in the following syntax:

```
<EMBED SRC="animate.dcr" HEIGHT=120 WIDTH=160>
<NOEMBED>
<IMG SRC="static.gif" HEIGHT=120 WIDTH=160>
</NOEMBED>
```

The example above would be seen in Navigator as an embedded Director document, while the browsers that do not recognize the <EMBED> tags would recognize the <IMG> tag contents. Including a link on the page to download the plug-in necessary to view the document is a good practice to adopt.

EMBED TAG USAGE

There are over forty plug-ins, along with their attribute usage and development programs, listed in Chapter 7. Several of the most important ones available today, including Shockwave, are included on the CD-ROM. The Web site on the CD-ROM has links to the plug-in sites to download the latest version of their products.

The <EMBED> tag allows Navigator to take advantage of additional functionality provided by plug-ins or helper applications. Plug-ins are software extensions to the Navigator application. These extensions, created by third-party developers, allow Navigator to display media in formats not otherwise available to HTML. In addition to the attributes on the previous page, plug-ins often require their own attributes. SCROLLABLE, for instance, is an attribute of Tumbleweed Software's Envoy. Details of tag usage and file creation are usually provided by the plug-in manufacturer.

The usage of the <EMBED> tag, along with the <NOEMBED> tag, allows for the development of high-end solutions to Web site design, while still maintaining an acceptable display in less-sophisticated browsers. As you shall see with the <FRAMES> and <NOFRAMES> tags, the usage of the embed tags enables the HTML designer to include an embedded object for those browsers that support the tags, and to have an alternative display for those browsers that do not support them. In this respect, the <NOEMBED> tag functions like the ALT attribute of the <IMG> tag from HTML 2. In the latter instance, the ALT attribute served two purposes: displaying the text in non-graphic browsers; and displaying text for those browsers that have had the automatic loading of images turned off.

From Netscape's home page, you can find many of the most recent plug-ins ("http://home.netscape.com"). Additional plug-ins can be found by using one of the search engines like Alta Vista or Yahoo to look for "Netscape" and "plug" or "plug-in." The CD-ROM has links to additional sites that regularly post new plug-ins. Other browser manufacturers, including Oracle, @Home, and Microsoft, either support the Netscape plug-ins, or have pledged to support them in the future.

FRAMES

With the introduction of frames, HTML designers are finally able to have parts of the page display stay fixed on the screen. (This was attempted with the <BANNER> tag from HTML 3, but the tag was never supported by browser developers.) It helps to be familiar with table design in approaching the development of frames. The biggest difference in table design and frame design is that *tables are designed one row at a time and frames are designed one rectangle at a time.* Although <TD> tags are used to define rectangular areas for page display, it is the <TR> tag that needs to be resolved one row at a time. In the case of a framed document, each rectangular area needs to be defined at its largest unit, then subunit. The frame tags are as follows:

<FRAMESET>   Used in the place of the <BODY> tag to define a framed document. Only <FRAME>, <NOFRAMES>, and nested <FRAMESET> tags are contained within the <FRAMESET> tag. All frame and frameset tags must be referred to by the ROWS and COLS attributes to be recognized. All body attributes will be specified by the HTML document referenced by the SRC attribute of the <FRAME> tag. The tag has two attributes:

ROWS   Determines the size and number of rectangular rows within a <FRAMESET>. Possible values are absolute pixel units, a percentage of screen height, or relative values using the asterisk (*) character. The latter enables the developer to allocate all unassigned vertical space proportionately. Values are given within quotation marks and separated by commas.

COLS   Determines the size and number of rectangular columns within a <FRAMESET>. Possible values are absolute pixel units, a percentage of screen width, or relative values using the asterisk (*) character. The latter enables the developer to allocate all unassigned horizontal space proportionately. Values are given within quotation marks and separated by commas.

<NOFRAMES>   All HTML within this tag is ignored by Navigator and other frame-capable browsers. Other browsers will ignore all frame tags, and interpret the <NOFRAMES> content, beginning with the <BODY> tag.

<FRAME>	This tag defines a single frame within a frameset. All frames and nested framesets must be accounted for in the COLS and ROWS attributes of the <FRAMESET> tag. This tag has the following attributes:

SRC	Provides the URL reference for the source of the frame.
NAME	Names the frame to allow targeting by other HTML documents. Works in conjunction with the TARGET attribute of the <A>, <AREA>, <BASE>, and <FORM> tags. See code below. All names must begin with an alpha-numeric value and not the underscore character. The exception is the special target names later in this chapter.
MARGINWIDTH	Optional attribute given in pixels. Determines horizontal space between the <FRAME> contents and the frame's borders.
MARGINHEIGHT	Optional attribute given in pixels. Determines vertical space between the <FRAME> contents and the frame's borders.
SCROLLING	Possible values are "yes," "no," and "auto." Default value is "auto," and will be available as necessary.
NORESIZE	Prevents viewers from resizing the frame's borders. Without this tag, viewers can stretch or shrink the frame's display by selecting the frame's border and moving it up, down, left, or right.

Finally, there is one additional attribute for some tags to which you have already been introduced. The TARGET attribute is used with the <A>, <AREA>, <BASE>, and <FORM> tags with the following syntax:

```
<A HREF="framedoc.htm" TARGET="Frame_window_name">;

<AREA SHAPE="RECT" COORDS="5,15,25,40" HREF="framedoc.htm"
TARGET="Frame_window_name">;

<BASE TARGET="Frame_window_name">; and

<FORM ACTION="cgi_bin/script" TARGET="Frame_window_name">;
```

Each of the comma-separated values in the ROWS and COLS attributes of the <FRAMESET> tag represents a single frame or frameset. Absolute pixel values, relative heights and widths, and/or all unused browser space, as represented by the asterisk (*) character, are acceptable values. Absolute values are often used together with the asterisk in the ROWS or COLS definitions. The following HTML defines a page with two frames: the left one 100 pixels wide; the other as wide as possible:

```
<FRAMESET COLS="100,*">
```

It is also possible for more than one frame or frameset to share the unused browser display, as in the following example:

```
<FRAMESET COLS="100,*,2*">
```

In this case, there are three frames: one 100 pixels wide; the second one taking up one third of the remaining browser display; and the third frame taking up the two remaining thirds of the browser display.

When dividing up the page for the purpose of HTML design, it is useful to contrast the approach taken for frames with that used with tables. In the figure below, the <FRAMESET> and <TR> divisions help us understand the page layout.

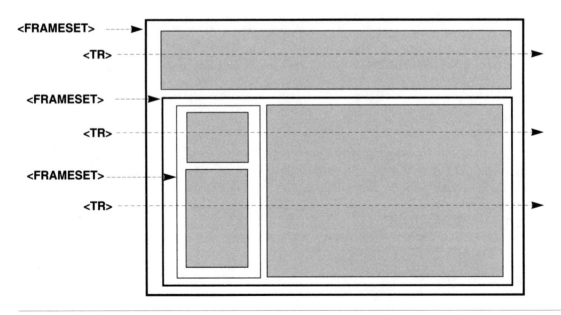

Consider the difference in the code behind the two methods:

```
<TABLE>

<! Notice that the table cells have absolute sizes, not relative sizes. Although a
table may take up the full page display with one monitor setting, this will not
be the case for larger monitors.>
<TR>
<TD COLSPAN=2 HEIGHT=65></TD>
</TR>

<TR>
<TD WIDTH=160 HEIGHT=65></TD>
<TD WIDTH=480 ROWSPAN=2></TD>
</TR>

<TR>
<TD HEIGHT=350></TD>
</TR>

</TABLE>
```

```
<FRAMESET ROWS="65, *">
    <FRAME SRC="frame1.htm"

    <FRAMESET COLS="160,*">

        <FRAMESET ROWS="65, *">

        <FRAME SRC="frame2.htm">
        <FRAME SRC="frame3.htm">

        </FRAMESET>

        <FRAME SRC="frame4.htm">
    </FRAMESET>
</FRAMESET>
```

In the example, there were three <FRAMESET> tags. It was possible to have more, but this was the least number necessary to describe the document. The <TABLE> tag could also have had one or more nested tables contained. The minimum number of rows that the table could have, however, was three. Both table design and frame design require the rectangular division of the viewing area. In the case of frames, it is the rectangular area itself that is topmost in the design hierarchy. For tables, all rectangles occur within <TR> tags, and each <TR> tag needs to be resolved one row at a time. Nested tables may be contained within table cells. When this occurs, the same rule regarding the resolution of rows applies.

Targets Revisited

The target attribute has several special names that cannot be assigned by the NAME attribute of the <FRAME> tag. Each of these reserved names serves a special function for the framed documents. These special names and functions are:

TARGET="_top"   This reloads the full main viewing area of the browser with the URL specified by the HREF attribute. This is particularly useful for navigating between framed documents.

TARGET="_blank" Opens a new browser window. The window is not named.

TARGET="_self"   Loads the document in the same window where the anchor was clicked. This is the default setting. This attribute would generally be used to override the TARGET attribute of the <BASE> tag.

TARGET="_parent" If the frame where this target is called from has a parent frame on the page (i.e., a frame that targeted and opened the frame), then the document will be loaded in the parent frame. If there is no parent frame, the attribute is ignored.

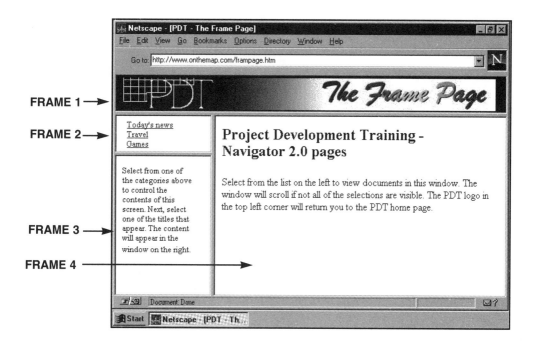

FRAME TAG USAGE

The above framed document illustrates how you would use one frame to control the contents of another. It also brings out the importance of communicating to your audience how they are expected to navigate through the framed page. The default body of the document (Frame 4) describes the framed page, and informs the viewer how to move through the frames. Selecting from the options in Frame 2 controls which list appears in Frame 3. Once the list in Frame 3 appears, selecting list items changes the display in Frame 4.

On the following pages, the HTML behind the document will be examined. Notice in Frame 1 the use of the client-side image map, along with its target reference. Also, notice the targets of Frames 2 and 3. Of the four frames, only two need to be named to serve as targets. Frame 2 is named for reference purposes. In addition to the four framed documents, "newsmarg.htm," a document that will be loaded in Frame 3, will also be displayed to see how it targets documents for Frame 4.

The Frame Page

```
<HTML>

<HEAD>
<TITLE>PDT - The Frame Page</TITLE>
</HEAD>

    <FRAMESET ROWS="65, *">
    <FRAME MARGINWIDTH="0" MARGINHEIGHT="0" SRC="frame1.htm" SCROLLING="NO">
        <FRAMESET COLS="160,3*">
            <FRAMESET ROWS="65, *">
             <FRAME SRC="frame2.htm" NAME="category" SCROLLING="NO" MARGINHEIGHT="0"
             MARGINWIDTH="5" >
             <FRAME SRC="frame3.htm" NAME="topic">
             </FRAMESET>
        <FRAME SRC="frame4.htm" NAME="targeted">
    </FRAMESET>
</FRAMESET>
</HTML>
```

Frame 1

```
<HTML>

<BODY BGCOLOR=000000>
<MAP NAME="homepage">
<AREA SHAPE="RECT" COORDS="0,0,148,50" HREF="index.htm" TARGET="_top">
</MAP>
<IMG BORDER=0 SRC="framhead.jpg" USEMAP="#homepage">
</BODY>

</HTML>
```

Frame 2

```
<HTML>

<BODY TEXT=000000 BGCOLOR=FFFFFF ALINK=FF0000 LINK=0000FF VLINK=0000FF>
<FONT SIZE=2.5><A HREF="newsmarg.htm" TARGET="topic">Today's news</A><BR>
<A HREF="travmarg.htm" TARGET="topic">Travel</A><BR>
<A HREF="gamemarg.htm" TARGET="topic">Games</A><BR>
</FONT>
</BODY>

</HTML>
```

Frame 3

```
<HTML>

<BODY TEXT=000000 BGCOLOR=FFFFFF>
<FONT SIZE=2.5>Select from one of the categories above to control the contents of
this screen. Next, select one of the titles that appear. The content will appear
in the window on the right.</FONT>
</BODY>

</HTML>
```

Frame 4

```
<HTML>

<BODY TEXT=000000 BGCOLOR=FFFFFF>
<FONT SIZE=5><STRONG>Project Development Training - <BR>Navigator 2.0
pages</STRONG></FONT><P>
Select from the list on the left to view documents in this window. The window
will scroll if not all of the selections are visible. The PDT logo in the top
left corner will return you to the PDT home page.<P>
</BODY>

</HTML>
```

newsmarg.htm

```
<HTML>

<BODY BGCOLOR=000000 TEXT=FFFFFF LINK=FFFF00 ALINK=FF0000 VLINK=FFFF00>
<STRONG><FONT SIZE=4>Today's News</FONT></STRONG><P>
<FONT SIZE=2.5>
<A HREF="http://www.timeinc.com/time/daily/time/1996/latest.html"
TARGET="targeted">TIME</A><BR>
<A HREF="http://www.fwi.com/wnt/wnt.html" TARGET="targeted">WWW World News</A><BR>
<A HREF="http://www.sfgate.com/chronicle/index.shtml" TARGET="targeted">SF
Chronicle</A><BR>
<A HREFf="http://www.cnn.com/US/index.html" TARGET="targeted">CNN - US News</A><BR>
<A HREF="http://www.abc.es/" TARGET="targeted">ABC - Spain</A><BR>
<A HREF="http://www.telegraph.co.uk/" TARGET="targeted">Telegraph</A><BR>
<A HREF="http://www.zfm.com/observador/" TARGET="targeted">El Observador
EconÛmico</A><BR>
<A HREF="http://www.unitedmedia.com/comics/" TARGET="targeted">United Media
Cartoons</A><BR>
</FONT>
<HR>
<FONT SIZE=2>Address all correspondence to <A HREF="mailto:sales@onthemap.com">
sales&#64 onthemap.com</A><P>
Copyright 1996 by Kevin Ready and Project Development Training
</FONT>
</BODY>

</HTML>
```

This last HTML document is a page that replaced the page that was originally in
Frame 3. Notice that the target for all of the individual list items is the largest visible
frame on the page, Frame 4. By using this model, you can quickly put together a
two-tiered descriptive list, such as a table of contents. Having one frame target
another is the first step, but it is the second step and beyond that really optimizes
the use of frames as an organizational tool. Using the frames as shown here,
integrated with the special TARGET references, a large amount of information
can be made readily available and easy to navigate through.

JavaScript

The scripting language native to Navigator allows for an extension to traditional HTML design. JavaScript enables developers to write code that is processed at the browser. The code is written to respond to events, such as a button click, a value being entered, or the opening of an HTML document. The HTML syntax is as follows:

<SCRIPT>   Contains the code to be executed at the browser level. The <SCRIPT> tag is generally included in the <HEAD> section to ensure that the code is loaded before being called from the HTML page. It has the following attributes:

                      LANGUAGE   The default is set to JavaScript, presently the only language available. This is an optional tag.

                      SRC   This is used to reference a URL containing the code to be accessed.

<! -- //>   The comment tag has a secondary use for JavaScript. Within the <SCRIPT> tag, it demarcates the area where functions are defined and loaded into memory. Although the scripts are loaded into memory, they are generally initiated on response to events.

Following is a brief example of the <SCRIPT> and <! -- > tags. For browsers that do not recognize the <SCRIPT> tag, none of the information below is displayed.

```
<SCRIPT LANGUAGE=LiveScript>

<! -- The comment field hides the script from other browsers

document.write("This is a simple script.")

//     Double slashes are used for comments within JavaScript.
//     The close of the comment tag ends the declaration section.>

</SCRIPT>
```

EVENT HANDLERS

In conjunction with the <SCRIPT> tag, the JavaScript language uses event handlers, which are included as attributes in tag definitions. Most of these are used with form tags, and enable designers to check for input and perform certain functions in response to user input. The available event handlers are the following:

onBlur
: This is used with the <SELECT> and <TEXTAREA> tags, and the text TYPE <INPUT> tag. Initiates a script when the form field is exited.

onChange
: This is used with the <SELECT> and <TEXTAREA> tags, and the text TYPE <INPUT> tag. Initiates a script when the form field value is changed.

onClick
: This can be used with most <INPUT> tag types and the <A> tag. In response to a mouse click, the script specified by this attribute would run.

onFocus
: This is used with the <SELECT> and <TEXTAREA> tags, and the text TYPE <INPUT> tag. Initiates a script when the form field is entered.

onLoad
: Executes a script once the window or all frames are loaded. Used with the <BODY> and <FRAMESET> tags.

onMouseOver
: This is used with <A> tags and other hot areas, such as the <AREA> tag. Determines the text to display in the status window. Default value is the URL reference.

onSelect
: This is used with the <TEXTAREA> tags, and the text TYPE <INPUT> tag. Initiates a script when text is selected.

onSubmit
: Executes a script upon form submission. Used with the <FORM> tag.

onUnload
: Executes a script when the document is exited. Used within the <BODY> or <FRAMESET> tags.

STATEMENTS

Statements are declared in the comments section within the <SCRIPT> tag. It is suggested that these be introduced in the <HEAD> section. Navigator reads HTML from top to bottom and from left to right. If the statement has not been declared prior to its use in the body of the document, it will not work. The following statements are supported in JavaScript:

break   Used to interrupt **while** or **for** loops. Remaining code after the interrupted loop statement is then interpreted.

comment   Comments are supported in two ways:
               // single line comment
               /* multiple line comment*/

               The top one is used for a single line of commented text; the bottom one is used for two or more lines of commented text.

continue   Terminates **while** or **for** loops. In a **while** loop, the test condition is returned to; in the **for** loop, the updated value or expression is passed.

for   The **for** loop consists of three optional expressions (separated by semicolons and contained within parentheses) and a block of statements. Their syntax is:
               for ([initial expression]; [condition]; [update expression]) {statements}

               The initial expression can use the var statement to declare a variable if necessary.

for....in Provides an interative function for variable var for all properties of object obj:
               for (var in obj) {statements}

function   See the following page for description and syntax.

if....else The if then format for JavaScript is as follows:
               if (condition) {
               statements
               } [**else** {
               else statements}]

               If a test condition is true, the statements are executed; if they are false, the else statements are execected. Statements may include nested if statements.

return   Specifies the value to be returned by a function.

var   Declares a variable. Variables may be declared by using the **var** statement or simply by assigning them a value. Consider the following:
               var varname[=varvalue]   or   varname=varvalue

while   Similar to the **for** loop, this statement evaluates an expression
                     condition, and if true, executes statements. It repeats this process as
                     long as the condition is true.

> **while** (condition)   {statements}

with   Establishes an object as the default object for multiple statements.

> **with** (object) {statements}

FUNCTIONS

A *function* is a special type of statement. Functions are triggered in response to event
handlers. The function definition contains three elements:

- The function's name
- The parameter(s) of the function enclosed in parentheses, and separated by
  commas
- The JavaScript statement(s) that define the function contained within braces

Here are the three elements in a simple script:

```
line 1       <SCRIPT LANGUAGE=LiveScript>
line 2       <! --
line 3       function square(x) {
line 4       document.write ("The square of ",x," is " )
line 5       return x * x
line 6       }
line 7       document.write(square(8),".")
line 8       <! -- >
line 9       </SCRIPT>
```

The first statement in the <SCRIPT> tag on line 3 is a function. The function's
name is "square"; the function's parameter is "x"; and the JavaScript statement is
contained within the braces from the end of line 3 to line 6. The second statement
uses the write property of the document object, and results in the square of 8 being
displayed. You have now seen the HTML to describe the JavaScript, the event
handlers that can trigger a function, and the manner in which the function is
organized within the <SCRIPT> tag. Next you shall consider the objects, properties,
and methods available in JavaScript.

OBJECTS

Objects are entities that can be interpreted or affected by using JavaScript. The primary objects in Navigator are the Window, Location, History, and Document objects. Following is the JavaScript object hierarchy:

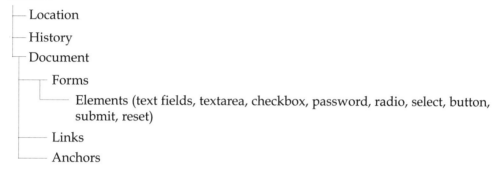

Some of these objects, such as History, can be interpreted by JavaScript. Others have properties that can be interpreted or affected through scripting. The BGCOLOR property of the Document object, for instance, can be interpreted by JavaScript, and it can also be affected, or changed, by JavaScript.

PROPERTIES

Object properties are aspects or features of an object that can be addressed by the JavaScript language. Following is an example of the syntax used to work with objects and their properties:

```
document.bgColor=#FF00FF
location.href="http://www.browserbydesign.com"
window.frames[1]="frame1.htm"
```

There are many properties that can be addressed by JavaScript. Appendix E and the CD-ROM provide online reference sources for further information on objects and properties. For the HTML designer, the important thing to be aware of is that many screen elements can be controlled through manipulation by JavaScript.

METHODS

A *method* is an action or operation affecting an object or its properties. Properties and methods have been compared to adjectives and verbs, respectively. Consider the following two examples:

Varname.value=1000
Math.abs(Varname)

The top example assigns a value to variable Varname. *Properties* can be thought of as ways to describe an object. The bottom example uses the abs method of the Math object to return a calculation using Varname as its initial value. *Methods* can be thought of as ways to transform or process an object. A quick way to recognize whether an element is a property or method is its use of the equal sign (=) or parentheses ((...)). Methods almost always require arguments or parameters contained within parentheses. Properties, on the other hand, are generally used with the equal sign to obtain an object's description or to assign it a value.

JAVASCRIPT USAGE

JavaScript can considerably expand the design of your HTML document. At this time, only Navigator will recognize the language. As a designer, it is important to know what kind of functionality is available to browsers. Using JavaScript, you can test for form entry values, launch applications in response to button clicks, and perform other functions that require server interaction.

The HTML on the following pages contains several useful JavaScript examples. Among the most common implementations of JavaScript are clocks, form entry checkers, navigation buttons, scrolling text boxes, and rollover mouse values. These provide a starting point for implementation of scripting in your pages.

Don't worry if you have trouble understanding the JavaScript the first time through. It is far more complex than HTML, even if it is a relatively simple programming language. There are resources available on the Internet that you can freely copy and insert into your documents—not all are freely distributed, however, so check before you include the code in your page. The HTML on the following pages can be freely copied and used for private or commercial purposes.

```
<HTML>
<HEAD>

<SCRIPT LANGUAGE="JavaScript">

var enabled=0;

// The first function sets the clock.

 function TimeOutfunc()
{ TIMEOUT = window.setTimeout( "TimeOutfunc()", 1000 );
var today = new Date();
document.forms[0].elements[0].value = today.toString();}

// The second and third functions test for form entry

function testentry(form)
{var foundError = false;
if(Blanktest(form.Box1))
{ alert("This field needs to be filled in.");
 foundError = true;}
 if(!foundError)
{alert("You have correctly entered text into the box.")}}

function Blanktest(theField)
{if(theField.value.length == 0)
  return true;
  else
  return false;}

// The fourth function is used by the scroll box.

var ScrollString="     This text can be changed for you to enter your own. It
will scroll across the page from right to left.                " var timer=0;

function Scrollon()
{document.box.boxtext.value = ScrollString

ScrollString=ScrollString.substring(1,ScrollString.length)+ScrollString.charAt(0)
    timer= setTimeout("Scrollon()",50)}
</SCRIPT>
```

```
<TITLE>JavaScript Demonstration Page</TITLE>

</HEAD>

<! The clock and scrolled text are initiated by the onLoad handler in the BODY
tag.>

<BODY onLoad="TimeOut = setTimeout( 'TimeOutfunc()', 1000 ); enabled=1;
Scrollon();}"
BGCOLOR=FFFFFF TEXT=000000 >

<H1>Clock with Date, Time, and Time Zone</H1>

<FORM>
<CENTER>
<INPUT TYPE="text" name="disp" value="" size=25 onFocus="this.blur()" >
</CENTER>
</FORM>

<H1>Test for Text Entry</H1>

<FORM NAME="TestforInput" METHOD="get">
Enter Text, then click outside the text box:<P>

<! By using the onBlur handler, the script is executed when the text box is left.>

<CENTER>
<INPUT TYPE="text" NAME="Box1" SIZE=30 onBlur="testentry(this.form)">
</CENTER>
</FORM>

<H1>Navigation Buttons</H1>

<FORM METHOD=POST>

<CENTER>
<! These buttons take advantage of the history object in Navigator.>
<INPUT TYPE="button" VALUE="Next Page" ONCLICK="history.go(1)">
<INPUT TYPE="button" VALUE="Reload" ONCLICK="history.go(0)">
<INPUT TYPE="button" VALUE="Previous Page" ONCLICK="history.go(-1)">
<INPUT TYPE="button" VALUE="Two Pages Ago" ONCLICK="history.go(-2)">
</CENTER>
</FORM>
```

```
<H1>Scrolling Text Box</H1>

<FORM NAME="box" onSubmit="0">

<CENTER>
<INPUT TYPE="text" NAME="boxtext" SIZE=45 VALUE ="">
</CENTER>
</FORM>

<H1>Mouse Over Text</H1>

<CENTER>

<! This little trick requires almost no code. Using the ONMOUSEOVER handler
enables you to write information that will display in the Status Bar when the
mouse is dragged over the element referred to by the anchor tag.>

<A HREF="index.htm" ONMOUSEOVER="window.status='Enter the text you wish here.';
return true">
<IMG SRC="pedestal.jpg" WIDTH=230 HEIGHT=200 BORDER=3></A>
</CENTER>

</BODY>

</HTML>
```

The examples here are simple applications of JavaScript, but they can at least get you started in the right direction. There are many excellent online resources, and you can copy much of the JavaScript straight from other people's pages. I would advise against doing such things verbatim, but they can certainly help you during the learning process.

You may have already experienced difficulties trying to read the document source from pages that use JavaScript or other client-pull methods to make the page change or be unreadable for one reason or another. If you want to see the HTML behind complex JavaScript pages that do not enable you to view the document source, open the page with a browser that does not support JavaScript, and then view its source. By not recognizing the <SCRIPT> or <META> tag, the browser will have no problem displaying these tags, which do not affect it. On the following page is the rendering of the HTML from the past three pages.

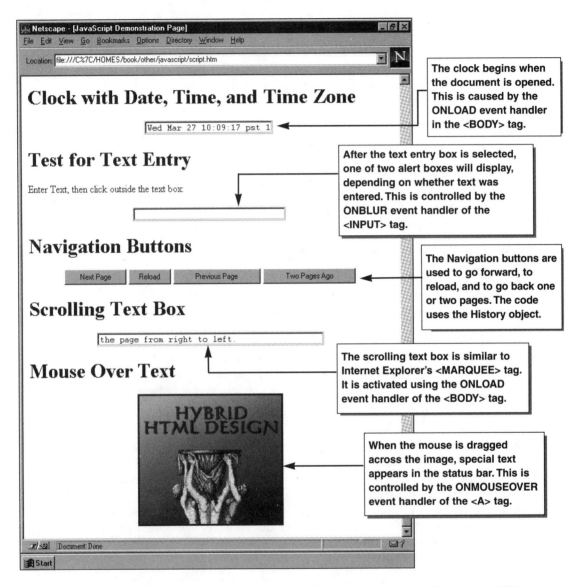

There are many excellent resources available for you to learn JavaScript. In addition to the CD-ROM and Appendix E, the Web site "http://www.browserbydesign.com/" has links to JavaScript, Java, and other related topics.

JAVA

Netscape Navigator supports the Java programming language developed by Sun Microsystems. This language was developed to be cross-platform and device-independent. It is a powerful language, yet unfortunately slow in its current implementation. An *applet*, for those not familiar with the term, is the name of the mini-applications created with the Java programming language. You will often be working with C programmers and others to provide your Java resources. If you are up to the challenge, online Java resources are listed in Appendix E and the CD-ROM. The HTML syntax for Java applets is as follows:

<APPLET>	Designates a Java applet. Instead of containing the code necessary to perform a task, this tag contains a reference to the code needed to perform the task. Contains one tag, the <PARAM> tag, that passes values to the applet. It has the following attributes:

CODEBASE	Directory or folder where the applet(s) are located.
CODE	Defines the compiled applet that is to be loaded.
WIDTH	Determines the width of the area reserved for the applet in the browser. Measured in pixels.
HEIGHT	Determines the height of the area reserved for the applet in the browser. Measured in pixels.

<PARAM>	This tag passes a parameter to the applet. It has two attributes:

NAME	Names the parameter for recognition by the applet.
VALUE	Defines a value for the parameter named by the NAME attribute. All data is passed to the applet as a string variable.

When using Java in your pages, it is important to be aware that most browsers do not currently support the language. If, like many authors, you are showcasing your use of Java on the page, it is advisable to include text in the document that alerts viewers to this fact. This is especially true when the applet itself is the centerpiece of the document. Java is expected to be supported by Internet Explorer, PowerBrowser, and others during 1996.

NAVIGATOR 3 AND BEYOND

At the end of March, 1996, Netscape introduced Atlas, a beta release for what is expected to be version 3.0 of its Navigator browser. This version recognizes the Microsoft attributes for tables and fonts, and it is rumored that VBScript may be supported by the time the commercial version is released. Most of the significant upgrades to Navigator 3 are related to security, mail, and chat functions.

Features added to the browser include being able to navigate through frame pages using the back and forward buttons. Instead of being brought back to the last full page that was loaded, you can now go back and forward to the previous or following frame. In the program's mail and news options, additional configurations are possible. Additional file formats will be supported by including plug-ins with the latest Navigator product. Presently, these include an audio plug-in that supports AIFF, AU, MIDI, and WAV formats; a video plug-in that supports the AVI format; and Live3D, a plug-in that supports the VRML file format.

CoolTalk is a helper application that ships with Navigator. This chat program enables you to engage in real-time audio and data collaboration with others over the Internet or Intranet. Unlike many other chat or collaboration programs, this helper application supports audio exchange, as well as a Shared Whiteboard for sharing graphic and text information.

Both Java and JavaScript have been enhanced for the Atlas release. The Macintosh version is Java-enabled, and several more Unix versions, such as IBM AIX and BSDI, support Java. JavaScript has been given the capability to recognize plug-ins and MIME-type support. This is facilitated through two additional properties for the global navigator object: the plug-ins object and the mimeTypes object.

Navigator has had several security features added to version 3.0. From the Options menu, the Security Preferences now let you enable or disable Java and JavaScript; to show alerts when interacting with secure and insecure Web sites; to password protect Navigator in a networked environment; to create or delete a personal security certificate; and to edit or delete a site certificate.

Certificates use public key cryptography technology developed by RSA Data Security. *Public key cryptography* involves the use of a public and private key to complete a transaction. This cryptography method has been adopted by most major browser manufacturers, as well as VISA and MasterCard.

PUBLIC KEY CRYPTOGRAPHY

As more and more attention is focused on security issues on the Internet, an understanding of the technology behind public key cryptography is useful. The technology involves the generation of two keys to conduct a secure transaction. The keys are actually two large, randomly generated prime numbers. The size of these numbers is measured in bit length. If the prime number is less than 256, or 2^8, it is an 8-bit prime number. If it is less than 1,048,576, or 2^{20}, it is a 20-bit number.

Government regulations restrict the export of encryption technology that can generate keys longer than a certain bit length (at one point this was 40 bits, but this is presently under review). Bank transactions typically use 512-bit keys (roughly 10^{150}), and are moving to even larger keys. The technology is based on a simple principle—large numbers are difficult to factor. The assumption is that if you have a number with 300 characters, it would be difficult to extract the two prime numbers that are its factors. So far, this assumption has been proven true.

The two large, randomly generated prime numbers are used to form the public key and the private key. The public key is published for all to see. It associates information with the individual or group that possess the key. An example of a public key is an e-mail address, or a published announcement. The other side of the transaction is the private key. This key is used to authenticate the identity of the sender. The public key is created by multiplying the two random numbers together. The private key is created using the two random numbers with an algorithm developed by RSA. Following is an example of public key crytography in action:

Random Number 1:	527
Random Number 2:	499
Public Key:	262,973 (527×499)
Private Key:	2,607 (($527 - 499$) + (527×3) + (499×2))

In this example, the first number is a 10-bit key (less than 2^{10}), and the second is a 9-bit key (less than 2^9). The public key is created by multiplying the two numbers, whereas the private key is generated with a specific algorithm. This is an example of such an algorithm, although this is not the one used by RSA. Netscape has added HTML tags to accommodate certificate-based transactions.

The only new tags, with the exception of the adoption of the Microsoft tags, that are known to be included in Navigator 3 involve the conduct of secure transactions. As VISA, MasterCard, and RSA make the Secure Electronic Transaction (SET) standard safe for Internet commerce, you can expect these tags or similar ones to appear as features in other browsers.

<CERTIFICATE>   This tag brackets a 64-bit encoded certificate. It is used to provide additional security to Internet transactions by encrypting form data. It has one attribute, as follows:

    NAME   This attribute is used by the server for processing form data. This is a required attribute.

<PAYORDER>   This is a special type of <INPUT> tag, and must be contained within a <FORM>. The contents of the tag are considered "the order." Used with the <CERTIFICATE> tag, this tag provides additional security to Internet transactions. It has two attributes, both of which are required:

    NAME   This attribute specifies the name to be paired with the <PAYORDER> contents.

    CERT   This attribute references a previously defined <CERTIFICATE> tag.

The review on the Atlas program was based on its initial beta release at the end of March, 1996. It is very likely that by the time this product ships, it will have additional tags, attributes, and features. Many of the features will be enhanced by using the Netscape server products in conjunction with the client browser. LiveWire, for instance, offers Web site development, database connectivity, and security features that are optimized for the Navigator browser.

The company's evolving product line also includes Chat and SmartMarks—two browser derivatives, which are included as part of Netscape's Power Pack. The first provides Navigator the same type of chat-room function as the online services, and will probably merge with CoolTalk. SmartMarks enables you to do offline browsing. This means that if you know that you want to go to a site on a particular day, or any time that it is updated, the caching of images can happen during the time that the browser is not busy doing other things. Check Netscape's home page regularly for the latest information on Atlas and other Web products and services.

NAVIGATOR 2.0 SUMMARY

When designing pages using Navigator 2 tags, you must consider the anticipated demographic audience. If your pages are for the World Wide Web and you expect everyone to be able to view your pages, you need to resolve the document's display in other browsers. If you are designing an internal Web site for a company that only uses the Navigator browser, then you can feel free to optimize your page display using the tags in this chapter without worrying about hybrid design techniques. The following chapter will examine the methods of designing hybrid pages for display in all browsers.

If you are designing pages that contain embedded objects, you should include a link to the site where the plug-in is available. It should be a reflex design response to include the <NOEMBED> tag when using the <EMBED> tag, as should be the inclusion of the ALT attribute for the <IMG> tag (see Chapter 3). This develops a hybrid design approach to HTML authoring, a trait you seek to fine-tune.

Frames are an important addition to your page design options. As with the <EMBED> tag, the framed document should always include a <NOFRAMES> tag with information to display in other browsers. This is generally included at the top of the framed document, but it can be at the bottom. The <NOFRAMES> tag must be included within the opening and closing <FRAMESET> tags. Remember that the <FRAMESET> tag takes the place of the <BODY> tag. The only place that a <BODY> tag belongs in a framed document is within the <NOFRAMES> tag.

Pages referenced by <FRAMESET> tags can be optimized for Navigator without too much consideration for other browsers. If the browser does not support frames, it will never read one of the framed documents. PowerBrowser and Explorer are beginning to support frames, and also recognize most of Netscape's other tags. This means that you will not generally have to worry about keeping the framed documents hybrid.

JavaScript works well as a check for input in form documents. This can save a lot of effort on the part of the server passing the CGI information (see Chapter 8). Filtering erroneous information at the browser reduces the drain on server resources. This will not affect browsers that do not recognize the code. Java, on the other hand, is not presently widely supported, and the pages that rely on it for display will have nothing to offer alternative browsers. In these cases, the only thing you can do is alert the viewer that they need a Java-enabled browser to view the document.

INTERNET EXPLORER 2.0

In August, 1995, Microsoft released the Windows 95 operating system. The fact that they packaged their Internet accessing software as part of their operating system generated a response from the U.S. Justice Department. This was due in large part to the perceived (and actual) advantage gained by Microsoft through their capability to access system resources of Windows 95. Ultimately, the government withheld their objections to the release of Windows 95, and Internet Explorer arrived as a component of the operating system. Recently, Microsoft made available a Macintosh version of the program, somewhat less functional than their own.

Microsoft has gone far to advance its own HTML tags. After a dismal introduction of the Explorer 1.0 browser, the company quickly released an upgraded version that not only recognized the <TABLE> tag and other HTML 3 tags, but that also launched a substantial number of its own tags and attributes. Microsoft tags are able to access system resources, such as fonts and OLE objects. With browsers that are supported in multiple operating systems, this has not been possible. This is changing quickly, however, as described in Chapter 9.

The majority of Internet Explorer's extensions to HTML are in the form of additional attributes. The tags extended by Explorer are the following:

1. <AREA>   This tag is used with the client-side image maps and includes non-rectangular shapes.

2. <BODY>   The tag has been expanded to include margins, a background watermark, and all of Netscape's extensions.

3. <FONT>   Font faces can now be set. Supports all HTML 3 attributes.

4. <HR>   The horizontal rule now supports color definition.

5. <IMG>   This has been considerably expanded to reference video and VRML files.

6. <TABLE>   Independent color control is now available for tabled areas. This is particularly helpful in page layout uses.

INTERNET EXPLORER TAGS

The new tags unique to Internet Explorer 2.0 are the <MARQUEE> tag and the <BGSOUND> tag. The tags and their attributes are as follows:

<MARQUEE>   Generates a scrolling marquee in the HTML document. For browsers that do not recognize the tag, the text within appears as regular text. Contains the following attributes:

ALIGN	Possible values are TOP, MIDDLE, or BOTTOM. Specifies where the text surrounding the marquee is positioned in relationship to the scrolling text.
BEHAVIOR	Possible values are SCROLL, SLIDE, or ALTERNATE. The default is set to SCROLL, which makes the text scroll across the page and disappear. SLIDE makes the text stop after it has scrolled into view. ALTERNATE makes the scrolled text go back and forth on the page.
BGCOLOR	Determines background color of the marquee. Possible values are hexadecimal colors or the color names described in Chapter 7.
DIRECTION	Determines the direction that the text scrolls across the screen. Possible values are LEFT or RIGHT.
HEIGHT	Determines height of marquee. Possible values are number of pixels or percentage of screen height.
WIDTH	Determines width of marquee. Possible values are number of pixels or percentage of screen width.
HSPACE	Determines left and right margins of marquee, measured in pixels.
VSPACE	Determines top and bottom margins of marquee, measured in pixels.
LOOP	Determines how many times the scrolled text will loop. Possible values are integers or INFINITE.
SCROLLAMOUNT	Specifies the number of pixels between loops of scrolled text.
SCROLLDELAY	Specifies the number of milliseconds between loops of scrolled text.

<BGSOUND>   Contains a sound file that is played when the page is loaded.
                   Supports .WAV, .AU, and .MID file formats. This tag is also
                   recognized by NCSA Mosaic 2.0. It has the following attributes:

                   SRC   Contains the URL reference for the sound file.

                   LOOP   Determines how many times the sound file will loop.
                                Possible values are integers or INFINITE.

INTERNET EXPLORER HTML ATTRIBUTES

The most substantial advance made by Internet Explorer has been its expansion of
existing tag attributes. By using tags that other browsers recognize, Explorer enables
you to optimize pages that are viewed differently in other browsers. The existing
HTML tags and their new attributes are as follows:

<AREA>   This HTML 3 tag that specifies hot areas in client-side image
                   maps now supports multiple shapes. Similar shapes can be
                   expected to be included in future HTML specifications.

                   SHAPE   Possible values are RECT, RECTANGLE, CIRC, CIRCLE,
                                POLY, or POLYGON. RECT and RECTANGLE use the
                                COORDS attribute, as described in HTML 3. The others
                                use the following syntax:

```
<AREA SHAPE="RECT" COORDS="10, 10, 60, 40" HREF="index.htm">
<! This creates a rectangular hotspot in the area from (10,10)
to (60,40).>
```

```
<AREA SHAPE="CIRC" COORDS="40, 40, 20" HREF="index.htm">
<! This creates a circular hotspot with a radius of 20 pixels
centered at (40,40).>
```

```
<AREA SHAPE="POLY" COORDS="10, 10, 20, 20, 5, 15"
HREF="index.htm">
<! This creates a polygon hotspot having vertices (10,10),
(20,20), and (5,15).>
```

<HR>   The horizontal rule now supports colors.

                   COLOR   Possible values are hexadecimal or special colors, as
                                described in Chapter 7.

<BODY>	This tag has had long-needed margin attributes added, as well as an ornamental background properties tag. These are as follows:

LEFTMARGIN	Determines the amount of blank space in pixels between the left and right margins and the edge of the page. This is defaulted to 0 in most browsers. In Microsoft's documentation, this is claimed to only affect the left margin, but testing has shown it to affect left and right margins.
TOPMARGIN	Determines the amount of blank space in pixels between the top and bottom margins and the edge of the page. This is defaulted to 0 in most browsers. This only affects the top margin in the Macintosh version, but it affects top and bottom margins in the Windows versions.
BGPROPERTIES	This is used with the BACKGROUND attribute. Only possible value is "FIXED," which makes the background image non-scrollable, a feature that Microsoft likes to call a watermark.

<FONT>	After not having recognized the tag in the Explorer 1.0 browser, Microsoft was able to leapfrog Netscape with its reference to its system resources. Windows 95 ships with over 30 font faces.

FACE	Specifies a specific font face. This will override the default font settings. The early beta versions for the Macintosh did not support this tag.

HTML Developer Tip #2

Microsoft, like Netscape, does not support tags equally in all operating systems. Developers are often forced to support the Microsoft OS due to its control of 90 percent of the desktop market. The higher degree of attention that Netscape and its plug-in software developers give to the Windows platform gives them the same ability to access Windows 95 system resources as Microsoft. This has worked to prevent Microsoft from dominating the PC browser market. Cross-platform differences present yet another consideration in HTML design.

IMAGE TAG ATTRIBUTES

The <IMG> tag contains several new attributes that provide support for richer content in HTML display. The new attributes offer an excellent alternative to the <EMBED> and <NOEMBED> tags of Navigator. All descriptive content is contained within the <IMG> tag. Browsers that do not recognize the additional attributes ignore them, resulting in no compromise in HTML display. For this reason, it is important to include a SRC reference in your <IMG> tag for alternative display.

The new <IMG> attributes are the following:

DYNSRC
Provides alternative content to the SRC attribute for Explorer. File types supported presently are .AVI and .VRM files. Uses the same syntax as SRC attribute.

CONTROLS
Displays control panel for DYNSRC files. Uses the following syntax:

```
<IMG SRC="test.gif" DYNSRC="test.AVI" CONTROLS>
```

This would result in the display of "test.gif" in browsers that do not support the DYNSRC attribute. For Explorer, a control panel will be present at the bottom of the .AVI display.

LOOP
Determines how many times the DYNSRC file will loop. Possible values are integers or INFINITE. Default is 1.

START
This attribute instructs the browser when to begin displaying the file referenced by the DYNSRC attribute. Possible values are FILEOPEN (the default) and MOUSEOVER. On FILEOPEN, the DYNSRC file will display upon document loading. On MOUSEOVER, it begins when the mouse is dragged across the page where the DYNSRC file is located. If used together, the LOOP attribute disables the FILEOPEN setting, so that only the MOUSEOVER method displays on the page.

TABLE TAG ATTRIBUTES

The table tags contain several new ornamental attributes. Be careful not to set the color of fonts within table cells to the color described by the BGCOLOR attribute of the <BODY> tag. Browsers that do not support the background table colors, but do support the BGCOLOR attribute and the TEXT attribute, may hide the text due to color conflicts. The following attributes affect the <TABLE>, <TH>, and <TD> tags. Most work in conjunction with the BORDER attribute, and use a 3D metaphor in lighting usage.

BGCOLOR	Determines the background color. Possible values are hexadecimal colors or special color names. This can also be used with the <TR> tag. The <TH> and <TD> attributes override the <TABLE> attributes.
BORDERCOLOR	This is used in conjunction with the BORDER attribute. Determines the color of the outer and inner borders. Possible values are hexadecimal colors or special color names. The attribute is overridden by the BORDERCOLORLIGHT and BORDERCOLORDARK attributes. The <TH> and <TD> attributes override the <TABLE> attributes.
BORDERCOLORDARK	This is used in conjunction with the BORDER attribute. For <TABLE>, this affects the outer top and left and inner right and bottom borders. For <TH> and <TD>, this affects the top and left borders. Possible values are hexadecimal colors or special color names. The <TH> and <TD> attributes override the <TABLE> attributes.
BORDERCOLORLIGHT	This is used in conjunction with the BORDER attribute. For <TABLE>, this affects the outer right and bottom and inner top and left borders. For <TH> and <TD>, this affects the right and bottom borders. Possible values are hexadecimal colors or special color names. The <TH> and <TD> attributes override the <TABLE> attributes.

EXPLORER TAG USAGE

As noted previously, most of Explorer's new features come in the form of additional attributes. In this manner, many possible conflicts are resolved due to the fact that when browsers do not recognize tags, they ignore them (as seen in Chapter 4, this is not always the case, but in the majority of cases, this rule applies). One good work habit to acquire is designing your Explorer-enhanced pages to be optimized for Navigator 2 and other browsers.

Consider the DYNSRC attribute of the <IMG> tag. If you address the same file with the SRC attribute of the <EMBED> tag as the DYNSRC attribute of the <IMG> tag, your rich media file will be recognized by Navigator, as well as Explorer. Using the <EMBED> and <NOEMBED> tags as described earlier in this chapter enables you to design pages without compromising your browser display. Including the SRC attribute in the <IMG> tag completes the hybrid design process by providing display for other browsers.

Dangers in designing pages for Internet Explorer come from the capability of other browsers to recognize HTML 3 tags, such as <FONT>, but not the Explorer tags. Consider the design of a page that has the BGCOLOR attribute of the <BODY> tag set to WHITE, or "FFFFFF", and a table with a black background and white text. This might look good in Explorer, but in other browsers that recognize the COLOR attribute of the <FONT> tag and the BGCOLOR attribute of the <BODY> tag, the effect is invisible text.

Following is a document that illustrates how to optimize HTML design for Internet Explorer. Comments in the code describe why the choice of tags and attributes are used. The attention is focused on the effective use of hybrid HTML methods.

```
<HTML>
<HEAD>
<TITLE>Integrating Internet Explorer Attributes into HTML Design</TITLE>
</HEAD>

<BODY BACKGROUND="texture.jpg" BGPROPERTIES="fixed" BGCOLOR=AAFFEA TEXT=000000
LEFTMARGIN=50 TOPMARGIN=20>
```

```
<H1>How to Integrate Explorer Attributes</H1>
```

As seen on the page, some browsers recognize some tags and not others. This page has had margins, background colors, and text colors added.<P>

```
<CENTER>
```

This section is supposed to be center aligned. Beneath are three images of a roulette wheel. Notice the HTML behind it. The code is a good example of hybrid design. The three examples are bringing out three different features: the use of EMBED tags, and DYNSRC and SRC attributes; the effects of height and width attributes on file display; and, when viewed on the CD-ROM, the effects of the LOOP and START attributes with FILEOPEN and MOUSEOVER options. <P>

```
<! Actual file size is 120×160. 26 was added to accept the size of the file name
beneath the image.>

<EMBED SRC="alchemy.avi" HEIGHT=120 WIDTH=160>
<EMBED SRC="alchemy.avi" HEIGHT=146 WIDTH=160>
<! The same again without size information>
<EMBED SRC="alchemy.avi">

<NOEMBED>

<! Notice that Navigator includes the document name that takes up part of the
space reserved for the .AVI file. Explorer does the same if you include the
CONTROLS attribute. For Explorer, add 26 to the IMG height to take the control
panel into consideration. The first example uses the actual file size.>
<IMG ALIGN=TOP HEIGHT=120 WIDTH=160 SRC="alchemy.gif" DYNSRC="alchemy.avi"
START=FILEOPEN >

<! Notice, however, that if you have CONTROLS, other browsers may have a
distorted image.>

<IMG ALIGN=TOP HEIGHT=146 WIDTH=160 SRC="alchemy.gif" DYNSRC="alchemy.avi"
START=FILEOPEN,MOUSEOVER CONTROLS>

<! And with no size description.>

<IMG ALIGN=TOP SRC="alchemy.gif" DYNSRC="alchemy.avi" LOOP=3 CONTROLS
START=FILEOPEN,MOUSEOVER>
</NOEMBED>
<P>

<TABLE BORDER BORDERCOLORLIGHT=FF0000 BORDERCOLORDARK=0000FF BGCOLOR=7FFF7F
CELLPADDING=10 CELLSPACING=10>
```

```
<TR><TD>
<FONT SIZE=4 FACE=MODERN><FONT SIZE=5 FACE=COURIER>This is </FONT>a test of TABLE
tags and </FONT>FONT tags. Both size and <FONT SIZE=-2>face</FONT>attributes of
<FONT SIZE=+2>the FONT tag</FONT> are being <FONT FACE=ARIAL>tested
here.</FONT><P>
</TD></TR></TABLE>
</CENTER>

<TABLE BORDER=5 BGCOLOR=FFFFFF CELLPADDING=5 CELLSPACING=5 WIDTH=100%
BORDERCOLOR=000000>

<TR><TD>

<TABLE BORDER BORDERCOLORLIGHT=FF0000 BORDERCOLORDARK=0000FF BGCOLOR=7FFF7F
CELLPADDING=10 CELLSPACING=10>

<TR><TD HEIGHT=250>This is a cell within a table. The cell attributes are the same
as the table attributes.</TD>

<TD HEIGHT=250 BORDERCOLORLIGHT=CFCFCF BORDERCOLORDARK=3F3F3F>This cell has its
own attributes.
</TD></TR>
</TABLE>

</TD>
<TD>

<TABLE BORDER BORDERCOLORLIGHT=FF0000 BORDERCOLORDARK=0000FF BGCOLOR=7FFF7F
BORDERCOLOR=000000 CELLPADDING=10 CELLSPACING=10>

<TR><TD>This is a cell within a table. The cell attributes are the same as the
table attributes.

</TD></TR>
<TR><TD BGCOLOR=000000>

<FONT COLOR=FFFFFF>This is a cell within a table. The font is changed to white,
and the table background to black.

</TD></TR>
</TABLE>

</TD></TR>
</TABLE>

</BODY>

</HTML>
```

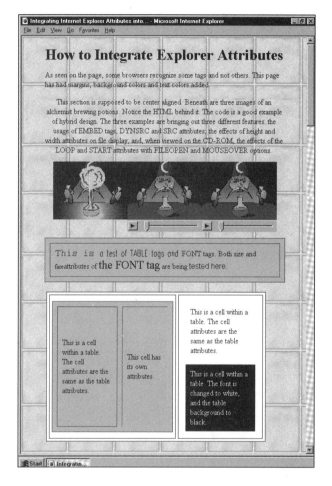

In the example, several settings were used to see how Internet Explorer treats its new tags. One item not mentioned in the Microsoft documentation is the fact that the CONTROLS attribute adds 26 pixels to the height of the embedded .AVI file. If you do the same test as shown here, setting the height to 120 (the actual file size height), the image becomes "squished." For various reasons, it is not recommended that you include size descriptions for your DYNSRC files. In the table beneath the images, the <FONT> tag is used in a manner that enables you to see the effects of nesting <FONT> tags. In theory, tags are opened and closed one at a time. In practice, multiple <A> tags can be closed with a single </A> tag, and multiple <FONT> tags are sometimes closed with a single </FONT> tag. Beneath the font example, you see how the new table tag attributes work. Notice the use of both <TABLE> and <TD> attributes, and the colors of the cell borders in the individual table cells.

By using the <EMBED> tag, relative consistency in Navigator's display of the file referenced by the DYNSRC attribute of the <IMG> file has been ensured. In doing a similar experiment with the size of the embedded object, you find that Navigator always displays the file name (in the place of the control panel). By using the size attributes, adding 26 pixels compensated for the extra height. The third image is without size attributes. The font size attributes are recognized, but not the face attribute. Finally, in the embedded tables at the bottom of the page, the table tags and font tag from Chapter 4 are supported, but not the new Explorer tags. This results in the compromised display, as seen here. The bottom right cell is particularly problematic. The white text is almost invisible on the background image.

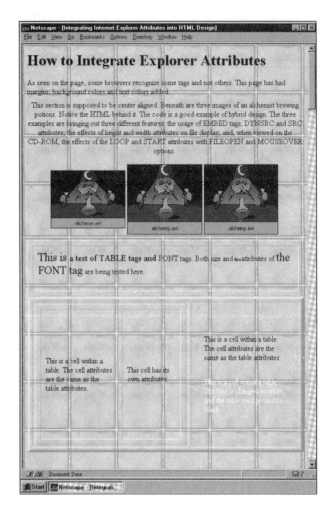

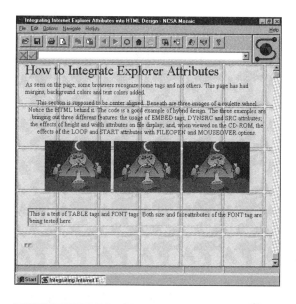

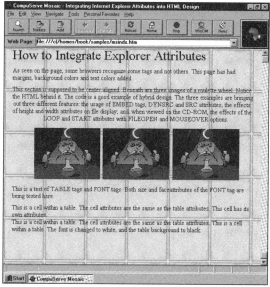

And what about other browsers? Mosaic, on the top, recognized the <CENTER> tag and the top <TABLE> tag. It did not recognize the <FONT> tags or SIZE attribute of the <IMG> tag, and, as seen in the last chapter, it does not display contents of nested tables. The background image tag is supported. The BGCOLOR attribute is used here in case any browsers did not support the BACKGROUND attribute. It did not affect these four browsers.

CompuServe's Spry Mosaic version .04.00.08.20 provided the display on the left. The latest version, .04.10.09.20, supports all of the Microsoft tags, including the FACE attribute of the <FONT> tag and table attributes. The version on the left did not recognize the <FONT> tags or the table tags, but, unlike Mosaic, it did display the text within the table cells. The <CENTER> tag and BACKGROUND attribute were recognized. The SIZE attributes of the <IMG> tag and all of the Explorer tags were ignored.

EXPLORER 3.0

Microsoft released the beta version of Explorer 3.0 in March, 1996. The latest version of Explorer considerably extends the browser's functionality. As seen in the image on the facing page, frames are now supported. The animated GIF was still not supported here, although the first frame of the animation was displayed. With the exception of the animated GIF, the display appears identical to Navigator 2.0 in Chapter 1.

The two most significant developments in Explorer 3 are VBScript and ActiveX technologies. VBScript, a dialect of Visual Basic, is comparable to JavaScript in functionality—that is, VBScript is written into the HTML document, and not distributed like Java. Remember that Java uses the CODE attribute of the <APPLET> tag much like the SRC attribute of the <IMG> tag. In Java's case, the file referred to by the CODE attribute resides on the host, or server, computer. In the case of VBScript, the code is contained within the <SCRIPT> tag, like JavaScript.

ActiveX technology, formerly code-named Sweeper, enables developers to port their Windows applications to the Internet through enhanced OLE controls, referred to as ActiveX controls. Eight Internet controls are contained in Microsoft's ActiveX Development Kit, including an FTP control, an HTTP control, and others. The new controls are embedded in the document using the <OBJECT> tag. Following are the new HTML tags supported by Explorer 3. See Appendix A for more information on the tags and attributes that the beta version supports.

<FRAME>	Explorer supports all of Netscape's frame tags and attributes. It introduces the following:	
	FRAMEBORDER	Possible values are "Yes" or "No." The default is set to "Yes." When "No" is selected, the border surrounding the frame is invisible.
	FRAMESPACING	This sets the space between frames measured in pixels.
<OBJECT>	This tag is part of the HTML 3 specifications and is used to embed ActiveX controls in the page. The attributes for this tag are determined by the ActiveX control type. The <OBJECT> tag generally requires <PARAM> tags, as introduced in the previous section on Navigator 3.	

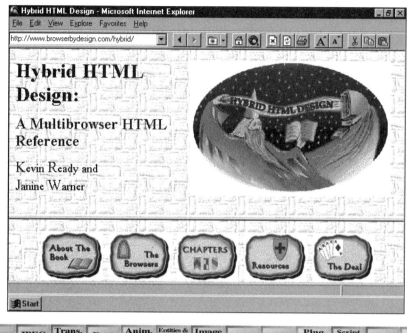

Forms	JPEG	Trans. GIFs	Font	Anim. GIFS	Entities & Sp Chars	Image Maps	Center	Tables	Plug ins	Script Langs.	Frames	Java

<SCRIPT>   Explorer now recognizes this tag, which has been adopted by the
                  W3C.

                  LANGUAGE   The only accepted value is VBS. Explorer is expected to
                               support JavaScript as well, but this is not presently the
                               case.

The VBScript included within the <SCRIPT> tag can interact with, and direct,
ActiveX controls in the page. For those already familiar with Visual Basic, Visual
Basic for Applications, Word Basic, and other derivatives, VBScript is easy to learn.
Other features include the integration of the Windows Explorer with Internet
Explorer, promised support for Java and plug-ins, and RealAudio functionality in
upcoming releases. The following pages contain an example of VBScript.

```
<HTML>
<HEAD>
<TITLE>Class Schedule</TITLE>

<SCRIPT LANGUAGE="VBS">

' The first subroutine is used for calculating the tuition.

SUB ClassFees
Dim Form
    Set Form = document.Scheduler
total = Form.Box1.checked + _
            Form.Box2.checked + _
            Form.Box3.checked + _
            Form.Box4.checked
Form.sum.value = "$" + CStr((total * 200)) + ".00"
END SUB

' This subroutine is used for displaying text in the textbox.

SUB SetText(strToSet)
   document.Scheduler.Text1.value = strToSet
END SUB

' This sub is for creating the alert box window.

SUB DoOrder
    ClassFees
    SetText"Your schedule will be mailed to you shortly."
Alert "Your total fees will be " + document.Scheduler.sum.value + "."
END SUB

' This is used to set the days boxes in the right-hand column.

SUB GetClasses(bOne, bTwo, bThree, bFour)
Dim Form
    Set Form = document.Scheduler
    Form.Box1.checked=bOne
    Form.Box2.checked=bTwo
    Form.Box3.checked=bThree
    Form.Box4.checked=bFour
    ClassFees
END SUB
```

```
' This sub is used to check the Monday and Wednesday boxes.

SUB OneandThree
   GetClasses True, False, True, False
   SetText"Your classes will meet on Monday and Wednesday."
END SUB


' This sub is used to check the Tuesday and Thursday boxes.

SUB TwoandFour
   GetClasses False, True, False, True
   SetText"Your classes will meet on Tuesday and Thursday."
END SUB


' This sub is used to check the Monday and Tuesday boxes.

SUB OneandTwo
   GetClasses True, True, False, False
   SetText"Your classes will meet on Monday and Tuesday."
END SUB


' This sub is used to check the Wednesday and Thursday boxes.

Sub ThreeandFour
   GetClasses False, False, True, True
SetText"Your classes will meet on Wednesday and Thursday."
END SUB

</SCRIPT>

</HEAD>

<BODY BGCOLOR=FFFFFF TEXT=00000 LINK=0000FF VLINK=FF00FF ALINK=FF0000>

<H1 COLOR=RED>The Class Schedule Form</H1>

<FORM Name="Scheduler">
<CENTER>
<TABLE WIDTH=100% BORDER=3>
<TR><TD VALIGN=TOP><STRONG>Select a Class Schedule</STRONG>

<TABLE BGCOLOR="#FFFFCC" WIDTH=60%>
```

```
<! The onClick event is used to run the scripts from the previous pages.>

<TR><TD>
<INPUT TYPE=RADIO NAME=RadioGroup onClick="OneandThree">Monday-Wednesday
</TD></TR>
<TR><TD>
<INPUT TYPE=RADIO NAME=RadioGroup onClick="TwoandFour">Tuesday-Thursday
</TD></TR>
<TR><TD>
<INPUT TYPE=RADIO NAME=RadioGroup onClick="ThreeandFour">Wednesday-Thursday
</TD></TR>
<TR><TD>
<INPUT TYPE=RADIO NAME=RadioGroup onClick="OneandTwo">Monday-Tuesday
</TD></TR>
</TABLE>
</TD>

<TD VALIGN=TOP>
<STRONG>Additional Class Days</STRONG>

<! The onClick event is used to run the scripts from the previous pages.>

<TABLE BGCOLOR="#FFFFCC" WIDTH=40%>
<TR><TD>
<INPUT TYPE=CHECKBOX NAME=Box1 onClick="ClassFees">Monday
</TD></TR>
<TR><TD>
<INPUT TYPE=CHECKBOX NAME=Box2  onClick="ClassFees">Tuesday
</TD></TR>
<TR><TD>
<INPUT TYPE=CHECKBOX NAME=Box3 onClick="ClassFees">Wednesday
</TD></TR>
<TR><TD>
<INPUT TYPE=CHECKBOX NAME=Box4 onClick="ClassFees">Thursday
</TD></TR>
</TABLE>
</TD></TR>
</TABLE>

<BR>

<CENTER>
```

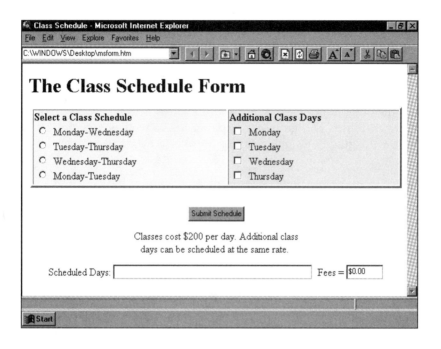

```
<INPUT TYPE=BUTTON VALUE="Submit Schedule" NAME="Order" onClick="DoOrder">
<P>

Classes cost $200 per day. Additional class<BR>days can be scheduled at the same
rate.

<P CLEAR=ALL>
Scheduled Days: <INPUT NAME=Text1 SIZE=80>
Fees = <INPUT NAME=Sum VALUE="$0.00" SIZE=10><BR>
</CENTER>

</FORM>

</BODY>

</HTML>
```

These uses of VBScript are very minimal. Web designers should not be intimidated by languages like JavaScript or Visual Basic. These simple scripting languages are easy to learn, and considerably expand your HTML documents.

SUMMARY OF INTERNET EXPLORER 2.0

Using Explorer tags presents a different type of design challenge than Navigator. With Navigator, you include <NOEMBED> and <NOFRAMES> tags to contain information for browsers that do not support embedded objects or frames. With Explorer, on the other hand, most of the additional features take place in the form of additional tag attributes. Designing for Explorer 3.0, as well as Explorer 2.0, requires that you follow the guidelines given earlier for hybrid frame pages, as well as those listed here.

In the example from the previous pages, problems occur at the high end and at the low end. At the high end, sophisticated browsers often support table and font tags, but not the Explorer extensions. At the low end, some browsers do not support the table and font tags, nor the center or body tag attributes. In the previous chapter, you confronted the issue of making tables presentable in all browsers. This technique is especially true when designing Explorer-enhanced pages. These enhanced pages often take advantage of the layout options made possible through the individual coloring of tabled sections. Including <BR> and <P> tags as necessary becomes particularly important.

The challenge presented by sophisticated browsers more directly impacts your design choices. Any color given to a font within an HTML document must contrast with the background color or background image that is described in the <BODY> tag. If this is not the case, the font can become obscured in browsers that support the body attributes and font tags, but not the BGCOLOR attribute of the <TABLE> tag. To confront this, you may choose to use black text and white body background with off-white table backgrounds. Remember that FFFFFF is the hexadecimal equivalent of white, and that the three pairs of numbers represent red, green, and blue, respectively. With that in mind, you can create off-white colors going toward the primary colors by lowering the values of the hexadecimal pairs, as follows:

Red off-white	FFCCCC	Cyan off-white	CCFFFF
Green off-white	CCFFCC	Magenta off-white	FFCCFF
Blue off-white	CCCCFF	Yellow off-white	FFFFCC

Anticipating the issues that arise from color conflicts, you can color-coordinate your page for Explorer, while not creating problems for browsers that recognize <FONT> and <BODY> tag attributes. Following these design guidelines will enable you to optimize your Explorer pages without compromising other browsers' displays.

ORACLE POWERBROWSER 1.0

Oracle introduced the beta version of its PowerBrowser in December, 1995. During its initial development, the company sought to support all of the Navigator and Explorer tags, as well as its own tags. PowerBrowser was the first to recognize Navigator's <FRAME> and <EMBED> tags, as well as Explorer's DYNSRC attribute of the <IMG> tag (plug-ins must be copied and put into Oracle's plug-ins directory). It has several impressive features of its own, including support for a new 360° file format developed by OmniView called PhotoBubbles.

As more and more browsers move to support the features of Netscape, Microsoft, Oracle, and others, you can anticipate conflicts arising from browsers that partially support the HTML definitions. This makes it difficult to write a hybrid HTML document to accommodate all browsers. After several incompatibilities stemming from partial tag support, the commercial version of PowerBrowser has corrected most of the bugs from the early beta versions. Examples of its early bugs are included in the next chapter for demonstration purposes and do not reflect the released version of PowerBrowser.

The browser performs respectably in its display of HTML 2 and 3 tags. In addition to supporting many Microsoft and Netscape extensions, Oracle has come out with several important features of its own. These are the following:

1. Network Loadable Objects	The Network Loadable Object provides support for additional file types.
2. Layout Frames/Sections	New Oracle tags allow for more control over sections of an HTML document.
3. Oracle Basic	The Oracle Basic language provides client-side form processing.

The fact that Oracle has gone out of its way to adopt the formatting tags of its competitors is encouraging. Additions made available through Oracle Basic and Network Loadable Objects are equally welcome additions to the development of HTML. Its personal server feature is also quite impressive. Using this feature, you can design locally hosted documents that use a variety of data sources to share over local area networks.

There are four primary tags supported by PowerBrowser that are not supported by other browsers. These are the <NLO>, <NONLO>, <LAYOUTFRAME>, and <LAYOUTFRAMERESET> tags.

NETWORK LOADABLE OBJECTS

The Network Loadable Object <NLO> functions similar to Navigator's embedded objects. PowerBrowser has several object types built into it that can be expanded to support additional user-defined objects. The <NLO> tag does not have a closing tag and is not seen in browsers that do not support it. You can, however, use the <NONLO> tag, like the <NOEMBED> tag, to support other browsers. Each NLO type can have additional attributes, which are defined in the "c:/windows/csp.reg" file on your hard disk. Attributes available to NLOs include the following:

TYPE

Required for all <NLO> tags, TYPE tells the browser which file type, or format, to load. Among the predefined object types are:

AVIHELPER

This file type supports .AVI video to be displayed in the HTML document. Uses the ALIGN, HEIGHT, WIDTH, SRC, SHOWBORDER, PLAYBAR or CONTROLS, AUTOREWIND, AUTOREPEAT or LOOP, and PLAY or AUTOSTART attributes.

MSGTICKER

This type defines a message that scrolls across the page from right to left. Uses SRC or TEXT, WIDTH, SHOWBORDER, HEIGHT, and ALIGN attributes.

PHOTOBUBBLE

This type displays a three-dimensional file format, .BUB. Supported attributes include SRC, ALIGN, HEIGHT, WIDTH, and FULLSCREEN.

SOUND

The sound type supports .AU, .AIFF, .VOC, and .WAV file formats. Uses PLAY or AUTOSTART, AUTOREWIND, AUTOREPEAT, NOPLAYBAR or NOCONTROLS, NOBORDER, RAISED, NOTIME, ALIGN, and CLICKPLAY attributes.

STOCKTIK

Like MSGTICKER, STOCKTIK defines a message that scrolls from right to left, within a text box, in a fixed-width font. Uses SRC, WIDTH, HEIGHT, NOBORDER, and ALIGN attributes.

NETWORK LOADABLE OBJECT ATTRIBUTES

ALIGN	Aligns the file in the HTML page. This can be used with most NLO file types. Possible values are left and right.
CONTROLS	Used with AVIHELPER NLO file type to display control panel for video images.
FULLSCREEN	Possible values are TRUE or FALSE. This is used with PhotoBubbles and other NLOs.
HEIGHT	Determines height of NLO measured in pixels.
HSPACE	Determines horizontal space between the right side of the NLO and the following text.
NOBORDER	Used with STOCKTIK and SOUND NLO file types. Removes the border from the file display.
NOCONTROLS	Used with SOUND NLO file type to hide control panel for sound documents.
SRC	This attribute is used with most NLO file types. In the case of MSGTICKER, it can be replaced with the TEXT attribute. Gives a reference address for the file to be displayed.
SHOWBORDER	Used with AVIHELPER and MSGTICKER NLO file types. Attaches a border to the file display.
TEXT	Used with MSGTICKER instead of SRC attribute. Provides text to scroll across the page.
VSPACE	Determines vertical space between the bottom side of the NLO and the neighboring text.
WIDTH	Determines width of NLO measured in pixels.

LAYOUT FRAME TAGS

The layout frame tags give considerable control over page display. Exact coordinates are given for the placement of text and other screen objects. Unlike tables, which work with exact, as well as relative, measurements, the layout frame tags are used with a level of precision associated with a coordinate-based system. When choosing between using these tags and table tags, you must not forget the display in other browers.

While not all browsers will recognize the table tags, only PowerBrowser recognizes the layout frame tags. Considerable attention must be given to your HTML design if you want to optimize using this tag without compromising the page display in other browsers. With layout frames, each section of a document is included within a layout frame area. When more than one <LAYOUTFRAME> tag is used, and if no <LAYOUTFRAMERESET> tags are present, then the whole document is a single layout frame section. Layout frame tags can be superimposed on each other.

Each area outlined by a <LAYOUTFRAME> tag is a columned area that is described using a modified Cartesian coordinate system.

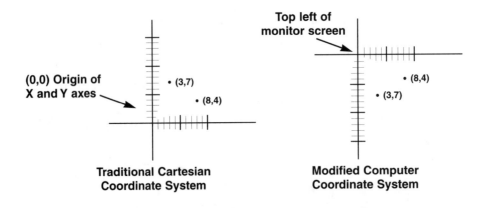

Traditional Cartesian Coordinate System

Modified Computer Coordinate System

With the traditional Cartesian coordinate system, the origin (0,0) is in the center of the world. In its computer counterpart, the origin is located at the top left of the monitor, or layout frame section.

<LAYOUTFRAME>   Establishes fixed position of text or other screen
                             object within a section of the HTML document.
                             Used with the <LAYOUTFRAMERESET> tag, exact
                             coordinates are given for text or image display. Has
                             three attributes:

                    X   The distance from the left edge of the
                             LAYOUTFRAME section to the left edge
                             of the columned area, measured in pixels.

                    Y   The distance from the top edge of the
                             LAYOUTFRAME section to the top edge of
                             the columned area, measured in pixels.

                    WIDTH   Determines the width of the columned area
                             measured in pixels.

<LAYOUTFRAMERESET>   Demarcates sections of HTML document. Until
                             this tag appears, all <LAYOUTFRAME> tags are
                             considered to be in the same section and can
                             overlap. The insertion of this tag begins a new
                             section. All following <LAYOUTFRAME> tags will
                             have their coordinates referenced to the insertion
                             point of the <LAYOUTFRAMERESET> tag.

NLO AND LAYOUT FRAME TAG USAGE

On the following page, the Network Loadable Objects and layout frame tags will be
displayed. Consider the effects that are possible as you see the superimposed text
and image in the example. If you are designing for an Intranet, you will not be
limited to the constraints of hybrid HTML design and can concentrate on the effects
and function of PowerBrowser without worrying about how other browsers display
the pages.

```
<HTML>
<HEAD>
<TITLE>Oracle PowerBrowser HTML Tags</TITLE>
</HEAD>
<BODY BGCOLOR=FFFFFF TEXT=000000>

<H1>Layout Frames</H1>
```

With the LAYOUTFRAME tag, exact alignment of screen elements is possible. Images and text can be superimposed or placed in specific places in the browser main viewing area.

```
<HR SIZE=2>

<LAYOUTFRAME X=75 Y=90 WIDTH=200>
```

Here, for instance, is a columned group of text information that begins at a point that is 75 pixels from the left margin, 90 pixels from the top margin, and is 200 pixels wide.

```
<LAYOUTFRAME X=285 Y=120 WIDTH=190>
```

And here is a columned group of text information that begins at a point that is 285 pixels from the left margin, 120 pixels from the top margin, and is 190 pixels wide. The text will continue down the page until the LAYOUTFRAMERESET tag reappears.

```
<LAYOUTFRAMERESET>

<LAYOUTFRAME X = 10 Y = 10 WIDTH = 108>
Here is a test of an image being superimposed on text.
<LAYOUTFRAME X = 10 Y = 10 WIDTH = 58>
<IMG SRC="../other/_wizard/wizard2.gif">

<LAYOUTFRAME X = 210 Y = 10 WIDTH = 58>
<IMG SRC="../other/_wizard/wizard2.gif">
<LAYOUTFRAME X = 210 Y = 10 WIDTH = 108>
And here is a test of Text being superimposed on an image.

<LAYOUTFRAMERESET>
<HR SIZE=2>
<H1>Network Loadable Objects</H1>
```

Network Loadable Objects feature the Message Ticker and the Stock Ticker. Here, the Message Ticker is given a border to appear like the Stock Ticker. Notice, however, that the font is not the preformatted font.

```
<P>
```

```
<CENTER>
<NLO TYPE="MSGTIKER" TEXT="This text will go across the screen from right to left.
It will repeat." WIDTH=300 HEIGHT=20 SHOWBORDER>
<NONLO>
<HR WIDTH=80% SIZE=4>

Download PowerBrowser to take advantage of a feature that your browser does not
recognize.

<HR WIDTH=80% SIZE=4>
</NONLO>
</CENTER>
```

```
The Stock Ticker is quite similar, except that it uses a .DAT file, as opposed to
a .TXT file for Message Ticker. The latter also enables you to assign the text as
an attribute for scrolling. Other NLOs can be used to extend PowerBrowser's
functionality. The browser also supports the EMBED tag and Netscape plug-ins.

<P>
<H2>PhotoBubbles</H2>

This is an incredibly rich file format. Three-dimensional views are possible by
clicking with your mouse button to navigate through the picture. When you bring
the mouse over the center of the screen, it becomes a magnifying glass. <P>

<CENTER>
<NLO TYPE="PHOTOBUBBLE" SRC="goldgate.bub" FULLSCREEN=FALSE HEIGHT=240 WIDTH=320>
<NONLO>
This object has depth in PowerBrowser<BR>
<IMG SRC="goldgate.gif" HEIGHT=240 WIDTH=320>
</NONLO>
</CENTER><P>
</BODY>
</HTML>
```

On the following pages, the HTML is displayed in PowerBrowser and Navigator. In the latter, the tags that are not recognized are ignored. The images are next to each other, and the text is inserted in the order that it appears in the HTML. The contents of the <NONLO> tags are displayed in the place of the Network Loadable Objects. Unless you know that PowerBrowser is your only browser audience, you should be careful about using layout frames, as well as NLOs. If you use them, make sure you test in other browsers, and make the page acceptable. The text may not be exactly where you planned it to be, but at least your visitors will have a clear view of your Web page content.

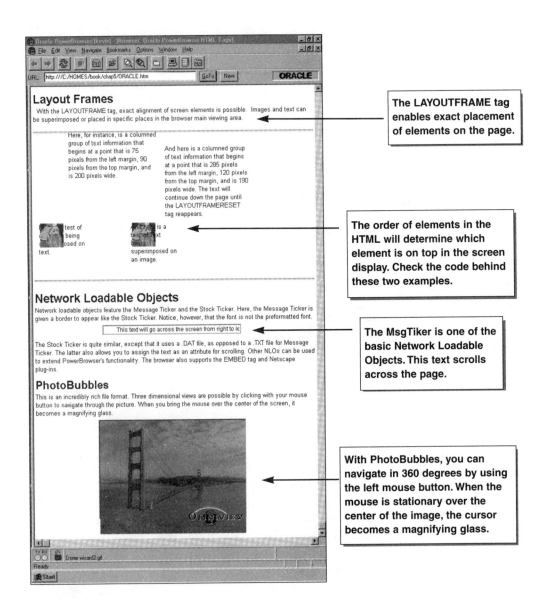

The LAYOUTFRAME tag enables exact placement of elements on the page.

The order of elements in the HTML will determine which element is on top in the screen display. Check the code behind these two examples.

The MsgTiker is one of the basic Network Loadable Objects. This text scrolls across the page.

With PhotoBubbles, you can navigate in 360 degrees by using the left mouse button. When the mouse is stationary over the center of the image, the cursor becomes a magnifying glass.

In Navigator, you can see how the PowerBrowser tags display when they are not recognized. In the case of the layout frames and Network Loadable Objects, the tags are ignored, and the information is displayed in the order that it appears in the HTML. When designing pages that are optimized for PowerBrowser, but are expected to be visited by other browsers, it is important that you test with several. Make sure that if <LAYOUTFRAMES> is not present, the page is acceptably displayed. Also, remember to include the <NONLO> tag for compatibility with browsers that do not support the <NLO> tag. Text and an image were inserted in the examples here by including this tag. If it had not been designed this way, nothing would have appeared in Netscape or other browsers in the place where the <NLO> tag was inserted.

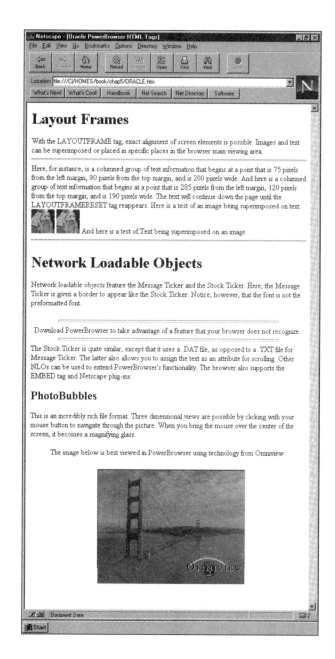

ORACLE BASIC

Oracle, like Netscape, has also introduced a programming language to extend its browser's functionality. Although, technically speaking, it is a scripting language, Oracle Basic is a powerful programming language that is able to exchange information with a variety of data sources. In respect to the strength and depth of function, the language can be compared to both Java and JavaScript. Although it is a scripting language like VBScript and JavaScript, the code is contained in a separate file with a .SCR file format. The language uses syntax common to many Basic programming languages.

The language supports object properties and methods. The principal objects available to Oracle Basic are the HTML object, the Browser object, and the Environment object. Each of these objects has its own methods, such as the HTML.BAS_startbody method of the HTML object (this method corresponds to the <BODY> tag in HTML). Using Oracle Basic, properties of these objects and their methods can be read or affected with or without user input. The CD-ROM contains examples on Oracle Basic, and its required syntax.

One browser feature that is particularly useful is the debugging mode selection from the Option menu. With this option selected, the code behind the HTML is revealed in response to user events in an independent window. In this way, you can trace your code, or that of other programmers right in the browser. This is a feature that Netscape and Microsoft should adopt as soon as possible. Being able to debug your code as you watch the HTML page will help reduce your development time.

A particular strength of PowerBrowser and Oracle Basic is their capability to work well with many different data formats, particularly those of a database nature. Using its expertise in database management, Oracle is likely to leverage its product quickly in the browser arena. Once developers discover the depth and breadth of functionality possible for PowerBrowser, it will likely be a favorite for programmers. These features are complemented by the Personal Server integrated into PowerBrowser.

Following is a brief example of Oracle Basic. The HTML document will be presented first, then the .SCR file. Consult the online documentation for more information on Oracle Basic. In addition to providing the syntax and language to Oracle Basic, there are examples to help you with your implementation. As you begin to use more Oracle-specific tags, make sure you test your pages on multiple browsers.

```
<HTML>
<HEAD>
<TITLE>Form Processing Using Oracle Basic</TITLE>
</HEAD>
<BODY BGCOLOR="#FFFFFF">
<FORM METHOD="POST" ACTION="/cgi-bin">
<H1>A Simple Calculation</H1>
<P>
Below is a demonstration of Oracle's capability to perform calculations on the fly.
<P>
<CENTER>
<TABLE WIDTH=80%>
<TR>
<TD ALIGN=RIGHT WIDTH=50%>Enter single digit hundreds value: </TD>
<TD WIDTH=50%>
<INPUT SIZE=8 NAME="Item1" VALUE="" METHOD = "ONEXIT:SCRIPT" ACTION =
"orascript.scr"></TD></TR><TR>
<TD ALIGN=RIGHT WIDTH=50%> Enter single digit tens value:</TD>
<TD WIDTH=50%><INPUT SIZE=8 NAME="Item2" VALUE="" METHOD = "ONEXIT:SCRIPT" ACTION
= "orascript.scr"></TD></TR><TR>
<TD ALIGN=RIGHT WIDTH=50%> Enter single digit units value: </TD>
<TD WIDTH=50%><INPUT SIZE=8 NAME="Item3" VALUE="" METHOD = "ONEXIT:SCRIPT" ACTION
= "orascript.scr"></TD></TR><TR>
<TD ALIGN=RIGHT WIDTH=50%> Double the amount:</TD>
<TD WIDTH=50%><INPUT TYPE=CHECKBOX NAME="zdoublebox" value="yes" METHOD =
"ONCLICK:SCRIPT" ACTION = "orascript.scr"></TD></TR><TR>
<TD ALIGN=RIGHT WIDTH=50%> Total:</TD>
<TD WIDTH=50%><INPUT SIZE=10 NAME = "zTotal">
</TD></TR></TABLE>
</CENTER>
</FORM>

</BODY></HTML>
```

```
Sub Main ()
        Dim Total As Long
        Total = (VAL(Item1) * 100) + (VAL(Item2) * 10) + (VAL(Item3) * 1)
        if zdoublebox = "yes" then
                Total = Total * 2
        end if
        zTotal = STR$(Total)
End Sub
```

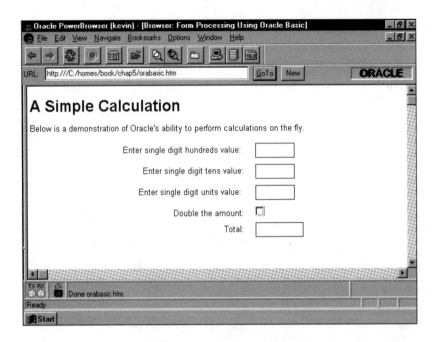

In the example, you can enter digits into either of the three textboxes above the checkbox. You can also select or deselect the "Double the amount" checkbox. Each time you leave a textbox or checkbox in the example, the script on the previous page will be performed. This is enabled by the ONEXIT:SCRIPT method of the <INPUT> tag. The other possible methods are ONENTER:SCRIPT and ONCLICK:SCRIPT. Additional methods are planned for future releases.

The CD-ROM contains a program, "oramirage.exe," which was designed with Oracle Basic. This program demonstrates how you can use the language to perform order operations locally, thus limiting the server workload. The script "search.scr" actually generates dynamic HTML pages in response to user input. Analyzing the code in this document will help you quickly uncover Oracle Basic's treatment of common Basic functions.

Future releases of PowerBrowser will support VBScript and JavaScript. Java, itself, will be supported in beta releases planned for Summer, 1996.

SUMMARY OF ORACLE POWERBROWSER 1.0

Oracle's PowerBrowser presents some special challenges to designers. In their effort to keep pace with Netscape and Microsoft, the company has gone to some length to include support for their most recent formatting tags. It supports frames, plug-ins with the <EMBED> tag, the DYNSRC attribute of the <IMG> tag, and the FACE attribute of the <FONT> tag.

On the down side, if the browser does not recognize the file type in the <EMBED> tag, you are not given the choice to find an application or viewer to assist PowerBrowser. The browser has, on the other hand, followed the lead of several plug-in developers to include the PLUGINSPAGE attribute in the <EMBED> tag description. This attribute provides the URL to download the plug-in. It also supports animated GIF file formats (see Chapter 7). Again, this was the first browser besides Netscape to support animated GIFs.

Intranet developers looking for an Oracle PowerBrowser-based solution for Web site projects can find a good deal of online information from Oracle, including the most recent release of the browser and accompanying documentation. Much of the power of the program lies in the Oracle Basic programming language, Network Loadable Objects, and its use of system resources.

Oracle designed its browser to perform many specific functions that complement its other product groups. Oracle Basic syntax illustrates the company's attention to database needs that PowerBrowser can fill. This need is also addressed with the company's Personal Server, which can create HTML documents on the fly.

If you are developing primarily for an Intranet, PowerBrowser will help you significantly in creating workgroup solutions. Sharing information with colleagues has been greatly simplified using the browser's personal server. This part of the program features several wizards for document creation, including a home page authoring wizard, a new HTML document wizard, and a data source wizard. The latter enables you to select several data sources from database, spreadsheet, and text file formats.

When developing for the Internet, make sure you test your pages in other browsers, especially if they make much use of <LAYOUTFRAMESET> or <NLO> tags. In most cases, you can expect the browser to look the same as Internet Explorer and Navigator when reading pages enhanced for these programs.

SUMMARY

When designing for individual browsers, you must be clear on your demographic audience. If you are designing for an Intranet, you are much freer to take advantage of browser-specific formatting than when designing for the entire Web community. Even if you are designing for the Internet, you can still take advantage of sophisticated formatting by using tags in a way that considers other browsers.

In the case of Netscape, the <NOEMBED> and <NOFRAMES> tags enable developers to present an alternative display to browsers that do not support the tags. These function like the ALT attribute in the <IMG> tag. If you use JavaScript or Java in your HTML documents, know that most browser programs do not support their instructions. In the case of JavaScript, you will often use the event handlers to respond to input contents that would be responded to at the server. For instance, an accidental sixth digit in a zipcode could be corrected before sending the information to a server, which must send back a new document requesting correctly formatted information.

Explorer's tags are easier, to some degree, to integrate with other browsers. Exceptions to this arise with table background colors. For browsers that support the TEXT attribute of the <BODY> tag or COLOR attribute of the <FONT> tag, care must be taken to not make text unreadable due to the color contrast between the text foregound and table background.

Designing for PowerBrowser involves a mix of the design styles for Navigator and Explorer, and the integration of its own. You are free to use frames and plug-ins, as well as font faces, in your page design. It's a good idea to include instructions for loading plug-ins on the page where they are required. If you are designing for the World Wide Web and want to take advantage of PowerBrowser's own tags, make sure that you test your pages on other browsers to ensure compatibility.

Other browsers can be expected to introduce more of their own tags as the Internet and Intranets continue to expand. Also, many of the HTML 3 tags are used only by the server, so it can be claimed that they are supported by all browsers. The fact that the gamut of HTML tags continues to expand does not, however, need to be intimidating. In the following chapter, the skills you have acquired over the past three chapters will be integrated into a design methodology. If the pages you design are intended for the Web, following hybrid HTML design methods will ensure the consistent acceptable display of your pages in all browsers.

THE ART OF HYBRID HTML DESIGN

Having been introduced to the HTML 2 and HTML 3 tags, as well as the browser-specific tags from Chapter 5, you are ready to face the challenge of hybrid HTML design. The creative use of tags, attributes, file types, and workarounds must be considered an artform in and of itself. To achieve and maintain mastery of this new age art, you must keep abreast of ongoing developments and integrate new design methods accordingly.

The focus of this book has been on creating Web pages that will be attractive regardless of the browser used to view them. In Chapters 4 and 5, this focus was relaxed for you to concentrate on learning new HTML tags. Hybrid design techniques were presented, but they did not have to be followed in the construction of your Web pages—particularly if you knew the intended browser audience.

In this chapter, attention is redirected to the design of hybrid HTML documents optimized for sophisticated browsers, yet supported in all browsers. "The Art of Hybrid HTML Design" encourages creative workarounds and advanced techniques to make your pages come to life in your favorite browsers without dying in the others.

INTRODUCTION

Hybrid HTML design requires authors to anticipate potential display conflicts and to mitigate them through the use of a design strategy. Potential HTML display conflicts stem from two primary causes:

1. Non-Recognition	As it sounds, this occurs when a browser does not recognize a tag. In most cases, this means that the tag is ignored and its contents are treated like other text.
2. Partial Recognition	This occurs when a browser only interprets a portion of the tag contents. Partial recognition is due to one of two reasons:

Attribute	One or more of the tag's attributes are not supported.
File Type	The document's file type is not supported.

An example of conflict arising from non-recognition is the table tag group. For browsers that do not recognize the <TABLE>, <TR>, and <TD> tags, their contents are treated as plain text. Generally, text is treated in the same fashion that it was prior to the unrecognized tag's appearance. In the case of Mosaic, however, embedded tables are not supported. This is the exception to the rule, and you can expect that unrecognized tags will be ignored, not their contents.

An example of conflict arising from partial recognition due to an unrecognized attribute would be the DYNSRC attribute of the <IMG> tag that is recognized by Internet Explorer and PowerBrowser, but not by others. Unsupported file types, such as the JPEG format in the HotJava browser, present the second partial recognition challenge to developers.

In addition to HTML sources of display conflicts, there are platform and hardware specific sources of conflicts, as well. Some of these are due to disparities in the browser software between platforms (see Navigator 2.0 in the previous chapter). Others are due to the operating system's color palette, to the size and depth of the monitor resolution, and to hardware performance and compatibility.

NON-RECOGNITION OF HTML TAGS

There are two distinct categories of tags that are not recognized by various browsers: browser-specific tags and HTML 3 tags. The first group are designed with the awareness that some browsers will not support them. The second group raises the standard of HTML to support, with less consideration given to browsers that do not recognize the tags. Each requires a different method of resolution.

BROWSER-SPECIFIC TAGS

Most of the browser-specific tags have their contents included within the tag definition and are invisible to browsers that do not support them. Some of these are accompanied by a second tag that contains elements for display in browsers that do not support the primary tag. An example of a tag that includes all of its content within its definition is PowerBrowser's <NLO> tag. Consider the following syntax:

```
<NLO TYPE="AVIHELPER" WIDTH=160 HEIGHT=120 SRC="video.avi">
```

If your browser does not recognize what is contained within the < and > symbols, the information is ignored. Following are browser-specific tags, along with their alternatives, that have all of their contents included in the tag definition.

HTML Tags with Contents Included in Tag Definition

Tag	Browser	Alternative Tag
<APP>	HotJava Alpha	Discontinued
<APPLET>	Navigator 2.0, Java Beta	None
<AREA>	HTML 3, others	None
<BGSOUND>	Internet Explorer	None
<EMBED>	Navigator 2.0, PowerBrowser	<NOEMBED>
<FRAME>	Navigator 2.0, PowerBrowser 1.0, Explorer 3.0	<NOFRAMES>
<FRAMESET>	Navigator 2.0, PowerBrowser 1.0, Explorer 3.0	<NOFRAMES>
<MAP>	HTML 3, others	None
<NLO>	PowerBrowser 1.0	<NONLO>
<OBJECT>	HTML 3, Explorer 3.0	None
<PARAM>	Navigator 2.0	None
<SCRIPT>	Navigator 2.0, PowerBrowser 1.0, Explorer 3.0	None
<!--->	All—used to hide <SCRIPT> contents	None

For those tags that do not have an alternative tag, their contents will not be displayed in browsers that do not recognize them. If you plan to include these tags in your pages for the Internet, you may want to inform viewers either on your home page, the page(s) that contain the tags, or both places that the page is optimized for a specific browser. This is not necessary if the tag does not affect the page display. For instance, <AREA>, <BGSOUND>, and <SCRIPT> tags do not affect the displayed page. You may want to alert visitors to your page that there is a background sound or that JavaScript will prevent them from entering invalid form information, but it is not necessary for the visitor to know that.

The <EMBED> and <FRAMESET> tags have counterparts for browsers that do not support them. The <NOEMBED> tag often contains a still image in the place of an animation or video. Other times text alone appears, informing the visitor that they need to use Netscape to view the document. In worst cases, the <NOEMBED> tag is not used. This is a great mistake for those designing for the Internet. Including the tag should be as much a design reflex as it is to include the ALT attribute for the <IMG> tag.

When frames are used, you are actually developing two primary pages, although they will share much of their content. The <FRAMESET> tags will generally contain an HTML document as their principal frame that corresponds with the contents of the <BODY> tag in the <NOFRAMES> section. In other words, the largest frame in the framed document will contain the same information as the <BODY> tag of the <NOFRAMES> section.

Besides the tags that have all of their information self-contained, there is Explorer's <MARQUEE> tag. This tag scrolls the contents across the page of the HTML document. When a browser does not recognize the tag, the text is stationary. Besides the obvious design compromise lost on browsers that do not support the tag, a secondary problem is posed by the tag's attributes. None of these will be recognized, so the space that the <MARQUEE> contents occupies may be different from one browser to the next. If you include the <BR> tag within the <MARQUEE> tag, Explorer will ignore it, although it may help the display in other browsers.

Finally, the <LAYOUTFRAME> tag from PowerBrowser presents a unique challenge to hybrid HTML design. Unlike the table tags that control relative areas of the screen display, the layout frame tags enable you to control exact coordinates in your Web page (see previous chapter). They even have the capability of superimposing text and graphic elements on the same area of the page.

The tricky part about including the layout frame tags in pages for the Internet is that most browsers will not recognize them, and the elements will appear on the screen in the order that they are written in the HTML code. Later in this chapter, you will see how this method was used to inverse the layout in the Navigator and PowerBrowser pages from Chapter 1.

Below is a document designed with browser-specific tags in hybrid fashion. The comment tags will explain what you can anticipate in various displays.

```
<HTML>

<HEAD>
<TITLE>Browser-Specific Tag Integration</TITLE>
</HEAD>

<! The BODY tag contains attributes that will not be recognized by many browsers.
For the least sophisticated, none of the attributes will be supported.>

<! The frame tags will not be presented in this example, due to their unique
nature. The example from the introduction will be examined later in this chapter.>

<BODY BGCOLOR=FFFFFF TEXT=000000 LINK=0000FF VLINK=FF00FF ALINK=FF0000>

<BGSOUND SRC="start.wav">

<H1>Browser-Specific Tag Integration</H1>

Here are some examples of how to integrate browser-specific tags into pages
destined for the World Wide Web. The <BLINK>Blink tag</BLINK> is distracting when
it does function; having it not work in other browsers is not such a loss.<P>
```

The EMBED tag, on the other hand, needs some attention:

<! The biggest problem posed by the EMBED tag is through its partial recognition by PowerBrowser. In this case, the tag is recognized, but the file format is not supported. The viewer receives an error message and a darkened rectangle in the object's place.>

<H2>An Embedded Object Example</H2>
<CENTER>
<EMBED SRC="shocked.dcr" WIDTH=320 HEIGHT=240>

<! The NOEMBED tag and the IMG tag are included for browsers that do not support the EMBED tag. Using a graphic element of the same size preserves page layout in multiple browser displays.>

<NOEMBED>
<IMG SRC="shocked.gif" WIDTH=320 HEIGHT=240>
</NOEMBED>
</CENTER>
<P>

<H2>A Marquee Example</H2>
<CENTER>
This is a test.
<MARQUEE WIDTH=200 HEIGHT=20 DIRECTION=LEFT HSPACE=10 VSPACE=10 SCROLLAMOUNT=10 SCROLLDELAY=250>

This text scrolls from right to left across the window in a box 200 pixels wide and 20 pixels high. In other browsers, this just appears like text.

</MARQUEE> This is a test.<P>
</CENTER>

<H2>A Layout Frame Example</H2>

This example is intended to illustrate the treatment of the elements contained within the LAYOUTFRAME tag<P>

One way the layout frame's control of a page can be demonstrated is by using it together with a table definition. To do this, the LAYOUTFRAMERESET tag will be inserted to reset the coordinate reference.<P>

<LAYOUTFRAMERESET>

<CENTER>

```
<! The table uses attributes that will distinguish it in browsers that support
them.>


<TABLE WIDTH=100% BORDER=5 CELLPADDING=5 CELLSPACING=5 BORDERCOLORDARK=FF0000
BORDERCOLORLIGHT=0000FF BGCOLOR=99FF99>
<TR>
<TD WIDTH=33% HEIGHT=50 ALIGN=RIGHT>
This table cell<BR>
is located in <BR>
the top right of <BR>
the top left cell.<P>
</TD>
<TD WIDTH=33% HEIGHT=50 ALIGN=CENTER>
This table cell<BR>
is located in the <BR>
center of the <BR>
middle cell.<P>
</TD>
<TD WIDTH=33% HEIGHT=50 ALIGN=LEFT>
This table cell<BR>
is located in the <BR>
top left of the <BR>
top right cell.
<P>
</TD>
</TR>
</TABLE>
<LAYOUTFRAME X=20 Y=2 WIDTH=100>
PowerBrowser <BR>
displays this<BR>
in the top left<BR>

</CENTER>
<LAYOUTFRAMERESET>
<P>
```

In the example above, PowerBrowser puts the contents beneath the table into the
left cell of the table. This is generally a dangerous thing to attempt in an
Internet environment. In controlled Intranet environments, you may want to use the
layout frame tags, but it is generally not advisable for the Internet.

```
</BODY>

</HTML>
```

Navigator is the only one (thank goodness!) to recognize the <BLINK> tag. This tag can be easily overused, so use it sparingly. Of the browsers tested here, Navigator is the only one that fully supported the <EMBED> tag. The image you see here is a Director file that has its own interactivity independent of the HTML page. In the Marquee example, you see that the words "This is a test." surround the contents of the <MARQUEE> tag. You are unaware that these should be scrolling, and the effect is not only lost, but it is unattractive. A <BR> tag before and after the contents of the Marquee (but within the <MARQUEE> tags) would break up the paragraph into three lines. The layout frame example is unrecognized, and the tag's contents display where you would expect them to be—beneath the table.

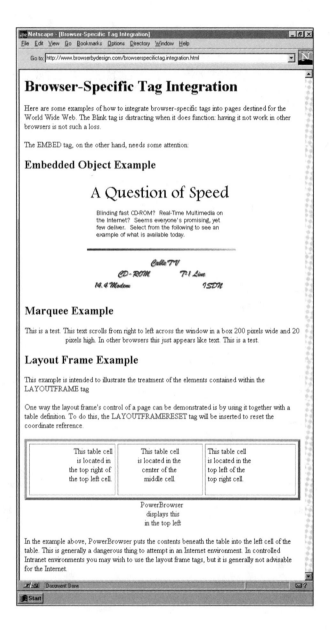

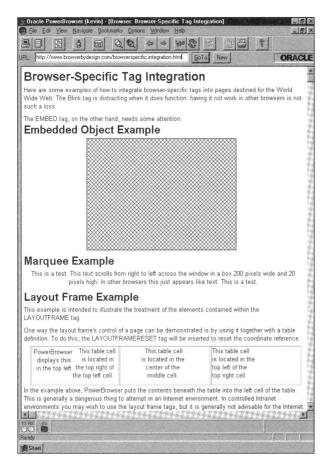

Here the <BLINK> and <MARQUEE> tags are unsupported, and their contents appear as though there were no tags. In this early beta version of PowerBrowser, an excellent example of partial support due to file incompatibilites is demonstrated. In the example, the <EMBED> tag is recognized, but the file format is not supported. Because of this, the browser displays a darkened rectangle in place of the object. This has since been corrected, but this is the type of problem that you will want to test as new file formats and technologies become available. In the layout frame example, you see the control that the coordinate system gives the designer. The <LAYOUTFRAMERESET> tag was needed twice in the example. Check the HTML behind it. Although this tag may be used in Intranet settings, it is wise to use tables in the place of layout frames. The latter should only be used to enhance your Web page, not to determine it.

Internet Explorer displays the contents of the <NOEMBED> tag as expected. The image on the screen is a .GIF file, not an interactive Director document. The Marquee was supported as expected. The words "This is a test." surround the scrolling text in the example. The contents of the layout frames were displayed after the table, as in Navigator and other browsers. The table itself illustrates much of the color control that Explorer has over its tabled areas. While most browsers only support the BGCOLOR attribute of the <BODY> tag (and many don't even support this), Explorer recognizes background colors, as well as border colors of tables. If the designer had wanted to animate the page in some way, a DYNSRC attribute could have been added to the <IMG> tag. This could refer to an .AVI or other file format supported by the present version of Explorer.

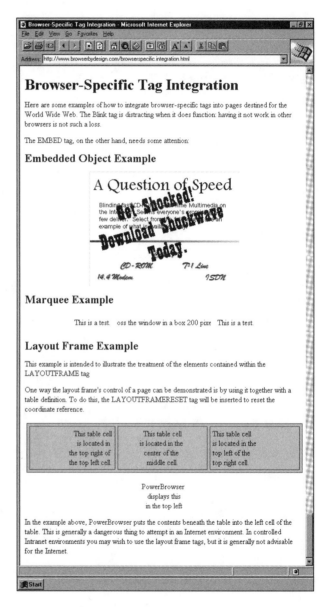

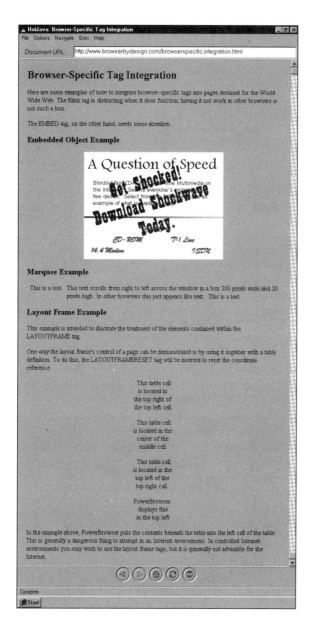

HotJava had the roughest time with the tags in the example. Most of its problems did not stem from the browser-specific tags, but from the HTML 3 tags. The BGCOLOR attribute of the <BODY> tag was not recognized. The table tags were also not recognized. The <CENTER> tag, still not included in the WWW HTML 3 specifications, is the only tag not from HTML 2 that is supported in this version of HotJava. The browser treated the contents of the <BLINK> and <MARQUEE> tags as plain text. It supported the .GIF file defined in the <IMG> tag within the <NOEMBED> tag. The layout frame tags were ignored, and their contents appeared underneath the table, as in the other browsers. Notice the distance between the table cell contents in the HotJava display. Their order is preserved here by alternating the <BR> and <P> tags. Between the lines of the table cell, <BR> tags are inserted. Between the cells of the table, <P> tags are used.

NON-RECOGNITION OF HTML 3 TAGS

In looking at the HTML 3 tags, the book is focused, as it was in Chapter 4, on those tags that are supported in the browsers available today. Therefore, the tags considered here are only the ones that have been previously discussed in this book. Tags such as <FIG>, <MATH>, <STYLESHEET>, and others that have not yet been implemented in browsers are included in Appendix A.

The HTML 3 attributes of HTML 2 tags will be explored in the following section. In this section, the <BIG>, <SMALL>, <SUB>, <SUP>, <FONT>, <DIV>, <META>, <CENTER>, and <TABLE> tags are considered in a multiple browser environment. The <MAP> and <AREA> tags are not included, due to their lack of effect on page display.

The first group, the text formatting tags, <BIG>, <SMALL>, <SUB>, <SUP>, and <FONT>, should be thought of as ornamental in a Web page. If you really need large text, use <H1> or <H2>, or a .GIF image of the font and size you want in your page. Otherwise, you risk losing the effect on browsers that do not support the tag. The <SUB> and <SUP> tags are particularly dangerous for designers. Unless you are only expecting advanced browsers to hit your page, you may want to use an image to express formulaic terms such as H_2O or πr^2.

As long as you do not mind that many browsers will not recognize the text formatting tags, use them at your discretion. The <DIV> tag is used to separate sections that are aligned differently. If your browser does not recognize the <DIV> tag, this will not matter. All the information in the page will be aligned left unless formatted by another tag. The <META> tag is either used by the server or, in the case of the HTTP-EQUIV="Refresh" attribute, for client-pull functions. As you will see later in this chapter, the <META> tag helped the author escape from a very tight back door in the design of the page in Chapter 1.

The <CENTER> tag is technically not an HTML 3 format. It is widely supported and should be a natural inclusion in HTML's evolution. Often <P ALIGN=CENTER> is used instead of, or along with, this tag; however, if a browser does not recognize one of these tags, they are often both unsupported. You can use the <IMG> or <PRE> tags to position an image or text a certain distance from the left margin. This method has severe limitations—primary of which is that neither performs the function of the <CENTER> tag. From a hybrid design perspective, center alignment can be considered ornamental and expendable for low-end browser display.

TABLE TAGS

The table tag group has traditionally presented a challenge to HTML designers. Not only were they difficult to learn, but they frustrated viewers using browsers that did not support them. This does not need to be the case, however—in this section, hybrid table design will help you to mitigate the differences between browsers.

Table design was introduced in Chapter 4, and the example in that chapter illustrated the effects of tables on a page that did not support tables. When designing hybrid tables, you must first consider that tables are used to organize information. The same relationships between table cells that are brought out in the table design need to be visible in the alternative display. This involves, in large part, using two devices to visually aid browsers that do not support tables.

1. **Effective Usage of <BR> and <P> Tags.**

   Effective usage of <BR> and <P> tags is the simplest way to organize table cell contents for browsers that do not recognize the table tags. The <BR> tag used after the <TD> contents, but before the </TD> tag, will force the contents of the next cell to a new line in browsers that do not support tables. The display in browsers that recognize the table tags will be unaffected. The <P> tag will insert a space beneath the line that contains it. In browsers that support tables, a space will be inserted within the table cell where the <P> tag occurs.

2. **Substituting <STRONG> and <TD> Attributes for <TH> Tags**

   Preserving the bold typeface on <TH> contents requires you to define them in a way that is independent of the <TH> tag. Use other formatting methods to identify the cell contents, such as the <STRONG> tag. If you want to preserve the location of the cell contents in browsers that recognize tables, use the <TD> attributes ALIGN=CENTER and VALIGN=MIDDLE.

SPECIAL CHARACTERS

There are many special characters, such as quotation marks, apostrophes, and others, that cannot be directly inserted into the HTML document. These special characters need to either be inserted as images or, the more usual alternative, described using one of two HTML methods. The special characters can be created using the ampersand, number sign, and integers from 34 to 255; or they can be created using entity names, displayed in Appendix C.

Special characters can be irritating for those who want consistency in multiple browsers. Using images is one way around this predicament; however, it is not a very practical or predictable solution in most situations. In places where your text is standing alone, as a header, perhaps, you can make the entire header an image instead of HTML text.

HYBRID HTML 3 TAG DESIGN

As mentioned in the introduction to this chapter, the HTML 3 tags raise the standard to which pages are expected to conform. For this reason, there are no built-in workarounds like there are with browser-specific tags. There is no <NOTABLE> tag, for instance, or <NOCENTER> tag. To confront the issues posed by browsers' non-recognition of HTML 3 tags, you have to either add formatting tags, such as the <BR> and <P> tags; use images in the place of special characters and new text formats; or accept the differences in display in the case of the text formatting, <CENTER> and <DIV> tags.

Integrating a hybrid approach to your Web page design should not be seen as a difficult feat. Much of the approach will become reflex activity in no time. In the same way that you include the ALT attribute in <IMG> tags for those viewers who have turned off the image loading functions, you will include <BR> and <P> tags in your table cells. The same way that you include <NOEMBED> tags to support embedded objects in browsers that do not support the <EMBED> tag, you will also include <STRONG> and ALIGN attributes for your <TD> tag contents for browsers that do not recognize tables.

On the following pages is an example of hybrid HTML 3 tag usage.

```
<HTML>

<HEAD>
<TITLE>HTML  3 Tag Integration</TITLE>
</HEAD>

<! Body attributes are often used to ensure that user settings will not obscure
the HTML page display. A white background with black foreground text is a common
background setting.>

<BODY BGCOLOR=FFFFFF TEXT=000000>

<H1>Text Formatting Tags</H1>

<! In the text formatting tag example, you can expect most of the tags to not be
recognized in many browsers. As long as the text format is not too important in
your page design, it will not be a problem. If the formatting is really important,
you may want to use an image.>


Unlike the H1 through H6 tags, the new <FONT SIZE=6>text formatting tags</FONT>
can affect text <FONT SIZE=1>within a line</FONT> without requiring their own
paragraph. For instance, <BIG>Big tag</BIG>, <SMALL>Small tag</SMALL>, <SUB>Sub
Tag</SUB>, and <SUP>Sup Tag</SUP> can occur within a sentence, while the <H1>H1
tag</H1>, <H2>H2 tag</H2>, and other Heading tags will force paragraph breaks. If
you really need a special symbol like &copy; or &#174;, especially in conjunction
with &#60;SMALL&#62;<SMALL>&copy;</SMALL>&#60;&#47;SMALL&#62; you may want to use
images like <IMG SRC="c.gif"> or <IMG SRC="r.gif">. You will often want special
characters at a larger or smaller size than other characters. Check Appendix C for
all the special characters.

<H1>The CENTER and DIV Tags</H1>

<! In browsers that do not support these tags, the paragraph will be
uninterrupted. For those that do recognize the tags, there will be five
paragraphs. The first, third, and fifth are left aligned, the second center
aligned, and the fourth right aligned.>


When including the CENTER and DIV tags, be aware that they will not be recognized
by many browsers. In this regard, both tags should be considered expendable.

<CENTER>

This does not need to affect your design much. It is unfortunate for those with
unsophisticated browsers that they do not recognize the CENTER and DIV tag, but it
cannot be avoided. Workarounds are not very accommodating, so you might as well
forget trying to make your display centered in all browsers.

</CENTER>
```

You will need P or BR tags before and after the CENTER and DIV tags for maintaining the paragraph consistency across browsers. Otherwise, there will be no paragraph break between sections in browsers that do not recognize the tag.

<DIV ALIGN=RIGHT>Alignment is not such a big deal for disseminating information. Not being able to control the alignment of images is more irritating for this author. Still, with so little control being made available to HTML authors, it is nice to use any help you can get.</DIV>

<! Beneath is the fifth paragraph of the section in browsers that support CENTER and DIV>

In many browsers, the CENTER and DIV Tags section will appear as one uninterrupted paragraph block, aligned left on the page. In browsers that recognize the tags, there will be five: the first, third, and fifth are left aligned; the second center aligned; and the fourth right aligned.

<P>
<H1>Table Tags</H1>

<! The table tags will be handled as described in the book. No TH tags will be used, and the BR and P tags will be used in an orderly fashion.>

In the table example, you will see one way of revealing the table contents. There will often be more than one way to design a table for browsers that do not support table tags. In the example, the table is centered in browsers that support the table tags, but the text is left aligned in browsers that do not recognize the tables. The table could have been built with a CENTER tag, three columns wide by one row high, using BR and P tags to space the contents within the cell. The CENTER tag was avoided because it was not desirable to have the information center aligned in the page. The STRONG tag was included within the CAPTION to preserve the title text format in other browsers.<P>

<! Instead of using a CENTER tag to center align the table cells, the ALIGN atttribute of the table tags is used to accomplish the same effect.>

<TABLE CELLSPACING=5 CELLPADDING=5 WIDTH=100% ALIGN=CENTER>
<CAPTION ALIGN=TOP><STRONG>Revenue vs. Expenditure by Region
</STRONG></CAPTION>

<! By using the ALIGN=CENTER attribute in the TABLE tag, and the WIDTH attributes of the TD tags, the table is centered in browsers that support the table tag, and left aligned in those that do not.>

```
<! By using the ALIGN=CENTER attribute in the TABLE tag, and the WIDTH attributes
of the TD tags, the table is centered in browsers that support the table tag,
left aligned in those that do not. The two blank TD tags made the alignment
work.>

<TR>

<TD WIDTH=14%>

<TD ALIGN=CENTER WIDTH=24% VALIGN=MIDDLE><STRONG>West </STRONG><BR>
$500,000,000<BR>
$450,000,000<P>
</TD>

<TD ALIGN=CENTER WIDTH=24% VALIGN=MIDDLE><STRONG>East</STRONG><BR>
$1,200,000,000<BR>
 $450,000,000<P>
</TD>

<TD ALIGN=CENTER WIDTH=24% VALIGN=MIDDLE><STRONG>South</STRONG><BR>
 $850,000,000<BR>
 $460,000,000<P>
</TD>

<TD WIDTH=14%>

</TR>

</TABLE>

</BODY>

</HTML>
```

In the following browsers, you will see what happens when tags are not recognized. Additional issues are presented by browsers that recognize some tags, and not others.

Navigator is the only one of the four browsers to recognize all four of the HTML 3 text formatting tags: <BIG>, <SMALL>, <SUB>, and <SUP>. The Netscape product also recognizes the <FONT> tag. The special characters were understood using both methods of display (i.e., using the numbering method and the entity method—see Appendix C). The <CENTER> and <DIV> tags were both recognized. As mentioned in the text, five paragraphs are visible. The first, third, and fifth are left aligned, the second is center aligned, and the fourth is right aligned. No <BR> or <P> tags were used in the CENTER and DIV Tags section. The table tags were all recognized. The <CAPTION> tag contents were aligned to the top of the table as expected. The <STRONG> tag was used, but is not necessary for display.

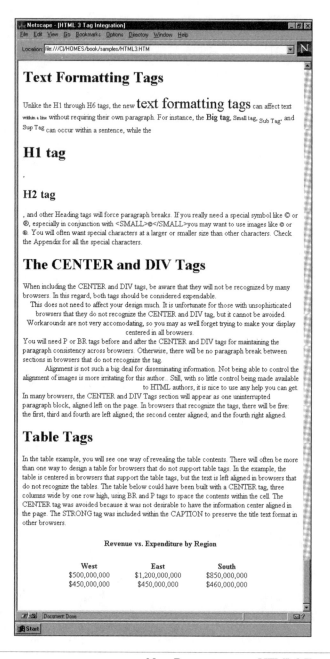

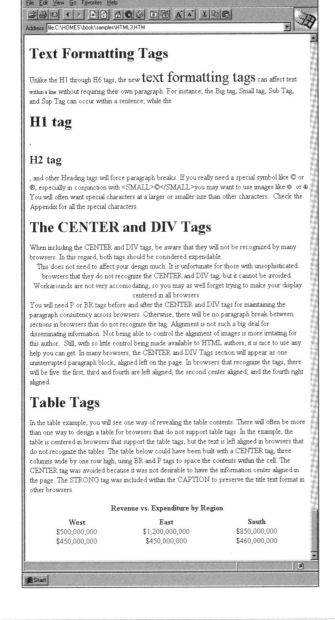

Internet Explorer recognized the <FONT> tag, but not the other text formatting tags. It recognizes additional attributes for the <FONT> tag, which will be looked at later in the chapter. The special characters were supported using both display methods. In the CENTER and DIV section, only the <CENTER> tag is recognized. Instead of one or five paragraphs, three are visible: the first left aligned; the second center aligned; and the third also left aligned. The <DIV> tag contents were not separated from the other paragraphs with <BR> or <P> tags, so it was treated as left aligned text after the </CENTER> tag. The table tags were all supported, including the <CAPTION> tag, located on top of the table. Explorer 3.0, released in March, 1996 in beta, will support the <BIG>, <SMALL>, <SUB>, and <SUP> tags.

PowerBrowser supports most of the text formatting tags. It supports the FACE and SIZE attributes of the <FONT> tag. It also recognizes the <BIG> and <SMALL> tags. PowerBrowser does not, however, recognize the <SUB> and <SUP> tags. The special characters were recognized using both numeric and entity reference methods. Like Explorer, the PowerBrowser recognized the <CENTER> tag, but not the <DIV> tag. Again, only three paragraphs are seen in the section where Navigator sees five. The <TABLE>, <CAPTION>, <TH>, and <TD> tags were all supported.

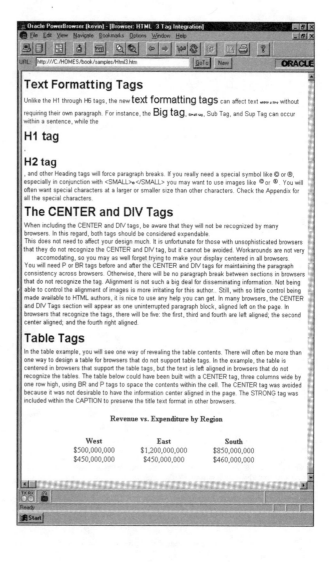

The America Online version 2.5 software shows you what will happen in a browser that does not support many of the HTML 3 tags. None of the text formatting tags, including <FONT>, are recognized by the program. The numeric and entity methods of special character construction are supported. In the CENTER and DIV section, it seems that two or three left-aligned paragraphs appear. If you look where the text "This does not need to affect your design much" is located, you will see that this is the beginning of the <CENTER> section, and does appear to have been forced to the left-hand margin. The hybrid approach to the table design shows how you can preserve the organization of your table contents if you design in anticipation of less-sophisticated browsers.

SUMMARY OF NON-RECOGNITION DESIGN STRATEGY

If you design HTML for the Internet and want to optimize your page display for one or more browsers, you do not have to sacrifice your page layout in other browsers. The page may be less attractive or functional in other browsers, but you can avoid many common mistakes by being aware of tag recognition issues.

When using browser-specific tags, realize that the browser manufacturer probably designed a "back door" in their HTML to accommodate other browsers. For Navigator, this would be the <NOFRAMES> or <NOEMBED> tag. Explorer uses another method that will be looked at in the next section. By allowing alternative displays for other browsers, software manufacturers and Web site developers ensure that the HTML documents do what they were intended to do—convey information.

The need for control over page layout should inspire designers to integrate hybrid techniques into their approach so that their pages don't end up out of control when viewed on the wrong browser. When resolving browser-specific tag issues, you are often able to use the workarounds provided with the tags themselves.

HTML 3 tags do not have back doors built into their formatting tags—there is no <NOTABLE> or <NODIV> tag, for instance. The new specification of HTML is supposed to raise the standard that all browsers are expected to support. With HTML 3, you have a few choices for resolving unrecognized tags. In the case of the <FONT> and text formatting tags, you can either treat their contents as ornamental and not worry about the sacrificed formatting, use HTML 2 formatting tags, or insert an image in place of the affected text.

The <DIV> and <CENTER> tags are ornamental in nature. Expect the <CENTER> and <DIV> contents to be left aligned in most browsers. At the beginning and end of <DIV> and <CENTER> sections, you will need <BR> or <P> tags to maintain paragraph integrity.

As noted elsewhere, special handling is required of tables. The structure of the information you want to display will control the way you design your hybrid tables. Remember to bold <TH> and <CAPTION> tag contents for support in other browsers. Effective use of the <BR> and <P> tags will help with your table organization.

Partial Recognition of HTML Tags

Partial recognition of tags poses an equally challenging design dilemma. There are two ways that browsers partially recognize tags: they either recognize the tag, but do not support one or more of the tag's attributes; or they recognize the tag, but do not support the file type.

Attributes

Whether or not the tag is HTML 3 or browser-specific, you will take a similar approach in resolving non-recognition of attributes. Unlike the tags in the previous section, the tags in this section are recognized by all browsers. It is only the attribute of the tag that is not supported. This can be a numbering method in the case of the <OL> tag, or a BORDER attribute for the <IMG> tag, for example.

The <HEAD> tags will not be included here due to the fact that they do not display in the browser. The following tags have attributes that are not included in their HTML 2 descriptions.

HTML 2 Tags with Additional Attributes

Tag	Supporting Browsers
<A>	Navigator
<AREA>	Navigator*, Explorer*
<BODY>	HTML 3, Explorer
 	HTML 3
<FONT>	Explorer*
<HR>	HTML 3
<P>	HTML 3
<IMG>	HTML 3, Explorer, Navigator, PowerBrowser
<TABLE>, <TR>, <TD>	Explorer*
<UL>	HTML 3
<OL>	HTML 3
<li>	HTML 3

* These tags have extensions to HTML 3 tag attributes. The tags did not exist in HTML 2.

PARTIAL RECOGNITION: ATTRIBUTES

In the same manner that you can consider the <CENTER> and text formatting tags of HTML 3 to be ornamental, it is safe to adopt a similar attitude toward many of the additional attributes for HTML 2 tags. It is frustrating to consider that many of the graphic elements that you will put into an HTML document will be unrecognized by less-sophisticated browsers; however, ignoring the fact that browsers will see your page differently will frustrate you more in the long run.

The only additional attribute of the <A> tag is TARGET, belonging to Navigator. This targets a frame for browsers that recognize it. For those that do not, it is ignored. Navigator also provides the TARGET attribute to the <FORM> tag and the <AREA> tag from HTML 3. In both cases, the TARGET attribute is ignored in other browsers.

The <AREA> tag also has attributes specific to Internet Explorer. The new attributes are additional definitions of SHAPE, such as CIRCLE and POLYGON. These attributes can be dangerous to use in a multiple-browser environment. For a browser like Navigator or PowerBrowser that understands client-side image maps, and that will not refer to the server-side image map for HREF information, the non-rectangular hotspots will be ignored. Even if browsers that do not recognize client-side image maps have alternative server-side HREF information, those that recognize the <MAP> and <AREA> tags, but not the SHAPE types, will not respond to non-standard shapes.

The <BODY> tag has additional attributes in HTML 3 and Explorer that should be thought of, to some degree, as ornamental. One important thing to remember when you set <BODY> tag attributes is that you cannot go knee deep in assuming control over the screen display. In other words, suppose you want a white background and black text, but you don't really care about the color of the link attributes. If a viewer has set browser settings to black background, white text, and off-white link colors, your partial control of his or her color scheme will leave the viewer squinting at the linked type. To overcome this, make sure you set the LINK, ALINK, and VLINK attributes when you set the BGCOLOR, BACKGROUND, and TEXT attributes. The BGPROPERTIES attribute does not fall into this group and will not generally affect screen display in other browsers. The TOPMARGIN and LEFTMARGIN attributes need to be considered expendable from a design perspective. You may want to use tables to create a similar effect that will be more widely supported.

The <BR>, <HR>, and <P> tags have all had similar attributes added. The CLEAR and ALIGN attributes work particularly well with other aligned screen elements, such as the <IMG> tag. The <HR> tag's CLEAR and ALIGN attributes were not recognized in the browsers tested here. A general rule of thumb to follow is that if your browser recognizes the ALIGN attribute of the <IMG> tag, it will probably recognize the CLEAR and ALIGN attributes of the <BR> and <P> tags. This means that you can design with both browser displays in mind by including the new tag attributes, while being aware that if they are not supported, the page contents will all be left aligned.

The <HR> tag has additional attributes that affect its display on the page. You should consider whether or not the SIZE, WIDTH, or NOSHADE attributes are needed for the overall appearance of the page. If you feel that your page would suffer substantially if the attributes were not supported, you may want to insert an image in its place that could maintain your page's consistency in other browsers.

The <FONT> tag from HTML 3 is looked at here due to the FACE attribute of Explorer. This attribute should definitely be thought of as ornamental. Either use one of the text formats of HTML 2 or HTML 3 that is closest to the font type that you want to use, include an image in the place of the tag, or resign yourself to the fact that most browsers will not support the attribute description. If it is really important, you can include a statement on your page to suggest that the viewers change their font preferences, but this is not advisable.

In addition to the ALIGN attribute, which is another ornamental tag description, the <IMG> tag has several attributes that are not supported in all browsers. The HTML 3 attributes of HEIGHT and WIDTH are often used to create larger screen images than the ones that are defined in the SRC attribute. While this is an efficient method of display in some browsers, in others the attributes will be ignored. The same is true of the HSPACE and VSPACE, BORDER, and UNITS attributes. The USEMAP is not supported in all browsers. The next chapter shows how you can have images positioned next to each other to work around the use of image maps.

Explorer also has some attributes for the <IMG> tag that are not supported in most browsers. The primary attribute is DYNSRC, which specifies a rich media format such as .AVI or .VRML for display. The CONTROLS, LOOP, and START attribute support the DYNSRC attribute. You should always include a SRC attribute for browsers that do not recognize the Explorer tags.

The listing tags can be resolved in one of two ways. Either use a text or image alternative to the bullet or number that is provided with the <li> tags, or accept the fact that your bullet or number specification may be ignored. For instance, if you wanted to have a square bullet, you can either enter the TYPE="square" attribute in the <UL> tag, or you could use <IMG SRC="bullet.gif"> instead. Using your own bullets will ensure that they are consistent. More important to many designers is the numbering method. If you must have "I. A. 1. a. i." structure in an outline format, you can nest <DL> tags, and have your numbering method included in the text line. Otherwise, accept the fact that not all browsers support the TYPE attribute, and that you may see "1. 1. 1. 1. 1." in the place of the outline structure that you are attempting to display.

Numbered List Using <OL> Tag

```
<OL TYPE=I>
<li>In Search of Ancient Cancer
Cures
<OL TYPE=A>
<li>Western Hemisphere
<OL TYPE=1>
<li>Secrets of the Incas
</OL>
</OL>
</OL>
```

Numbered List Using <DL> Tag

```
<DL>
<DD>I. In Search of Ancient Cancer
Cures
<DL>
<DD>A. Western Hemisphere
<DL>
<DD>1. Secrets of the Incas
</DL>
</DL>
</DL>
```

Finally, the table tags have additional attributes provided by Explorer. These need to not only be considered ornamental; they also need to be designed in a way that does not conflict with the display of other tags—specifically, with the color attributes of the <BODY> and <FONT> tags. You may be tempted to use a strongly contrasted table cell with a font color that is closer to the background color of the HTML page than the text color of the HTML page. In browsers that recognize the <FONT> and <BODY> attributes, the text will be obscured and hard to read.

PARTIAL RECOGNITION: FILE TYPES

Even though you may have followed all the HTML design techniques described in this book, you may still find that your pages are not well displayed due to file type recognition. This happens when a browser understands the tag and the attributes necessary for its display, but it has no way of displaying the file type that is referenced.

Most of the file type recognition issues stem from images. Chapter 7 deals specifically with image and other media file types, and their production and usage. In this section, the focus is on HTML design, and on mitigating display conflicts in multiple browsers. Being aware that not all images are supported in all browsers will influence your image type and HTML choice.

For images, the CompuServe .GIF87 file format is the most widely supported by browsers. The transparent .GIF89 format was introduced more recently and is supported by an increasing number of browsers. Even those browsers that do not support its transparency will recognize this image type. The animated .GIF file is a much more recent arrival. Most browsers that were used to test this image format recognized the first or last cell of the animation, if not the animation itself. The exception was PowerBrowser, which displayed a darkened rectangle in place of the image. One problem with the animated .GIF file is that it is much larger than a regular .GIF file and some browsers need to load it entirely before displaying.

The JPEG file format is increasingly supported in browsers. Designing for all browsers may make you consider using only .GIF files, but the percentage of browsers that do not recognize JPEG is small and shrinking. Other image file formats, such as .TIF or .WMF, can be seen in some browsers, usually by plug-ins or other software extensions to the browser architecture.

Most browsers enable you to use helper applications that greatly extend the range of file formats that you can use. Some of these are reviewed in the following chapter. Another device used by designers is to make files available for download that can be viewed using a traditional application. An example may be a Lotus Freelance graphic, which has no accompanying viewer, but can be viewed nonetheless with the creating program on your hard disk.

PARTIAL RECOGNITION: OBSERVATIONS

The examples that are presented in the following pages bring to light several potential conflicts for browser display. Fewer browsers support percentage width values than pixel values for images and other tags. In the example, you will see how PowerBrowser displays certain images much smaller than Navigator or Explorer. This is because it ignores the % mark after the number 100, and the browser displays an image 100 pixels wide. Not all browsers will support the HEIGHT and WIDTH attributes for the <IMG> tag, so you may want to make the image the exact size that you intend it to be in the main viewing area.

As you compare the screen display in the various browsers, be aware that the appearance of the page in the various browsers is an accurate representation of the page as it looks in the main viewing area of the browser. Explorer had particular difficulties making the resized gradient images look convincing. For the reasons cited, you may want to direct your attention to the bottom image in each group, and consider using a longer image in your screen display. The unfortunate part of the design process here is that you cannot include the WIDTH=100% attribute if you intend all browsers to display your page. Rather than ignore the contents, browsers like PowerBrowser (and there are others, believe it) interpret the attribute's instructions, except for one detail—they don't recognize the % sign, and they will display an image 100 pixels wide.

Also notice that the CLEAR attribute of the <BR> tag is not supported in all browsers that recognize the ALIGN attribute of the <IMG> tag. Browsers often recognize tag groups and their attributes. For instance, if a browser recognizes the <FONT> tag, it will usually recognize the color attributes of the <BODY> tag. And usually, if a browser recognizes the ALIGN attribute of the <IMG> and <HR> tags, it will also recognize the CLEAR and ALIGN attributes of the <BR> and <P> tags. At some point, you cannot avoid a certain degree of conflict in your browser display. In this regard, being aware of possible display conflicts is important, but catering to browsers that are inconsistent in their tag recognition can create more problems than it resolves.

Check out the HTML behind the browser display. The text in the screen, as well as in the comments, describes what is going on in the main viewing area.

```
<HTML>

<HEAD>
<TITLE>Partial Tag Recognition</TITLE>
</HEAD>

<! The body attributes in this example are included to demonstrate good HTML
grammar. If you are going to control the background or text colors, you must also
set the link colors if you use links on your page. If a visitor to your site has
their link colors set to a color that is close to your background or text colors,
the linked text will not be visible. >

<BODY BACKGROUND="bkground.gif" BGCOLOR=FFFFFF TEXT=000000 LINK=0000FF
VLINK=6666FF ALINK=FF0000>

<H1>Attribute Recognition</H1>

The BODY tag has color attributes set, including a background .GIF file for those
that read the BACKGROUND attribute. Below are several different lines from which
you can get ideas. The smallest is only 11 colors and is 10 pixels by 1 pixel.
The graphic takes less than 2 bytes of memory. The biggest ones at the bottom of
the list take up less than 1 kilobyte.<P>

<! The gradient images here are separated by individual black lines. Some browsers
will not recognize the percentage sign in the WIDTH attribute, and will make their
contents 100 pixels wide, instead of 100 percent of the screen width.>

<IMG SRC="bgblend.gif" HEIGHT=10 WIDTH=100%><BR>
<IMG SRC="black.gif" HEIGHT=1 WIDTH=100%><BR>
<IMG SRC="bgblnd2.gif" HEIGHT=10 WIDTH=100%><BR>
<IMG SRC="black.gif" HEIGHT=1 WIDTH=100%><BR>
<IMG SRC="bgblnd3.gif" HEIGHT=10 WIDTH=100%><BR>
<IMG SRC="black.gif" HEIGHT=1 WIDTH=100%><BR>
<IMG SRC="bgblnd4.gif" HEIGHT=10 WIDTH=100%><BR>
<IMG SRC="black.gif" HEIGHT=1 WIDTH=100%><BR>
<IMG SRC="bgblnd5.gif" HEIGHT=10 WIDTH=100%><BR>
<IMG SRC="black.gif" HEIGHT=1 WIDTH=100%><BR>
<IMG SRC="bgblnd6.gif" HEIGHT=10 WIDTH=100%><BR>
<IMG SRC="black.gif" HEIGHT=1 WIDTH=100%><BR>
<IMG SRC="bgblnd7.gif" HEIGHT=10 WIDTH=100%><BR>
<IMG SRC="black.gif" HEIGHT=10 WIDTH=100%><BR>
<HR SIZE=4 WIDTH=50% ALIGN=CENTER>
```

```
<IMG SRC="black.gif" HEIGHT=10 WIDTH=100%><BR>
<IMG SRC="bgblend.jpg" HEIGHT=10 WIDTH=100%><BR>
<IMG SRC="black.gif" HEIGHT=1 WIDTH=100%><BR>
<IMG SRC="bgblnd2.jpg" HEIGHT=10 WIDTH=100%><BR>
<IMG SRC="black.gif" HEIGHT=1 WIDTH=100%><BR>
<IMG SRC="bgblnd3.jpg" HEIGHT=10 WIDTH=100%><BR>
<IMG SRC="black.gif" HEIGHT=1 WIDTH=100%><BR>
<IMG SRC="bgblnd4.jpg" HEIGHT=10 WIDTH=100%><BR>
<IMG SRC="black.gif" HEIGHT=1 WIDTH=100%><P>
```

The first seven images are .GIF files, created using an image one pixel high by 10, 20, 40, 80, 160, 320, and 640 pixels wide. They are separated by a pixel that is 1 × 1. Beneath them, separated by two 10 pixel-high lines surrounding a horizontal rule, are four JPEG images: one pixel high by 10, 40, 160, and 640 pixels wide. The horizontal rule is centered and is 50% of the screen width. All the images have been stretched to the full screen width. <P>

```
<! The FONT tag is used to affect the border color of the IMG tag.>

<FONT COLOR=FF0000>
<IMG SRC="checker.gif" HEIGHT=180 WIDTH=240 BORDER=5 HSPACE=10 VSPACE=10
ALIGN=RIGHT>
</FONT>
```

This section will look at the image, paragraph, and line break attributes. In browsers that support the attributes, this paragraph will be on the right side of the checkerboard image that is 240 pixels wide by 180 pixels high. It should have a red border if it read the COLOR attribute of the FONT tag. The original is 10 × 10 pixels.

```
<P CLEAR=LEFT>
```

This paragraph should also be to the left of the top image.

```
<P CLEAR=ALL>

<A HREF="HTML3.HTM"><IMG SRC="checker.gif" HEIGHT=140 WIDTH=140 BORDER=0 HSPACE=10
VSPACE=10 ALIGN=LEFT></A><BR>
```

This paragraph is to the right of the second checkerboard image. The image functions as a link, but the border has been turned off and should not be seen.

```
<BR CLEAR=ALL>
```

```
<A HREF="HTML3.HTM"><IMG SRC="checker.gif" HEIGHT=140 WIDTH=140 BORDER=5 HSPACE=10
VSPACE=10 ALIGN=RIGHT></A>

This paragraph is to the left of the second checkerboard image. The image to the
right is linked to a page. It should have a border around it that is the color of
the linked text.<BR>


<! Here are a few HR tags with attributes. The first two should appear to the
left of the second checkerboard image.>

<HR SIZE=10 WIDTH=50% ALIGN=RIGHT><BR>
<HR NOSHADE SIZE=5 WIDTH=75% ALIGN=LEFT><BR CLEAR=ALL>
<HR NOSHADE SIZE=5 WIDTH=75% ALIGN=CENTER><BR>

<! Here is a test of the two methods of centering text available to most
browsers.>

<P ALIGN=CENTER>This is a test of the ALIGN=CENTER attribute of the P tag.<P>
<CENTER>This is a test of the CENTER tag.</CENTER>
<P>

<! And finally, here is a revisit to the listing tag groups.>

<H2>Listing Tags</H2>

Here are the OL and UL listing tag groups.<BR>

<H3>The OL Tags</H3>
<OL TYPE=I>
<li>The Big Project
<OL TYPE=A>
<li>Introduction
<li>Proposal
<OL TYPE=1>
<li>Identifying the Problem
<OL TYPE=a>
<li>Urban Setting
<li>Suburban Setting
</OL></OL></OL></OL>
<P>
<H3>The UL Tags</H3>
<UL TYPE="square">
<li>Filled in Bullet
<li TYPE="disc">Default Bullet
</UL>
<P>

</BODY>

</HTML>
```

The Navigator browser recognizes all of the <BODY> attributes. The BGCOLOR attribute is not seen, because the BACKGROUND attribute lies over the background color. At the top of the HTML document are several images with height and width attributes. This example brings out several points. It is possible to use small images and make them take up a much larger space on your Web page. It also demonstrates that convincing gradient effects can be made without large files being used. Unlike the image referenced by the BACKGROUND attribute of the <BODY> tag, the image referenced by the <IMG> tag has its size multiplied, rather than repeated across the screen. The background image is 100 × 100 pixels. It is repeated from left to right, top to bottom, over and over down the page. When the <IMG> tag is resized, on the other hand, the entire image is multiplied, so that if a color occupied one pixel, and you double its length, the color would occupy two pixels. Navigator recognized the ALIGN and CLEAR attributes of the <BR> and <P> tags; the COLOR attribute of the <FONT> tag; the WIDTH and ALIGN tags of the <HR> and <IMG> tags; the NOSHADE and SIZE attributes of the <HR> tag; the BORDER attribute of the <IMG> tag; and the TYPE attribute of the <OL>, <UL>, and <li> tags.

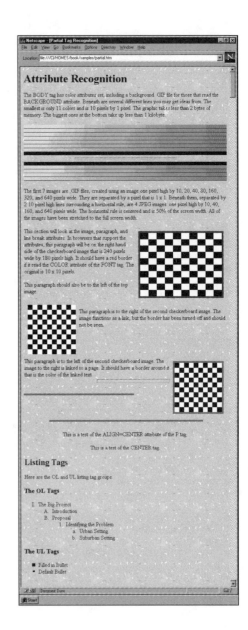

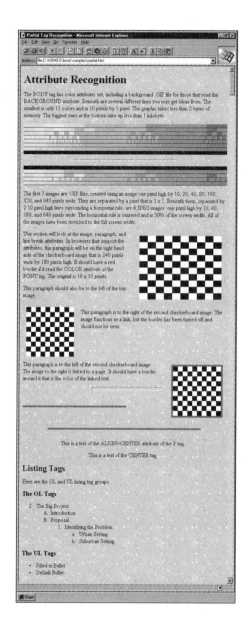

Internet Explorer recognizes most of the tags and their attributes presented here. Its first difficulties come in its interpretation of the gradient images. Unlike Navigator, which gives a smooth representation of the images, Explorer appears to have difficulties differentiating and displaying the colors in the image. The choppiness in the first four .GIF files is particularly pronounced, which suggests that you would probably be safer using a longer image, like the bottom one in each group. Down the page, you see that Explorer recognizes the ALIGN, HEIGHT, and WIDTH attributes of the <IMG> and <HR> tags; the ALIGN and CLEAR attributes of the <BR> and <P> tags; the NOSHADE and SIZE attributes of the <HR> tag; the BORDER attribute of the <IMG> tag; and the TYPE attribute of the <OL>, <UL>, and <li> tags. The browser did not support the COLOR attribute of the <FONT> tag, where it attempted to define the border color of the top image. In Navigator, this same image has a red border, as specified in the <FONT> tag. Apparently, the BORDER attribute of Explorer only affects the image when it functions as an anchor (e.g., using the <A> tag). In other uses, Explorer does support the COLOR attribute of the <FONT> tag, as seen previously.

PowerBrowser recognizes the <BODY> tag attributes in the example. It also supports the HEIGHT, WIDTH, and ALIGN attributes of the <IMG> tag— sort of. The gradient images at the top of the page all use the SIZE attribute, but the 100% value is interpreted as 100 pixels. The browser recognizes the SIZE attribute, but only when used with exact pixel units of measurement. As stated with Navigator and Explorer, it is probably safer to use a long gradient image without giving it width attributes to ensure consistency in multiple browsers. The height attribute is supported in a greater number of browsers. PowerBrowser had a rough time with the CLEAR attribute of the <BR> and <P> tags. Although it recognizes the ALIGN attribute of the <IMG> tag, it does not recognize the spacing tag attributes. It supports all the attributes of the <HR> tag, except CLEAR. All of the listing tags are supported, as well as the ALIGN attribute of the <P> tag. The COLOR attribute of the <FONT> tag is not supported in its use of defining the image border color. It recognizes the BORDER attribute of the <IMG> tag.

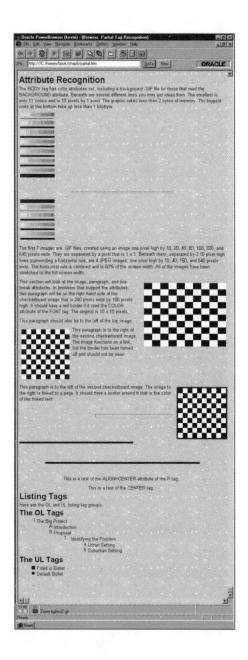

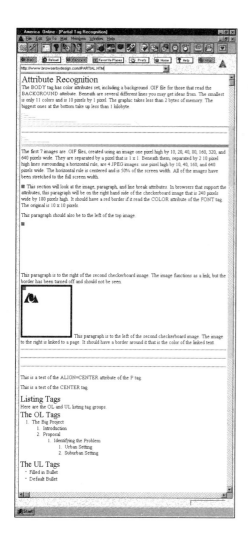

The America Online version 2.5 browser provides an excellent example of what can happen to your Web page display in other browsers. None of the attributes in the <BODY> tag are supported; nor are the ALIGN, HEIGHT, and WIDTH attributes of the <IMG> tag. If you want to use a gradient line to separate your document into sections, the display here suggests that you use a wide image to ensure consistency in multiple browsers. It is important to observe that even this early version of America Online's browser supported the JPEG format (as did the other browsers). Image issues will be looked at in the following chapter. None of the <BR>, <HR>, or <P> attributes are supported; neither are the attributes of the <OL>, <UL>, and <li> tags. For the <IMG> tag, only the BORDER attribute is supported when the image functioned as an an anchor. The checkerboard image used in the other browsers is finally seen as it really exists: as a 10 × 10 image. The strange thing is that the HEIGHT and WIDTH attributes of the <IMG> tag affect the size of the hotspot that responds to the <A> tag instructions, yet it does not affect the display of the image. While America Online is introducing its new browser, you cannot expect the Nielsen family in Peoria to rush online and update their software. HTML 2 will continue to be the lowest common denominator for some time to come.

SUMMARY OF PARTIAL RECOGNITION DESIGN STRATEGY

When designing for all browsers, the fact that many do not recognize some tag attributes or certain file types requires you to be aware of what other browsers do with the information that they receive. In a worst-case example, consider the following HTML:

```
<IMG DYNSRC="video.avi" CONTROLS HEIGHT=120 WIDTH=160>
```

If this HTML appeared on a page intended for the Internet, most browsers would not display anything. All the author needed to do was to insert a SRC attribute:

```
<IMG SRC="video.gif" DYNSRC="video.avi" CONTROLS HEIGHT=120 WIDTH=160>
```

By including an attribute that other browsers recognize, a conflict was avoided. Most tags do not have such a simple solution as this one. More often than not, your choice is either to ignore the fact that your page will not be optimized the way you would like it to be in all browsers, or you can insert an image in the place of the unsupported HTML tags.

The table tag group always needs to be given special attention. After you become comfortable with one or more table models that incorporate hybrid design, it will become second nature. Using the <BR>, <P>, and <STRONG> tags, along with the ALIGN and VALIGN attributes of the table tags, you can optimize your table's appearance in browsers like Navigator, without losing its information structure in less-sophisticated browsers.

File type issues can be mostly resolved by sticking with .GIF87 and .GIF89 file types for images. Animated .GIF files are encouraged, which can be designed using GifBuilder on the CD-ROM. Browser manufacturers like Netscape, Oracle, and Microsoft have designed their new HTML tags to accommodate other browsers. When individual browsers are unsuccessful in adopting their competitors' HTML tags, you should not abandon DYNSRC or <EMBED> content, animated .GIF files, or the ALIGN attributes of the <BR>, <IMG> and <P> tags. As with the lack of support for embedded tables in Mosaic, you have to draw the line on how far you will go to make your page acceptable in all browsers. Follow the tips and techniques in this book to the extent that you feel necessary for your audience. A single browser display should not be allowed to ruin a design strategy (unless, of course, it represents a substantial enough market share of your anticipated audience).

HARDWARE AND PLATFORM INCOMPATABILITIES

In addition to browser display conflicts, the operating system and hardware used to view Web pages will also affect the screen display. Among the biggest mistakes made by developers is to only test a document on one platform or one monitor size and resolution. Although it is not very costly to pick up multiple browsers for testing (they are often free), buying a second computer or monitor is an expense that many HTML authors are reluctant to incur.

If designing Web pages becomes an increasingly important source of your income, and if you design for a multiple platform audience like the Internet, you will probably want to at least have a PC-compatible computer and a Macintosh. A Unix system, such as Sun or Silicon Graphics, will be an excellent addition to your hardware testing facilities. There are certainly going to be niche industries that predominantly use Unix workstations to visit Web sites. If your business is one where this is to be expected, the third computer will be more important than otherwise. One excuse for buying a Unix system is provided to you if you want to host your own domain. This alternative is reserved for those who are willing to commit the level of resources necessary to maintain a server. Server issues are addressed in Chapter 8.

Many of the issues posed by multiple platforms concern the system palette and resources available for display. Image and color issues are explored in some length in Chapter 7. In addition to the operating system, the color depth and resolution size of the monitor will significantly affect the browser display. As a lowest common denominator, designing for 256 colors (8 bit) at 640×480 pixel resolution (14-inch monitor display) is quite safe. Although you will have a number of visitors using smaller screens, with black-and-white or 16-color display, at some point you have to define the demographic audience you want to consider in your HTML.

Hardware incompatabilities in addition to those regarding colors and image display increase as you take advantage of browser-specific tags. It has already been noted that both Netscape and Microsoft ship their browser products with different functionality. This is extended through the use of plug-ins, and other extensions, that will increasingly leverage their functionality through their access of system resources of the operating system. In actuality, this translates to further dominance of Windows, as all browser manufacturers and third-party developers increasingly tailor their products for Windows 95 and NT.

Advanced Table Design Using Hybrid HTML

Now that you have been introduced to many of the tools and techniques for creating hybrid HTML documents, it is time to consider a more complex document. The document that follows uses embedded tables, a method that is not recognized by NCSA Mosaic. In this case, it was considered demographically acceptable. Unless you strictly follow HTML 2 tag usage, there is always a chance that individual browsers will have difficulty in displaying your Web page. In this book, you are encouraged to test and experiment with all possible combinations of tags, with as many browsers as possible.

The Web page described here is highly customized to take advantage of the placement possible using embedded tables. As you look at the first division of the page, realize that it will again be subdivided—tables will be contained within table cells. Tables are embedded to provide a frame for the picture and a fixed position for customized bullets. Notice that the <CENTER> tag was avoided at the top of the page by using the ALIGN=CENTER attribute in a table containing the displayed table. This was done so as not to center the information in browsers that recognize the <CENTER> tag, but not the <TABLE> tag.

In the diagram below, several nested tables will be used within the initially described table cells. The cells in the outermost table are defined as follows:

The design is a relatively simple three column by three row table. The top row has two cells, the second row has two cells, and the third row has one cell. In the design, you will see an embedded table in the second cell of the first row that is used to give a frame to the picture that will occupy that space. In the second row, both table cells contain embedded tables with custom bullets to stay aligned with wrapped text in the cell to the right of it. When using custom bullets, you have to consider that if the text wraps to the next line, it will be under the bullet. Using the listing tags, the text will wrap to the next line underneath the first line of text, and not the bullet or number. Comments will be provided to make the HTML understandable.

```
<HTML>
<HEAD><TITLE>PDT Associates - Kevin Ready</TITLE></HEAD>
<BODY BGCOLOR=FFFFFF TEXT=000000 LINK=0000FF VLINK=8000FF ALINK=FF0000>

<! The first table is used in place of the CENTER tag to preserve the document
layout in browsers that do not support tables.>

<TABLE BORDER=3 ALIGN=CENTER WIDTH=100%>
<TR>
<TD ALIGN=CENTER>

<! This begins the actual table that is described using the diagram in this
chapter.>

<TABLE  WIDTH=95%>

<TR>

<TD VALIGN=MIDDLE COLSPAN=2  HEIGHT=30><FONT SIZE=6><STRONG>
Kevin Ready</STRONG></FONT><BR>

<EM>President, Project Development Training</EM><HR SIZE=4></TD>

<! The width attribute is set to a value that could conflict with the display
needs of the browser. In this case, the browser generally forces the issue and
makes the space available determined by the contents, as well as the tags and
their attributes.>

<TD WIDTH=20% VALIGN=TOP HEIGHT=180 ROWSPAN=2>
```

```
<! The cell actually has a second embedded table. This was done to allow the
picture to be framed, while having the linked text appear beneath it. The second
table was not necessary: you could have just had a single table, followed by the
linked text. This method was chosen after experimenting with several
combinations.>

<TABLE>
<TR>
<TD>

<! This is the table that gives the frame to the picture.>

<TABLE BORDER=2 CELLSPACING=2 CELLPADDING=2>
<TR><TD>
<IMG SRC="kevin.jpg"><BR>
</TD></TR>
</TABLE>

</TD>
</TR>

<TR>
<TD ALIGN=CENTER>
<A HREF="Mailto:kready@onthemap.com">Click Here to E-Mail</A><BR>
</TD>
</TR>

</TABLE>

</TD>
</TR>

<! At the beginning of the second row, you will see the tables within tables that
support the customized bullets. Notice that you have to use the FONT tag in every
table cell.>

<TR>
<TD VALIGN=TOP WIDTH=40%>
<TABLE >
<TR ALIGN=CENTER><TD COLSPAN=2 ALIGN=CENTER><STRONG>Skills<BR> </STRONG></TD></TR>
<TR>
<TD><IMG SRC="square.gif"> </TD>
<TD VALIGN=MIDDLE><FONT SIZE=2>Website and Database Design<BR></FONT></TD>
</TR>
```

```
<! This is the HTML behind the custom bulleted list. Notice that a UL list could
have performed a very similar function.>
<TR>
<TD><IMG SRC="square.gif"> </TD>
<TD VALIGN=MIDDLE><FONT SIZE=2>DTP and HTML Page Layout/Design<BR></FONT></TD>
</TR>

<TR>
<TD><IMG SRC="square.gif"> </TD>
<TD VALIGN=MIDDLE><FONT SIZE=2>Software Training and Curriculum
Development<BR></FONT></TD>
</TR>

<TR>
<TD><IMG SRC="square.gif"> </TD>
<TD VALIGN=MIDDLE><FONT SIZE=2>Business Software Integration and
Automation</FONT><BR></TD>
</TR>
</TABLE>
</TD>

<! Here is the second cell with the embedded table with custom bullets.>

<TD VALIGN=TOP WIDTH=40%>
<TABLE>
<TR ALIGN=CENTER><TD ALIGN=CENTER COLSPAN=2><STRONG>Clients/Projects<BR>
</STRONG></TD></TR>

<TR>
<TD><IMG SRC="square.gif"> </TD>
<TD VALIGN=MIDDLE><FONT SIZE=2><STRONG><A
HREF="http://www.enternet.com/platt">Platt College</A></STRONG>
<BR>Multimedia Instructor</FONT><BR></TD></TR>

<TR>
<TD><IMG SRC="square.gif"> </TD>
<TD VALIGN=MIDDLE><FONT SIZE=2><STRONG><A HREF="http://www.segaoa.com">
Sega of America</A></STRONG>
<BR><A HREF="kr_sega.htm">4 Color Newsletter</A><BR></FONT></TD>
</TR>
```

```
<TR>
<TD><IMG SRC="square.gif"> </TD>
<TD VALIGN=MIDDLE><FONT SIZE=2><STRONG>On The Map</STRONG><BR>
Website under construction<BR></FONT></TD>
</TR>

<TR>
<TD><IMG SRC="square.gif"> </TD>
<TD VALIGN=MIDDLE><FONT SIZE=2><STRONG><A HREF="http://www.visa.com">
VISA International</A></STRONG>
<BR><A HREF="kr_visa.htm">VBA Macro Programming</A><BR></FONT></TD>
</TR>

</TABLE>
</TD>

</TR>

<! Finally, here is the last row. The TARGET attribute loads the document into the
main viewing area of the browser. This is one way to make sure that your page is
not framed within someone else's.>

<TR>
<TD COLSPAN=3 ALIGN=CENTER VALIGN=TOP>
<A HREF="home.htm" TARGET="_top"><IMG BORDER=0 SRC="home2.gif"></A>
<A HREF="assoc.htm" TARGET="_top"><IMG BORDER=0 SRC="assoc2.gif"></A>
<A HREF="price.htm" TARGET="_top"><IMG BORDER=0 SRC="price2.gif"></A>
<A HREF="info.htm" TARGET="_top"><IMG BORDER=0 SRC="info2.gif"></A>
<A HREF="sites.htm" TARGET="_top"><IMG BORDER=0 SRC="design2.gif"></A>
</TD>
</TR>

</TABLE>

</TD>
</TR>

</TABLE>

</BODY>
</HTML>
```

Navigator and Explorer demonstrate the control that table design can give the HTML author. The layout of the cells closely corresponds with what you may have anticipated from the discussion on pages 264-65. You can see the five cells that make up the table (the name and title, picture, skills, clients/projects, and the icons along the bottom). You can also see how the table cells were subdivided into additional tables. The Skills and Clients/Projects lists both take advantage of the formatting that tables provide. The picture has a frame around it made possible by an embedded table surrounding it. Notice the difference in the width of the table cells between Navigator and Explorer. Both of the cells in the second row (the bulleted lists) have their WIDTH attribute set to 40%. Explorer provided more space for the first cell than it did for the second.

Mosaic, as seen on the right, ignored the embedded table contents completely. This is rather incredible, and it really does need to be seen to be believed. The four pages of HTML behind the document created the filled in box shape in the top left of the browser window.

The 2.5 version of America Online shows what happened to the code in a less-sophisticated browser display. Notice the order of information appears in the order of the cell contents of the table. If you had wanted the skills and clients to come before the picture, you could have made a two column by two row table, then formed a table out of the name, skills and clients/projects areas. Knowing that tables can be created in many different configurations will strengthen your ability to design hybrid documents. The custom bullets worked well here, too. A space was inserted between the <IMG> tag and the </TD> tag so that a space would be entered before the text began.

The screen at the bottom shows how the page would appear if a hybrid method was not used. The <BR> tags that are present help the table display and are not used to separate the page for unsophisticated browser displays. Notice how the text runs together uninterrupted. In bigger tables, this can be really horrible. Using the <BR> and <P> tags in your table design will preserve the structure for your information to be under-stood in browsers that do not recognize the table tags.

ADVANCED FRAME DESIGN USING HYBRID HTML

The last example of the chapter is the HTML behind the document in Chapter 1. Many browser-specific tags were used in that Web page, although these would probably not be used together in most situations. In designing a framed document, you are actually designing three or more pages. The main document will be used as both the <FRAMESET> parent document, as well as the HTML description for browsers that do not recognize frames. All framed documents need two or more frames to be functional. Often the largest frame shares considerable information with the <BODY> contents of the <NOFRAMES> section.

There was a fair amount of trickery in the design of the pages for the first chapter. There should have only been three documents involved, but due to a file type conflict, a devious workaround was used to optimize the display in all browers requiring four documents. The trickery involved Navigator and the beta version of PowerBrowser. The latter was offering partial support to the Netscape tags. It insisted on recognizing frames, but it did not support animated .GIF files.

After some investigation, it was discovered that PowerBrowser did not recognize the LOWSRC attribute of Navigator. This provided no solution, however, because after Navigator went through the trouble to download the relatively large file through the LOWSRC attribute, it was immediately replaced by the image referenced by the SRC attribute, the one that PowerBrowser recognized. After almost giving up on designing the document as desired, another discovery was made—PowerBrowser did not recognize the HTTP-EQUIV="Refresh" attribute from the <META> tag. This provided the back door that was needed.

To overcome the challenge posed by PowerBrowser, the <META> tag was used along with the LOWSRC attribute of the <IMG> tag. By using the LOWSRC attribute, the animated .GIF file was cached. When the <META> tag forced the loading of the second page for Navigator—but not for PowerBrowser, which did not recognize the tag—the SRC attribute of the <IMG> tag was able to use the cached animated .GIF file. PowerBrowser and others were able to be ignored, because only Navigator understood the unique combination of tags.

Unfortunately (or fortunately, depending on your perspective), the commercially released version of PowerBrowser 1.0 had resolved all of the conflicts for which such sophisticated workarounds were created. It presently has the same appearance as it does in the introduction, except that it supports the animated .GIF file.

```
<HTML>
<HEAD>
<TITLE>Hybrid HTML Design</TITLE>
</HEAD>

<FRAMESET ROWS="*, 100">

<! NOFRAMES is generally inserted at the top of framed documents. It has to occur
before the final closing FRAMESET tag. The content of the NOFRAMES section is
ignored by Navigator and PowerBrowser. Other browsers will start recognizing the
code from the BODY tag.>

<NOFRAMES>

<BODY BGCOLOR=FFFFFF TEXT=000000 LINK=0000FF VLINK=7F7FFF ALINK=FF0000
BACKGROUND="castle2.gif" TOPMARGIN=0>
<CENTER>

<! The order of the table cell contents will determine the order of elements in
browsers that do not support tables. The wizard is the first screen element to be
seen.>

<TABLE WIDTH=100% CELLPADDING=3 CELLSPACING=3>
<TR>
<TD><! Blank cells were used to make sure that the screen elements were well
placed.</TD>
<TD ALIGN=CENTER COLSPAN=3 ROWSPAN=2><IMG BORDER=0 SRC="wizard.gif"> <BR></TD>
<TD><!A second blank cell></TD>
</TR>

<TR><! Only two cells are in the second row, because the wizard took up two rows
and three columns. The third row has only one cell: the document title.>

<TD ALIGN=CENTER ><A HREF="about.htm"><IMG BORDER=0 SRC="about.gif"></A></TD>
<TD ALIGN=CENTER ><A HREF="deal.htm" <IMG BORDER=0 SRC="deal.gif"></A></TD></TR>
<TR><TD ALIGN=CENTER COLSPAN=5>
<H2>Hybrid HTML Design: an HTML Programming Reference</H2></TD></TR>

<TR><! Table cell backgrounds are only supported in Explorer. Other browsers
ignored it.>

<TD WIDTH=20% ALIGN=CENTER VALIGN=MIDDLE>
<TABLE ALIGN=CENTER VALIGN=MIDDLE ><TR>
<TD BGCOLOR=FF7F7F WIDTH=20 HEIGHT=20></TD>
<TD BGCOLOR=FFFFFF WIDTH=20 HEIGHT=20></TD>
<TD BGCOLOR=FF7F7F WIDTH=20 HEIGHT=20></TD>
</TR>
```

```
<TR>
<TD BGCOLOR=FFFFFF WIDTH=20 HEIGHT=20></TD>
<TD BGCOLOR=FF7F7F WIDTH=20 HEIGHT=20></TD>
<TD BGCOLOR=FFFFFF WIDTH=20 HEIGHT=20></TD>
</TR><TR>
<TD BGCOLOR=FF7F7F WIDTH=20 HEIGHT=20></TD>
<TD BGCOLOR=FFFFFF WIDTH=20 HEIGHT=20></TD>
<TD BGCOLOR=FF7F7F WIDTH=20 HEIGHT=20></TD>
</TR></TABLE>
</TD>
<! The table above will display a checkered background in Explorer.>


<TD WIDTH=20% ALIGN=CENTER ><A HREF="browser.htm"><IMG BORDER=0
SRC="browser.gif"></A></TD>
<TD BGCOLOR=FFFFFF WIDTH=20% ALIGN=CENTER><A HREF="chapter.htm"><IMG BORDER=0
SRC="chapter.gif"></A></TD>
<TD WIDTH=20% ALIGN=CENTER ><A HREF="resource.htm"><IMG BORDER=0
SRC="resource.gif"></A></TD>
<TD WIDTH=20% ALIGN=CENTER VALIGN=MIDDLE>
<TABLE ALIGN=CENTER VALIGN=MIDDLE ><TR>
<! Here is a second group of background table color tags.>
<TD BGCOLOR=FF7F7F WIDTH=20 HEIGHT=20></TD>
<TD BGCOLOR=FFFFFF WIDTH=20 HEIGHT=20></TD>
<TD BGCOLOR=FF7F7F WIDTH=20 HEIGHT=20></TD>
</TR><TR>
<TD BGCOLOR=FFFFFF WIDTH=20 HEIGHT=20></TD>
<TD BGCOLOR=FF7F7F WIDTH=20 HEIGHT=20></TD>
<TD BGCOLOR=FFFFFF WIDTH=20 HEIGHT=20></TD>
</TR><TR>
<TD BGCOLOR=FF7F7F WIDTH=20 HEIGHT=20></TD>
<TD BGCOLOR=FFFFFF WIDTH=20 HEIGHT=20></TD>
<TD BGCOLOR=FF7F7F WIDTH=20 HEIGHT=20></TD>
</TR></TABLE>

</TD></TR></TABLE>
</CENTER>
</BODY>

</NOFRAMES>

<! This is the end of the section designed for browsers that do not support
frames.  The instructions for Navigator and other frame-enabled browsers continue
on the next page.>
```

```
<FRAME SRC="index2.htm" NAME="targeted">

<FRAME NORESIZE MARGINWIDTH="0" MARGINHEIGHT="0" SRC="banner.htm" SCROLLING="NO">

</FRAMESET>

<! There are two frames in the framed document. These were defined at the top of
the document, and the FRAME tags above give the source of the sub-HTML files.
Sub-HTML refers to their usage within an HTML document.>

</HTML>
```

The following document fills the bottom frame of the framed document. The same
icons as the ones used in the BODY section provide navigation for the framed
document. The document name is "banner.htm."

```
<HTML>

<! No head section is required for framed documents.>

<BODY BGCOLOR=FFFFFF TEXT=000000 LINK=FFFFFF VLINK=FFFFFF ALINK=FF0000
BACKGROUND="castle2.gif">

<CENTER>
<TABLE VALIGN=TOP CELLPADDING=3 CELLSPACING=3><TR VALIGN=TOP>
<TD VALIGN=TOP ALIGN=CENTER>
<A HREF="about.htm" TARGET="targeted"><IMG SRC="about.gif"></A></TD>
<TD VALIGN=TOP ALIGN=CENTER>
<A HREF="browser.htm" TARGET="targeted"><IMG SRC="browser.gif"></A></TD>
<TD VALIGN=TOP ALIGN=CENTER>
<A HREF="chapter.htm" TARGET="targeted"><IMG SRC="chapter.gif"></A></TD>
<TD VALIGN=TOP ALIGN=CENTER>
<A HREF="resource.htm" TARGET="targeted"><IMG SRC="resource.gif"></A></TD>
<TD VALIGN=TOP ALIGN=CENTER>
<A HREF="deal.htm" TARGET="targeted"><IMG SRC="deal.gif"></A></TD>
</TR></TABLE>
</CENTER>

</BODY>

</HTML>
```

The two pages below fill the top frame of the framed document. The first one, "index2.htm," is the default that loads when the document loads. The <META> tag in the second line instructs the browser to search immediately after loading the document for "index3.htm," the document at the bottom of the page. Notice that the <LAYOUTFRAME> tag is not required in the lower document.

```
<HTML>
<META HTTP-EQUIV="REFRESH" CONTENT="0;URL=index3.htm">
<BODY BGCOLOR=FFFFFF TEXT=000000 LINK=0000FF VLINK=7F7FFF ALINK=FF0000
BACKGROUND="castle2.gif">

<LAYOUTFRAME X=10 Y=10 WIDTH=330>
<IMG BORDER=0 ALIGN=RIGHT LOWSRC="bdwizard.gif" SRC="wizard.gif">
</LAYOUTFRAME>
<LAYOUTFRAME X=340 Y=10 WIDTH=260>
<H1>Hybrid HTML Design: </H1>
<H2>An HTML Programming Reference </H2>
<FONT SIZE=4><FONT SIZE=5>K</FONT>evin
<FONT SIZE=5>R</FONT>eady and<BR>
<FONT SIZE=5>J</FONT>anine
<FONT SIZE=5>W</FONT>arner
</FONT>
</LAYOUTFRAME>
</BODY>
</HTML>
```

```
<HTML>

<BODY BGCOLOR=FFFFFF TEXT=000000 LINK=0000FF VLINK=7F7FFF ALINK=FF0000
BACKGROUND="castle2.gif">
<IMG BORDER=0 ALIGN=RIGHT SRC="bdwizard.gif">
<H1>Hybrid HTML Design: </H1>
<H2>An HTML Programming Reference </H2>
<FONT SIZE=4><FONT SIZE=5>K</FONT>evin
<FONT SIZE=5>R</FONT>eady and<BR>
<FONT SIZE=5>J</FONT>anine
<FONT SIZE=5>W</FONT>arner
</FONT>
</BODY>

</HTML>
```

SUMMARY

In Chapter 1, you saw a dramatically different page display of a single HTML document in the browsers reviewed. Having been introduced to the methods used to create the page, compare the code in the last four pages of this chapter with the images in the first chapter. Viewing the document with the individual browsers will reveal additional functionality that the printed page cannot.

In most cases, you can expect to maintain your page layout in sophisticated browsers, while integrating tags and attributes that will make it acceptable in other browsers. Designing hybrid HTML documents occasionally requires you to compromise your screen appearance to some degree in the advanced browsers. The extent to which the display of your Web page will need to be compromised is dependent on the demographic audience you want to design for and the nature of the content in your HTML document.

Of the tags and attributes reviewed here, a strong difference between non-recognition of tags and partial recognition of tags was made evident. Additionally, HTML 3 and browser-specific tags were handled very differently in hybrid design due to the latter group's built-in workarounds to display inconsistencies. It is important for the developer to be aware of the fundamental differences in the methods used to mediate display conflict between HTML 3 and browser-specific tags. These methods were covered in the first section of this chapter.

Of the tags that were only partially supported, a distinction was made between the support of attributes and the support of file types. Most of the conflicts noted were as a result of attribute non-recognition. These can be mitigated using several methods, which were presented in the second section. Issues presented by file type were relatively minor. For Navigator, this is in large part due to the usage of the <EMBED> tag for non-standard file formats. For Explorer, this is handled with the DYNSRC attribute of the <IMG> tag. PowerBrowser recognizes both.

The most important thing you can do to enhance your hybrid design techniques is to test your documents on multiple browsers. Do not rush to throw away your old browsers: you will need to refer to them to see how many visitors will see your pages. This is particularly true if you are expecting the worldwide audience of the Internet to arrive at your home page. Who knows what browser your audience could be using?

RICH MEDIA FILE FORMATS

HyperText Markup Language, as the name implies, provides a text-based method of graphically displaying information. The principal form of data that it was intended to transfer was text. As the tremendous growth of the World Wide Web has pushed the language to accommodate non-text elements, the HTML developer is increasingly expected to become expert in fields other than strict programming or text editing.

Understanding and working with diverse media file formats, browser extensions, and programming languages beyond HTML have suddenly become very important to Web page designers. In the first part of this chapter, you will be introduced to image, audio, video, animation, and VRML files. The second part of the chapter is dedicated to helper applications, especially plug-ins, and how to use them effectively. The last part of the chapter looks at distributed applications over the Internet using languages like Java and Visual Basic. As a Web site designer, you must continually update your knowledge of available resources. Things that work one way one day may be inefficient or obsolete the next.

IMAGE FILES

There are many file types presently available for HTML developers to use. In addition to the traditional .GIF files, the .JPEG file format, VRML file format, and animation, video, and audio file formats have become recent additions to the developer's tool kit. In this section, you will be introduced to the file types to the extent you can expect to be working with each of them as an HTML programmer.

Of all the file types that you will be working with, the image files are likely to be the most common. Before making a choice about which format to use, some understanding of the digital method of representing color is necessary.

DIGITAL COLOR

When displaying colors on a monitor, you will be using the RGB color method. RGB stands for Red, Green, and Blue—the three primary digital colors. All colors displayed on your monitor are made up of a combination of Red, Green, and Blue values. The other principal method of working with color is CMYK, which stands for Cyan, Magenta, Yellow, and Black. The CMYK method is the print media counterpart to RGB. Cyan, Magenta, and Yellow are the opposite colors to Red, Green, and Blue, respectively. The fourth color is Black, which is used for additional color control.

Print media uses a 32-bit four-color system for working with colors. Monitor display, which is what you will be designing Web pages for, uses the RGB method and has a maximum of 24-bit color display. Each color value has 8 bits, or one byte, of information assigned to it. This represents an integer value from 0 to 255 for each color, or zero to 100 percent.

When RGB values are all set to zero, the color displayed is black. When all values are set to 100%, the color displayed is white. If one of the values is brought to 100% while the others stay at zero, the color becomes pure red, pure green, or pure blue. To create the basic colors of the CMYK system, you do so in a reverse method to the one used to make RGB. Cyan is the opposite of Red. To create the CMYK opposite for an RGB primary color, you set the RGB value of the color to zero, and the value of the other two RGB colors to 100 percent. For Cyan, you set Red to zero, and Green and Blue to 100%. For Magenta, you set Red and Blue to 100%, and Green to zero. Finally, for Yellow, you set Red and Green to 100%, and Blue to zero.

RGB, CMYK, and Hexadecimal Color Systems

There are many converters available on the Web that will translate CMYK and RGB into hexadecimal numbers. It is strongly suggested that you use these to the extent that they familiarize you with the conversion system and help you quickly define the color that you are looking for. For those with a print background who are accustomed to adding more Yellow, or making something less Black, an understanding of the conversion system will help you make a lot of your hexadecimal changes without consulting these resources.

Adding or subtracting Cyan, Magenta, and Yellow from a color is easy using hexadecimal. To add Cyan, for instance, you need to lower the value of Red in the color. To subtract Magenta, you will actually be adding Green. While working with opposites is one thing, adding and subtracting black requires a bit more thought. To make a color brighter or darker, you increase and decrease the individual RGB values proportionately to the distance that they are from zero and 100%.

In the diagram below, three color bars with five color settings are looked at: Black; White; an RGB color; and the color with 50% Black added and 50% Black taken away. To add Black, you need to move each RGB value proportionately toward zero. To add White, you need to move each RGB value proportionately toward 100%. Each of the intermediate RGB values should be half the distance between the original color and zero, or between the original color and 255. This can be slightly off, as seen in the numbers below, but in theory, it should be exactly correct.

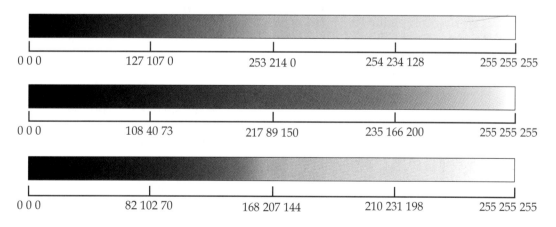

0 0 0	127 107 0	253 214 0	254 234 128	255 255 255
0 0 0	108 40 73	217 89 150	235 166 200	255 255 255
0 0 0	82 102 70	168 207 144	210 231 198	255 255 255

In the first bar of the example, the RGB color selected was 253 214 0. To find the RGB number halfway between it and White, calculate the number halfway between each individual RGB value and 255. For Red, this is 254; for Green, this is 234; for Blue, this is 128. Using the same method, you can test the values on the other two bars.

To find the RGB number halfway between each number and Black, you calculate the number halfway between each and zero. For Red, the number halfway between zero and 254 is 127. For Green, this is 107, and for Blue, the number halfway between zero and zero is zero. This example worked exactly, although it is typical for one or two values to be off by one or two, since all numbers are rounded to the nearest integer.

It will take some time to become familiar with the RGB color system if you have not yet been introduced to it. You can learn a lot by just choosing colors from your program's color picker and looking at the RGB description. The hexadecimal color system was introduced in Chapter 4 and is based on the RGB system. The system uses sixteen alphanumeric characters: the ordinal numbers from 0 to 9, and A through F of the alphabet. Using two digit places to express each RGB value, a total of 256 number combinations are possible: 0 to 255 in the RGB system.

Using the hexadecimal color system, you can describe millions of colors, yet many monitors can only display 256, or 8-bit color. In a perfect world, you could tell the computer which 256 colors you wanted to use, but in actuality, you are forced to accept some colors you may not even use and forced to do without some you may really want to use.

When using 8-bit color, you have access to 256 colors. In many instances, these colors are dynamic and will respond to user requests for individual colors. Although both Macintosh and Windows have system palettes, you are able to use colors that you create yourself using the RGB or CMYK method. In this manner, you reserve one or more of the 256 colors for your own usage.

At any moment in an 8-bit monitor display, all of the screen elements, including the menu bar, icons, images, and other objects, share a maximum of 256 colors. Some of these colors are reserved by the operating system, whether or not they are required by the user. This becomes very important when you include more than one indexed image in a page, as shown later in this section.

COLOR PALETTES

The Macintosh, Windows, and Unix operating systems each have their own system palettes and their own methods of interpreting image data. It has been generally noted that the Macintosh screen display is brighter than Windows, which is brighter than that of most Unix displays. More important than the relative brightness of the screen displays is the way that the operating systems treat color palettes.

Images and background colors will change from monitor to monitor, let alone from operating system to operating system. Many browsers are recognizing the 216 basic colors that can be generated by using the hexadecimal values 00, 33, 66, 99, CC, and FF for each of the three RGB colors. The squares in the color table below represent the 216 basic colors that are available using this method. The legend illustrates the three axes used in making the colors.

In each table, the Red value is increased from zero to 100% from top to bottom. The color in the top cell of each table has no Red. The color in the bottom cell of each table has 100% Red. The Green value is increased from left to right. Each cell against the left margin of a table has no Green; cells against the right side have 100% Green. The Blue value is increased from the top left table to the bottom right table. All cells in the first table have no Blue. All cells in the second table have 20% Blue, and so on until the last table, in which all cells have 100% Blue.

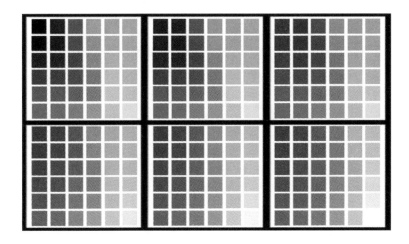

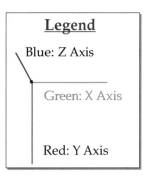

Using hexadecimal numbering, you would reference the top left cell of the first table as 000000, or Black. The Red value increases as you move down: 330000; 660000; 990000; CC0000; and FF0000. The Green value increases as you move to the right: 003300; 006600; 009900; 00CC00; and 00FF00. If you move from one table to the next in the same relative cell (the top left corner), the Blue value increases: 000033; 000066; 000099; 000000CC; and 0000FF. All the cells within the tables use the same referencing technique.

When working in Photoshop or other image editing programs, you will soon discover that even if you make sure that all your RGB values are set correctly, their hexadecimal counterparts may still be a little off. This is unfortunate, but for those from print media backgrounds who have been nailed over color issues, it does give you a good excuse when reviewing color with a client. The differences in operating system, monitor, and browser types will each affect the color that you see.

If you design your images with colors from the previous page—which correspond to 0, 51, 102, 153, 204, and 255; or 0%, 20%, 40%, 60%, 80%, or 100% in RGB color—you can expect acceptable display in 8-bit monitors from the various operating systems.

SPECIAL COLOR NAMES

In addition to the hexadecimal numbering method, there are several special color names that can be used to reference colors. The colors, along with their special names, hexadecimal number, and traditional color names are displayed on the facing page. Notice that the special colors use CMYK and RGB names that do not necessarily correspond with their print counterpart. The color "Green," for example, is darker than RGB Green, which is represented by the color "Lime." The color "Magenta" has been renamed "Fuchsia," and the color "Cyan" has been renamed "Aqua."

If these colors are close to what you want, you can adjust them as described on the preceding pages. For instance, if you want a lighter Olive, add a proportionately equal amount to each of the RGB values. If you want a darker Olive, substract a proportionately equal amount from each RGB value. Not many browsers support these colors presently. Of the ones tested, only Navigator 2 and Explorer 2 recognized the special color names. It is likely that more will follow suit, but you should stick to hexadecimal for consistency in multiple browsers.

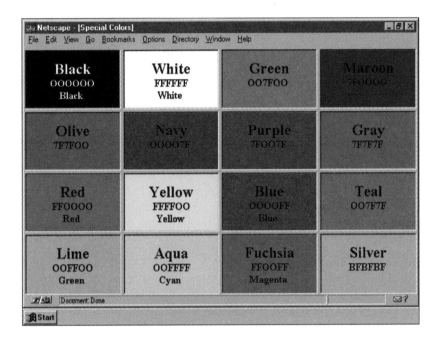

IMAGE FILE FORMATS

Of all the image file types, the CompuServe Graphics Interchange Format, or GIF, is by far the most widely supported. The .GIF file is an indexed image, which uses no more than 256 colors. It is generally a good idea to do image design with your monitor set to 256 colors in order to anticipate how your browser audience will view colors. At this monitor setting, you can observe potential display conflicts that come from the indexing of colors. When you index a color, you are assigning it to one of the 256 colors available in the palette. If more than 256 colors are defined in the screen, the monitor will substitute one of the 256 available colors for those that it cannot accommodate in its palette.

You should save your images with as few colors as possible. This will reduce file size, which results in quicker loading. From Photoshop, change the Mode to Indexed Color, and select 8-bit, 7-bit, 6-bit, and so forth to see how much detail is lost in the image. Images with few colors and rectangular shapes are the best candidates for a .GIF file format.

There are several types of .GIF files available for developers. The original, GIF87a, has been around for over eight years. The GIF89a format arrived two years later. With the latter format, designers can create transparent .GIFs, images that have one color blocked out so as to appear transparent against the background color or image. You can also create interlaced images with GIF89a, images that load in several passes so that part of the image is seen almost immediately.

The most recent addition has been animated .GIFs. These were developed at the end of 1995 and are made up of several .GIF87a or .GIF89a files together. The images load sequentially and appear as an animation. Presently, Navigator is the only browser to support the animation, while most browsers will recognize the first or the last image in the animation. For this reason, you will want to make sure that the first and last frames in your animated .GIF file are acceptable if seen alone. A few browsers will not be able to support the file format at all, but these are in the minority.

The second most popular image file format on the Web was devised by the Joint Photographic Experts Group and is called JPEG. The suffix for this file type is usually .JPG or .JPEG. The JPEG file format supports millions of colors and is quite presentable on 256-color displays. Images with complex shapes and many colors, such as photographs, are best served with the JPEG format. Most browsers today support this image file format, although this has not always been true.

A new arrival on the scene is the Portable Network Graphics format, .PNG. This was introduced in 1995, partially in response to CompuServe and Unisys, who are attempting to force royalties from developers of .GIF files. None of the browsers tested presently support the file type, but it is promised to be a major advance over the other two format types.

On the facing page, several images are presented with their compression method and file size. The photograph suffered tremendously with the .GIF compression, both in appearance and file size. The image of four solid colors, on the other hand, was much larger in .JPEG than in .GIF format. Using less colors also affects the size of the .GIF file, as the individual pictures demonstrate. Other factors that influence file size include horizontal and vertical orientation, complexity of the image, and compression method, as seen on page 286.

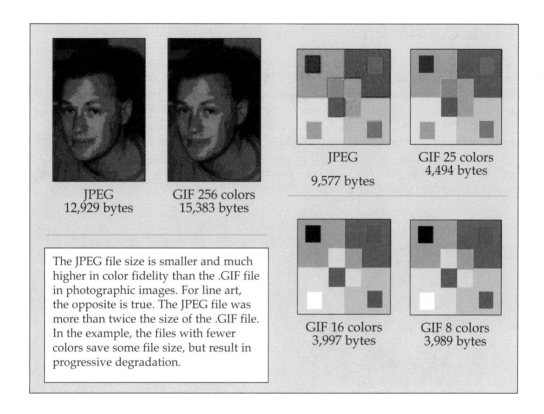

JPEG
12,929 bytes

GIF 256 colors
15,383 bytes

JPEG
9,577 bytes

GIF 25 colors
4,494 bytes

The JPEG file size is smaller and much higher in color fidelity than the .GIF file in photographic images. For line art, the opposite is true. The JPEG file was more than twice the size of the .GIF file. In the example, the files with fewer colors save some file size, but result in progressive degradation.

GIF 16 colors
3,997 bytes

GIF 8 colors
3,989 bytes

Until other file formats become more widely supported, using .GIFs and JPEGs will ensure that your images are able to be seen in almost all browsers. For the most part, you are quite safe to include animated .GIFs in your design, as long as you ensure that the first and last frames can stand alone in those browsers that do not recognize the animation.

Additional file formats will be introduced later in this chapter in the plug-ins section. Many of these are proprietary and are supported only by the manufacturer that made the plug-in. Use .GIFs for flat images, line art, and graphics that do not have complex colors. Try to use as few colors as possible to reduce the file size. Use the JPEG file format for photographic images and other complex colors and shapes. Wavelet compression, available in some plug-ins, is a very promising future development.

IMAGE COMPRESSION

JPEG and GIF files use different compression methods. The latter, as seen on the previous page, uses a system of mapping pixels to indexed colors. When the number of colors is reduced, greater compression is enabled. The distribution of the indexed colors will also affect file size, as seen in the figures at the bottom of the page. JPEG uses lossy compression. *Lossy compression* is a method that approximates the colors in an image. It works best with photographic images, and you can choose the degree of compression that you want your picture to undergo. Using maximum compression, your files are smaller, yet not as true to the original. Using low compression, your files are large, but they accurately reflect the content of the original image.

137,284 bytes
This high-resolution image was saved using low compression.

52,213 bytes
This low-resolution image was saved using maximum compression.

3,913 bytes
Horizontally distributed GIFs are the smallest.

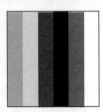

7,170 bytes
Vertically distributed GIFs are almost twice the size of horizontal GIFs.

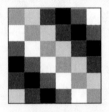

7,318 bytes
The simple checkered GIF does not add much to the file size over vertically distributed GIFs.

11,423 bytes
No two same-colored pixels are adjoining. This is the largest file size.

IMAGE MAPS VERSUS ADJACENT IMAGES

One way you can avoid using server scripts to process image maps, introduced in the following chapter, is to break your image into pieces and butt them against each other. If you use tables to do this, you can come up with pretty cool effects with placement of graphics against a background image or color. You can follow the guidelines for table creation introduced earlier to ensure backwards compatibility. When designing an image that requires more than one line to provide the images needed for navigation (e.g., there are two different hotspots in a single vertical line in your image), you should separate the lines using a <BR> tag. The <P> tag will insert a space beneath the top graphic and can be undesirable.

Contrast the following HTML:

```
<A HREF="cgi-bin/map.map"><IMG SRC="spiro.jpg" ISMAP></A>
```

and

```
<TABLE CELLPADDING=0 CELLSPACING=0 BORDER=0>
<TR>
<TD><A HREF="whatnew.htm"><IMG SRC="whatnew.jpg" BORDER=0></A>
</TD>
<TD ROWSPAN=2><A HREF="home.htm"><IMG SRC="home..jpg" BORDER=0></A> </TD>
<TD><A HREF="product.htm"><IMG SRC="product.jpg" BORDER=0></A>
</TD></TR><TR>
<TD><A HREF="support.htm"><IMG SRC="support.jpg" BORDER=0></A>
</TD>
<TD><A HREF="about.htm"><IMG SRC="about.jpg" BORDER=0></A>
</TD></TR><TR>
<TD COLSPAN=3><IMG SRC="twisty.jpg"></A>
</TD></TR>
</TABLE>
```

On the following page, you will see these in two different browsers. America Online 2.5 was selected to demonstrate that this technique will enable browsers that do not recognize image maps to navigate your pages. Notice that the "home.jpg" could have been broken in two if we were really concerned about making it acceptable in all browsers.

In the top example, the effects of a table that enclosed the two methods can be seen. Using a table, it was possible to place each method into its own table cell for observation. The adjacent images had slightly more space between the images than the image map. This can be mitigated through trial and error, and perhaps a slight shaving of the original images. All of the links work, but the image map links require server processing.

In the bottom example, using America Online's browser, the display is quite different. Although their browser will be changing and recognizing more sophisticated tags, remember that there are a lot of others that will not. The browser did not recognize the image map. In the adjacent images, the page would have been helped if the second image in the top row was split in half. This way, all three lines could be in alignment.

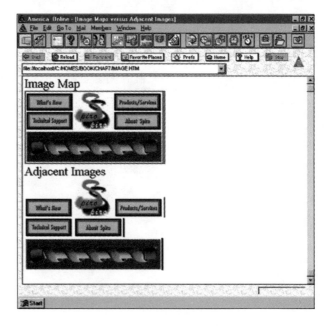

Tips for Image File Usage

Sticking to .GIF and JPEG files will ensure that your images will be seen by almost all browsers. If you are planning on using more than one .GIF image on a page, realize that 256 is the total number of colors that the monitor can display. That means that in addition to the images in the page, the menu bar, toolbar, and all other screen elements are sharing the same palette.

It is safe to consider your actual palette size as being limited to the 216 colors and special color names introduced earlier. Even if you use different colors, you should try to work within 216 colors of your choice. In other words, your operating system, browser, and any additional programs that are running on your computer will reserve at least 16, and often 32 or more, colors for their display. The special colors are among the reserved colors.

Consider a page where you have three .GIF files. Between the three, they can use up to 216 colors. If you save one at 6-bit color, or 64 colors, you have 152 left for the other two to use. The second one may be a 7-bit color, or 128-color, image, leaving 24 for the third image. The third one may also be a 7-bit color image, needing 128 colors for its own usage. For this reason, it is a good idea to save your indexed images in exact number of colors. If the 6-bit image could be brought down to 50 colors, and the first 7-bit image could be brought down to 80 colors, you would have 86 colors left over for the third. More than likely, all three images would withstand the slight loss of quality that may accompany this economizing.

It is not only for the display of graphics that you want to reduce the number of colors you use. It is also due to file size. The fewer colors that need to be described, the smaller the image files that are restricted to those colors. It is a good idea to test with fewer colors than the original image requires. If you can make an 8-bit graphic into a 4-bit graphic without overly compromising the image, your graphics can experience substantial reductions in file size.

The issue with JPEG is fidelity, not bit-depth. JPEG images are designed to find the closest match on the available system palette at any given monitor depth. Any compromise in quality occurs when the image is produced. It is often the case that a degree of quality is traded for the speed in download time. Unfortunately, it is more often the case that graphic artists choose not to trade any quality and have Web pages that are less frequented due to download times. Many companies work within a specified size limit per page so as not to lose any mouse-happy surfers.

AUDIO FILE FORMATS

Although audio file formats have been around as long or longer than most of the image files here, they have not traditionally been included in Web pages. Navigator, Explorer, Mosaic, PowerBrowser, and others support audio files. The most widely supported are the audio interchange file format (.AIFF), the Sun audio file format (.AU and .SND), the RIFF Wave file format (.WAV), and the Musical Instrument Digital Interface file format (.MID), or MIDI.

Apple developed the .AIFF during the early 1980s. At the same time, Sun and NeXT, and Microsoft and IBM were working on their own audio file formats. The first two supported the .AU and .SND file formats, initially developed for the telephone industry. The latter group worked on the .WAV file type definitions, which has seen a dramatic increase in usage since the introduction of Windows 95.

MIDI is very different from the other audio file types. The other three each describe the waveform of the physical sound. MIDI describes note information that is interpreted by either a MIDI standard instrument, included in many sound cards, or by another MIDI-compatible musical instrument. For this reason, MIDI files are much smaller than the others looked at here. There are additional file types that are supported by Netscape plug-ins that will be looked at later in this chapter.

The quality of most audio file formats, including .AIFF, .AU, and .WAV files, is determined in large part by its sampling rate and sound depth. *Sampling rate* refers to how many times in one second a soundwave is recorded. *Sound depth* refers to the amount of information that is recorded during each recording. The first is measured in cycles per second, or Hertz (Hz). The second is measured in bits (8-bit, 16-bit, and so on). that describe the dynamic envelope of the soundwave. Roughly stated, the dynamic envelope determines the distance between the highest and lowest volumes in the recorded sound. The greater the bit size, the higher the dynamic response, as measured in decibels, that can be included in the sound description.

The range of human hearing is approximately 20 Hz, or 20 cycles per second, to 20 KHz, or 20,000 cycles per second. Middle C on the piano is 261 Hz; sopranos reach up to 1 KHz, and beyond; a string bass has its lowest note at 56 Hz or lower frequency. In addition to the sounded note, your ear also distinguishes the note's overtone series: natural sounds occurring in nature made by integer multiples of the note's frequency. That means that in addition to 261 Hz, for example, your ear also hears 522 Hz, 783 Hz, and 1,044 Hz at progressively lower volumes. The overtone series provide much of the richness and color in a sound.

The higher the frequency, the poorer the quality of sound reproduction. For instance, if you have an electric guitarist playing a note at 1,300 Hz, and your sample rate is 11 KHz, that means that you will have less than nine individual images of the soundwave made by the guitar. In the figure below, one of the cycles from a continuous sound source is displayed. The image to the left shows the points at which the soundwave was photographed, or sampled. On the right, three soundwaves are displayed: the original; a 22 KHz sample; and an 11 KHz sample.

By drawing lines through the intersection points at a given sampling rate, you can approximate the generated soundwave. Considerable detail in the sound becomes lost as the sampling rate decreases, with the highest notes being the first to become obscured. Usually the lower sampling rate is accompanied with a smaller bit size in dynamic response. For instance, 11 KHz sampling is usually paired with an 8-bit dynamic range. The nature of your audio content will strongly influence the quality that you want it to have. Voice is often acceptable at 11 KHz, while music is not. If possible, stick to 44.1 or 48 KHz for higher-quality recordings.

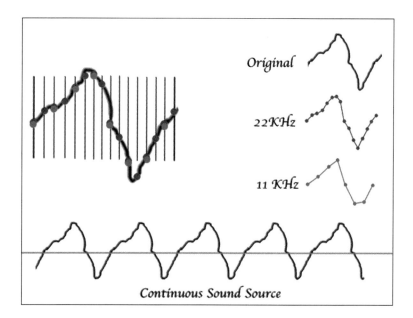

Original

22 KHz

11 KHz

Continuous Sound Source

Dynamic response describes the incrementation of the volume of sound as measured in decibels (dB). This is more noticeable at some frequencies than others. At 1 KHz, your ear can detect 0.2 dB changes in volume levels at 80 dB; at 40 Hz, your ear can only detect changes of 5 dB or greater at 10 dB volume levels. CD quality audio is considered 16-bit, which gives enough definition to the sound for imperfections to be relatively unnoticed by the human ear.

High-end digital to analog (D/A) and analog to digital (A/D) converters often use 22- or 24-bit envelopes to ensure capturing the high end. Whether measuring sound depth or sampling rate, it is always the higher frequencies that suffer from the digitization process. For sound depth, this is caused by the fact that the higher frequencies are often at higher volumes than the other sounds, and that their interpretation by the ear is more scrupulously interpreted than other frequencies.

MIDI FILE FORMAT

Unlike the others looked at here, the MIDI file format involves the passing of note information for a music device to interpret into sound. In this respect, MIDI acts like HTML, where a small amount of information is input for processing, and the client device interprets the code into pitch, timbre, and duration information. As developers turn to MIDI as an effective method to transfer sound files, you can expect browsers to increasingly support it. A Netscape plug-in is available for MIDI support, and Explorer already supports MIDI in its <BGSOUND> tag.

QuickTime presently supports the MIDI file format, and other video file formats are promised to support the format in the future. The MIDI standard has been around in the music industry for almost two decades. Using MIDI information to pass to musical instruments and devices is extremely efficient, and will hopefully become an Internet standard. Using standard MIDI instruments, a 60-minute orchestral piece with 20 instruments can be described with a couple of megabytes of storage space or less. The same file using many other methods would be compressed to 10 megabytes per minute, or 600 megabytes for the piece.

The ideal audio format of the future will integrate the digital recording needs of voice and other acoustic sources with the power and efficiency of MIDI. Sampled sounds and the human voice will not likely find a compression method as effective as MIDI is for note information.

Tips for Audio File Usage

In addition to the plug-ins and sound capabilities of Navigator, Explorer, and other browsers, helper applications, as introduced later in this chapter, may be used to facilitate audio file transmission. If you had a browser that did not support the audio file within the browser, for instance, you could set the helper application in your preferences or options menu item to an application that reads audio files. Anticipating that many of your visitors will not have audio capabilities, referring them to an online audio resource will enable these visitors to experience the audio file.

As more and more products with sound and music capabilities come online, keep your ears open for new compression methods to be announced. In addition to RealAudio, Toolvox, and other audio product vendors, many interactive authoring tools are available for you to include sound in embedded documents. Director, Astound, and other plug-ins give you the ability to include sound in your multimedia presentations.

When designing pages that contain embedded audio elements, remember that your audience becomes narrower as you introduce non-traditional files. Even if you consider Navigator to be your only target audience, there is nothing to ensure that your visitors will have downloaded the plug-in necessary to view or hear your page. On pages where the sound is important to the overall content, you may want to include links to the browser(s) needed to hear the page, and to the plug-in that supports the file type.

There is often more than one way to include audio in your Web pages. Your choices will depend on the anticipated browser demographics of your audience and your particular usage of audio devices. If you are exchanging audio information with co-workers or clients, you can make sure that everyone is using the necessary hardware and software. If you are designing for the Internet, be aware that a large segment of your audience is probably not going to hear your page. In this respect, sounds should be generally treated like the ornamental tags from HTML 3. Not being able to hear the sound should not detract from the information-based reason that a visitor came to your Web page. If the reason that someone goes to your page is because of the sound, however, this is another case.

VIDEO AND ANIMATION

As with audio file types, embedded animation or video files in your page will not be seen by all of your visitors. Things are moving fast, though, and you can expect your visitors to catch up soon. Even more than audio, there are several ways to incorporate motion into your HTML pages. You can embed .AVI, .MOV, .QT, or .MPEG documents, use animated .GIF files, Java, JavaScript, Shockwave, and other embedded objects that often combine audio and video effects.

The first group—the .AVI, .MOV or .QT, and .MPEG formats—represents the three most common file types. The Audio Video Interleaved (.AVI) format is Microsoft's digital video standard. The .MOV and .QT file formats, QuickTime, is Apple's original digital video standard. The Motion Pictures Expert Group came up with the .MPEG file format. Up until recently, .MPEG required additional hardware to be viewed, and in most cases this is still true. There are plug-ins available that can enable your browser to display .MPEG files without additional hardware, which will be introduced in the following section.

In the short-term horizon, MPEG II and ActiveMovie will both influence the choices available to developers. These should both become available in the second quarter of 1996. MPEG II has been developed over the past several years by the same group that developed the original MPEG. The new MPEG II standard also provides audio support, including an impressive compression system. Both MPEG file formats have traditionally needed hardware for their images to be seen. Lately, the functions performed by hardware are increasingly being performed in the software.

ActiveMovie, announced in March 1996 by Microsoft and to be included in Explorer 3.0, is a cross-platform digital video technology that will support all the preceding file formats, as well as the audio file formats examined on the previous pages. According to Microsoft, the software will be capable of decoding MPEG without requiring an MPEG chip. As with all new technologies, its claims will need to be proven in the market if it is to become the standard that Microsoft is hoping.

It is still too early to tell which digital video file format is likely to emerge as the standard, or whether or not there will continue being several to choose from. QuickTime and .AVI are the most widely supported presently. The original MPEG format is fading into history, and the new MPEG II and ActiveMovie technologies are just now coming online.

VIDEO AND ANIMATION ALTERNATIVES

Using video files gives you an excellent opportunity to design a hybrid HTML document. As seen in Chapter 5, including the <NOEMBED> tag with the <EMBED> tag from Navigator will enable your Netscape audience to see the embedded object, while your other visitors will see the contents of the <NOEMBED> tag. In the same document, you can include the SRC attribute with the DYNSRC attribute for the <IMG> tag. This way, Navigator, Explorer, and other sophisticated browsers may display the video, while the other browsers will have an image to look at:

```
<EMBED SRC="alchemy.avi" HEIGHT=120 WIDTH=160>
<NOEMBED>
<IMG SRC="alchemy.gif" DYNSRC="alchemy.avi" HEIGHT=120 WIDTH=160>
</NOEMBED>
```

The preceding example enables Navigator and Explorer to see the .AVI file, while displaying the .GIF file in other browsers. This type of design will be needed for quite a while, as it is likely that a large number of Internet users will continue to be unable to view video files.

ANIMATED GIFS

Animated GIF files, introduced earlier in this chapter, provide a simple workaround for including animated images in a document. The only problem is that Navigator is the only browser that currently recognizes the animation feature of the file. If you want movement on your page, this is one way to go that is quite simple to implement and that has a workaround built into it. Browsers that do not support the animation will see either the first or last frame.

OTHER ANIMATION DEVICES

In addition to the video file formats and animated GIFs, HTML developers can take advantage of plug-ins, such as Shockwave, that enable multimedia presentations to be embedded into the page. These can range from a simple logo animation to a full-featured interactive program. In addition to plug-ins, you can also use Java, JavaScript, or other languages to help your page come alive. These will be looked at later in this chapter. A final, discouraged, animation device is the use of the HTTP-EQUIV="Refresh" attribute of the <META> tag, as seen in Chapter 4. This tag forces the reloading of a page in the place of the current one.

VRML

In 1993, Mark Pesce and Tony Parisi developed a three-dimensional interface that could be used to navigate the World Wide Web. Soon after the introduction of their interface, the term Virtual Reality Modeling Language (VRML) was coined. Using VRML, developers can give size, shape, texture, and linking properties to objects. Once defined, the "world" file (.WRL) can be embedded in an HTML page, or directly accessed by opening the document itself.

As with audio and video files, VRML files are not widely supported in browsers at this writing. They can, however, be viewed with helper applications, as described later this chapter. Early in 1996, Silicon Graphics, Sony, and other hardware and software developers agreed on a proposal for a VRML 2.0 standard. The proposal, named Moving Worlds, has wide industry support. This new file format promises to be a major development for the Web and should usher in a shift to three-dimensional navigation on the Internet.

The VRML file format is one way of viewing three-dimensional worlds. Another is the Object Oriented Graphics Library (.OOGL) file format. This format is only available for workstations and more powerful computers such as SGI, NeXT, Sun, HP, and DEC Alpha chips. It was developed in 1992 at the Geometry Center at the University of Minnesota and uses an interactive 3D geometry viewing program named Geomview.

Designing worlds in VRML requires considerable expertise. There are presently several books available on the topic, including *VRML: Browsing and Building in Cyberspace* by Mark Pesce, which describes how to create and navigate through virtual worlds. Several skill sets will be involved in creating virtual worlds, including programming, image design, and three-dimensional and Internet navigation skills.

OTHER FILE FORMATS

In addition to these file formats, other file formats can be viewed using helper applications or browser extensions. These greatly expand the number of files you can include for display in your Web pages. Applications and compressed files, such as .EXE, .ZIP, .GZ, .TAR, and others, are typically available for downloading, and are not viewed by the browser. There will be many platform-specific file formats that your operating system will not be able to recognize.

HELPER APPLICATIONS

Early Web browsers were not intended to display the many file format types that are presently available for download on the Internet. One way that this was remedied early on was with the use of *helper applications*—applications designated to run when a particular file type was opened. In most browsers, you can select your helper applications from the options or preferences menu item.

Helper applications may be used in a variety of instances. From e-mail and ftp functions to movie and graphics viewing, helper applications enable you to do things that go well beyond typical browser features. Many of these features have been integrated into browser design, or are available through plug-ins. *Plug-ins* are special types of helper applications that do not launch their own window to display documents. Their documents are referred to as embedded objects, and they are contained within the HTML page.

Following is a list of helper applications, their manufacturers, the platforms and files they support, and the URLs where they can be found. You can also use most programs on your hard disk as helper applications. For instance, if you wanted to use Adobe Persuasion as the helper application for .PRS files, you can set the relationship in your browser's preferences.

GRAPHICS

JPEGView   **Aaron Giles**   **Macintosh**

    This viewer resides at the Cornell University Medial College, and was written by Aaron Giles. It upports JPEG, PICT, GIF, TIFF, BMP, and MacPaint file formats.

              `http://www.med.cornell.edu/jpegview.html`

LView Pro   **Leonard Haddad Loureiro**   **Windows 3.1, 95**

    This program works as both a viewer and an editor. This is convenient if you have limited disk space for applications. LView Pro supports JPEG, BMP, GIF 87a, GIF 89a, PCX, TARGA, TIFF, and PPM file formats.

              `http://world.std.com/~mmedia/`

Imagenation Viewer   **Spicer Corporation**   **Windows, Macintosh, Unix planned**

Spicer is a developer of CAD and Raster Imaging software. Their viewer, Imagenation, supports over 130 formats, including AutoCad, TIFF, DXF, JPEG, and others.

`http://www.magi.com/spicer/`

GifBuilder, Clip2Gif   **Yves Piguet**   **Macintosh**

Yves Piguet has made excellent contributions to the freely available products on the Internet. GifBuilder is a program used for making animated .GIF files and is included on the CD-ROM. Clip2Gif is a utility program that converts PICT, TIFF, GIF, and JPEG file formats.

`http://iawww.epfl.ch/Staff/Yves.Piguet/clip2gif-home/GifBuilder.html`
`http://iawww.epfl.ch/Staff/Yves.Piguet/clip2gif-home/`

AUDIO

GoldWave   **Chris Craig**   **All Windows**

GoldWave is a digital audio editor that can also act as a helper application. It features real-time amplitude, spectrum, and spectrogram views. It can open, play, and convert .AIFF, .AU, .WAV, and many others.

`http://web.cs.mun.ca/~chris3/goldwave/`

RealAudio Player   **Progressive Networks**   **Macintosh, Windows 3.1, 95, Unix**

This player is one of the most widely used. RealAudio Player will be bundled with the next version of Windows 95. The company also makes a plug-in for Navigator. It supports .RA and .RAM file formats.

`http://www.realaudio.com/release/download.htm`

VIDEO

Sparkle   **The Texas Higher Education Network**   **Macintosh**

THEnet provides a mirror site for this much needed program. Sparkle decodes MPEG and converts it to QuickTime format for display in Macintosh computers.

`ftp://ftp.the.net/mirrors/ftp.utexas.edu/graphics/sparkle-245-fat.hqx`

MPLAYER.EXE   **NCSA**   **All Windows**

This viewer from NCSA supports QuickTime movies in Windows OS.

`http://ncsa.uiuc.edu/SDG/Software/WinMosaic/Viewers/qt.htm`

AviLxp AVI Movie Viewer   **Scientific CD Movies**   **Windows 95, NT**

This company specializes in the quick turnaround of digitized video. Their freely available viewer supports .AVI file format. It provides zoom, crop, speed, and copy functions.

`http://www.scdm.com/`

MPEG2PLY.EXE   **Stefan Eckart**   **Windows 32s, Windows 95, NT**

This program is available at Netcom's FTP site. It supports MPEG I and MPEG II formats.

`ftp://ftp.netcom.com/pub/cf/cfogg/mpeg2/`

VIRTUAL WORLDS

Fountain   **Caligari**   **Windows 95**

Caligari provides a VRML browser and creator in one program. It supports and creates .WRL files for three-dimensional views.

`http://www.caligari.com/lvltwo/2product.html`

Webspace Navigator   **Silicon Graphics, Template Graphics**   **Unix, Windows NT, 95**

This product was one of the first VRML navigators. It supports .WRL files.

`http://www.sgi.com/Products/Evaluation/; http://www.sd.tgs.com/`

CyberGate   **Black Sun Interactive**   **Windows 95, NT**

Black Sun has introduced a VRML browser that is integrated with a chatroom feature. You use avatars to navigate in a world with other visitors.

`http://www.blacksun.com/`

QuickTime VR   **Apple Computers**   **Macintosh, Windows 3.1, 95**

The QuickTime VR format uses twelve pictures 30° apart to create a 360° view of a photographed image. It supports .QTVR files.

`http://qtvr.quicktime.apple.com/`

PhotoSphere Viewer   **OmniView**   **Windows, Macintosh**

OmniView has taken the lead from Apple in developing a file format that supports three-dimensional photographic imagery. The file type that it recognizes is .BUB, PhotoBubbles.

`http://207.217.86.10/`

Utilities

Eudora   **Qualcomm, Inc.**   **Macintosh, Newton, All Windows**

> Eudora is one of the first e-mail programs to become available to both
> Macintosh and Windows users. The company has a Eudora Light Freeware
> version, as well as a Eudora Pro version for retail purchase.

> `http://www.qualcomm.com/ProdTech/quest/light.html`

PKZip   **PkWare**   **Windows**

> PKZip is one of the most used freeware/shareware programs in existence.
> This company led the way in PC compression, and a large percentage of
> compressed files use the .ZIP file format.

> `http://www.pkware.com/`

Stuffit   **Aladdin Systems**   **Macintosh, Windows**

> This program is almost as popular on the Macintosh as PKZip is on the PC.
> Stuffit Lite, Stuffit Pro, Stuffit Expander, and others are available from their
> Web site.

> `http://www.aladdinsys.com/`

WinZip   **Nico Mak Computing**   **Windows 3.1, 95, NT**

> This compression utility has become very popular with the Windows 95
> audience. It uses .ZIP file formats, and can be used to decompress TAR,
> gzip, and other file formats.

> `http://www.winzip.com/`

Any program on your hard disk may be used as a helper application. The preceding
are just a few of the many you will find on the Internet. Check out the CD-ROM
for other resources, and lists of sites where you can find more specific helper
applications. You can also try using Alta Vista, Yahoo, or other search engines to
locate a document type, or a program you know that creates it.

Helper applications are launched independently of the browser. The next pages deal
with a special kind of helper application—a plug-in. The line that differentiates
plug-ins from helper applications is not always apparent. For the most part, plug-ins
run in the background, and are not visible in the application menu or application
bar. Helper applications, by definition, run independently of the browser.

Plug-ins

Plug-ins extend the architecture of the Navigator browser. Since their introduction at the end of 1995, there have been over 40 plug-ins developed by third-party manufacturers for the Netscape product. The extensions to the Navigator architecture access file types that the browser could not otherwise recognize. They do this by being inserted using the <EMBED> tag.

When the <EMBED> tag is used, the file type referenced by the SRC attribute is matched with a plug-in or helper application. One problem noticed when testing the plug-ins is that sometimes more than one want to recognize the same file type. You can only use one plug-in to recognize a file type. This is set in the Options menu under the General Preferences menu item.

Companies that use plug-ins within an Intranet strategy can benefit from knowing that their employees all have access to the same functionality from the browser. Being able to share and edit spreadsheet information, or being able to take other employees on a tour of relevant Web sites are among the many uses that plug-ins can serve in the workplace.

Other browser manufacturers, such as Oracle and Microsoft among others, have been moving to support the Netscape Application Programming Interface, NSAPI. Explorer 3 had not yet recognized the <EMBED> tag when this book went to print, but PowerBrowser had managed to resolve much of its initial conflicts with plug-ins. To support plug-ins in PowerBrowser, you must install them in the Navigator directory, and then copy or move them to the "c:/orapb95/plugins/" directory.

Remember when using plug-ins that the most recent ones installed will override your file suffix recognition settings. In other words, if you have installed a plug-in that recognizes .TIF documents, and then you install another one to support JPEG documents that also recognizes the .TIF file, the most recently installed plug-in will support the .TIF file. This can be irritating, so test several of the plug-ins alone and in combination so that you may better suggest to visitors how to view your site.

Plug-ins open up the browser's architecture dramatically. They can be used to recognize sound files, MPEG files, interactive presentations, chat rooms, and many other formats that have not yet been developed. Refer to the Netscape plug-ins page for the latest updates and new plug-ins.

```
http://home.netscape.com/comprod/products/navigator/version_2.0/plugins/index.html
```

Adobe   **Acrobat Amber Reader**   **Macintosh, Windows 95, NT**

Adobe has made available its .PDF format for display in the Navigator browser. At this time, the Acrobat Reader is launched when .PDF files are visited, opening the .PDF files directly. It is a good idea to alert visitors on the page that links to the .PDF file that they need the plug-in or Acrobat Reader to view the document. The file format can be created with many applications on the Macintosh, Windows, and Unix platforms in conjunction with the Acrobat Distiller program. From the program you want to publish from, you select the .PDF file output the same way that you normally target a printer. The Acrobat Reader has its own control panel, which gives considerable navigation control and zoom features.

```
http://www.adobe.com/Amber/Download.html
```

Apple   **QuickTime**   **Macintosh, Windows**

Apple has been a long time coming with its own plug-in. Several other developers have already arrived to market with their own versions. The plug-in supports .QT and .MOV file types. In addition to SRC, ALIGN, HEIGHT, and WIDTH attributes, the plug-in supports the following:

AUTOPLAY=TRUE or FALSE
CONTROLLER=TRUE or FALSE
LOOP=TRUE, FALSE, or PALINDROME
PLAYEVERYFRAME=TRUE or FALSE
PLUGINSPAGE=URL

It is expected that the plug-in may support additional attributes. QuickTime is expected to be released by Summer, 1996.

```
http://quicktime.apple.com/internet/
```

Business@Web   **OpenScape**   **Windows 3.1, 95, NT**

OpenScape is one of two plug-ins that support OLE objects and .OCX controls. As with other file formats, Navigator generally uses the most recently installed plug-in to recognize file types. Business@Web provides both the development tool and the plug-in to view custom-created and general application OLE objects, .VBX controls, and more within Web pages. Embedded documents have the .OPP suffix. The plug-in supports the HEIGHT, WIDTH, SRC, and FORM attributes. FORM identifies the object type, such as Excel, frmStockQuotes, and so on.

```
http://www.busweb.com
```

Carberry Technology/EBT   **FIGleaf Inline**   **Windows 95 and 3.1**

This plug-in enables you to view many image file formats, including .cgm, .tiff, .eps, .epsi, .epsf, .tg4, .bmp, .wmf, .ppm, .pgm, .pbm, .sun, .gif, and .jpeg. FIGleaf competes with several other plug-ins that recognize multiple image file formats, which can result in conflicts. The right mouse button enables viewers to select the palette, zoom in or out, view the image, save the image or its location, and learn about the plug-in. Besides HEIGHT, WIDTH, and SRC, the plug-in supports the following attributes:

COLORMAP= DITHERED or PRIVATE

BORDER=pixel_value

Additional information can be found from the Carberry Home Page:

                        http://www.ct.ebt.com/

Chaco Communications   **VR Scout**   **Windows 95, NT**

Chaco is one of several VRML plug-ins available for Navigator. As with the other ones, VR Scout recognizes the .WRL file format. The company also makes a stand-alone helper application. The plug-in features a navigation bar at the bottom of the screen that is not as sleek as some of its competitors. The right mouse button features navigation mode setting; refreshing and resetting the camera; setting the headlight, dimmer, and preferences settings; and product, company, and help information. Remember, only the most recently installed plug-in for a specific file type will be used.

                        http://www.chaco.com/

Corel   **CMX Viewer**   **Windows 95, NT**

The maker of Corel Graphics has provided this plug-in to view the .CMX file format. CorelDraw is the development tool needed to generate .CMX files. Using the right mouse button, you can view the .CMX file in its own window, save the file, flip the image vertically or horizontally, rotate the image 90° in either direction, zoom in or out, and refresh the window image. The plug-in uses the SRC, HEIGHT, and WIDTH attributes. Corel is presently working on a Java-based plug-in code named Viking that is expected to be released during the second quarter of 1996.

                        http://www.corel.com/corelcmx/

Farallon   **Timbuktu Plug-in**   **Windows, Macintosh planned**

Farallon gives you the ability to work on a hard disk at a distance. Long
known for its networking software, the plug-in requires both parties to
have the software in order to exchange information.

```
http://collaborate.farallon.com/www/look/ldownload.html
```

Future Wave Software   **FutureSplash**   **Macintosh, Windows**

This program uses files created with CelAnimator, a vector-based drawing
and animation product in the .SPL file format. Both editor and plug-in are
available presently for free from their Web site.

```
http://www.futurewave.com/
```

GEO   **Emblaze**   **Macintosh, Windows 3.1, 95**

This plug-in supports images animated with the Emblaze Creator. Of all the
methods to transfer animations, Emblaze was the fastest tested by a
substantial margin. Supports the .BLZ file format. Presently recognizes the
HEIGHT, WIDTH, and SRC attributes.

```
http://www.geo.co.il/technology/emblaze/index.html
```

Gold Disk   **Astound Web Player**   **Windows 95, NT, 3.1**

Gold Disk provides this plug-in to support multimedia presentations
created by Astound, a cross-platform development tool. The document
suffix is .ASN. The plug-in presently uses only the HEIGHT and WIDTH
attributes, and the right mouse button is not enabled.

```
http://www.golddisk.com/
```

ICB   **ViewMovie**   **Macintosh**

This plug-in was released ahead of Apple's own QuickTime plug-in. It
recognizes .QT and .MOV file formats. In addition to HEIGHT, WIDTH,
and SRC attributes, the plug-in supports several of its own, as follows:

CONTROLLER=TRUE or FALSE

AUTOPLAY=TRUE or FALSE

LOOP=TRUE or FALSE

More information is available from the following URL:

```
http://www.well.com/user/ivanski/download.html
```

Ichat, Inc.   **ichat Plug-in**   **Windows 95, NT**

The ichat plug-in enables groups of visitors to carry on a chat-room conversation as they cruise through the Web. One person can lead others through Web sites, and comments can be made to other visitors as you share your view of Web pages. It is also available as a helper application.

http://www.ichat.com/

Infinet Op   **Lightning Strike**   **Macintosh, Windows 95, NT**

This plug-in enables you to download large bitmap files saved using the Lightning Strike Compressor and Decompressor (codec). It does this through what it terms a wavelet-based compression method, which averaged close to 100:1 in the sample images provided by the company. Using the right mouse button, you can get information about the image, save the image as a bitmap file, and toggle back and forth between the picture's own palette and the Netscape browser palette. Presently only supports the SRC, HEIGHT, and WIDTH attributes.

http://www.infinop.com/

Inso Corporation   **Word Viewer Plug-in**   **Windows 95, NT, 3.1**

Inso provides this plug-in that enables you to embed Microsoft Word documents into your Web page. This conflicts with KEYview and other conversion programs. The right mouse button enables visitors to activate the object, save it, copy it, or make an Internet Shortcut. Uses the SRC, HEIGHT, and WIDTH attributes, as well as ALIGN and ALT.

http://www.inso.com/

Integrated Data Systems   **VRealm**   **Windows 95, NT**

This is another VRML plug-in, one of the first introduced. Quite innovative, the plug-in uses a control panel at the bottom of the screen that you use to navigate with, set options, and perform other functions in a virtual world. The company also makes a stand-alone helper application. It supports the .WRL file format, which means that it will conflict with other plug-ins that attempt to recognize virtual worlds. You may want to test drive a few until you find the one that feels best. In addition to its control panel, the plug-in features many right-mouse functions, including navigation mode setting; headlight, collision, and gravity settings; viewing options; and product information.

http://www.ids-net.com/ids/downldpi.html

InterCAP Graphics Systems   **InterCAP InLine**   **Windows 95, NT**

Another graphic plug-in, InterCAP supports Computer Graphics Metafiles (.CGM), which are made with many graphics programs. This plug-in supports zooming, panning and magnification, animation, and hyperlinked CGM images. This plug-in will conflict with other plug-ins that attempt to recognize the same file type. If you want to use InterCAP after installing another plug-in, reset the application from the general preferences option.

```
http://www.intergraph.com/icap/
```

Intelligence at Large   **MovieStar Plug-in**   **Windows 95**

This plug-in enables PC users to view QuickTime files. It supports .MOV and .QT files.

```
http://130.91.39.113
```

InterVU   **PreVU**   **Windows 95, NT**

This plug-in feeds your screen streaming MPEG videos as files download. With all the streaming, screaming speed, video still continues to suffer if your modem connection is slower than 56 Kbps. This plug-in may conflict with other video plug-ins. No additional functions are provided with the right mouse button. In addition to HEIGHT, WIDTH, and SRC, the plug-in supports these additional attributes:

AUTOPLAY=YES or NO
FRAMERATE=Number of Frames per Second
LOOP=NUMBER or TRUE
DOUBLESIZE=YES or NO
HALFSIZE=YES or NO
CONBAR=YES or NO
STRETCH=TRUE or FALSE

Additional information can be found at the InterVU home page:

```
http://www.intervu.com/prevu.html
```

Live Update   **Crescendo**   **Macintosh, Windows 95, NT, 3.1**

This plug-in recognizes the .midi file format. Using this format, sound files can be extremely compressed. Standard MIDI files can be created using many music software programs and devices. In addition to SRC, HEIGHT, and WIDTH, Crescendo presently supports one additional attribute:

AUTOSTART=TRUE or FALSE

```
http://www.liveupdate.com/midi.html
```

Iterated Systems   **CoolFusion**   **Windows 95**

CoolFusion supports .AVI files for Windows 95 users. A simple control
panel (Stop and Pause) appears at the bottom of .AVI files, with a second
icon present when using the right mouse button. From the right mouse
button, you can play, rewind, or stop the video; get company and product
information; save the file; or enable the alternate menu (which displays the
second control bar icon). With the second icon, and the alternate menu for
the right mouse button, you can resize the video; change its speed; copy the
video; configure the video display; or send an MCI String Command. No
information was available on which attributes were supported.

```
http://www.iterated.com/
```

Iterated Systems   **Fractal Viewer**   **Windows 95**

Fractal Viewer recognizes the .FIF (Fractal Interchange File) file format. This
format enables you to zoom into pictures and maintain an incredibly high
resolution quality. With the right mouse button you can select a zoom
option; set the color resolution; flip, rotate, scale, and stretch the image;
copy the image or its location; set preferences; save the image or get
information about it; and get information about the company and product.
Check out the company's Web site for attributes. It has a large number of
its own attributes that enable you to protect the file; define the progression
method; align, crop, and rotate the image; and perform other functions.

```
http://www.iterated.com/
```

Macromedia   **Shockwave for Director**   **Windows 95, 3.1, Macintosh**

Of all the plug-ins to be introduced thus far, Shockwave has probably
received the most fanfare. This plug-in allows interactive applications
created with Macromedia Director to be embedded into the HTML page.
Recognizes .DCR and .DIR files. When considering how to animate your
pages, this plug-in is good for larger, more functional applications. For
simpler animations, the download time takes longer than other methods.
Supports SRC, HEIGHT, and WIDTH attributes.

```
http://www.macromedia.com/
```

Macromedia   **Shockwave for Freehand**   **Windows 95, 3.1, Macintosh**

This plug-in supports documents created with Freehand 5.0 and later. This
plug-in is scheduled for release before Summer, 1996.

```
http://www.macromedia.com/
```

Mark Carolan   **Play3D**   **Windows 95**

This plug-in supports a three-dimensional file format, .P3D. It is expected
to be made available through DirectX technology to Explorer by Fall, 1996.
It is presently available as a plug-in.

```
http://www.magna.com/au/pub/users/mark_carolan/HeadsOff.html
```

MDL Information Systems   **Chemscape Chime**   **Windows 95**

This plug-in supports many scientific file formats, including MDL Molfile,
PDB, MSC, XMolXYZ, Gaussian Input, IEMBL Nucleotide Format,
Chemical Structure Markup Language, and others. In addition to the
HEIGHT, WIDTH, and SRC attributes, the plug-in has many of its own
attributes. Check out the following URL for more information.

```
http://www.mdli.com/chemscape/chime/download.html
```

mBED   **mBED Software**   **Windows, Macintosh**

This program integrates well with Java and enables animation on your Web
pages. It supports .MBD files, known as emBedlets. Check their site for tag
and attribute descriptions.

```
http://www.mbed.com/index.html
```

Microcom   **Carbon Copy**   **Windows 95**

This plug-in provides remote PC control functions for Navigator. When two
people share the plug-in, or its stand-alone product, they can treat each
other's files as though they lived on their local disks. Examples are
provided by Microcom for you to try this out with one of their computers.
More information is available from their Web site:

```
http://www.microcom.com/
```

MVP Solutions   **Talker 2.0**   **Macintosh, Windows**

This plug-in takes advantage of Apple's Text-to-Speech software and
enables visitors to hear several computer voice types. Talker recognizes the
.TALK file format, a voice-recognition-based format. In addition to SRC,
WIDTH, and HEIGHT, it also recognizes the PLUGINSPAGE attribute,
which points to the page where Talker can be located on the Web.

```
http://www.mvpsolutions.com/PlugInSite/Talker.html
```

NCompass   **OLE Control Plug-in**   **Windows 95, NT**

NCompass was one of the first plug-ins to become available for Navigator. The plug-in supports OLE objects and controls. The embedded objects are in .OPF file format. Supports HEIGHT, WIDTH, and SRC attributes.

`http://www.excite.sfu.ca/NCompass/nchome.html`

Netscape   **Live3D**   **Windows, Macintosh, Unix**

Netscape's Live3D enables visitors to move around a three-dimensional space using several methods of navigation. Uses .WRL file types. Files are often accessed directly. When used with the <EMBED> tag, BORDER and ALIGN are available in addition to HEIGHT and WIDTH. When accessed directly, a control panel is available at the bottom of the page. You can select the navigate method using the control buttons, as well as get help or reset the VRML file to its original position. The right mouse button enables you to control your navigation method, set the lighting, set the level of rendering, set the screen information display, set user options, and find out more about Live3D.

`http://home.netscape.com/comprod/products/navigator/live3d/index.html`

Progressive Networks   **RealAudio**   **All Windows, Macintosh, Unix**

This plug-in was the first of its kind and competes with, though does not conflict with, Toolvox and others. Supports .RPM files as embedded objects, or .RA and .RAM formats with RealAudio Player. Unlike .AIFF, .AU, and .WAV file formats, plug-ins often use proprietary compression methods. This results in faster loading documents than those made with the traditional methods. RealAudio works as both helper application and plug-in. In addition to SRC, HEIGHT, WIDTH, and ALIGN attributes, RealAudio supports the following:

AUTOSTART=TRUE or FALSE

CONTROLS=ALL/CONTROLPANEL/INFOVOLUMEPANEL/ INFOPANEL/STATUSBAR/PLAYBUTTON/STOPBUTTON/ VOLUMESLIDER/POSITIONSLIDER/ POSITIONFIELD/ STATUSFIELD

CONSOLE=ConsoleName (Used for synchronizing controls)

NOLABELS=TRUE or FALSE

`http://www.realaudio.com/`

RadMedia   **MediaViewer**   **Windows 95, NT, Macintosh, Unix**

RadMedia's multimedia development tool, PowerMedia, supplies the .RAD documents for MediaViewer. This cross-platform application will have plenty of competition in the multimedia plug-in arena. The company is going after many of the same users as Macromedia, Gold Disk, SPC, and others. The development tool and browser can be found at their site:

http://radmedia.com/

SmartBrowser   **HistoryTree**   **Windows 95, Macintosh planned**

This plug-in works more like a helper application in some respects. It loads up when Navigator loads, and enables you to access your entire history, not just the latest limb of your Web surfing, as is typical in browsers.

http://www.smartbrowser.com/

SoftSource   **DWG/DXF Plug-in**   **Windows 3.1, 95, NT**

This plug-in supports SVF, DXF, and AutoCAD file types. SoftSource also provides a development program necessary to create the file types. This plug-in supports both percentage and pixel values for WIDTH and HEIGHT attributes. Many of the attributes that it supports work in conjunction with the right mouse button, which enables you to zoom, pan, manipulate layers, and get product information. In addition to HEIGHT and WIDTH, the plug-in supports SRC and the following:

NAMEDVIEW=VIEWNAME
LAYERON=VIEWNAME1, VIEWNAME2, ETC.
LAYEROFF=VIEWNAME1, VIEWNAME2, ETC.
STATUS="Text for status bar"
ZOOM=TRUE or FALSE
PAN=TRUE or FALSE
LAYERS=TRUE or FALSE
LINKS=TRUE or FALSE

More information can be found on their home page:

http://www.softsource.com/softsource/

SSEYO   **Koan Plug-in**   **Windows 95, 3.1**

This plug-in supports files created by Koan Pro, a digital recording program also available from its Web site. It supports the .SKP file format. Check the Web site for attribute syntax:

http://www.sseyo.com/

Software Publishing   **ASAP WebShow**   **Windows 3.1, 95**

The ASAP WebShow plug-in uses files created by ASAP WordPower, a presentation software program. Beneath the embedded file is a control panel, which can be hidden. This is used to navigate or explode the object to full screen. With the right mouse button, you can go to a specific slide, play and pause the presentation, save the object (if not disabled), print or edit the object, zoom in and out, and get information about the company and product. The presentations are able to take advantage of many custom attributes. The attributes that it supports are the following:

STARTABOUT="ON" or "OFF"
AUTOPLAY="TRUE" or "FALSE"
BGCOLOR=HEXADECIMAL
BORDER=RAISED, RECESSED, SLIDE, SHADOWED, SIMPLE, or NONE
FULLPAGE="ON" or "OFF"
HELP="ON" or "OFF"
MENU="ON" or "OFF"
SAVEAS="ENABLED" OR "DISABLED"
DELAYTIME="12"
EFFECT=Numerous; visit their Web site
BORDER="WINDOW"
ORIENTATION=FREEFORM, LANDSCAPE, PORTRAIT, or X:Y RATIO
DITHERING="ON" or "OFF"
NAVBAR="ON" or "OFF"
NAVBUTTONS="ON" or "OFF"
PAUSEBUTTON="ON" or "OFF"
WIDTH=PIXEL OR PCT
HEIGHT=PIXEL OR PCT
PALETTE=FOREGROUND or BACKGROUND
VSPACE="PIXELVALUE"
HSPACE="PIXELVALUE"
SOUND="URL"
SRC="URL"
LOOPBACK="TRUE" or "FALSE"

More information can be found for ASAP and its attribute usage at the Software Publishing Corporation's Web site:

```
http://www.spco.com/
```

Starfish Software   **EarthTime**   **Windows 95, NT**

This timekeeper plug-in enables viewers to select eight cities worldwide, out of a list of 350 cities, to know what time it is there. EarthTime does not function like most plug-ins. You cannot use it with the embed tag; it uses its own file format, which is referenced directly by the browser. The company also sells personal organizing software, which is what it hopes users will come back for.

```
http://www.starfishsoftware.com/getearth.html
```

Summus   **Wavelet Image Plug-in**   **Windows 95, NT, 3.1**

This plug-in recognizes images that use wavelet compression. Like Lightning Strike, the compressed image averaged approximately 100:1 the size of the original image. Its file type, .WI, is created through a proprietary compression method that Summus offers in the form of a Software Development Kit (SDK). In addition to the HEIGHT, WIDTH, and SRC attributes, the plug-in supports the following:

PROGRESSIVE=TRUE or FALSE
BUFSIZE=Number_of_bytes

Additional information can be found on their site:

```
http://www.summus.com/
```

TMS   **ViewDirector Plug-in**   **Windows 3.1, 95, NT**

This plug-in recognizes many common graphic formats, including .TIF, .JPG, .BMP, .PCX, .DCX, .MIL, .CAL, and .PDA. The right mouse button offers zoom control, the option to save or print the image, the capability to scale the image to gray or smooth its colors, product information, and an advanced feature list for the professional version. In addition to the SRC, HEIGHT, and WIDTH attributes, the plug-in also accepts the BORDER attribute.

```
http://www.tmsinc.com/
```

Totally Hip Software   **Sizzler**   **Macintosh, Windows 95, NT, 3.1**

This plug-in recognizes animations that are generated by the company's development tool. Sizzler supports the .SPRITE file type and WIDTH, HEIGHT, and SRC attributes. More information can be found at the company's Web site:

```
http://www.totallyhip.com/
```

Tumbleweed Software   **Envoy**   **Macintosh, Windows 3.1, 95**

This plug-in works with the Novell-sponsored Envoy file format. Envoy performs a similar function to Acrobat. Tumbleweed Publishing Essentials is the developer kit needed to create Envoy documents, which can be generated from most PC and Macintosh printable file formats. In addition to the HEIGHT and WIDTH attribute, the plug-in supports the following:

INTERFACE=FULL, SCROLL, or STATIC
PAGE=PAGENUMBER
BOOKMARK=BOOKMARKNAME
ZOOM=FITWIDTH, FITHEIGHT, FITPAGE, or ZOOM_IN_PCT
RECT=LEFT, TOP, WIDTH, RIGHT
HORI=FIT, LEFT, CENTER, or RIGHT; PAGE or RECT
VERT=FIT, CENTER, TOP or BOTTOM; PAGE or RECT

Visit their Web site for additional information on attribute usage:

http://www.twcorp.com/

Visual Components   **Formula One/Net**   **Windows 95, NT**

This plug-in enables you to embed a spreadsheet into an HTML document. It supports formulas, functions, and other spreadsheet features, including forms and error checking. The plug-in uses the .VTS file format, but also enables you to work with Excel 4 and 5 file formats, as well as tabbed text documents. Using the right mouse button, you can open and save files, print the spreadsheet; cut, copy, and paste; edit the document, or find information about the company and the product. Presently only uses the HEIGHT and WIDTH attributes.

http://www.visualcomp.com/

VDOnet   **VDOLive**   **All Windows, Macintosh**

This is the first streaming video plug-in to be available for browsers. In addition to the plug-in, the company also makes a stand-alone player as a helper application. With the right mouse button, you can play or stop the video, or get company information. The plug-in recognizes the .VDO file format. In addition to the HEIGHT, WIDTH, and SRC attributes, VDOLive supports the following:

AUTOSTART=TRUE or FALSE
LOOP=TRUE or FALSE
STRETCH=TRUE or FALSE

More information can be found at their Web site:

http://www.vdolive.com/

VREAM   **WIRL Interactive 3D Plug-in**   **Windows 95**

This is another VRML plug-in that supports virtual worlds, but not in the standard file format. WIRL recognizes .VRW files. These are created using VREAM's Development Tool. Supports HEIGHT, WIDTH, and SRC attribute, as well as the NAME attribute. The right mouse button provides file functions, edit functions, world attributes, object attributes, viewer position, device controls, options, and help information.

`http://www.vream.com/`

Voxware   **ToolVox for the Web**   **Macintosh, Windows 95, 3.1**

This plug-in adds streaming audio functionality delivered from any server, and is also available as a helper application. Supports .VOX files. The sound file has a play or stop button, and a speed control when the VISUALMODE is set to EMBED. In addition to the ALIGN, HEIGHT, WIDTH, and SRC attribute, this plug-in also recognizes two of its own attributes:

PLAYMODE=AUTO or USER
VISUALMODE=EMBED or ICON

Other attributes and values for these attributes can be found on their site:

`http://www.voxware.com/`

Wayfarer   **Wayfarer Plug-in**   **Windows 95, NT**

This plug-in supports .WFX files, which are served from a Wayfarer server. Many leading programming languages, such as Visual Basic, Visual C++, PowerBuilder, and Java, are leveraged to match the right tool for the right task. It's even possible to integrate objects from multiple languages and present them as embedded files or with a stand-alone application. In addition to HEIGHT, WIDTH, and SRC attributes, the plug-in also recognizes a MAXIDLEMINS attribute.

`http://www.wayfarer.com/`

In addition to going to Netscape's site for the latest plug-ins, you can also try searching for them with Alta Vista, Yahoo, or other engines. Try "navigator" and "plug" for match words, or "plug-in" as a single word. As more plug-ins and helper applications become available, it is likely that you will find the file types that you are most comfortable with will arrive as embedded objects.

Tips on Using Plug-ins and Helper Applications

When you design pages that use file formats that require plug-ins or helper applications, you are creating documents that visitors with standard browser software alone will not be able to experience. It is up to you to both alert the visitor that this is the case, and to provide a link on your page to the helper application or plug-in that will enable the visitor to interpret the rich media file format.

Using plug-ins and helper applications can greatly enhance the appearance and function of your pages. There is a strong tendency for helper applications and plug-ins to conflict. You can mediate this by only installing plug-ins as needed, and not by reflex. If there is a specific plug-in that you know you will want to recognize one file type, while a conflicting plug-in is needed to recognize another file type, there are two ways to resolve this.

If you already know that you will be needing both plug-ins, install the one needed to view the conflicting file after the one needed to recognize another file type. If the conflicting plug-ins are already installed, reset the browser's helper application preferences or reinstall the plug-in needed to recognize the file type.

As plug-ins become supported in more browsers, you will want to test your pages in programs other than Navigator. Conflicts stemming from partial recognition of tags, as described in Chapter 6, are increasingly likely to occur. Browsers that are able to recognize the <EMBED> tag, but do not support the file type, may display a darkened rectangle or broken icon in place of the embedded object.

Designers need to be especially aware of conflicts arising from more than one helper application or plug-in attempting to recognize a file type, and by those browsers that do not support a particular plug-in. As with all of your code, testing on more than one browser is a good place to start. Including <NOEMBED> tags is all but essential. Including notice on your page that a particular plug-in or helper application is needed is generally appreciated by visitors.

Having a link to the browser(s) that support the object, in addition to the plug-in itself, will help your visitors view the page as you intended. Some plug-in manufacturers, as well as Oracle, have begun to support the PLUGINSPAGE attribute, which will enable visitors to link to the page without going through the effort of finding the page.

Distributed Applications

You were introduced to scripting languages in Chapter 5 with JavaScript, VBScript, and Oracle Basic. This section is dedicated to applications distributed on the Internet, not scripts embedded into the HTML document. The difference is that the scripts are contained within the HTML code, while the distributed applications are written in another language—increasingly Java or Visual Basic.

Java

The Java programming language, developed by Sun Microsystems, has received the most attention thus far as an Internet programming standard. Its features, according to Sun, are its cross-platform portability; secure environment; object-oriented programming; multi-threaded, high performance code; and ease of use. In reality, Java is best learned by C programmers and others with computer programming skills much more advanced than those needed for HTML.

Since its inception, Java has undergone a number of transformations. HotJava, Sun's own browser, originally recognized applets using the <APP> tag. Navigator, Explorer, HotJava, and other browsers now all use the <APPLET> tag. Java can be used to create self-contained applications, or applets, to be distributed over the Internet.

Applets are mini-applications that run within the browser interface. They can either be embedded within the page, or command their own windows, or a combination of the two. Applications, as opposed to applets, run independently of the browser. HotJava itself is an application created using Java.

Java has attracted an enormous amount of attention from software developers. At this time, Borland, Symantec, RogueWave, and others have already come to market with GUI development tools. Using a GUI environment, developers can hope to have much shorter learning curves and be able to create Java applets and applications much quicker than previously.

With all the attention and support given it by major software manufacturers, Java will be here for some time to come. More information can be found from Sun's Java Web site:

```
http://java.sun.com/
```

VISUAL BASIC

There are three strands of Visual Basic that Microsoft currently offers. VBScript is a strict subset of Visual Basic for Applications (VBA). VBA is an application scripting language. Finally, Visual Basic (VB) 4.0 is Microsoft's GUI application development environment, and is the most appropriate for developing distributed applications.

In March of 1996, Microsoft launched the beta version of Internet Explorer 3.0 and ActiveX™ Controls. The latter are the latest evolution of OLE controls and are specifically designed for the Internet. The Microsoft Internet Control Pack consists of eight controls based on Internet protocols.

Microsoft's integration of Visual Basic into its Internet strategy promises to allow many OLE controls to easily migrate into Web pages. This is facilitated using VBScript. The full-featured program, VB, will generally be used to distribute applications that run independently of the browser. An example of VBScript appears in Chapter 5.

This book was completed as these latest product announcements were being made by Microsoft. Additional information can be found on their Web site:

```
http://www.microsoft.com/
```

DISTRIBUTED APPLICATION USAGE

There are several books available on Java and Visual Basic. These can be very powerful tools in expanding the functionality of your HTML pages. Like most of the file formats looked at in this chapter, distributed applications cannot be expected to be seen in all browsers. Notifying your visitors that there is an applet or program available for supporting browsers is a good idea.

Although the advent of Java and Visual Basic are very promising developments for the Web, programming distributed applications requires a much more sophisticated skill set than HTML. For those of you who want to learn more, there are many online resources available, some of which are listed on the CD-ROM.

SUMMARY

The file types introduced in this chapter cannot be expected to be supported in all browsers. There is, however, an increasing number of options available to developers for including rich media in Web site design. Being aware of the limitations and possibilities offered by rich media formats, as well as the HTML needed to avoid display conflicts, should guide your format choice.

Once you have decided to use a plug-in, for instance, try not to forget those that do not have browsers to view the embedded object. The <NOEMBED> tag should always be used when designing Web pages, as should the SRC attribute whenever the DYNSRC attribute of the <IMG> tag is used. Having an image in the place of the animation or other object will enable other visitors to see something—even if it's just a notice saying they need another browser.

If you are concerned about your visitors being able to see or hear your page the way you intended, provide a link to the browser, plug-in, and/or helper application necessary to view or hear the media. Including both the plug-in and helper application will enable those with browsers that do not support plug-ins to experience your Web site.

A large number of online resources are provided on the CD-ROM. There are links to all the programs and plug-ins listed here, as well as many graphics, audio, video, VRML, and programming resources. The World Wide Web has exploded this year to allow far richer page displays than those possible just twelve months ago. Much of the depth and diversity is facilitated through the use of plug-ins and helper applications.

Distributed applications, although not examined in depth here, will be at the center of the new paradigm envisioned by Oracle, Sun, and others. According to them, the computer of the future, the NC, will download applications as needed, and then dispose of them with other elements of RAM when the computer is turned off. Although it is doubtful that the PC is on the way out, distributed applications will become increasingly common throughout the decade.

In addition to file type considerations, there are many issues involved with server interaction. Whether or not you are just trying to get your Web site online, or are wanting to process forms and create image maps, you will need to have some familiarity with server-side issues.

SERVER SIDE ISSUES

HTML is only part of developing a Web site. The rest involves putting your files on a server connected to the Internet. Web servers run on a variety of software programs and operating systems, including Unix, Windows NT, and Macintosh. Each has its own features and limitations, but all of them do essentially the same thing—deliver HTML and other files through the HyperText Transfer Protocol (HTTP) to a "client," usually a browser. In essence, these computers "serve" files to your audience.

Some servers are designed to handle one Web site, others handle many sites simultaneously. The latter are generally run by universities, government organizations, and private companies. The decision to set up your own server or lease space on an established system should be based on your budget and expertise and the requirements of the Web site you build. In the following pages, you'll learn how to select a service provider, when setting up your own server is worthwhile, how to transfer files to a remote computer, and the basics of working with CGI scripts such as image maps and forms.

RUNNING YOUR OWN SERVER VS. USING A SERVICE PROVIDER

Many people setting up a Web site for the first time think they also need to run a Web server, but maintaining a server can be a complicated and expensive process that requires very different skills from developing HTML pages. Unless you are building a large and complex Web site, setting up a server may not be necessary, especially at first.

At the lowest end, a Web server can be set up on almost any desktop computer with a connection to the Internet. On a 14.4 or 28.8 modem, however, such a system will be very slow and require a dedicated connection. At the high end, a good Unix computer, a fast and dedicated Internet connection, and the staff to keep everything working can cost tens of thousands of dollars. The alternative is to find a service provider with an established Web server and lease a small piece of it for your own site, which can cost as little as $20 a month. Some service providers will also enable you to co-locate your own equipment at their location and share the Internet connection.

DOMAIN NAMES AND MOVING A WEB SITE

Registering a domain name for your Web site is one of the first things you should consider, no matter how you put your site online. A domain name serves as a unique and permanent address on the Internet, even if you move to a different Web server later. If you want to see if a domain name is already in use, you can look it up at "http://rs.internic.net/." A domain name also makes your address easier to remember and advertise. If you do not register a domain name, expect your URL to be longer and more complicated, as shown in the following:

```
http://www.serviceprovider.com/businesses/yourname/
```

If you have your own domain name, it might look like this:

```
http://www.yourname.com/
```

The Internic currently charges $100 to register a domain name for two years, and $50 a year after that. Most Internet Service Providers (ISPs) will register a domain name for you for a fee. If you run your own server and want to register the name yourself, be aware that the Internic now requires that you have a second server in place as a backup to register a name. If you don't have a second system in place, you may be able to use an ISP for this purpose. Expect it to take one to three weeks to have a name registered.

Commercial Internet Service Providers

Most ISPs that provide Internet connections also lease Web space. In addition, an increasing number of companies provide server space in conjunction with other services such as custom programming and database management. Most commercial servers lease space to individuals, companies, and other organizations and can set up your access in a few days. Pricing varies dramatically but is generally based on the amount of space you lease on the server and the amount of traffic your site attracts. (References to Web service providers can be found in Appendix E.)

Running a Web server is a relatively new and volatile business and not all companies offer the latest features, such as security or the ability to accommodate a large number of users. Before you select a service provider, consider what you will want on your Web site. Not all servers support database systems or other custom programming, such as CGI scripts for forms and image maps. CGI scripts will be explained in greater detail later in this chapter, but it is important to realize that not all Web servers let you use your own scripts and others may charge to review them before putting them on their server. Technical support also varies, as many service providers do not consider this part of their contract with Web site clients. Before selecting a commercial server, you'll want answers to these questions:

1. **Do they provide technical support? When can you expect to find a knowledgeable person to answer your questions?**

    Technical support can be crucial. Each server has different features and limitations, and it may be hard to know how to use the service if you can't reach their staff. Some service providers have knowledgeable technical support on-call 24 hours a day; others may never answer the phone. A good test is to call several service providers and see how long it takes them to respond to your initial questions. Most service providers offer a place to serve your site, but expect HTML development, scripts, and other options to be your responsibility.

2. What kind of backup systems do they have in place?

Backup systems can be crucial on the Internet where technical problems are common and servers go down regularly. Many providers are still not established well enough to have an alternate computer, on-call technical staff, and an emergency power supply. But if you *have* to ensure that your Web site is always available, it may be worth paying for a high-end server where backup systems are in place.

3. Do they provide CGI scripts and/or limit the use of your own?

Many service providers offer common scripts, such as image maps and basic forms, to all of their Web site clients, and will enable you to use your own scripts. Others may limit your use of scripts or charge you to test them before they will put them on the server. These providers are concerned about security issues and the fact that a poorly written script can slow down the server and even cause it to crash. Some service providers will let you set up your own directory and give you full access to install any CGI scripts.

4. How many Web sites do they serve and how much traffic do they attract?

Even with a very fast connection to the Internet, if the server has too many Web sites, or those sites attract a lot of traffic, you may find your Web site responds at a slower rate. Viewers on a Web server are like cars on a freeway: the more people on the road, the longer it takes to get home. Even if the server has only one other Web site, if that site gets heavy traffic, it may slow down the entire system. On the other side of this issue is the potential that your service provider may ask you to leave or charge you much higher rates if you attract too many viewers. Ask your provider about usage charges, and be prepared to upgrade if you expect a large number of users.

A good way to test the speed of a server before you sign on is to visit a few of the Web sites already on the provider's machine and compare loading times with other service providers. Note that the size of graphics and other files also affects speed—try to compare similar HTML pages on each server.

5. How fast is the server's connection to the Internet?

The speed of a service provider's connection to the Internet will affect how quickly your pages and graphics can be accessed by your viewers. Speeds range from a connection called a T3 line, which allows for transfer speeds of up to 45 Mbps, to a more common T1 line, which yields 1.54 Mbps. Smaller servers may share a T1 line or even run a server through a POTS line (that's Plain Old Telephone Service) with a modem. The faster the connection, the better the server should perform. Some service providers have more than one connection, allowing them to balance the traffic on their servers.

6. Can they set up a secure server? How secure? What software do they use?

A secure server means traffic between the client and server is encrypted. The level of encryption varies depending on the type of service you use. Some common protocols include Secure Socket Layer (SSL), used by Netscape servers, and Pretty Good Protection (PGP), used by Mosaic servers. Expect to pay considerably more for your Web space if you want a secure server. The current range is about $400/month to $2,000/month—and that only gets you the secure server software. If you want password access, for example, you'll probably have to do your own custom programming to set it up. If you want to offer credit card transactions that will be verified online, you'll also need a processing service such as Cybercash. If your provider has established a relationship with these kinds of services, it may be easier and less expensive to arrange.

7. Do they set up a unique directory and CGI directory for your Web site?

Many commercial servers run all of their Web sites through the same server software and put all CGI scripts in one shared directory. While this is probably the most common practice, it can cause problems. As a result, such servers are more likely to restrict your use of custom scripts. If your provider sets up a unique directory for your Web site, however, you should be able to develop and run your own CGI directory. That means you'll have full access for your own scripts.

SELECTING A SERVICE PROVIDER

The questions presented on the preceding pages should provide a basis for determining whether a server fits your unique needs. The answers will vary dramatically and your goal should be to match a provider's services with your Web site and budget. As you look for a server, keep in mind that unlike dial-up connections—where a local phone number will save you long distance phone charges—your Web server does not need to be in the same geographic location. With File Transfer Protocol (FTP) software, you can use a PPP or SLIP account to send files anywhere on the Internet. If you have the opportunity, however, being able to visit the facility is one of the best ways to assess what a service provider has to offer. It's impossible to determine if someone is running a server from their closet or from a penthouse suite just by viewing a Web site online. Legitimate and reliable service providers should be open to letting you see their offices and equipment.

MIRRORING A WEB SITE

If you have a large number of viewers in another geographic area, you may want to make your site available from more than one location. Web sites are "mirrored" by sending copies of the same files to different servers. International companies often set up sites on more than one server and recommend their viewers select the nearest location. This is especially common among software companies because downloading programs uses more resources on the server than viewing HTML pages. As a general rule, the farther a viewer is from a Web server, the longer it takes to retrieve information. If you have a large enough audience, the vast distances allowed by the Internet may be best accommodated by more than one server. If you do this regularly, you may want to find or create a program that automatically sends files to all of the servers you use. Many Web sites are dynamic, changing daily or weekly, and keeping all sites up-to-date can get complicated if you do not have a good system in place. One potential conflict to be aware of: if the servers run on different platforms or use different server software, you may have to do special programming for each one.

Web Site Organization and Relative Links

Good Web site organization warrants some planning. The process of diagramming or story boarding, as it is known in other design fields, is also an excellent approach to Web design. As a site grows, creating new directories for distinct sections, such as organizing issues of a publication in distinct directories named by date, or keeping all commonly referred to files in a folder called resources, is a good way to keep track. Because adding a folder for existing files usually requires changing links, building in several directories in the early development can save time later.

As you develop your HTML pages, you need to keep track of where your directories and files are in relationship to one another in order to set their links. Local links, those that go to HTML documents or other files within your Web site, should be set as relative, not absolute, links. An absolute link might look something like this: <A HREF="http://www.domain_name.com/file_name.html">. A relative link might simply look like this: <A HREF="file_name.html">. Absolute links should be reserved for links to other Web sites. For local files, relative links will work faster for your viewers. If you keep all of your HTML and other files in one folder, all of the links will be that simple: <A HREF="file_name.html">. However, as Web sites grow to hundreds or even thousands of pages, storing all of your files in one folder may make it hard to keep track.

Setting the path for relative links comes easily for people who have worked in DOS or Unix because a text-based operating system forces you to understand the structure of directories. (Note that in DOS, however, the slash marks go the opposite direction. In DOS, you use the backward slash mark \ as a delimiter. In Unix, use the forward slash /.) If you've only worked in Windows or Macintosh operating systems, setting relative links may seem a little confusing at first because you have been sheltered by a graphic interface. Although some new HTML authoring tools (described in Chapter 2) provide a graphic view of local links, it is still important to understand how a site is organized and how links are set.

On the following page, you see a diagram of a simple Web site with examples of how links are created. Essentially the path in the link tag tells the browser where to find the page, graphic, or other file that is described in the HTML reference. Paths are set the same way for links to HTML pages as they are to graphics and other files. To describe the path, you must direct the browser up or down the hierarchy of the Web site, indicating the name of the targeted file, as well as the directories that are between the original HTML file and the one that is linked to it.

SETTING RELATIVE LINKS

An example of the files and directories in a simple Web site is shown below. Use this diagram to see how links are set. Look at the link examples on the left and follow the path through the files and directories on the right. Note that if you want to link to a file within another folder, you need to include the directory name in the path. If the original file is in a sub-directory, use the "../" to indicate the path to a higher level. A link from the index page to the staff file located in the resources folder would look like this: <A HREF="resources/staff.html">; the return link from staff back to index would look like this: <A HREF="../index.html">.

EXAMPLES OF RELATIVE LINKS

Set a link to contact.html from index.html:

```
<A HREF="resources/contact.html">
```

Set a link to index.html from contact.html:

```
<A HREF="../index.html">
```

Set a link to contact.html from staff.html:

```
<A HREF="contact.html">
```

Set a link to staff.html from page1.html:

```
<A HREF="../resources/staff.html">
```

To display logo.gif on the index page:

```
<IMG SRC="graphics/logo.gif">
```

To display staff.gif on the staff.html page:

```
<IMG SRC="../graphics/staff.gif">
```

index.html
resources
contact.html
staff.html
graphics
logo.gif
staff.gif
august_issue
page1.html

WEB SITE ORGANIZATION AND CROSS-PLATFORM ISSUES

Before you send your Web site to a server, it's a good idea to test your links locally. This can be done by simply opening any linked HTML file on your computer with any browser and selecting the links. Be aware, however, that just because your graphics and links work on the hard drive you use to design your Web site doesn't mean they will work on the server you use to put them online. Unix, Macintosh, and Windows computers have distinct naming requirements that can cause problems when you move a site from one computer to another. This surprises many new developers because HTML files are ASCII text and can be opened by any text editor on any computer system.

The most common problems occur when you create a Web site on a Macintosh or Windows computer, and then send it to a Unix server. Because most of the servers on the Internet are Unix machines, you should be aware of one of the biggest differences right away: Unix systems are case-sensitive, and Windows and Macintosh are not. That means that you can create a file called "index.html" and refer to it in your HTML links as "INDEX.HTML" and it will work on a Macintosh or Windows system, but not on a Unix server. Many HTML authors have tested and retested their work locally, only to see all of their links fall apart when it was put online.

Another naming difference for Macintosh users is that file names in a Web site cannot include spaces. Many people use the _ mark to make up for this, creating names such as "the_file.html." A file name with a space, such as "the file.html," will not work on most servers. On a Windows machine, you may be further limited to names with no more than eight characters and a three-digit extension. That means limiting names such as "this_is_too_long.html" to "it_works.htm." Notice that the extension must be shortened to .htm instead of .html. Other extensions must also be shortened, such as .jpeg to .jpg. (For a list of common extensions by platform, see Appendix D.)

If you want to ensure that your Web site will work on any server or hard drive, you may want to limit file names in your Web site, even if you are working on a system that allows greater flexibility. If you start out with the longer file names allowed by Unix and Macintosh, you may face changing every link on the site if you ever want to move it to a Windows machine. This brings up another problem—when you move files from a Windows system to a Macintosh, all of the file names will be changed to capital letters on the Macintosh system.

PUTTING A WEB SITE ONLINE: FTP SOFTWARE

Most Web sites are created on a desktop computer and then transferred to a Web server with File Transfer Protocol (FTP) software. Even if you run your own server, you may use FTP software to send and retrieve files between computers. Many Internet users are familiar with FTP programs because they have downloaded software, often using anonymous FTP to retrieve programs from public sites. Sending files *to* a Web site, however, requires a unique user ID and password. If you use a commercial server, you should be assigned a password when you set up your account so that you can control who has access to your directory. If you are at a university or other organization with its own server, you'll need to get this access information from the system administrator.

There are a number of FTP programs available on the Web for Macintosh and Windows. On Unix machines, FTP functions are generally built into the system software. If you don't have an FTP program, you can download one using a browser such as Netscape. Most of these programs are small (as little as a 300 KB), and simple to install and use. They are easily configured to work with almost any server, and most can store logon information for more than one host computer.

When using FTP software, keep in mind that as you send files to a server, you are making live changes to your Web site. As soon as the new files are loaded, they will be accessible to your viewers. That means you should make changes at off hours, when you know fewer people will be viewing your site. Assuming you haven't made any mistakes, the FTP process shouldn't disrupt your site much because as soon as each file loads, it becomes available to your viewers. Loading time depends on the speed of your connection and the size of the file. Graphics are usually larger and take longer to load, so it's a good practice to load graphic files before you load the HTML pages on which they will appear. That way you avoid the risk that someone will view an HTML page before the graphics get to the server. Some developers create a special directory where they can test files online before linking them to the rest of the site. If you don't do this, it's a good idea to at least test your site with a browser immediately after loading new files. Because FTP programs use little RAM, most computers can run a browser simultaneously. If you keep your FTP program open while you test with your browser, it will be easier to make corrections quickly. This is one place that a small text editor such as SimpleText or Notepad can be handy for quick changes.

FTP programs can be used to upload, download, or delete entire directory trees, sub-directories, and individual files. You must, however, send files to the proper directory on the server. Your home directory will be assigned by your service provider or system administrator and all of your files and sub-directories should reside in that directory. Within your directory, you can organize files and sub-directories in any combination as long as you maintain relative links. Using the sample Web site and links you saw earlier in this chapter, consider that all files must stay in the same relative locations on the server. That means the "index.html" file and directories would be sent to the top level of the home directory on the server. If, as an example, you wanted to send "staff.gif" as an individual file, you would first need to open the "graphics" directory on the server, and then send the graphic into that directory. Within most FTP programs, you can easily move from one directory level to another to ensure your files are sent to the right location and maintain their relative links. Although many FTP programs will enable you to rename or delete a file on a server, most will not let you move the file once it has been uploaded. In the next few pages, you'll learn the basics of the most common FTP programs for Windows and Macintosh and where to find them online.

HTML Developer Tip #1

A new category of commercial Web server has emerged. Designed for those who know little or nothing about HTML, these companies bundle a WYSIWYG HTML editor or form-based development system with FTP software preset for their server. These systems take much of the hassle—and control—out of Web site development. Although some offer high-end services such as secure servers and custom programming, most of these all-in-one development packages are limited to the most basic HTML design, with little or no room for customization.

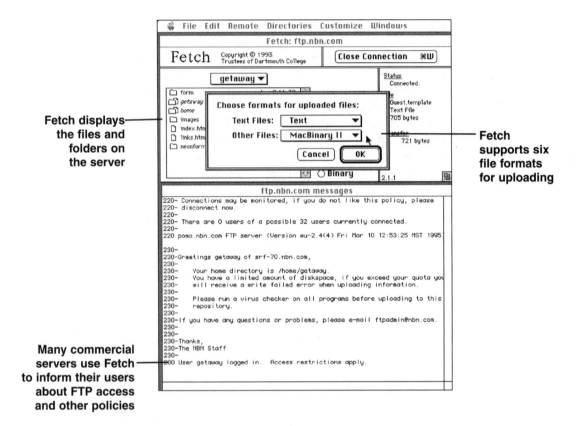

Fetch displays the files and folders on the server

Fetch supports six file formats for uploading

Many commercial servers use Fetch to inform their users about FTP access and other policies

FETCH 3.0

Macintosh

Fetch was created in 1989 at Dartmouth to allow Macintosh computers to take advantage of the University's newly acquired Internet connection. Since then, it has grown to be one of the most popular FTP programs for the Macintosh. Fetch allows point-and-click, drag-and-drop file transfers, and works with any FTP server over a TCP/IP network.

Features include support for multiple connections, bookmark lists, AppleScript, Internet Config, and Open Transport. Fetch also provides Apple Event Object Model support for easier scripting with languages such as AppleScript, Frontier, and others. Fetch is recordable, so writing a script can be as simple as hitting the Record button in your script editor.

Files can be uploaded in AppleSingle, BinHex, and MacBinary II format, as well as the common Text and Raw Data formats. This gives you many options as you send files, but make sure you use the appropriate format for your server. Most Web browsers cannot display files encoded in a format such as MacBinary. You can set the default options in preferences where you can set suffix mapping. To ensure that your files will work, use the "Raw Data" format for graphics and other binary files and the common "Text" option for HTML files. You may use the "Wrapped Text" option, which forces a line break after a specific number of characters. This is usually set to 80 characters, but it can be changed in preferences. This option is offered to prevent text files from loading as one very long line on a Unix machine.

Fetch comes with a list of suffix mappings that relate file-name extensions, such as .html and .gif. You can also add your own. Suffixes are automatically added to all files, unless you change the preferences in the default mappings. Because you should have added suffixes to your files as you created them, you will probably want to turn this feature off. Otherwise, Fetch will add a second suffix as it loads your files on the server.

Fetch can display text files, directory listings, and server messages in its own windows. On the previous page, you see a message from a commercial service provider that is automatically displayed in Fetch each time a Web site is accessed. Fetch only supports simple (userid@host style) proxy servers. Fetch is free to users affiliated with educational institutions or non-profit organizations and may be downloaded as shareware. A single user license costs $25. For more information on Fetch, check out their online users manual, complete with a tutorial and reference topics, at the following:

Dartmouth College, Software Sales. (603) 646-2643; Fax: (603) 646-2810
http://www.dartmouth.edu/

A commercial version is also available through the following:

Adobe, (415) 961-4400 or (800) 833-6687
http://www.adobe.com/

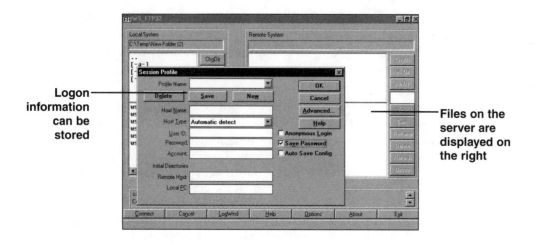

Logon information can be stored

Files on the server are displayed on the right

WS_FTP

Windows

WS_FTP is an FTP application for Windows that offers a point-and-click interface and features such as saving site profile information and facilitating multi-file transfers. A WinSock-compliant application, this program works on Windows 3.x and Windows 95 operating systems.

When you log onto a site, WS_FTP displays the local directories and files in the left half of the screen and the remote server in the right. There are two lists displayed: one on each half of the main window. The top half lists your directories, and the lower half lists files. To transfer multiple files, use the standard window methods of selecting multiple files or directories with the Shift or Control keys. You can also select multiple files by clicking on the first file that you want and dragging the mouse down to the last file in the group. After selecting the desired files, press the transfer button for the function you want to use.

WS_FTP enables you to save logon information for a remote host so that you can return to the server as simply as choosing the host from the list and clicking on the OK button. With this program, as with any FTP program, you must be careful to use the proper File Transfer Modes. For text files, use the ASCII option; for all other files, use Binary. If your server's computer and development machines use the same operating system, you can always use Binary mode.

The simplest way to upload or download files with WS_FTP is to double click on a file name. If you double click on the local file, it will transfer to the server. If you double click on a remote file, it will transfer to your hard drive. If you double click on a remote file, it will be transferred in binary mode to the Windows temporary directory. You can execute a file locally in WS_FTP by clicking on a file name and then selecting Execute.

If the file name has an extension other than .EXE, .COM, .BAT, or .PIF, then the file associations from the file manager are used. If the extension has no association, you will be allowed to specify the association at run time. This association is saved in the WIN.INI file in the Extensions section and will also be valid for the file manager. You can set associations by selecting Options and then selecting Associations.

You can also click on a directory or file to change the name. You can drag one or more files from the Windows file manager anywhere on the main computer and they will be transferred to the current directory of the remote host. You cannot drag and drop directories on the remote computer, however, nor can you drag or drop from the remote host to another application. If you can connect to a remote host, but don't get a directory listing, try changing the host type in the connect or options dialog boxes. "Auto detect" and host types works on about 90 percent of all servers, but may have to be set manually for some systems.

WS_FTP is available for download from many Windows FTP directories. For more information, direct your browser or other appropriate application to the following:

```
http://csra1.csra.net/junodj/ws_ftp.htm
```

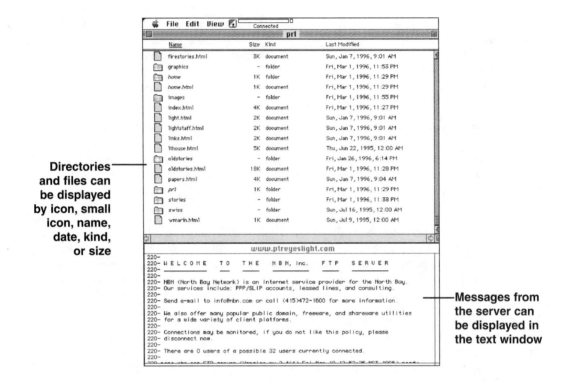

Directories and files can be displayed by icon, small icon, name, date, kind, or size

Messages from the server can be displayed in the text window

SNATCHER

Macintosh

Snatcher is an FTP client designed to look like the Macintosh Finder. A drag-and-drop interface lets you move files and directories from your desktop computer to your server simply by dragging icons around.

Snatcher uses Finder-like windows to display files and folders with the same options as you'll find in the finder in your system software on the Macintosh. You can view the files and directories by icon, small icon, name, date, kind, or size. To transfer files, simply drag and drop icons between Snatcher's display and the finder on your hard drive, and they will automatically upload or download.

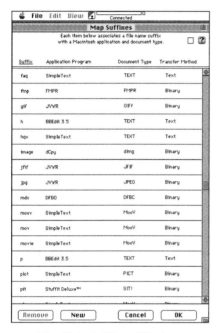

The Map Suffixes Window

Using AppleScript, you can create scripts to perform complicated or recurring actions. Snatcher also handles simultaneous connections, enabling you to send data to several sites at one time and transfer data to and from sites simultaneously. A link manager enables you to create icons representing remote servers so that it is easy to return to them.

You can watch the progress of uploading or downloading in Snatcher's progress indicator. Similar to the one used for copying files in the Finder, it shows items remaining, the speed at which the transfer is taking place, and the estimated time to completion. Expand the progress indicator to show detailed information for individual connections. Using the queuing facility, Snatcher will enable you to cancel individual items, even in the midst of being transferred.

One of the most unique aspects of this program is the ability to view the file size on the server. This is important because many service providers limit your space and will prevent additions to the site if you reach your limit and have not arranged for more space. This feature is useful because file sizes on your hard drive may be different from file sizes on your server. To view file sizes on the server, highlight the file by selecting it in Snatcher's display, and then select Get Info from the File menu. You can also Get Info to see the size, type, location, date of creation, owner, permissions, and URL of any file or folder.

Snatcher requires System 7.0, Macintosh Drag and Drop 1.1, and AppleScript 1.1 (or System 7.5), 800 KB application RAM, 1 MB of free disk space, and a PPP, SLIP, or TCP/IP network connection. For more information, direct your browser or other appropriate application to the following:

> **Software Ventures Corporation,** (510) 644-3232; Fax: (510) 848-0885.
> http://www.svcdudes.com/Welcome.html/

Common Gateway Interface (CGI) Scripts

Many of the interactive features you can implement on a Web site require a Common Gateway Interface (CGI) script. CGI is a standard that was created to provide an interface between programs and World Wide Web servers. This interface allows the server to pass information from the clients to the application with the CGI specification. Adding this interface, CGI took the Web from static HTML documents to dynamic information that can be tailored to each visitor.

From an application as simple as an image map to one that creates dynamic HTML pages from a database, CGI scripts are powerful components of a Web site. Most scripts are form-based, meaning information is entered through an HTML form and then submitted through the browser. Form-based scripts can also be used for numerical calculations, such as a program that tallies a user's purchases. In this case, the script could add the price of each item and generate the HTML necessary to display the total amount in the browser. Search engines can be created by matching a form with a database so that information can be retrieved based on a user's query. Another script could automatically post user responses to an HTML page, creating a simple conferencing system.

CGI scripts may be written in a number of programming languages, including perl, C, C++, TCL, AppleScript, Visual Basic, and any Unix shell programming language. It is difficult to describe CGI scripts generally because they can be written in so many different languages and must be tailored to the operating system and other software on your server. An experienced programmer should have little trouble learning the unique aspects of creating CGI scripts because most of the development issues are the same. If these languages are new to you, however, you'll find that learning to create CGI scripts is significantly more difficult than learning HTML.

Fortunately, most HTML designers don't need to write their own scripts—they simply need to learn to use them. Common scripts, such as image maps and form processors, are provided with most Web server software and may already be available on your server. Using scripts can be as simple as adding a reference line in your HTML document to call a script that can process a form. Some scripts may also require that you create a supplemental file, such as a document with the coordinates and URLs for an image map. Commercial servers often provide a list of scripts for their customers, and some offer special instructions on using them. In the following pages, you'll get a general overview of how scripts work and how to use some of the most common applications.

CGI Scripts: How They Work

When a client requests a URL corresponding to a CGI script, the server executes the application and typically the program will do some actions based on the input from the client and send a response to the browser or another specified destination. Note that if the script is written properly and there are no problems with the Internet connections, the entire process should only take a few seconds. One of the goals in good CGI programming is to create programs that are quickly executed so that information is returned to the browser with no noticeable delay. The example below demonstrates what happens when a simple script is used to handle a guestbook form, sending a confirmation response back to the browser and an e-mail message with the data to a remote computer.

Diagram of a Simple CGI Script in Action

Step One: A message is sent to the server when a visitor submits a form through a browser.

Step Two: That message is received by the server and passed through CGI to the application that will process it.

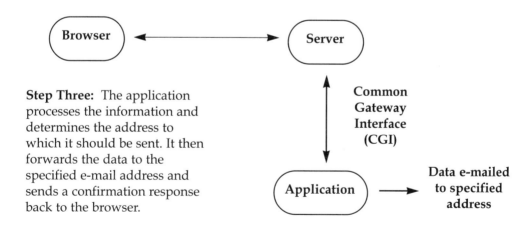

Step Three: The application processes the information and determines the address to which it should be sent. It then forwards the data to the specified e-mail address and sends a confirmation response back to the browser.

CGI SCRIPTS

There are dozens of CGI scripts freely available on the Internet, but many still require knowledge of the programming language they were written in because they will need to be tailored to your server and unique project. In addition, CGI applications usually have to be loaded to a special directory on the server, usually called the cgi-bin. Unless you run your own server or have your own CGI directory, you will probably have to request that the system administrator install the script for you. Not all service providers will do this; others may charge a fee for the service.

If you have access to use CGI scripts, but don't know how to write them, you may want to hire an experienced programmer to create or tailor applications for you. Many of the scripts commonly used on the Internet can be written in a few hours by a good programmer and can add valuable features to your Web site. Many service providers have programmers on staff or offer referrals to programmers they work with regularly. This may be the best way to find someone because the programmer will be familiar with the system and requirements of your service provider. As mentioned earlier, it is difficult to generalize about CGI scripts because they can be written in so many different languages and must be tailored to the system and server software on your server's computer. Finding someone who already knows how to work with your server may save you considerable time and money. (A list of other references and available scripts can be found in Appendix E.)

If the CGI script you need is already on the server, you may only need to refer to it in your HTML documents to put it to use. That can be as simple as calling a script for a form at the top of an HTML page. On the following pages, you'll get an overview of how to use a script for an image map, as well as a script that will process a basic HTML form and send the response back in an e-mail message. These examples should serve as a guideline to using scripts, but the HTML and other files you create will have to be tailored to the unique script or requirements of the server you use. To find out what's available on your server, you'll have to talk to your system administrator. Some of this information may be available on your service provider's Web site.

Using an Image Map Script

Although image map scripts may vary from server to server, the basic functions and requirements should be consistent. Unlike client-side image maps, server-side image maps are processed on the server and require a CGI application to make them work. As a result, server-side image maps cannot be tested offline or implemented locally. After you create all of the necessary components of an image map, you'll have to put it online to test it. (Refer to Chapters 4, 5, and 7 for more information on client-side image maps.)

Before you can use an image map script, you need to create a graphic file in GIF or JPEG format and determine the shape and coordinates of the areas you want to link. Using the traditional Cartesian x,y coordinate system, you'll need to chart the coordinates on the image that correspond to each hotspot you want to link. Those coordinates are based on the method, or shape, you use to describe the area. Once you have determined the coordinates, you'll need to create a configuration file that includes their respective link references. The configuration file, HTML page, and graphic file must be properly loaded on the server for the image map to work. (An example of a common configuration file is provided on the following page.)

The areas in an image may be described using the following methods:

> **Default**—This sets the default URL and requires no explicit coordinates. It defines all coordinates not defined by other methods.

> **Circle**—This uses a circle to designate the hot area and requires the coordinates be set at the center and radius.

> **Poly**—This uses a polygon of, at most, 100 vertices to designate the hot area and requires that each vertex is a coordinate.

> **Rect**—This uses a rectangle to designate the hot area and requires the coordinates be set at the upper-left and lower-right corners.

> **Point**—Sets the hotspot closest to a point and requires the specific location of that point as the coordinate.

As you set the coordinates, try to keep the hot areas in the map spread far enough apart so users will clearly know what they are clicking on. There are a number of programs available on the Internet that will help you find these coordinates. Some provide a WYSIWYG editing environment, where you can select a shape from the tool palette, click on the area of the image you want to make hot, and use the mouse to create the shape to cover the area you want to indicate on the image. Once you have defined the area, these programs determine the x,y coordinates automatically. Some will even prompt you to enter the URL for the link and create a basic configuration file. (For a list of links to image map programs, see Appendix E.)

Image maps may include relative or absolute URLs and may be used to call local files, other Web sites, or as a mailto link. Within the configuration file, methods and coordinates are prioritized in the order in which they are listed. If you have overlapping areas, such as a polygon inside a circle, you should list the one you want evaluated first in the configuration file. It is not good practice to use the default method with the point method because if even one point is specified, anywhere you click may be considered close to the point. That means the URL specified by point will be given priority for retrieval.

As an example, consider the image map application included with the NCSA server software package, a common system on Unix servers. Within the HTML document where the image appears, you will have to add a reference to the CGI script. The following is an example of what that reference line could look like. If you are not sure what the path is, you may have to ask your system administrator.

```
<A HREF="http://www.service_provider.com/cgi-bin//home/imagemap/your_map.map">

<IMG SRC="/graphics/cool_map.gif" ISMAP></A>
```

The configuration file that must accompany your HTML document has to include the method, URL, and coordinates. Here is an example:

```
default /directory/any_file.html

circle link1.html  110,91, 22
rect link2.html  20,21  77,101
rect http://www.domain name.com 117,122 175,158
```

The first line of the configuration file on the previous page specifies the URL to be called if the region of the image selected does not correspond to any of the stated methods and coordinates. The following lines specify a circle and two rectangles as the methods, followed by their respective URL references and finally their coordinates. It is important to note that on many servers, you cannot put your configuration map file at the top level of the directory because the image map CGI script may have trouble referencing it. If you are having trouble getting your image map to work, try placing your map file in a subdirectory or in the CGI directory.

Again, remember that each server may have different requirements. On a CERN server that comes with the htimage script, your image map should look something like this:

```
default /cgi-bin/file_name.html


rect (20,21) (77,101) /example/file.html
poly (89,23) (132,23) (132,65) (90,23) /example/file2.html
circle (25,75) 25 /example/file2.html
rect (245,86)   (504,143) mailto:yourname@server.com
```

Anytime you are working with scripts, it's a good idea to test your work before it is available to your users. A good way to do this is to set up a test directory on your server so that you can run CGI scripts to make sure they work before linking them into your site. Testing an image map is pretty simple. Load the HTML, graphic, and configuration files, view the page in a browser that supports server-side image maps, click somewhere on the image, and see what happens.

HTML Developer Tip #2

Client-side image maps offer a new alternative to the server-side variety. If your users have browsers that support client-side image maps, you may want to consider them as a simpler, and often faster, alternative. Better yet, use both, so that your users who can take advantage of client-side image maps have the opportunity without excluding viewers with limited browsers. (For more on client-side image maps, see Chapter 7.)

USING A BASIC FORMS SCRIPT

Forms scripts are commonly used to create guestbooks, collect market research, or take orders on a Web site. Creating an HTML form is pretty straightforward once you understand the tags required to create radio buttons, textboxes, and other features. (For information on how to create HTML forms, see Chapter 3.) After you create the form, you'll need a script to process the data your visitors enter with their submissions. As with all of the scripts that are discussed generally in this chapter, the unique aspects of your server and the programming language used to create the application will determine how you interact with the script. In the following pages, you'll learn the basics of how to use common forms scripts.

A simple form script could put the information entered into a form into an e-mail message and forward it to a specified address, usually sending a simple confirmation page back to the browser. If your server provides a forms-processing script, you may only need to reference the script in a line at the top of your HTML file to put it to use. Again, depending on the script, you may also need a configuration file to indicate the e-mail address and other unique functions. The following is an example of how the reference could appear in the HTML document:

```
<FORM METHOD="POST"
    ACTION="/cgi-bin/form_process.pl/home/directory/form/Guest.conf">
```

The first thing you may notice is the method. Forms may use either the "POST" or "GET" methods. Which one you use depends on the script, but "POST" has emerged as the more common option for basic forms processing. Next you notice the action value that is the URL for the CGI script. When you write the HTML code for a form, each of your input fields must have a corresponding symbolic name NAME=VALUE relationship. When your user types data into the input areas of the form, the NAME value is encoded with the form data. Thus, form data consists of NAME=VALUE pairs. When an e-mail is sent as a result of the script, the NAME is matched with the data so you can see what category on the form corresponds with each user entry. When you create a form, NAME=VALUE pairs are usually defined as part of the script, but each CGI program may have its own unique requirements.

A BASIC FORM

On the following pages, you see an example of a simple form in HTML code, the e-mail message that was returned, and the configuration that directed it to the proper e-mail address. The HTML page and e-mail response are shown below.

```
<HTML> <HEAD><TITLE>Guest Book</TITLE></HEAD>
<BODY>

<FORM METHOD="POST"
          ACTION="/cgi-bin/form_process.pl/home/prl/coastal/form/Guest.conf">

<CENTER><H1>Guest Book</H1></CENTER>

<TABLE>
<TR><TD>First Name:</TD>
    <TD><input type="text" size=45 name="First_Name"><br></td></tr>

<TR><TD>Last Name:</TD>
    <TD><input type="text" size=45 name="Last_Name"><br></td></tr>

<TR><TD>Email address:</TD>
    <TD><input type="text" size=30 name="Email"><br></td></tr>

<TR><TD valign=top>Comments:</TD>
    <TD><input type="text" size=45 name="comments"><br><br></td></tr>

</TABLE></FORM></BODY></HTML>
```

E-MAIL RESPONSE WITH DATA

This information request was submitted from your Web site.

First name: Janine

Last name: Warner

E-mail address: janine@well.com

Comments: This is a cool form.

The Configuration File

The configuration file below is called "Guest.conf," and contains the mailto reference indicating where the data should be sent. Guest Book is entered as the mailsubject and will appear in the subject line of the message, and the template line refers the script to the template file displayed below. Not all forms scripts require a template, which is generally used to organize the data in the e-mail message. The success_message controls the response to the browser, usually thanking the user for submitting the form. After the success_message line, you can enter any text you want, and can use HTML code to insert formatting and links at the end of the confirmation message.

```
MAILTO name@serviceprovider.com
MAILSUBJECT Guest Book
TEMPLATE /home/your_directory/form/Guest.template
SUCCESS_MESSAGE <BR>
<HR>
<CENTER><A HREF="/home/directory/index.html">Back to main
page</A></CENTER>
```

Template Files

Some forms scripts also require a template file. This file arranges the order and any other message that should appear in the e-mail with the forwarded data.

This information request was submitted from your Web site.

First name: &First_Name

Last name: &Last_Name

E-mail address: &Email

Comments: &comments

Only the name=value fields matter to the script. As you can see, the name=value is indicated by the &. Notice that this file corresponds to the HTML code on the previous page.

Web Statistics and Determining Your Audience

Hit statistics report the number of times your pages were requested by a browser. Many Web sites include a script that calculates the number of requests and displays it at the top or bottom of the page. Hit statistics can be very misleading because they represent the number of requests made on a page, not the number of visitors. It's important to understand that each page may count as more than one request. Hit statistics are generally counted in this way: one request for each page, another request for each graphic on the page, and still another request for each external link. That means that a page with five graphics and two external links will register eight hits each time one user requests the page. If you are using frames, each document called into a frame window will also be counted.

The software on your server should be capable of recording the number of requests your Web site receives, and most service providers make that information readily available to their clients. Some also record where those users come from and will provide you with a report listing the domain names for all of your visitors. With that information, it is possible to get a good idea of what browsers are landing on your site simply by noting that they came from aol.com or compuserve.com.

Many scripts have been written to determine the exact browsers, including version numbers, of the users at a site. There are many places on the Web that claim to report the percentage of Web surfers using the various browsers. If you want to know exactly what's happening on your site, however, you'll need your own script. With a more complex script, it is also possible to direct users to HTML pages designed specifically for that browser. Using the hybrid HTML techniques described in Chapter 6, such practices should not be necessary. But if you are determined to design for a specific browser, you can write a script that directs users to the appropriate page when they access your site. It is also possible to create a script to determine the user's system software. If you are concerned about color palettes or other differences among platforms, you may also want to direct users to different HTML pages based on their system software and hardware.

SUMMARY

After learning the basics of working with a Web server, you should have all the information you need to get your Web site online. Remember, good Web site organization is a key ingredient to ensuring your links will work on the server. Make sure you understand the limitations or special requirements of your server, such as case sensitivity in file names and extensions. Test your work locally before sending it to the server, and consider creating a special test directory for scripts and other functions that only work online.

When working with CGI scripts, keep in mind that programming languages and server software will affect how you interact with scripts. If you are unsure about what is available on a commercial server, check their Web site. Many service providers list the scripts they offer to their clients and provide basic instructions on how to use them. If you have no programming background and want to have sophisticated features, such as search engine, consider hiring an experienced programmer to do it for you.

Selecting an appropriate server is an important first step toward ensuring you'll be able to add all of the features you want to your Web site. If you know you will want access to common scripts, for example, make sure your service provider offers them. If you want to use your own programs, you'll want to confirm that your service provider will let you put them in a cgi-bin or other directory where you can use them. Service providers vary dramatically and there are many options available on the Web. The questions provided in this chapter should help you as you consider where to put your Web site. If you decide to run your own server, you'll need information that is specific to the platform you are using and the server software you use with it. There are many software packages available to run a Web server: some are available for free; others cost thousands of dollars.

Consider registering a domain name early in the development process as it can take up to three weeks to get it confirmed. And remember, one of the best reasons to get a domain name is that you can always move your site to a new server later without having to changing your address with your users.

ON THE HORIZON

You can anticipate a continuing need for hybrid HTML development in the foreseeable future. Many visitors to your Web pages will be using the latest browser versions, while many others will stick to older browsers. You will also need to consider how file type and size, bandwidth, and other issues affect the content in your design.

Throughout this book, you have been taking advantage of the latest HTML tags and extensions to the browser. Using hybrid design techniques, you have learned to mitigate potential display conflicts in multiple browsers. If you have arrived at this final chapter after reading through the first eight, it can be assumed that you are, indeed, a highly skilled Webmaster.

It is important as a master of any art to be current on trends and events that affect your craft. In no craft is this more true than the art of the Web. In the very near future, you will see style sheets, fonts, VRML functions, chat functions, and others included in browser features. You will see a growing number of sites supporting high-bandwidth content. And you will see companies spending billions of dollars competing to set the standards of this new era.

THE EVOLUTION OF HTML

In early 1996, several events occurred that will affect the evolution of HTML. The World Wide Web Consortium (W3C), supported by Netscape, IBM, Microsoft, and others, agreed to a standard for style sheets. Style sheets enable HTML developers to specify font face, size, leading, and other typographic controls, and associate them with individual styles. Up until this point, this has not been possible due to the different font types in multiple operating systems. It should be noted that Marc Andreessen and others had suggested the inclusion of style sheets since at least 1993.

Two competing font technologies have arrived to make cross-platform style sheets possible. Netscape, Adobe, and Apple have joined to offer one font alternative, while Microsoft has proposed another. The first group integrates the technologies behind Adobe Type 1 and Apple TrueType fonts into HTML design; the second brings Microsoft's TrueType technology to the Web. The degree to which you can hope for compatibility between the font types remains to be seen.

A potential Trojan Horse in the middle of it all could be Bitstream. Their OpenType technology enables font shapes to be replicated in any operating system with very small file sizes. Their new technology is supposed to work with any of the existing browsers and font systems, and will be available by Summer, 1996.

Working with competing font systems is one potential source of conflict for HTML authors. Another is the continuing stratification of HTML design. The W3C is supposed to be the grand arbiter of HTML specifications. However, browser manufacturers, such as Netscape and Microsoft, have been introducing their own tags at a much quicker rate than those proposed by the W3C.

Initially, Navigator's innovations were adopted by the W3C and soon copied by other browser vendors. By the end of 1994, however, the W3C began to resist the new changes introduced by Netscape. It seemed as though they were following the lead of Netscape, rather than the other way around. When Netscape introduced the <CENTER> tag, which performed the same function as the <P ALIGN=CENTER> tag of HTML 3, the lockstep relationship appeared to end.

By the end of 1995, more browsers supported the <CENTER> tag of Netscape than the <P ALIGN=CENTER> tag of the W3C. During this time, Navigator introduced frames. Although the opportunity was there for the W3C to adopt the tag, it chose not to, even though two of Netscape's primary competitors, Microsoft and Oracle, had chosen to support it.

It must be noted that the majority of the HTML 3.0 proposed specifications have not been adopted by any of the major browsers. The <MATH>, <FIG>, and <INSERT> tags are three of the more visible that have not yet been implemented. The Portable Network Graphics (PNG) file format is another example of the failure of the W3C to set the path for others to follow. It has thus far been the case that tags have become standardized after appearing as a feature in the market leader first, rather than as a result of the W3C debate.

As this book was being completed, Explorer 3.0 was just being released. Microsoft, like Oracle, has pledged to recognize Netscape's plug-ins (although this was not yet functional in their beta version). As more and more browsers rush to support each other's tags, partial recognition of tags is likely to increase due to differences in browser architectures. Partial recognition will stem from both file type and attribute incompatibilities (see Chapter 6).

Up until this point, Netscape has set the trends in tag recognition and many other browser features. With the introduction of ActiveX objects, however, Microsoft may have finally arrived with something worth copying. It may be the case that the objects will be able to be integrated as easily into Navigator's architecture as into Explorer's. It is not yet clear how Netscape plans to respond to Microsoft's move. With the release of Navigator 3.0, Netscape has already demonstrated that it can follow Microsoft's lead in supporting the BGCOLOR attribute of the table tags. It is likely that the company will continue to implement the formats of the W3C, as well as those of other browsers.

Security on the Internet will also influence browser choice. Both Netscape and Microsoft have been pushing forward with their own security protocols, which are each optimized for their own browser. VISA and MasterCard have joined forces to back Secure Electronic Transactions (SET), which Microsoft has also pledged to support. It is too early to see how security will affect browser choice, though it will certainly be a concern for companies.

Browser features, such as chat functions and VRML recognition, have been promised by the end of the year. These features are presently available using plug-ins or helper applications. Once browsers support the features without the need for the browser extensions, designers will be able to take further advantage of virtual worlds and group surfing. Keeping up on news releases of the major browser manufacturers and checking the browser FTP sites regularly for the latest versions will help you to stay on top of rapidly changing Web developments.

NEW HTML DESIGN STRATEGIES

Stratification in HTML tag recognition will continue to pressure Webmasters to design hybrid Web sites. There is no substitute for testing your pages in multiple browsers to make sure that the combination of tags that you use does not become unreadable. The <SCRIPT> tag, for instance, should almost always be included in the <HEAD> section. The <EMBED> tag should always have a <NOEMBED> tag. These strategies were discussed in Chapters 5 and 6.

Another strategy has to do with the file type that you select to perform a particular function. Once you have decided to animate a page, for instance, there are several ways to implement that feature. If you require no audio, your choices could be to use the Emblaze plug-in by GEO, an animated GIF, the Shockwave plug-in by Macromedia, Java, the <META> tag, and several other proprietary presentation methods. Factors that influence your choice include browser demographics of your audience, the type of animation, and the size and speed of different Web media.

If your animation is not very complex, and contains no interactivity (i.e., no clickable areas within the animation), then you will probably want to use Emblaze or the animated GIF. The Emblaze document is supportable in browsers that recognize the NSAPI architecture. With the animated GIF file, most browsers will support the first or last frame. The Emblaze document is much richer and more efficient in its compression than the animated GIF, but the animated GIF is supported in more browsers (although it is not animated in most).

The Shockwave document would probably not be your first choice due to the relative time lag it has when loading. The same applies to Java. Loading an applet takes time, even if it is efficient after it has been loaded. If your animation was bigger, interactive, or with sound, Shockwave and Java would definitely be considerations. Remember that when you use the <EMBED> tag, inserting a <NOEMBED> tag containing an image will provide display for other browsers.

It is strongly recommended to test various methods to deliver the media that you want to embed in your HTML document. Much of your testing could consist of checking out other people's documents to see how they load. If you see how the different file types are treated by one or more browsers, it may influence you to select one method over another. The important thing to remember is that all of these file types are evolving. What is true today may not be true tomorrow. Once you have settled on your file format, make sure you have a reference on your page to the browser(s) and helper application or plug-in necessary to view your document.

In addition to developments in HTML, companies such as Quark, Powersoft, Oracle, and others are introducing new document types independent of Web browsers. QuarkImmedia is a product that will be released during the first half of 1996. This program enables QuarkXPress users to create interactive documents similar to Director. The viewer will be distributed freely, while the developer product will cost about the same as QuarkXPress.

Powersoft's media.splash is both a helper application and plug-in. This new media type will take advantage of Sybase and Powersoft technologies, and integrate them with a graphical design interface. You will then be able to make documents that are visually rich and sophisticated in their performance of database functions. Oracle's Media Objects has also been promised as a plug-in, though now it can be used for creating stand-alone applications.

Demographics: Browsers and Bandwidth

When designing HTML in the coming year, you will be more and more concerned with two demographic issues: which browser supports the file type or HTML formatting required in your pages; and what size files your pages will require. The first of these has been the focus of this book. The latter involves modem connection speed and download time.

You have learned how to design sophisticated pages, while maintaining a page for browsers that do not support particular tags or file types. This has been facilitated through tags like <NOEMBED> and <NOFRAMES>, as well as through attributes like DYNSRC. As long as you continue to use these tags and attributes in the manner prescribed in Chapters 5 and 6, you will not have to worry too much about supporting multiple browsers. Problems may arise when a browser supports a tag, but not an attribute or file type, but if you follow the techniques discussed within, your pages should be relatively resistant to unacceptable browser displays.

Bandwidth refers to the size of the modem connection to your computer. With existing technology, the fastest modems using telephone lines operate at 28,800 bits per second, or 28 Kbps. In a growing number of cities, Integrated Services Digital Network (ISDN) lines are now available. Their capacity is 128 Kbps, although many connecting devices only support slower transmission speeds, like 112 Kbps or 56 Kbps.

At the high end, there are frame relay connections, which are in multiples of 56 Kbps; T1 connections, which are 1.2 megabits; and cable modems, which operate at over a megabit per second. Of these, the cable modem is the most likely to be adopted by a wide commercial audience due to existing cable television infrastructure.

Hand-in-hand with bandwidth issues is the issue of compression. As compression methods advance, and file size and loading times decrease, even slower connections will provide richer Web pages. AT&T has announced a compression method that is supposed to give full-frame, full-motion video over standard telephone lines. Progressive Networks and Microsoft have made a similar announcement.

An important consideration for designers is that you will generally need to create a duplicate site to support high bandwidth content, if you intend to publish pages for mass consumption. Consider the following workaround:

```
<EMBED HIGHBANDWIDTH="fullmovie.dcr" SRC="lowresmovie.dcr">
```

In this case, the HIGHBANDWIDTH attribute loads the "fullmovie.dcr" file if the modem connection is over a certain threshold. (This doesn't exist, so don't start using the attribute!) For high-bandwidth sites, hybrid HTML methods can generally be ignored, as you will probably be designing for a single browser. For its low-bandwidth counterpart, however, the hybrid HTML methods introduced in this book will help you to be more inclusive in your Web site design.

As you use larger file sizes and more sophisticated compression methods, it is very important to notify your visitors of the special browser or software needed to fully experience your Web page. It will often be the case that your visitors will need guidance through the installation process. You may want to either include instructions on your site, or provide a link to the instructions page on the site of the software manufacturer.

One high-bandwidth content company to watch in the future will be @Home. As cable modems are introduced into major metropolitan areas over the next 18 months, you can expect to see an increasing amount of high-bandwidth content on the Web. At this point, only ISPs and corporations that require the use of large file transfers will be demographically targeted with many of the rich media documents. Until high-bandwidth infrastructure is in place, you can expect the volume of rich media content on the Web to remain relatively minimal.

Once technology and economy-of-scale production catch up, you can expect to see full-screen, full-animation, full-sound, virtual wonderlands cascade from your computer monitor. At the rate that things are changing, that point will arrive within the next two years, if not sooner. When that occurs, the integration of entertainment, information, communications, and other industries will be far more evident.

SUMMARY

As new technologies become available, and browser features proliferate, an increasing number of options become available to HTML developers. As the Netscapes, Microsofts, and Oracles of the world continue to wage browser battles, Web wars, and server slug-outs, there is no need for the designer to suffer from such fratricide.

The competition for standards on the Web is taking place at many levels. It's not just the browser, the server, the fonts, the tags, the file formats, and the protocols—it's all that and more. Industries that have not yet even been conceived will be strongly influenced by the standards wars of today. As consumers and designers, all of us can hope to benefit from the richness of products spawned by such fierce competition. We can also anticipate suffering from inevitable monopolies and oligopolies forming in cyberspace, if these are not kept in check.

Over the last several years, the Web has become increasingly commercialized and stratified. Popular sites now have advertising—visitors often arrive to see icons stating that the site is best viewed with a single browser. The commercial advertising that now appears on Web sites has helped to drive the growth of the Web industry. This has created or contributed to several other fields, such as iconography, image design, CGI programming, and others.

Following the guidelines set forth in *Hybrid HTML Design*, you can take control of this new medium and prepare for the inevitable evolution of the Web. As you become familiar with the functionality that exists and that is coming available, it will be apparent that you will be working with other professionals for much of the rich media content in your Web pages. Familiarizing yourself with the limits and tradeoffs of each of the media file formats you seek to incorporate will help you communicate effectively with the individuals responsible for creating them.

Being a Webmaster requires not only learning the skills you need today to create rich Web pages. It also requires that your education process be an ongoing commitment. Your visitors and clients will demand it. The more you are able to be proactive in both mitigating display conflicts and incorporating multimedia effects, the more your audience will appreciate your design skills. As things change very quickly in cyberspace, the only way that you will continue being able to do this is by keeping yourself up to date with ongoing developments.

This book is accompanied by appendices and a CD-ROM that will help you today and into the future. The links from the CD's Web site will lead you to sites that will be even more current than the software on the CD itself. Many of the products are beta versions or demo versions, and you are encouraged to go online yourself to make sure you have the most current version.

Additionally, the book is supported by a Web site at the following URL:

```
http://www.browserbydesign.com/
```

This site will have updates to the chapters within, as well as information about new editions, online resources, and other tips and pointers for HTML developers. Please feel free to stop by and check out the latest updates to the book. Any comments you have about this book can be directed through the Web site, or through New Riders Publishing.

Appendices

APPENDICES

The appendices are intended to extend the information provided in the book, as well as to provide a quick reference for Web site designers. Appendix A, "HTML Tag and Attribute Support," provides a comprehensive list of all known HTML tags and the browser where they were first introduced. Appendix B, "HTML Editors," details the level of HTML support available in the Text and WYSIWYG editors from Chapter 2.

Appendix C, "Special Characters," lists all the special characters formed by numbered HTML descriptions, or with HTML entities. Appendix D contains a listing of various MIME types. Finally, Appendix E references a large number of online resources for additional information—this appendix is broken into several categories, including browsers, browser resources, HTML, Java, JavaScript, audio, video, and others.

Many of the HTML tags listed in Appendix A were introduced by Netscape and have been referred to here as HTML 2 or HTML 3 tags. This certainly does not attempt to downplay the contribution made by Netscape in the evolution of HTML tag design. It is an effort to show how tags, once accepted by all players, become standards. Many of the tags introduced by a single company are replicated by others, often in favor of the HTML 3 specifications.

In addition to the resources in the appendices, the CD-ROM has many software products and its own Web site that links to many online destinations not listed in this book. You can also visit "http://www.browserbydesign.com/" for updates to the information contained in this book. If you have comments or suggestions for inclusion in later editions, send them to the following:

authors@browserbydesign.com

APPENDIX A
HTML TAG AND ATTRIBUTE SUPPORT

Tag / Attribute	Name	Origin	A	B	C	D	E	F	G	H	I	J	K	L
`<A></A>`	Anchor	HTML 2	X	X	X	X	X	X	X	X	X	X	X	X
NAME=String		HTML 2	X	X	X	X	X	X	X	X	X	X	X	X
HREF=URL		HTML 2	X	X	X	X	X	X	X	X	X	X	X	X
REL=Relationship		HTML 3	-	-	-	-	-	-	-	-	-	-	-	-
REV=Reverse Relationship		HTML 3	-	-	-	-	-	-	-	-	-	-	-	-
TARGET=Target Frame Name		Netscape	X	X	-	O	-	O	O	O	O	O	O	O
TITLE=Title of Name		HTML 3	-	-	-	O	-	O	O	O	O	-	O	O
`<ADDRESS></ADDRESS>`	Address	HTML 2	X	X	X	X	X	X	X	X	X	X	X	X
`<APP>` Discontinued		HotJava	-	PL	PL	X	-	-	-	-	-	-	-	-
`<APPLET></APPLET>`	Applet	Netscape	X	X	X	X	X	X	X	X	X	X	X	X
CODEBASE=URL		Netscape	X	X	O	X	O	O	O	O	O	X	O	X
CODE=URL		Netscape	X	X	O	X	O	O	O	O	O	X	O	X
ALT=String		Netscape	X	X	O	X	O	O	O	O	O	X	O	X
NAME=String		Netscape	X	X	O	X	O	O	O	O	O	X	O	X
WIDTH=Pixel Value		Netscape	X	X	O	X	O	O	O	O	O	X	O	X
HEIGHT=Pixel Value		Netscape	X	X	O	X	O	O	O	O	O	X	O	X
ALIGN=Left/Right/Center/*		Netscape	X	X	O	X	O	O	O	O	O	X	O	X
HSPACE=Pixel Value		Netscape	X	X	O	X	O	O	O	O	O	X	O	X
VSPACE=Pixel Value		Netscape	X	X	O	X	O	O	O	O	O	X	O	X
`<AREA>`	Area	HTML 3	X	X	X	-	O	O	O	O	O	X	O	X
COORDS=X,Y		HTML 3	X	X	X	-	O	O	O	O	O	X	O	X
HREF=URL		HTML 3	X	X	X	-	O	O	O	O	O	X	O	X
NOHREF		HTML 3	X	X	X	-	O	O	O	O	O	X	O	X
SHAPE=RECT/CIRC/POLY/*		HTML 3	X	P	P	-	O	O	O	O	O	P	O	X
`<B></B>`	Bold	HTML 2	X	X	X	X	X	X	X	X	X	X	X	X
`<BANNER></BANNER>`	Banner	HTML 3	O	X	X	X	O	O	O	O	O	O	O	O
`<BASE>`	Base	HTML 3	X	X	X	X	X	X	X	X	X	X	X	X
HREF=URL		HTML 3	X	X	X	X	X	X	X	X	X	X	X	X
TARGET=Target Frame Name		Netscape	X	X	O	O	O	O	O	O	O	O	O	O
`<BASEFONT>`	Basefont	Netscape	X	O	-	O	O	O	O	O	O	O	O	O
COLOR=Hexadecimal or COLOR Name		Netscape	PL	X	-	O	O	O	O	O	O	O	O	O
FACE=Font		Microsoft	PL	X	-	O	O	O	O	O	O	O	O	O
SIZE=1-7; 1 is smallest; 7 is largest		Netscape	X	X	-	O	O	O	O	O	O	O	O	O
`<BGSOUND>`	Background Sound	Microsoft	O	X	-	O	O	PL	O	O	O	O	O	O
SRC=URL		Microsoft	X	X	-	O	O	O	O	O	O	O	O	O
LOOP=INFINITE or Number		Microsoft	X	X	-	O	O	O	O	O	O	O	O	O
`<BIG></BIG>`	Big	HTML 3	X	X	X	O	O	O	O	O	O	X	X	X
`<BLINK></BLINK>`	Blink	Netscape	X	O	O	O	O	O	O	O	O	X	O	O
`<BLOCKQUOTE></BLOCKQUOTE>`	Blockquote	HTML 2	X	X	X	X	X	X	X	X	X	X	X	X

A=Netscape Navigator 3.0; B=Microsoft Internet Explorer 3.0 Alpha; C=Oracle PowerBrowser 1.0; D=HotJava Alpha Release; E=NCSA Mosaic 2.0; F=America Online Windows 2.5; G=CompuServe Spry Mosaic 1.0; H=Prodigy 2.0d; I=Apple CyberDog Beta 2; J=Navigator 2.0; K=Navigator 1.1; L=Internet Explorer 2.0. X=Supports the tag; O=Does not support the tag; P=Partial support; PL=Planned support; "-"=Server-side or N/A. An asterisk indicates additional attributes.

Tag Attribute	Name	Origin	A	B	C	D	E	F	G	H	I	J	K	L
<BODY></BODY>	Body	HTML 2	X	X	X	X	X	X	X	X	X	X	X	X
ALINK=Hexadecimal or COLOR Name		Netscape	X	O	X	O	O	O	O	O	O	X	X	O
BACKGROUND=URL		Netscape	X	X	X	X	X	X	X	X	X	X	X	X
BGCOLOR=Hexadecimal or COLOR Name		Netscape	O	X	O	O	O	O	O	X	O	X	X	X
BGPROPERTIES=FIXED		Microsoft	O	O	O	O	O	O	O	O	O	O	O	X
LEFTMARGIN=Pixel Value		Microsoft	O	O	O	O	O	O	O	O	O	O	O	X
LINK=Hexadecimal or COLOR Name		Netscape	X	X	X	X	X	X	X	X	X	X	X	X
TEXT=Hexadecimal or COLOR Name		Netscape	X	O	O	O	O	O	O	X	O	X	X	X
TOPMARGIN=Pixel Value		Microsoft	O	O	O	O	O	O	O	O	O	O	O	X
VLINK=Hexadecimal or COLOR Name		Netscape	O	X	O	O	O	O	O	X	O	X	X	O
  Line Break		HTML 2	X	X	O	X	X	X	X	X	X	X	X	X
CLEAR=LEFT, RIGHT, ALL		HTML 3	X	O	O	X	X	X	X	X	X	X	X	X
<CAPTION></CAPTION>	Caption	HTML 3	X	O	O	X	X	X	X	X	X	X	X	X
ALIGN=LEFT/RIGHT/CENTER/*		HTML 3	X	X	X	X	X	O	X	X	X	X	X	X
VALIGN=Top or Bottom		HTML 3	X	X	X	O	O	O	O	X	O	X	O	O
<CENTER></CENTER>	Center	Netscape	X	O	O	O	O	X	X	X	O	X	X	X
<CERTIFICATE></CERTIFICATE>	Certificate	Netscape	X	-	-	-	-	-	-	-	-	-	-	-
NAME=Unique Identifier		Netscape	X	-	-	-	-	O	O	X	-	-	-	-
<CITE></CITE>	Cite	HTML 2	X	X	X	X	X	X	X	X	X	X	X	X
<CODE></CODE>	Code	HTML 2	X	X	X	X	X	X	X	X	X	X	X	X
<DD>	Definition Description	HTML 2	X	X	X	X	X	X	X	X	X	X	X	X
<DIR></DIR>	Directory List	HTML 2	X	X	X	X	X	X	X	O	X	X	X	X
<DIV></DIV>	Division	HTML 3	X	O	O	O	O	O	O	X	O	O	O	O
ALIGN=LEFT/RIGHT/CENTER/*		HTML 3	X	-	-	-	-	-	O	-	-	-	-	-
CLASS=String		HTML 3	X	-	-	-	-	O	O	-	-	-	-	-
CLEAR=LEFT/RIGHT/ALL/Pixel Value		HTML 3	X	-	-	-	-	O	X	-	-	-	-	-
ID=SGML Identifier		HTML 3	X	-	-	-	-	-	-	-	-	-	-	-
NOWRAP		HTML 3	X	-	-	-	-	-	-	-	-	-	-	-
<DL></DL>	Definition List	HTML 2	O	X	O	X	X	X	X	X	X	X	X	X
COMPACT		HTML 3	X	O	X	O	X	X	X	X	X	X	X	X
<DT>Definition Term		HTML 2	X	X	X	X	X	X	X	X	X	X	X	X
<EM></EM>	Emphasis	HTML 2	X	X	X	X	X	X	X	X	X	X	X	X
<EMBED>	Embed	Netscape	X	PL	X	O	O	O	O	O	-	-	-	-
ALIGN=LEFT/RIGHT/CENTER		Netscape	X	PL	X	-	-	-	-	-	-	-	-	-
HEIGHT=Pixel Value		Netscape	X	PL	X	-	-	-	-	-	-	X	X	-
PLUGINSPAGE=URL		Oracle	O	O	X	-	-	-	-	-	-	O	O	-
SRC=URL		Netscape	X	PL	X	-	-	-	-	-	-	X	X	-
WIDTH=Pixel Value		Netscape	X	PL	X	-	-	-	-	-	-	-	-	-

A=Netscape Navigator 3.0; B=Microsoft Internet Explorer 3.0; C=Oracle PowerBrowser 1.0; D=HotJava Alpha Release; E=NCSA Mosaic 2.0; F=America Online Windows 2.5; G=CompuServe Spry Mosaic 1.0; H=Prodigy 2.0d; I=Apple CyberDog Beta 2; J=Navigator 2.0; K=Navigator 1.1; L=Internet Explorer 2.0 X=Supports the tag; O=Does not support the tag; P=Partial support; PL=Planned support; "-"=Server-side or N/A. An asterisk indicates additional attributes.

Tag Attribute	Name	Origin	A	B	C	D	E	F	G	H	I	J	K	L
`<FIG></FIG>`	Figure	HTML 3	O	O	O	O	O	O	O	O	O	O	O	O
ALIGN=LEFT/RIGHT/CENTER		HTML 3	-	-	-	-	-	-	-	-	-	-	-	-
CLASS=String		HTML 3	-	-	-	-	-	-	-	-	-	-	-	-
CLEAR=LEFT/RIGHT/ALL		HTML 3	-	-	-	-	-	-	-	-	-	-	-	-
HEIGHT=Pixel Value		HTML 3	-	-	-	-	-	-	-	-	-	-	-	-
ID=SGML Identifier		HTML 3	-	-	-	-	-	-	-	-	-	-	-	-
IMAGEMAP=URL		HTML 3	-	-	-	-	-	-	-	-	-	-	-	-
NOFLOW		HTML 3	-	-	-	-	-	-	-	-	-	-	-	-
SRC=URL		HTML 3	-	-	-	-	-	-	-	-	-	-	-	-
WIDTH=Pixel Value		HTML 3	-	-	-	-	-	-	-	-	-	-	-	-
`<FONT></FONT>`	Font	HTML 3	P	X	P	O	O	O	P	P	O	X	X	X
COLOR=HEXADECIMAL or COLOR Name		HTML 3	O	X	O	X	X	X	X	X	X	X	O	X
FACE=Font		Microsoft	X	X	O	X	X	X	X	X	X	X	X	X
SIZE=1-7: 1 is smallest; 7 is largest		HTML 3	X	X	X	X	X	X	X	X	X	X	X	X
`<FORM></FORM>`	Form	HTML 2	X	X	X	X	X	X	X	X	X	X	X	X
ACTION=URL		HTML 2	X	X	X	X	X	X	X	X	X	X	X	X
METHOD=GET/POST		HTML 2	X	X	X	X	X	X	X	X	X	X	X	X
`<FRAME>`	Frame	Netscape	X	X	X	O	O	O	O	O	O	O	O	O
FRAMEBORDER=YES or NO		Microsoft	PL	X	PL	-	-	-	-	-	-	-	-	-
FRAMESPACING=Pixel Value		Microsoft	PL	X	PL	-	-	-	-	-	-	-	-	-
MARGINWIDTH=Pixel Value		Netscape	X	X	X	-	-	-	-	-	-	-	-	-
MARGINHEIGHT=Pixel Value		Netscape	X	X	X	-	-	-	-	-	-	-	-	-
NAME=String		Netscape	X	X	X	-	-	-	-	-	-	-	-	-
NORESIZE		Netscape	X	X	X	-	-	-	-	-	-	-	-	-
SCROLLING=YES/NO/AUTO		Netscape	X	X	X	-	-	-	-	-	-	-	-	-
SRC=URL		Netscape	X	X	X	-	-	-	-	-	-	-	-	-
`<FRAMESET></FRAMESET>`	Frameset	Netscape	X	X	X	O	O	O	O	O	O	O	O	O
COLS=Pixel Value/Percentage		Netscape	X	X	X	-	-	-	-	-	-	-	-	-
ROWS=Pixel Value/Percentage		Netscape	X	X	X	-	-	-	-	-	-	-	-	-
`<H1...6></H1...6>`	Header 1 through 6	HTML 2	X	X	X	X	X	X	X	X	X	X	X	X
ALIGN=LEFT/RIGHT/CENTER		HTML 3	O	O	O	X	X	X	X	X	X	X	X	X
CLEAR=LEFT/RIGHT/ALL		HTML 3	-	-	-	-	-	-	-	-	-	-	-	-
`<HEAD></HEAD>`	Head	HTML 2	X	X	X	X	X	X	X	X	X	X	X	X
`<HR>`	Horizontal Rule	HTML 2	X	X	X	X	X	X	X	X	X	X	X	X
ALIGN=LEFT/RIGHT/CENTER		HTML 3	O	X	O	X	X	X	X	X	X	X	X	X
COLOR=HEXADECIMAL or COLOR Name		Microsoft	O	X	O	O	O	O	O	O	O	O	O	X
SIZE=Pixel Value		HTML 3	X	X	X	X	X	X	X	X	X	X	X	X
WIDTH=Pixel Value/Percentage		HTML 3	O	X	O	X	X	X	X	X	X	X	X	X
NOSHADE		HTML 3	X	X	X	X	X	X	X	X	X	X	X	X
`<HTML></HTML>`	HTML	HTML 3	X	X	X	X	X	X	X	X	X	X	X	X
`<I></I>`	Italic	HTML 2	X	X	X	X	X	X	X	X	X	X	X	X

A=Netscape Navigator 3.0; B=Microsoft Internet Explorer 3.0 Alpha; C=Oracle PowerBrowser 1.0; D=HotJava Alpha Release; E=NCSA Mosaic 2.0; F=America Online Windows 2.5; G=CompuServe Spry Mosaic 1.0; H=Prodigy 2.0d; I=Apple CyberDog Beta 2; J=Navigator 2.0; K=Navigator 1.1; L=Internet Explorer 2.0. X=Supports the tag; O=Does not support the tag; P=Partial support; PL=Planned support; "-"=Server-side or N/A. An asterisk indicates additional attributes.

Tag / Attribute	Name	Origin	A	B	C	D	E	F	G	H	I	J	K	L
<IMG>	Image	HTML 2	X	X	X	X	X	X	X	X	X	X	X	X
ALIGN=LEFT/RIGHT/CENTER/*		HTML 3	X	X	X	X	X	X	X	X	O	X	X	X
ALT=Text		HTML 2	X	X	X	X	X	X	X	X	X	X	X	X
BORDER=Pixel Value		HTML 3	X	X	X	X	P	X	X	X	X	X	X	X
CONTROLS		Microsoft	O	O	X	O	O	O	O	O	O	O	O	O
DYNSRC=URL		Microsoft	X	X	X	O	X	O	O	X	O	O	O	X
HEIGHT=Pixel Value		HTML 2	X	X	X	O	X	O	O	O	O	X	X	O
HSPACE=Pixel Value/Pct of Image		Netscape	O	O	O	O	X	O	O	O	O	O	O	O
ISMAP		HTML 2	X	X	O	O	X	X	O	X	X	X	X	X
LOOP=INFINITE or Number		Microsoft	O	X	O	O	X	O	O	O	O	O	O	O
LOWSRC		Netscape	X	X	X	X	X	X	X	X	O	X	X	X
SRC=URL		HTML 2	X	X	X	O	X	X	O	X	O	X	O	X
START=FILEOPEN/MOUSEOVER		Microsoft	O	X	X	O	X	X	X	X	X	X	X	X
USEMAP=Map Name		HTML 3	X	X	X	O	X	X	O	O	O	X	O	X
VSPACE=Pixel Value/Pct of Image		Netscape	X	X	X	O	X	X	O	O	O	X	X	O
WIDTH=Pixel Value		HTML 2	X	X	X	O	X	X	O	O	O	X	X	O
<INPUT>	Input	HTML 2	X	X	X	O	X	X	X	X	X	X	X	X
ACTION=URL		HTML 3	X	X	O	O	X	X	X	X	X	X	X	X
ALIGN=TOP/MIDDLE/BOTTOM		HTML 3	X	X	X	O	X	X	X	X	X	X	X	X
CHECKED=True or False		HTML 2	O	O	O	O	X	O	O	O	O	O	O	O
DISABLED		HTML 3	O	O	O	O	X	O	O	O	O	O	O	O
ERROR		HTML 3	O	O	O	O	X	O	O	O	O	O	O	O
MAX=Number; Maximum Permitted Value		HTML 3	O	O	O	O	X	O	O	O	O	O	O	O
MAXLENGTH=Number of Characters		HTML 2	O	O	O	O	X	O	O	O	O	O	O	O
METHOD=Script		Oracle	O	O	O	O	X	O	O	O	O	O	O	O
MIN=Number; Lowest Permitted Value		HTML 3	O	O	O	O	X	O	O	O	O	O	O	O
NAME=String		HTML 2	X	X	X	O	X	X	X	X	X	X	X	X
SIZE=Width in Pixels, Height in Pixels		HTML 2	X	X	X	O	X	X	X	X	X	X	X	X
SRC=URL		HTML 2	P	P	P	P	O	O	O	O	O	P	O	P
TYPE=CHECKBOX/FILE/HIDDEN/IMAGE/PASSWORD/RADIO/RANGE/READONLY/RESET/SCRIBBLESUBMIT/TEXT/TEXTAREA		HTML 2 and HTML 3	X	X	X	X	X	X	X	X	X	X	X	X
VALUE=String or Number		HTML 2	X	X	X	X	X	X	X	X	X	X	X	X
<ISINDEX>	Index	HTML 2	-	-	-	-	-	-	-	-	-	-	-	-
ACTION=String		HTML 3	-	-	-	-	-	-	-	-	-	-	-	-
PROMPT=String		HTML 3	-	-	-	-	-	-	-	-	-	-	-	-
<KBD></KBD>	Keyboard	HTML 2	O	X	X	X	X	X	X	O	O	X	X	X
<LAYOUTFRAME></LAYOUTFRAME>	Layout Frame	Oracle	O	O	X	O	O	O	X	O	O	O	O	O
WIDTH=Pixel Value		Oracle	O	O	X	O	O	O	X	O	O	O	O	O
X=X Coordinate		Oracle	O	O	X	O	O	O	X	O	O	O	O	O
Y=Y Coordinate		Oracle	O	O	X	O	O	O	X	O	O	O	O	O
<LAYOUTFRAMERESET></LAYOUTFRAMERESET>	Layout Frame Reset	Oracle	X	X	X	X	X	X	X	X	X	X	X	X
<LH>	List Header	HTML 3	X	O	O	O	X	X	X	O	O	X	O	O

A=Netscape Navigator 3.0; B=Microsoft Internet Explorer 3.0; C=Oracle PowerBrowser 1.0; D=HotJava Alpha Release; E=NCSA Mosaic 2.0; F=America Online Windows 2.5; G=CompuServe Spry Mosaic 1.0; H=Prodigy 2.0d; I=Apple CyberDog Beta 2; J=Navigator 2.0; K=Navigator 1.1; L=Internet Explorer 2.0

X=Supports the tag; O=Does not support the tag; P=Partial support; PL=Planned support; "-"=Server-side or N/A. An asterisk indicates additional attributes.

Tag Attribute	Name	Origin	A	B	C	D	E	F	G	H	I	J	K	L
`<LI>`	List Item	HTML 2	X	X	X	X	X	X	X	X	X	X	X	X
TYPE=See `<OL>` and `<UL>`		HTML 3	X	P	O	O	O	O	O	O	O	X	X	X
VALUE=Number for `<OL>` lists		HTML 3	-	P	O	O	O	O	O	O	O	X	X	X
`<LINK>`	Link	HTML 2	-	-	-	-	-	-	-	-	-	-	-	-
HREF=URL		HTML 2	-	-	-	-	-	-	-	-	-	-	-	-
NAME=String		HTML 2	-	-	-	-	-	-	-	-	-	-	-	-
REV=Reverse of REL attribute		HTML 2	-	-	-	-	-	-	-	-	-	-	-	-
REL=Banner/Copyright/Glossary/Help/Home/Index/Toc/*		HTML 2/3	-	-	-	-	-	-	-	-	-	-	-	-
REL=STYLESHEET (New)		HTML 3	-	-	-	-	-	-	-	-	-	-	-	-
TITLE=String		HTML 2	-	-	-	-	-	-	-	-	-	-	-	-
TYPE=Identifying Stylesheet		HTML 3	-	-	-	-	-	-	-	-	-	-	-	-
`<MAP></MAP>`	Map	HTML 3	X	X	X	O	O	O	O	O	O	X	O	X
NAME=Unique Identifier		HTML 3	X	X	X	O	O	O	O	O	X	X	O	X
`<MARQUEE></MARQUEE>`	Marquee	Microsoft	O	X	O	O	O	O	O	O	O	X	X	X
ALIGN=TOP/MIDDLE/BOTTOM		Microsoft	X	O	O	O	O	O	O	O	O	O	O	O
BEHAVIOR=SCROLL/SLIDE/ALTERNATE		Microsoft	O	X	O	O	O	O	O	O	O	O	O	O
BGCOLOR=Hexadecimal or COLOR Name		Microsoft	X	O	O	O	O	O	O	O	O	O	O	O
BORDER=Pixel Value		Microsoft	X	O	O	O	O	O	O	O	O	O	O	O
DIRECTION=LEFT or RIGHT		Microsoft	X	O	O	O	O	O	O	O	O	O	O	O
HEIGHT=Pixel Value or Percentage		Microsoft	X	O	O	O	O	O	O	O	O	O	O	O
HSPACE=Pixel Value		Microsoft	X	O	O	O	O	O	O	O	O	O	O	O
LOOP=Infinite or Number		Microsoft	X	O	O	O	O	O	O	O	O	O	O	O
SCROLLAMOUNT=Pixel Value		Microsoft	X	O	O	O	O	O	O	O	O	O	O	O
SCROLLDELAY=Value in Milliseconds		Microsoft	X	O	O	O	O	O	O	O	O	O	O	O
VSPACE=Pixel Value		Microsoft	X	O	O	O	O	O	O	O	O	O	O	O
WIDTH=Pixel Value or Percentage		Microsoft	X	O	O	O	O	O	O	O	O	O	O	O
`<MENU></MENU>`	Menu	HTML 2	X	X	X	X	X	X	X	X	X	X	X	X
COMPACT		HTML 3	O	O	O	O	X	X	X	X	X	O	O	O
`<META>`	Meta	HTML 3	X	X	X	P	X	P	P	P	P	X	P	X
CONTENT=String		HTML 3	X	X	X	X	X	P	P	X	X	X	P	X
HTTP-EQUIV=String		HTML 3	X	X	X	X	X	P	P	P	X	X	P	X
NAME=String		HTML 3	X	-	X	X	X	X	X	X	X	X	X	X
`<NEXTID>`	Next ID	HTML 3	-	-	-	-	-	-	-	-	-	-	-	-
N=String		HTML 3	-	-	-	-	-	-	-	-	-	-	-	-
`<NLO>`	Network Loadable Object	Oracle	-	X	X	-	-	-	-	-	-	-	-	-
ALIGN=LEFT or RIGHT		Oracle	-	X	-	-	-	-	-	-	-	-	-	-
CONTROLS		Oracle	-	X	-	-	-	-	-	-	-	-	-	-
HEIGHT=Pixel Value		Oracle	-	X	-	-	-	-	-	-	-	-	-	-
HSPACE=Pixel Value		Oracle	-	X	-	-	-	-	-	-	-	-	-	-
NOBORDER		Oracle	-	X	-	-	-	-	-	-	-	-	-	-
NOCONTROLS		Oracle	-	X	-	-	-	-	-	-	-	-	-	-
SHOWBORDER		Oracle	-	X	-	-	-	-	-	-	-	-	-	-
SRC=URL or String		Oracle	-	X	-	-	-	-	-	-	-	-	-	-

A=Netscape Navigator 3.0; B=Microsoft Internet Explorer 3.0 Alpha; C=Oracle PowerBrowser 1.0; D=HotJava Alpha Release; E=NCSA Mosaic 2.0; F=America Online Windows 2.5; G=CompuServe Spry Mosaic 1.0; H=Prodigy 2.0d; I=Apple CyberDog Beta 2; J=Navigator 2.0; K=Navigator 1.1; L=Internet Explorer 2.0
X=Supports the tag; O=Does not support the tag; P=Partial support; PL=Planned support; -="Server-side or N/A. An asterisk indicates additional attributes.

Tag Attribute	Name	Origin	A	B	C	D	E	F	G	H	I	J	K	L
`<NLO>` (continued)														
SRC=URL or String		Oracle	X	–	X	–	–	–	–	–	–	–	–	–
TEXT=String		Oracle	X	–	X	–	–	–	–	–	–	–	–	–
TYPE=MSGTICKER/STOCKTIK/AVIHELPER/SOUND/*		Oracle	X	–	X	–	–	–	–	–	–	–	–	–
VSPACE=Pixel Value		Oracle	–	–	X	–	–	–	–	–	–	–	–	–
WIDTH=Pixel Value		Oracle	–	–	X	–	–	–	–	–	–	–	–	–
`<NOBR>`	No Break	Netscape	X	P	X	–	–	–	–	–	–	X	X	P
`<NOEMBED>`	No Embed	Netscape	X	PL	X	–	–	–	–	–	–	X	X	–
`<NOFRAMES></NOFRAMES>`	No Frames	Netscape	X	X	X	–	–	–	–	–	–	X	–	–
`<NONLO></NONLO>`	No NLO	Oracle	–	–	PL	–	–	–	–	–	–	–	–	–
`<OBJECT>`	Object	HTML 3	PL	X	PL	O	O	O	O	O	O	O	O	O
ALIGN=LEFT/RIGHT/CENTER		HTML 3	–	X	–	–	–	–	–	–	–	–	–	–
BORDER=Pixel Value		HTML 3	–	X	–	–	–	–	–	–	–	–	–	–
CLASS=Class Identifier		HTML 3	–	X	–	–	–	–	–	–	–	–	–	–
DATA=URL		HTML 3	–	X	–	–	–	–	–	–	–	–	–	–
HEIGHT=Pixel Value		HTML 3	–	X	–	–	–	–	–	–	–	–	–	–
NAME=Identifier		HTML 3	–	X	–	–	–	–	–	–	–	–	–	–
TYPE=Data Type		HTML 3	–	X	–	–	–	–	–	–	–	–	–	–
WIDTH=Pixel Value		HTML 3	–	X	–	–	–	–	–	–	–	–	–	–
`<OL></OL>`	Ordered List	HTML 2	X	X	X	O	X	X	X	X	X	X	X	X
CLEAR=LEFT/RIGHT/ALL		HTML 3	–	–	–	–	–	–	–	–	–	–	–	–
COMPACT		HTML 3	–	–	–	–	–	–	–	–	–	–	–	–
CONTINUE		HTML 3	–	–	–	–	–	–	–	–	–	–	–	–
SEQNUM=Number		HTML 3	–	–	–	–	–	–	–	–	–	–	–	–
START=Number		Netscape	X	X	X	O	O	O	O	O	O	X	X	X
TYPE=1/A/a/I/i		HTML 3	X	X	X	O	O	O	O	O	O	X	X	X
`<OPTION></OPTION>`	Option	HTML 2	X	X	X	X	X	X	X	X	X	X	X	X
NAME=String		HTML 2	X	X	X	X	X	X	X	X	X	X	X	X
SELECTED		HTML 2	X	X	X	X	X	X	X	X	X	X	X	X
VALUE=String or Number		HTML 2	X	X	X	X	X	X	X	X	X	X	X	X
`<P></P>`	Paragraph	HTML 2	X	X	X	O	X	X	X	X	X	X	X	X
ALIGN=RIGHT/LEFT/CENTER		HTML 3	X	X	X	O	O	O	O	O	O	O	O	O
CLEAR=RIGHT/LEFT/ALL		HTML 3	X	O	O	O	O	O	O	O	O	O	O	O
`<PARAM>`	Parameter	Netscape	X	O	O	P	O	O	O	O	O	O	O	O
`<PAYORDER></PAYORDER>`	Pay Order	Netscape	P	O	O	P	O	O	O	O	O	O	O	O
NAME=Unique Identifier		Netscape	X	P	P	P	P	P	P	P	P	P	P	P
CERT=Certificate Name		Netscape	X	X	P	X	X	X	X	X	X	X	X	X
`<PLAINTEXT></PLAINTEXT>`	Plain Text	HTML 2	P	O	X	O	X	X	X	X	X	X	X	P
`<PRE></PRE>`	Preformatted Text	HTML 2	X	X	X	X	X	X	X	X	X	X	X	P
`<RANGE>`	Range	HTML 3	O	–	O	O	–	–	–	–	–	O	O	O
CLASS=String		HTML 3	–	–	–	–	–	–	–	–	–	–	–	–
FROM=Start of Range		HTML 3	–	–	–	–	–	–	–	–	–	–	–	–
ID=Name		HTML 3	–	–	–	–	–	–	–	–	–	–	–	–
UNTIL=End of Range		HTML 3	–	–	–	–	–	–	–	–	–	–	–	–
`<S></S>`	Strikeout	HTML 2	O	X	O	X	X	O	O	O	O	O	X	X

A=Netscape Navigator 3.0; B=Microsoft Internet Explorer 3.0 Alpha; C=Oracle PowerBrowser 1.0; D=HotJava Alpha Release; E=NCSA Mosaic 2.0; F=America Online Windows 2.5; G=CompuServe Spry Mosaic 1.0; H=Prodigy 2.0d; I=Apple CyberDog Beta 2; J=Navigator 1.1; K=Navigator 2.0; L=Internet Explorer 2.0
X=Supports the tag; O=Does not support the tag; P=Partial support; PL=Planned support; "–"=Server-side or N/A. An asterisk indicates additional attributes.

Tag / Attribute	Name	Origin	A	B	C	D	E	F	G	H	I	J	K	L
<SAMP></SAMP>	Sample	HTML 2	X	X	X	X	X	X	O	X	X	X	X	X
<SCRIPT></SCRIPT>	Script	Netscape	X	X	X	X	O	O	O	O	O	O	O	O
LANGUAGE=Language Name		Netscape	O	X	O	O	O	O	O	O	O	O	O	X
SRC=URL		Oracle	O	X	O	O	O	O	O	O	O	O	O	O
<SELECT></SELECT>	Select	HTML 2	X	X	X	X	X	X	X	X	X	X	X	X
MULTIPLE		HTML 2	X	X	X	X	X	X	X	X	X	X	X	X
NAME=String		HTML 2	X	X	X	X	X	X	X	X	X	X	X	X
SIZE=Height in Number of List Entries		HTML 2	X	X	X	X	X	X	X	X	X	X	X	X
<SMALL></SMALL>	Small	HTML 3	X	X	O	X	X	X	X	O	X	X	X	O
<STRIKE></STRIKE>	Strikeout	HTML 3	X	X	X	X	X	X	X	X	X	X	O	X
<STRONG></STRONG>	Strong	HTML 2	X	X	X	X	X	X	X	X	X	X	X	X
<STYLE></STYLE>	Style	HTML 3	O	O	O	O	O	-	O	O	O	O	O	O
Name=SGML Notation		HTML 3	-	-	-	-	-	-	-	-	-	-	-	-
	Subscript	HTML 3	X	X	X	O	O	O	O	O	O	O	O	O
	Superscript	HTML 3	X	X	X	O	O	X	O	O	O	O	O	O
<TABLE></TABLE>	Table	HTML 3	X	X	X	X	X	O	X	X	X	X	X	X
ALIGN=LEFT/RIGHT/CENTER/*		HTML 3	O	X	O	X	X	-	X	X	X	X	X	X
BGCOLOR=Hexadecimal or COLOR Name		HTML 3	O	X	O	X	X	X	X	X	X	X	X	X
BORDER=Pixel Value		HTML 3	X	X	O	O	O	-	O	O	O	O	O	X
BORDERCOLOR=Hexadecimal or COLOR Name		Netscape	O	X	O	X	O	X	O	O	O	O	O	X
BORDERCOLORDARK=Hexadecimal or COLOR Name		Microsoft	O	X	O	-	O	-	O	O	O	O	O	X
BORDERCOLORLIGHT=Hexadecimal or COLOR Name		Microsoft	O	X	O	-	O	-	O	O	O	O	O	X
CELLPADDING=Pixel Value		Microsoft	X	X	-	-	O	-	O	O	O	O	O	X
CELLSPACING=Pixel Value		Netscape	X	X	O	O	O	O	O	O	O	O	O	X
CLEAR=LEFT/RIGHT/ALL		HTML 3	-	-	-	O	-	O	-	-	-	-	-	-
COLSPEC=Column Widths and Alignments		HTML 3	-	-	-	O	-	-	-	-	-	-	-	-
HEIGHT=Pixel Value		HTML 3	X	X	X	O	O	X	O	O	O	X	X	X
NAME=String		HTML 3	X	X	O	O	O	O	O	O	X	X	X	X
WIDTH=Pixel Value or Percentage		HTML 3	O	X	X	O	O	-	O	O	X	X	X	X
<TD></TD>	Table Data	HTML 3	O	X	O	O	O	O	O	O	O	O	O	X
ALIGN=LEFT/RIGHT/CENTER/*		HTML 3	O	X	O	O	O	-	O	O	O	O	O	X
BGCOLOR=Hexadecimal or COLOR Name		HTML 3	O	X	X	O	O	O	O	O	O	O	O	X
BORDER		Microsoft	X	X	O	O	O	O	O	O	O	O	O	X
BORDERCOLOR=Hexadecimal or COLOR Name		Microsoft	X	X	X	O	O	O	O	O	O	O	O	X
BORDERCOLORDARK=Hexadecimal or COLOR Name		Microsoft	X	X	X	O	O	O	O	O	O	O	O	X
BORDERCOLORLIGHT=Hexadecimal or COLOR Name		Microsoft	X	X	X	O	O	O	O	O	O	O	O	X
COLSPAN=Number of Columns		Netscape	X	X	X	X	X	O	X	X	X	X	X	X
HEIGHT=Pixel Value		HTML 3	X	X	O	O	O	O	O	O	O	O	O	X
HSPACE=Pixel Value		Netscape	X	X	O	O	O	O	O	O	O	O	O	X
NOWRAP		HTML 3	X	X	O	O	O	O	O	O	O	O	O	X
ROWSPAN=Number of Rows		Netscape	X	X	X	O	O	O	O	O	O	X	X	X
VALIGN=TOP/MIDDLE/BOTTOM/BASELINE		HTML 3	X	X	O	X	X	O	X	X	X	X	X	X
VSPACE=Pixel Value		Netscape	X	X	O	O	O	O	O	O	O	O	O	O
WIDTH=Pixel Value or Percentage		HTML 3	X	X	X	X	X	-	X	X	X	X	X	X

A=Netscape Navigator 3.0; B=Microsoft Internet Explorer 3.0; C=Oracle PowerBrowser 1.0; D=HotJava Alpha Release; E=NCSA Mosaic 2.0; F=America Online Windows 2.5; G=CompuServe Spry Mosaic 1.0; H=Prodigy 2.0d; I=Apple CyberDog Beta 2; J=Navigator 2.0; K=Navigator 1.1; L=Internet Explorer 2.0. *An asterisk indicates additional attributes.*

X=Supports the tag; O=Does not support the tag; P=Partial support; PL=Planned support; "-"=Server-side or N/A.

Tag Attribute	Name	Origin	A	B	C	D	E	F	G	H	I	J	K	L
`<TEXTAREA></TEXTAREA>`	Text Area	HTML 2	X	X	X	X	X	X	X	X	X	X	X	X
COLS=Number		HTML 2	X	X	X	X	X	X	X	X	X	X	X	X
NAME=String		HTML 2	X	X	X	X	X	X	X	X	X	X	X	X
ROWS=NUMBER		HTML 2	X	X	X	X	X	X	X	X	X	X	X	X
WRAP		HTML 3	O	O	O	O	P	O	O	P	O	O	O	O
`<TH></TH>`	Table Header	HTML 3	X	X	X	X	X	X	X	X	X	X	X	X
ALIGN=LEFT/RIGHT/CENTER/*		HTML 3	O	X	O	O	X	–	O	O	X	O	X	X
BGCOLOR=Hexadecimal or COLOR Name		HTML 3	O	O	O	O	O	–	O	O	O	O	O	X
BORDER		HTML 3	O	X	O	O	O	–	O	O	O	O	O	X
BORDERCOLOR=Hexadecimal or COLOR Name		Microsoft	O	X	O	O	O	–	O	O	O	O	O	X
BORDERCOLORDARK=Hexadecimal or COLOR Name		Microsoft	O	X	O	O	O	–	O	O	O	O	O	X
BORDERCOLORLIGHT=Hexadecimal or COLOR Name		Microsoft	O	X	O	O	O	–	O	O	O	O	O	X
COLSPAN=Number of Columns		Netscape	X	X	X	X	X	X	X	X	X	X	X	X
HEIGHT=Pixel Value		HTML 3	X	O	O	O	O	–	O	O	O	O	X	X
HSPACE=Pixel Value		Netscape	X	X	X	X	X	X	X	X	X	X	X	X
NOWRAP		HTML 3	X	X	X	X	X	X	X	X	X	X	X	X
ROWSPAN=Number of Rows		Netscape	X	X	X	X	X	X	X	X	X	X	X	X
VALIGN=TOP/MIDDLE/BOTTOM/BASELINE		HTML 3	X	X	X	X	X	X	X	X	X	O	X	O
VSPACE=Pixel Value		Netscape	X	X	X	X	X	X	X	X	X	X	X	X
WIDTH=Pixel Value or Percentage		HTML 3	X	X	X	X	X	X	X	X	X	X	X	X
`<TITLE></TITLE>`	Title	HTML 2	X	X	X	X	X	X	O	X	X	X	X	X
`<TR></TR>`	Table Row	HTML 3	X	X	X	X	X	O	O	O	X	X	X	X
ALIGN=LEFT/RIGHT/CENTER/*		HTML 3	O	X	O	O	X	–	O	O	X	O	X	X
BGCOLOR=Hexadecimal or COLOR Name		HTML 3	O	O	O	O	O	–	O	O	O	O	O	X
BORDER		HTML 3	O	X	O	O	O	–	O	O	O	O	O	X
BORDERCOLOR=Hexadecimal or COLOR Name		Microsoft	O	X	O	O	O	–	O	O	O	O	O	X
BORDERCOLORDARK=Hexadecimal or COLOR Name		Microsoft	O	X	O	O	O	–	O	O	O	O	O	X
BORDERCOLORLIGHT=Hexadecimal or COLOR Name		Microsoft	O	X	O	O	O	–	O	O	O	O	O	X
HEIGHT=Pixel Value		HTML 3	X	O	O	O	O	–	O	O	O	O	X	X
HSPACE=Pixel Value		Netscape	X	X	X	X	X	X	X	X	X	X	X	X
VALIGN=TOP/MIDDLE/BOTTOM/BASELINE		HTML 3	X	X	X	X	X	X	X	X	X	O	X	O
VSPACE=Pixel Value		Netscape	X	X	X	X	X	X	X	X	X	X	X	X
WIDTH=Pixel Value or Percentage		HTML 3	X	X	X	X	X	X	X	X	X	X	X	O
`<TT></TT>`	Typewriter Text	HTML 2	X	X	X	X	X	X	X	X	X	X	X	X
`<U></U>`	Underline	HTML 2	O	O	O	O	O	X	O	O	X	X	X	X
`<UL></UL>`	Unordered List	HTML 2	X	X	X	X	X	X	X	X	X	X	X	X
COMPACT		HTML 3	X	X	X	O	O	X	O	X	O	X	X	X
TYPE=CIRCLE/SQUARE		HTML 3	X	X	X	O	O	X	O	O	O	O	O	O
`<VAR></VAR>`	Variable	HTML 2	X	X	X	X	X	X	X	X	X	X	X	X
`<WBR>`	Word Break	Netscape	X	X	X	O	O	O	O	O	O	X	X	X
`<XMP></XMP>`	Example	HTML 2	X	X	X	X	X	O	O	X	X	X	X	X

A=Netscape Navigator 3.0; B=Microsoft Internet Explorer 3.0 Alpha; C=Oracle PowerBrowser 1.0; D=HotJava Alpha Release; E=NCSA Mosaic 2.0; F=America Online Windows 2.5; G=CompuServe Spry Mosaic 1.0; H=Prodigy 2.0d; I=Apple CyberDog Beta 2; J=Navigator 2.0; K=Navigator 1.1; L=Internet Explorer 2.0
X=Supports the tag; O=Does not support the tag; P=Partial support; PL=Planned support; "–"=Server-side or N/A. An asterisk indicates additional attributes.

HTML TEXT EDITORS

Features	HTML Assistant Pro 2	HotDog	World Wide Web Weaver	Aardvark Pro	BBEdit	HTMLed Pro	Arachnid
Macintosh platform	O	PL	X	O	X	O	X
Windows platform	X	X	O	X	O	X	X
HTML 2 tags	X	X	X	X	X	X	X
HTML 3 tags	P	P	P	VL	P	P	VL
Netscape extensions	P	P	P	VL	P	P	VL
Microsoft extensions	O	P	O	O	O	O	O
Ability to add custom tags	X	X	X	X	X	X	O
Tables builder	VL	VL	P	P	P	P	VL
Form builder	X	X	X	X	X	X	O
Graphic conversion	O	O	O	O	O	O	O
Point and click link setting	X	X	X	X	X	X	X
Preview option	X	X	X	X	X	X	X
Ability to use any browser	X	X	X	X	X	X	X
Conversion of word processing docs	O	O	O	O	P	O	O
Spell checker	X	O	O	O	X	X	O
Special character tags	VL	VL	P	P	P	P	VL
Hexadecimal colors	X	O	X	O	PL	O	X

X=Supports the feature; O=Does not support the feature; P=Partial support; VL=Very limited support; PL=Planned support

HTML WYSIWYG EDITORS

Features	FrontPage	*SiteMill	HotMetal Pro	GNNPress	Navigator Gold
Macintosh platform	PL	X	X	X	X
Windows platform	X	PL	X	X	X
HTML 2 tags	X	X	X	X	X
HTML 3 tags	PL	PL	P	P	VL
Netscape extensions	PL	PL	P	P	VL
Microsoft extensions	PL	O	P	P	O
Ability to add custom tags	O	O	X	X	PL
Tables builder	O	O	X	X	PL
Form builder	X	X	X	O	PL
Graphic conversion	O	X	O	O	PL
Point and click link setting	X	X	X	X	PL
Preview option	X	X	X	X	X
Ability to use any browser	O	O	X	O	O
Conversion of word processing docs	O	O	X	O	PL
Spell checker	X	O	X	O	O
Special character tags	P	VL	P	VL	P
Link Manager	X	X	O	O	PL
CGI scripts	X	O	O	O	O

X=Supports the feature; O=Does not support the feature; P=Partial support;
VL=Very limited support; PL=Planned support

* Includes PageMill Editor

Appendix C
Special Characters

Numbered HTML	Intended Display	HTML Entities	Numbered HTML	Intended Display	HTML Entities	Numbered HTML	Intended Display	HTML Entities
&#34;	"	&quot;	&#74;	J		&#114;	r	
&#35;	#		&#75;	K		&#115;	s	
&#36;	$		&#76;	L		&#116;	t	
&#37;	%		&#77;	M		&#117;	u	
&#38;	&	&amp;	&#78;	N		&#118;	v	
&#39;	'		&#79;	O		&#119;	w	
&#40;	(		&#80;	P		&#120;	x	
&#41;	)		&#81;	Q		&#121;	y	
&#42;	*		&#82;	R		&#122;	z	
&#43;	+		&#83;	S		&#123;	{	
&#44;	,		&#84;	T		&#124;			
&#45;	-		&#85;	U		&#125;	}	
&#46;	.		&#86;	V		&#126;	~	
&#47;	/		&#87;	W		&#127;	none	
&#48;	0		&#88;	X		&#128;	•	
&#49;	1		&#89;	Y		&#129;	™	
&#50;	2		&#90;	Z		&#130;	,	
&#51;	3		&#91;	[		&#131;	ƒ	
&#52;	4		&#92;	\		&#132;	„	
&#53;	5		&#93;	]		&#133;	…	
&#54;	6		&#94;	^		&#134;	†	
&#55;	7		&#95;	_		&#135;	‡	
&#56;	8		&#96;	`		&#136;	^	
&#57;	9		&#97;	a		&#137;	‰	
&#58;	:		&#98;	b		&#138;	…	
&#59;	;		&#99;	c		&#139;	‹	
&#60;	<	&lt;	&#100;	d		&#140;	Œ	
&#61;	=		&#101;	e		&#141;	Ÿ	
&#62;	>	&gt;	&#102;	f		&#142;	/	
&#63;	?		&#103;	g		&#143;	∂	
&#64;	@		&#104;	h		&#144;	Δ	
&#65;	A		&#105;	i		&#145;	'	
&#66;	B		&#106;	j		&#146;	'	
&#67;	C		&#107;	k		&#147;	"	
&#68;	D		&#108;	l		&#148;	"	
&#69;	E		&#109;	m				
&#70;	F		&#110;	n				
&#71;	G		&#111;	o				
&#72;	H		&#112;	p				
&#73;	I		&#113;	q				

Numbered HTML	Intended Display	HTML Entities
&#149;	•	
&#150;	–	
&#151;	—	
&#152;	~	
&#153;	™	
&#154;	°	
&#155;	›	
&#156;	œ	
&#157;	ˇ	
&#158;	1	
&#159;	Ÿ	
	non-breaking space	
&#161;	¡	&iexcl;
&#162;	¢	&cent;
&#163;	£	&pound;
&#164;	¤	&curren;
&#165;	¥	&yen;
&#166;	|	&brvbar;
&#167;	§	&sect;
&#168;	¨	&uml;
&#169;	©	&copy;
&#170;	ª	&ordf;
&#171;	«	&laquo;
&#172;	¬	&not;
&#173;	–	&shy;
&#174;	®	&reg;
&#175;	¯	&macr;
&#176;	°	&deg;
&#177;	±	&plusmn;
&#178;	2	&sup2;
&#179;	3	&sup3;
&#180;	´	&acute;

Numbered HTML	Intended Display	HTML Entities
&#181;	µ	&micro;
&#182;	¶	&para;
&#183;	·	&middot;
&#184;	¸	&cedil;
&#185;	1	&sup1;
&#186;	º	&ordm;
&#187;	»	&raquo;
&#188;	π	&frac14;
&#189;	∏	&frac12;
&#190;	≤	&frac34;
&#191;	¿	&iquest;
&#192;	À	&Agrave;
&#193;	Á	&Aacute;
&#194;	Â	&Acirc;
&#195;	Ã	&Atilde;
&#196;	Ä	&Auml;
&#197;	Å	&Aring;
&#198;	Æ	&AElig;
&#199;	Ç	&Ccedil;
&#200;	È	&Egrave;
&#201;	É	&Eacute;
&#202;	Ê	&Ecirc;
&#203;	Ë	&Euml;
&#204;	Ì	&Igrave;
&#205;	Í	&Iacute;
&#206;	Î	&Icirc;
&#207;	Ï	&Iuml;
&#208;	‹	&ETH;
&#209;	Ñ	&Ntilde;
&#210;	Ò	&Ograve;
&#211;	Ó	&Oacute;
&#212;	Ô	&Ocirc;
&#213;	Õ	&Otilde;
&#214;	Ö	&Ouml;
&#215;	x	&times;

Numbered HTML	Intended Display	HTML Entities
&#216;	Ø	&Oslash;
&#217;	Ù	&Ugrave;
&#218;	Ú	&Uacute;
&#219;	Û	&Ucirc;
&#220;	Ü	&Uuml;
&#221;	†	&Yacute;
&#222;	fi	&THORN;
&#223;	ß	&szlig;
&#224;	à	&agrave;
&#225;	á	&aacute;
&#233;	é	&eacute;
&#234;	ê	&ecirc;
&#235;	ë	&euml;
&#236;	ì	&igrave;
&#237;	í	&iacute;
&#238;	î	&icirc;
&#239;	ï	&iuml;
&#240;	›	&eth;
&#241;	ñ	&ntilde;
&#242;	ò	&ograve;
&#243;	ó	&oacute;
&#244;	ô	&ocirc;
&#245;	õ	&otilde;
&#246;	ö	&ouml;
&#247;	÷	&divide;
&#248;	ø	&oslash;
&#249;	ù	&ugrave;
&#250;	ú	&uacute;
&#251;	û	&ucirc;
&#252;	ü	&uuml;
&#253;	‡	&yacute;
&#254;	fl	&thorn;
&#255;	ÿ	&yuml;

Appendix D
MIME Types

Description	MIME Type	File Extensions
Text files	text/HTML	html, htm
	text/text	txt
	text/richtext	rtx, rtf
	text/MS Word	doc
	text/WordPerfect	wp
	text/Windows Write	wri
	text/Postscript	ps, eps, ai
	text/Tool Command Language	tcl
	text/Tab Separated	tsv
Graphics	image/gif	gif
	image/jpeg	jpeg, jpg, jpe
	image/tiff	tiff, tif
	image/pict	pict, pic
	image/x-cmu-raster	ras
	image/x-rgb	rgb
	image/x-bitmap	xbm, pbm
	image/x-portable-networkgraphic	pmg
	image/x-portable-pixmap	ppm
	Image exchange format	ief
	image/x-xwindowdump	xwd

Description	MIME Type	File Extensions
Audio players	audio/basic	au, snd
	audio/aiff	aiff, aif
	audio/wav	wav
	audio/Real Audio	ra, ram
Movie players	video/mpeg	mpeg, mpg, mpe
	video/quicktime	qt, mov
	video/msvideo	avi
	video/sgi-movie	movie
Compressed file extensions	application/zip	zip
	application/gzip	gzip, gz, tgz, z
	application/Mac-binhex	hqx
	application/gtar	gtar
	application/tar	tar
	application/stuffit	sit, sea
	application/UU	uu
	application/acr	arc
	application/bin	bin

APPENDIX E
ONLINE RESOURCES

BROWSERS

Netscape Navigator
http://home.netscape.com/comprod/products/navigator/version_2.0/index.html

Microsoft Internet Explorer
http://www.microsoft.com/ie/msie.htm

Oracle PowerBrowser
http://www.oracle.com/

Sun HotJava
http://java.sun.com/HotJava/index.html

NCSA Mosaic
http://www.ncsa.uiuc.edu/SDG/Software/Mosaic/Docs/help-about.html

Spry Mosaic
http://www.spry.com/

CompuServe Mosaic
http://www.compuserve.com/

America Online
http://www.aol.com/

AOL 3.0 Web Browser
http://www.aol.com/help/specs/browser.html

Prodigy
http://www.prodigy.com/

Apple Cyberdog
http://cyberdog.apple.com/

PointCast PCN Browser
http://www.pointcast.com/

GNN
http://www.gnn.com/gnn/

Ubique

    `http://www.ubique.com/`

Netcom

    `http://www.netcom.com/`

NetManage WebSurfer

    `http://www.netmanage.com/netmanage/download.html`

Cello

    `http://www.law.cornell.edu/cello/cellotop.html`

CyberGate

    `http://www.blacksun.com/`

Accent Multilingual Mosaic

    `http://www.accentsoft.com/`

Lynx

    `http://kuhttp://cc.ukans.edu/about_lynx/about_lynx.html`

BROWSER RESOURCES

Browser by Design

This site provides the online accompaniment to this book. It contains many pages for testing your browser, links to hundreds of sites, and updates to the materials in this book.

    `http://www.browserbydesign.com/`

BrowserWatch

This page is one of several online browser resources.

    `http://www.browserwatch.com/`

Yahoo - Browser Usage Statistics

This site can help you plan for your demographic audience. The number of people still using Navigator 1.1 and other questions can be answered here.

    `http://www.yahoo.com/Computers_and_Internet/Internet/World_Wide_Web/`
    `Browsers/Browser_Usage_Statistics/`

The Browser Tuneup

This page provides some testing for browsers.

```
http://www.eit.com/goodies/tuneup/
```

CNET Browser Review

CNET provides ongoing reviews of computer hardware and software products.

```
http://www.cnet.com/Content/Reviews/Compare/Browsers/
```

BrowserCaps

This site has links to browser resources.

```
http://www.objarts.com/bc/
```

BrowserWatch - Plug-In Plaza!

This site may have some late-breaking plug-ins not otherwise available.

```
http://www.browserwatch.com/plug-in.html
```

WWW Browser Plug-Ins!

Here is another site that provides a list of plug-ins.

```
http://www.edinic.com/software/plugin.html
```

PC Magazine InternetUser - Plug-In Central

Here is *PC Magazine*'s plug-in central.

```
http://www.zdnet.com/pcmag/IU/plugins/plugins.htm
```

Plug-ins

This is Netscape's list of plug-ins.

```
http://home.netscape.com/comprod/products/navigator/version_2.0/plugins/
index.html
```

HTML

Creating Net Sites

Netscape provides these pages that describe traditional HTML, as well as the Netscape specific tags, like <FRAME> and <EMBED>.

```
http://home.netscape.com/assist/net_sites/
```

Yale HTML Style Manual

This site gives some good design guides. It is administered by Patrick Lynch at the Yale Center for Advanced Instructional Media.

```
http://info.med.yale.edu/caim/StyleManual_Top.HTML
```

Cascading Style Sheets, Level 1

This is the World Wide Web Consortium draft on style sheets.

```
http://www.w3.org/pub/WWW/TR/WD-css1.html
```

Inserting Objects into HTML

This describes how the <OBJECT> tag is treated in HTML. Microsoft refers developers to this page for tag usage.

```
http://www.w3.org/pub/WWW/TR/WD-object.html
```

HTML DTDs (and other public text)

This page discusses the many HTML dialects that are appearing. It provides and has links to Document Type Definitions, including HTML 2, HTML 3, Netscape, and Explorer extensions.

```
http://www.w3.org/pub/WWW/MarkUp/html-pubtext/
```

HTML Reference Manual

This site is maintained by the Sandia National Laboratories. It has links to HTML tutorials and many online resources.

```
http://www.sandia.gov/sci_compute/html_ref.html
```

HyperText Markup Language Specification 3.0

This site is generally considered to be the official HTML 3.0 specifications. The site is maintained by Dave Raggett of Hewlett-Packard Laboratories.

```
http://www.hpl.hp.co.uk/people/dsr/html/Contents.html
```

W3C Tech Reports

This site has a list of working drafts for the proposed HTML specifications.

```
http://www.w3.org/pub/WWW/TR/
```

HTML 3 Linking and Embedding Model

This page describes how HTML 3 implements the <INSERT> tag, contrasting it with <EMBED> and DYNSRC of Netscape and Microsoft, respectively.

```
http://www.w3.org/pub/WWW/TR/WD-insert-951221.html
```

HyperText Markup Language (HTML): Working and Background Materials

This is one of the W3 Consortium's principal sites. There are links to historic documents, proposed specs, and other W3C documents.

`http://www.w3.org/pub/WWW/MarkUp/`

Internet Explorer - ActiveX Gallery

This site showcases the ActiveX objects in Explorer 3.0.

`http://www.microsoft.com/ie/appdev/controls/`

Microsoft ActiveX Development Kit

Download the ActiveX Development Kit and Explorer 3.0 from this site. Also links to gallery and related sites.

`http://www.microsoft.com/intdev/sdk/`

Microsoft Internet Explorer 3.0 HTML Support

Microsoft provides a pretty extensive list of HTML tags here.

`http://www.microsoft.com/ie/author/html30/html_toc.htm`

VBScript: Working Description

Visual Basic and VBScript are presented here.

`http://www.microsoft.com/INTDEV/vbs/vbscript.htm`

Internet Control Pack

This page describes the ActiveX Controls.

`http://www.microsoft.com/icp/`

JavaScript

Gamelan's JavaScript

This page has a large number of links to JavaScript sites.

`http://www.gamelan.com/frame/Gamelan.javascript.html`

JavaScript

Netscape provides this list of JavaScript resources.

`http://home.netscape.com/comprod/products/navigator/version_2.0/script/`
`script_info/index.html`

JavaScript Index

This site is an excellent resource for JavaScript links.

`http://www.c2.org/~andreww/javascript/`

JavaScript Authoring Guide

This is Netscape's own JavaScript authoring guide. Links are available to describe all of the syntax in the language.

`http://home.netscape.com/eng/mozilla/Gold/handbook/javascript/index.html`

White Paper: Verifying Form Input with JavaScript

This site is maintained by Gordon McComb, author of *The JavaScript Sourcebook*. It has some good examples for form input checking.

`http://gmccomb.com/javascript/valid.htm`

JAVA

Java: Programming for the Internet

This is Java's home page. The site is maintained by Sun and has links to documentation and other resources.

`http://java.sun.com/`

FutureTense, Inc.

This is a new Java-based Web authoring tool. The company also provides a viewer.

`http://www.futuretense.com/`

Concurrent Programming in Java

This page links to many sites dealing with designing multithreaded code.

`http://g.oswego.edu/dl/pats/aopintro.html`

Making Sense of Java

This site is a down-to-earth look at Java, and answers a lot of often-asked questions.

`http://reality.sgi.com/employees/shiffman_engr/Java-QA.html`

Borland's Internet Tools

This is Borland's Java products page. They have introduced several GUI Java development tools.

`http://www.borland.com/Product/java/java.html`

Symantec Java Central

This is Symantec's main Java products page. There are links to Symantec information, as well as general Java.

`http://cafe.symantec.com/javacentral/index.html`

GUI Programming Using Java

This tutorial was put together by Jan Newmarch of the University of Canberra.

`http://pandonia.canberra.edu.au/java/tut.html`

The Java™ Developers Kit

This page enables you to download the Java Developers Kit for designing applets.

`http://java.sun.com/JDK-1.0/index.html`

The Java Package Tutorial

This tutorial deals specifically with the creation of packages.

`http://192.225.81.232:2000/JavaPackages.html`

Trail Map: The Java Language Tutorial

This is Sun's Java tutorial.

`http://java.sun.com/tutorial/`

Gamelan

This has to be the greatest collection of things Java on the Internet.

`http://www.gamelan.com`

JavaWorld

This online 'zine is maintained by IDG.

`http://www.javaworld.com/cgi-bin/w3com/start?JW+main`

GRAPHICS

Lynda's Homegurrl Page

This page is maintained by Lynda Weinman. There are some excellent links to graphics resources from her site, as well as information on her book.

`http://www.lynda.com/`

Clip2Gif and GifBuilder

These programs, contained on the CD-ROM, are two excellent programs by Yves Piguet.

`http://iawww.epfl.ch/Staff/Yves.Piguet/clip2gif/`

Netscape Technical Note 10117

This site is the original "magic palette." The 216 colors that are supported cross-platform by Netscape are provided.

`http://www.netscape.com/assist/support/client/tn/windows/10117.html`

Royal Frazier's INTERcoNnEcTions

This site has links to all sorts of animated GIF resources.

`http://www.reiworld.com/royalef/royal.htm`

Computer Graphics

This is an international collection of computer graphics college programs maintained by the Perceptual Science Laboratory at the University of California Santa Cruz. This site is an excellent resource for those who want to study computer graphics.

`http://mambo.ucsc.edu/psl/cg.html`

INFO-MAC HyperArchive ROOT

This site has a large volume of Macintosh freeware, shareware, demos, updates, and more.

`http://hyperarchive.lcs.mit.edu/HyperArchive.html`

The Graphics File Format Page

Martin Reddy provides an excellent resource for describing image file formats. Links to pages describing 2D and 3D image formats, and downloadable utility programs are listed.

`http://www.dcs.ed.ac.uk/~mxr/gfx/`

OAK Repository - SimTel Windows Mirror Index

This is a repository for every type of Windows application, including a big list with all sorts of categories.

```
http://www.acs.oakland.edu/oak/SimTel/SimTel-win3.html
```

Aaron's Graphic Archive

This site has links to graphics on the Web. There is a copyright disclaimer (the small print) that instructs visitors on the use of graphics.

```
http://hoohoo.ncsa.uiuc.edu/Public/AGA/
```

WebImage Information

WebImage is a suite of applications that is designed for creating Web graphics.

```
http://www.group42.com/webimage.htm
```

PNG (Portable Network Graphics) Home Page

The home pages of the PNG file format are maintained by Greg Roelofs. There are links to all things PNG from this page.

```
http://quest.jpl.nasa.gov/PNG/
```

AUDIO

MAZ Sound Tools Page

This page features links to all kinds of audio software, including sample editors, converters, and recorders.

```
http://www.th-zwickau.de/~maz/sound.html
```

Waveform File Formats

This site lists various waveform types. Of these, only the AIFF and Sun AU files are presently supported on the Internet.

```
http://www.cs.rochester.edu/u/ringger/htk/node57.html
```

midiSource QuickHelp

This site gives descriptions for commonly used MIDI terms.

```
http://netris1.corpcomm.net/~jjorgensen/mshlp-lg.html
```

GoldWave Digital Audio Editor

Chris Craig has designed an excellent audio editor available from this site. The site is hosted by the Computer Science Department of Memorial University in Newfoundland, Canada.

```
http://web.cs.mun.ca/~chris3/goldwave/
```

DD's Cyberhome

David Dight put this list together that links to original shareware and WaveGen. There is also a French version on this site that resides in Australia.

```
http://people.interconnect.com.au/~davidd/
```

Digital Music Zone

Jack Orman put together this list of links to pages related to electronic music creation.

```
http://users.aol.com/jorman/
```

VIDEO

Cross-Platform QuickTime

This site is managed by Robert Lentz at Northwestern University. It has links to QuickTime viewers and other utilities.

```
http://www.astro.nwu.edu/lentz/mac/qt/
```

Desktop Video

Guy Mullins put together an incredible tutorial on Desktop Video Production. It resides on the Arizona State University server.

```
http://godzilla.inre.asu.edu/~guy/Video1.html
```

MPEGe Lib

This MPEG library is maintained by Alex Knowles. There are links to an MPEG editor, as well as MPEG resources.

```
http://www.tardis.ed.ac.uk/~ark/mpegelib/
```

Yahoo - Computers and Internet:Multimedia:Video:Collections

This is Yahoo's catalog of online digital video collections.

```
http://www.yahoo.com/Computers_and_Internet/Multimedia/Video/Collections/
```

Watch Videos

Here are some videos that can be watched using the VDOlive plug-in.

```
http://www.vdolive.com/watch/
```

VRML

Virtual Reality Modeling Language (VRML) Forum

Mark Pesce and Brian Behlendorf put together this site. Links to historic VRML documents, bios of key VRML participants, and the VRML mailing list are available. The mailing list also has a rule of etiquette to which you can link.

```
http://vrml.wired.com/
```

VRML World Hotlinks Forum

This site, submitted by Dave Blackburn, is on the Mecklermedia iworld pages. There are links to new VRML sites, VRML Architecture Group sites, sites using VRML since its inception, and some odd links to Java and HotJava resources.

```
http://www.iworld.com/netday/VRML/hotlinks.html
```

QuickTime VR

Apple offers its own 3D, photorealistic standard with the QuickTime VR player. The player is available cross-platform, and requires that QuickTime, itself, is already installed.

```
http://qtvr.quicktime.apple.com/
```

VRML Browser Links

This page links to a handful of the most popular VRML browsers. From the company's home page, other VRML sites and displays can be located.

```
http://www.arkspace.com/vrml/browser.html
```

Caligari Home World

Caligari is a company specializing in VRML design. They make a browser and development product. Lots of links on their site.

```
http://www.caligari.com/
```

WebSpace™ Availability

WebSpace was one of the first VRML browsers, and is available in several platforms.

```
http://www.sd.tgs.com/~template/WebSpace/monday.html
```

VRML Library Archive: "History of VRML"

This page gives a history of VRML as notated by one of its founders, Mark Pesce. The discussion is rather broad and traces the history of the Web, as well as VRML. Relatively short, concise, easily readable.

```
http://webspace.sgi.com/Archive/VRML-history/index.html
```

Moving Worlds Design - A Proposal for VRML 2.0

This page describes the Moving Worlds Proposal for VRML 2.0. This standard is being supported by Silicon Graphics, Netscape, Sun Microsystems, Apple, and others.

```
http://webspace.sgi.com/moving-worlds/Design.html
```

VRML Repository

This site is maintained by the San Diego Supercomputer Center. Of all the sites listed here, this could be the most complete. A large number of browsers, software libraries, texture libraries, geometry converters, and other links are available.

```
http://sdsc.edu/vrml/
```

INTERNET SERVICE PROVIDERS

Internet Services Group

A service provider offering mirrored sites in 26 countries and 64 U.S. cities.

```
http://www.thehost.com/
```

Internet Services (General Products and Services)

ISPs and other Internet-related resources.

```
http://www.einet.net/galaxy/Business-and-Commerce/General-Products-and-
Services/Internet-Services.html
```

Yahoo: Web Presence Providers

Yahoo's list of Web service providers.

```
http://www.yahoo.com/Business_and_Economy/Companies/Internet_Services/
Web_Presence_Providers/
```

World Wide Web Servers

A list of registered Web servers listed alphabetically by continent, country, and state.

`http://www.uni-kl.de/Weitere-WWW-Server/Geographical.html`

Wisconsin Web Resources: Internet Services

A comprehensive list of ISPs in Wisconsin.

`http://www.inmarket.com/wisconsin/internet.htm`

California Internet-Services WWW Servers

A comprehensive list of ISPs in California.

`http://www.calif.com/ca/internet.services.html`

Web Developer's Virtual Library: Providers

Service providers in the U.S. that offer Web servers.

`http://www.stars.com/Vlib/Misc/Providers.html`

Providers of Commercial Internet Access (POCIA)

More than 850 ISPs from the U.S., Canada, and 46 other countries.

`http://www.celestin.com/pocia/index.html`

Internet Access Providers Around the World

ISPs from Africa, America - Central and South, Asia, Europe - Central, Europe - Eastern, Europe - Western, Middle East.

`http://www.best.be/iap.html`

U.S. Internet Service Providers List

A list of ISPs from throughout the U.S.

`http://www.primus.com/staff/peggy/provider.html`

SERVER SCRIPTS

Learn to Write CGI Forms

A beginner's tutorial for writing cgi-bin scripts in perl.

`http://www.catt.ncsu.edu/~bex/tutor/index.html`

Tutorial: Scripts, Forms, and Server-Side Things

Basic CGI scripts; requires some familiarity with shell scripts. The few places where server-specific issues are discussed refer to CERN and NCSA servers.

`http://pluto.ulcc.ac.uk/~cziwkga/server-side-tutorial.html`

Use of CGI Forms and Scripts Tutorial

How to write and use basic scripts in C.

`http://huckleberry.sfsu.edu/%7Ehodges/FormsScriptUse.html`

CGI Scripts

A comprehensive tutorial on how to write scripts in perl.

`http://oscar.teclink.net/~noumen/cgi.html`

Scripts for WWW

A tutorial for writing scripts in perl 5.

`http://dslab.csie.ncu.edu.tw/resource/www_script.html`

CTC Tutorial on Shell Scripts

How to use and write shell scripts.

`http://www.tc.cornell.edu/Edu/Tutor/Basics/shell/`

Introduction to CGI Programming

Introduction to CGI programming in Unix Bourne Shell language (sh) and perl.

`http://www.usi.utah.edu:80/cgi-programming/`

MSG Tutorial: Much Ado about Perl

Basic information about perl and links to many other CGI references.

`http://www.msg.net/tutorial/cgi/perl.html`

Perl

The perl programmer's handbook (a comprehensive guide).

`http://www.atmos.washington.edu/perl/perl.html`

perlWWW

An extensive list of perl programs available on the Web.

`http://www.oac.uci.edu/indiv/ehood/perlWWW/`

UF/NA Perl Archive

The University of Florida perl archive.

```
http://www1.cis.ufl.edu/perl/
```

Perl Reference Materials

A list of books and other perl resources.

```
http://www.eecs.nwu.edu/perl/perl.html
```

DG Scripts

Scripts tutorial for C with a focus on creating games.

```
http://www.cypronet.com/~dg/bresource/scripts/
```

An Introduction to Shell Scripts

A short course on shell scripts from Rice University.

```
http://riceinfo.rice.edu/Computer/Documents/Classes/Unix/script/script.html
```

Computer Science

Resources for C++ programming and scripts.

```
http://gnofn.org/whs1/education/subjects/compsci.html
```

CGI

A basic CGI tutorial for perl.

```
http://www.acprog.ifas.ufl.edu/~glf/Forms_and_Gateways/cgi2.html
```

The Common Gateway Interface Specification

The NCSA Common Gateway Interface Specification.

```
http://hoohoo.ncsa.uiuc.edu/cgi/interface.html
```

MMS Literature: CGI

An online course in perl and CGI scripts.

```
http://media.it.kth.se/mms/cgi/
```

Overview of CGI

The World Wide Web Consortium (W3C) overview on CGI scripts.

```
http://www.w3.org/hypertext/WWW/CGI/
```

IMAGE MAPS

MapServe Home Page

An image mapping CGI program for use with MacHTTP or WebSTAR.

http://www.spub.ksu.edu/other/machttp_tools/mapserve/mapserve.html

MapMarker Home Page

A Unix program for editing image maps.

http://www.dl.ac.uk/CBMT/mapmarker/HOME.html

Mac-ImageMap Home Page

A CGI script for image maps on a Macintosh WWW server, which runs with the software WebSTAR or MacHTTP.

http://weyl.zib-berlin.de/imagemap/Mac-ImageMap.html

MapMaker

An online image map editor.

http://www.tns.lcs.mit.edu/cgi-bin/mapmaker

WebMap for the Macintosh

An image map editor for the Macintosh.

http://www.city.net/cnx/software/Webmap.html

Web Hotspots

An image map editor that supports client- and server-side image maps for Windows 3.1 and Windows 95.

http://www.cris.com/~automata/hotspots.shtml

Map THIS! Home Page

A free image map editor for Windows 3.1x with Win32s 1.25 or later, Windows NT 3.5x, or Windows 95.

http://www.ecaetc.ohio-state.edu/tc/mt/

Mapmaker v1.1 Home Page

An image map editor for Unix.

http://icg.resnet.upenn.edu/mapmaker.html

glorglox Advanced Image Mapper

An NCSA server-specific image map editor that lets you map each pixel to a distinct URL.

```
http://www.uunet.ca/~tomr/glorglox/
```

SEARCH ENGINES

Alta Vista

Alta Vista is an extremely powerful search engine with billions of words in millions of Web pages.

```
http://www.altavista.digital.com/
```

Yahoo

Yahoo is one of the most well-known search engines.

```
http://www.yahoo.com/
```

Search.com

Search.com was started in March 1996 by CNET. It searches other search engines.

```
http://www.search.com/
```

Switchboard

Switchboard helps you locate individuals.

```
http://www.switchboard.com/
```

Who is

This internic service helps you find domain names.

```
gopher://rs.internic.net/7waissrc%3A/rs/whois.src
```

Lycos, Inc.

This is one of the original search engines.

```
http://www.lycos.com/
```

Metasearch

Metasearch uses other search engines to conduct searches.

```
http://metasearch.com/
```

The Electric Library

This engine uses newspapers, periodicals, books, and other printed sources for its searches.

`http://www.elibrary.com/id/2525/`

Shareware.com

This site is maintained by CNET, and has links to all the shareware you can eat.

`http://www.shareware.com/`

Submit It!

Submit It! helps you publicize your Web site.

`http://www.submit-it.com/`

WebPromote™

WebPromote also helps publicize Web sites.

`http://www.webpromote.com/`

Thanks to all of the people involved in making available the Web sites listed in this appendix. They have been excellent sources of reference to us throughout this book. This list will be updated at the Browser by Design Web site. Check back regularly for updated Web site listings. The list will be operated and maintained by the authors and will be a preview of future editions of *Hybrid HTML Design*. So go ahead, check it out!

`http://www.browserbydesign.com/`

INDEX

Symbols

<!..comment> extension (Netscape), 88, 179
non-recognition, 229
2 HTML (conversion program), 40
4W Publisher (database conversion program), 52

A

<A> extension (Netscape Navigator), 109, 249
Aardvark Pro V2.0.4 (editor), 60-61
features, 365
Aaron's Graphic Archive (Web site), 379
absolute links, defined, 325
absolute references
defined, 110
table design, 140
accent marks, HTML tag, 32
Accent Multilingual Mosaic, 24
Web site, 372
Acrobat Amber Reader (plug-in), 302
ActiveMovie, 294
Address Bar, Internet Explorer 2.0, 6
<ADDRESS> tag, 92
adjacent images, comparisons to image maps, 287-288
Adobe, 84
Acrobat Amber Reader (plug-in), 302
AIFF files (Audio Interchange File Format), 290
ALIGN attribute
Internet Explorer HTML extensions
<HSPACE>, 195
<MARQUEE>, 195
<NLC>, 215

HTML 3 tags
<CAPTION>, 141
<DIV>, 156
<HR>, 129
<IMG>, 130
</P>, 129
<TD>, 142
<TH>, 142
<TR>, 141
ALINK attribute, <BODY> HTML 3 tag, 127
Alis, Multilingual Browser, 25
Alta Vista, Web site, 387
Amber Reader (plug-in), 302
America Online (AOL), browsers, 16
HTML 3 tags example, 160
HTML 3 attributes to HTML 2 tags, 137
HTML 2 listing tags, 106
HTML extensions (table), 357-364
HTML tag attribute support (table), 357-364
HTML text formatting tags, 97
interface, 16-17
non-recognized HTML 3 tags, 238
partially recognized HTML tags, 261
table design techniques, 270
Web controls, 16
Web site, 17, 371
anchor tag (HTML 2), 109
animation files, 295
ANT_HTML (conversion program), 39
apostrophe ('), HTML tag, 32
<APP> extension (HotJava), non-recognition, 229
Apple
browsers, see Cyberdog
plug-ins, QuickTime, 302

<APPLET> extension (Netscape Navigator), 189
non-recognition, 229
applets (Java), defined, 316
applications
distributed applications, 316-317
helper applications
audio, 298
AviLxp AVI Movie Viewer, 299
Cybergate, 299
defined, 297
Eudora, 300
Fountain, 299
GifBuilder, Clip2Gif, 298
GoldWave, 298
graphics, 297
Imagenation Viewer, 298
JPEGView, 297
LView Pro, 297
media.splash, 351
MPEG2PLY.EXE, 299
MPLAYER.EXE, 298
PhotoSphere Viewer, 299
PKZip, 300
QuickTime VR, 299
RealAudio Player, 298
Sparkle, 298
Stuffit, 300
tips, 315
utilities, 300
video, 298
virtual worlds, 299
WebSpace Navigator, 299
WinZip, 300
Arachnid (editor), 65
features, 365
<AREA> extension (Internet Explorer), 249
attributes, 196
<AREA> HTML 3 tag, 156
attributes, 156

non-recognition, 229
Netscape Navigator, 249
ASAP WebShow (plug-in),
311
Astound Web Player
(plug-in), 304
attributes
HTML 2 tags, browser-
support (table),
357-364
HTML 3 attributes in
HTML 2 browsers,
132-138
integrating, 139
HTML 3 tags
<AREA>, 156
<BODY>, 127
<CAPTION>, 141
<DIV>, 156
<FONT>, 155
<HR>, 129
<IMG>, 130
<li>, 131
<LINK>, 124
<MAP>, 156
<META>, 125
<OL>, 131
</P>, 129
<TABLE>, 141
<TD>, 142
<TH>, 142
<TR>, 141
<UL>, 131
version-specific,
249-252, 357-364
HTML tags, browser-
specific, 249-252
Internet Explorer HTML
extensions
<AREA>, 196
<BGSOUND>, 196
<BODY>, 197
<FONT>, 197
<HR>, 196
<IMG>, 198
<MARQUEE>, 195
<NLC>, 215
<TABLE>, 199

Netscape HTML
extensions
<APPLET>, 189
<CERTIFICATE>, 192
<FRAME>, 171, 174
<FRAMESET>, 170
<PARAM>, 189
<PAYORDER>, 192
audio files, 293
formats, 290-292
AIFF files (Audio
Interchange File
Format), 290, 292
MIDI files (Musical
Instrument Digital
Interface), 290
helper applications, 298
players, MIME types
(table), 370
resources, Web sites,
379-380
sampling rate, 290
sound depth, 290
Audio Interchange File
Format files (AIFF), 290
Audio Video Interleaved
(AVI files), 294
authoring tools
converters, 30, 80
BeyondPress
(QuarkXPress), 29,
80-82
Collect HTML
(QuarkXPress), 83
FrameMaker, 85
HexWeb XT
(QuarkXPress), 83
PageMaker, 84
databases, 45-47
4W Publisher, 52
choosing, 47
Cold Fusion, 51
dbWeb, 49
drivers, 47
HTMakeL Database
Merge, 52
Illustra, 48
Oracle WebServer 2.0,
50

development of, 30
editors, 53
Aardvark Pro V2.0.4,
60-61, 365
Arachnid, 65, 365
BBEdit, 62-63, 365
defined, 30
HotDog V2.0, 56-57,
365
HTML Assistant Pro 2,
54-55, 365
HTML Easy! Pro, 66
HTMLed Pro, 64, 365
table, 365
Webber, 66
WebEdit, 66
World Wide Web
Weaver V1.1.1,
58-59, 365
spreadsheets, 41
application design, 42
converters, 43-44
macros, 42
trial versions, 86
word processors, 32
2 HTML, 40
ANT_HTML, 39
converters, 37-40
Cyberleaf, 38
HTML Transit
program, 37
Internet Assistant for
Microsoft Word, 38
macros, 35
mail merge feature, 36
search and replace
feature, 35
special characters,
32-34
spell check, 35
templates, 35
thesaurus, 35
Web Author, 40
Web Publisher, 39
WordPerfect Internet
Publisher, 40
WYSIWYG editors, 67
FrontPage, 68-69, 366
GNNPress, 76-77, 366

HotMetal Pro, 78-79
Navigator Gold, 74-75,
   366
PageMill, 70-71, 366
SiteMill, 72-73, 366
table, 366
AVI files (Audio Video
   Interleaved), 294
AVIHELPER attribute,
   <NLO> extension
   (Internet Explorer), 214
AviLxp AVI Movie Viewer
   helper application, 299

B

<B> tag, 91
BACKGROUND attribute,
   <BODY> HTML 3 tag, 127
bandwidth, defined, 351-352
Base 10 system, 128
Base 16 system, 128
<BASE> tag, 89-90
<BASEFONT> extension
   (Netscape), 165
BBEdit (editor), 62-63
   features, 365
BEHAVIOR attribute,
   <MARQUEE> extension
   (Internet Explorer), 195
BeyondPress (QuarkXPress
   conversion extension), 29,
   80-82
BGCOLOR attribute
   HTML 3 tags, <BODY>,
      127
   Internet Explorer HTML
      extensions
         <MARQUEE>, 195
         <TABLE>, 199
BGPROPERTIES attribute,
   <BODY> extension
   (Internet Explorer), 197
<BGSOUND> extension
   (Internet Explorer), 196
   non-recognition, 229
<BIG> HTML 3 tag, 155
<BLINK> extension

Internet Explorer,
   non-recognition, 234
Netscape Navigator, 165
<BLOCKQUOTE> tag, 92
blue support level, 3
body element tags
   HTML 2, 91-92
   HTML 3, 127-129
      image tag, 130
      listing tags, 131
<BODY> extension
   Internet Explorer, 249
      attributes, 197
   Netscape Navigator, 166
<BODY> HTML 3 tag, 88,
   127, 249
   attributes, 127
   hexadecimal color coding
      system, 128
bold formatting, HTML 2
   tags, 91
Bookmark window,
   PowerBrowser 1.0, 8
Bookmarks menu, Netscape,
   4
BORDER attribute, HTML 3
   tags
      <IMG>, 130
      <TABLE>, 141
BORDERCOLOR attribute,
   <TABLE> extension
   (Internet Explorer), 199
BORDERCOLORDARK
   attribute, <TABLE>
   extension (Internet
   Explorer), 199
BORDERCOLORLIGHT
   attribute, <TABLE>
   extension (Internet
   Explorer), 199
Borland's Internet Tools
   (Web site), 377

 extension, 107
   attributes, 251
Break statement, JavaScript,
   181
Browser By Design (Web
   site), 372

Browser Tuneup, The (Web
   site), 372
browser-specific tags, *see*
   individual browser
   extensions
BrowserCaps (Web site), 373
browsers
   America Online, 16
      HTML extensions,
         357-364
      HTML tag attribute
         support, 357-364
      interface, 16-17
      non-recognized HTML
         3 tags, 247
      partially recognized
         HTML tags, 261
      Web controls, 16
      Web site, 17
   Cyberdog (Beta Release
      2), 20
      Cybericons, 20
      HTML extensions,
         357-364
      HTML tag attribute
         support, 357-364
      interface, 20-21
      OpenDoc components,
         20
      running dog icon, 20
      Web site, 21
   defined, 1-2
   development of, 2
   display, bar beneath
      display, 3
   GNN Works, 26
   hardware incompatibili-
      ties, 263
   HotJava (Alpha 1.0), 10
      hiding screen elements,
         10
      HTML extensions,
         357-364
      HTML tag attribute
         support, 357-364
      interface, 10-11
      navigating pages, 10

non-recognized HTML
    extensions, 237
Web site, 11
HTML 2 tags
    form tags, 116-119
    listing tags, 103-106
    text formatting, 95-98
HTML 3 tags, 87
    embedded table tags,
        146-147
    examples, 159-161
    in HTML 2 browser
        examples, 133-138
    integrating in HTML 2
        browsers, 139
    table tags in business
        letters, 152-153
HTML tag extensions
    Internet Explorer,
        194-205, 212
    Internet Explorer 3,
        206-211
    Netscape Navigator,
        179-193
    Netscape Navigator 3,
        190-192
    Oracle Basic, 222-224
    PowerBrowser,
        213-221, 225
Internet Explorer 2.0
    HTML extensions,
        357-364
    HTML tag attribute
        support, 357-364
    interface, 6-7
    non-recognized HTML
        3 tags, 245
    non-recognized HTML
        extensions, 236
    partially recognized
        HTML tags, 259
Internet Explorer 3.0
    HTML extensions,
        357-364
    HTML tag attribute
        support, 357-364
levels of support, 3
Lynx, 25

Mosaic (NSCA Mosaic
    2.0)
    collaboration sessions,
        12
    development of, 12
    HTML extensions,
        357-364
    HTML tag attribute
        support, 357-364
    interface, 12-13
    Presentation Mode, 12
    Web site, 13
Multilingual Browser
    (Alis), 25
Multilingual Mosaic
    (Accent), 24
Netscape Navigator 1.1
    HTML extensions,
        357-364
    HTML tag attribute
        support, 357-364
Netscape Navigator 2.0, 4
    frames, 4
    HTML extensions,
        164-178, 357-364
    HTML tag attribute
        support, 357-364
    interface, 4-5
    logo, 4
    non-recognized HTML
        3 tags, 244
    non-recognized HTML
        extensions, 234-235
    partially recognized
        HTML tags, 258
    Web sites, 5
Netscape Navigator 3.0
    HTML extensions,
        357-364
    HTML tag attribute
        support, 357-364
non-recognized HTML
    tags, 248
    browser-specific
        extensions, 229-237
    defined, 228
    HTML 3 tags, 238-247
Opera, 27

partially recognized
    HTML tags, 262
    attributes, 249-252
    defined, 228-249
    examples, 254-261
    file types, 253
platform
    incompatibilities, 263
PointCast PCN
    interface, 22-23
    Web site, 23
PowerBrowser (Oracle
    PowerBrowser 1.0), 8
    hiding screen elements,
        8
    HTML extensions,
        357-364
    HTML tag attribute
        support, 357-364
    interface, 8
    menus, 8
    non-recognized HTML
        3 tags, 246
    partially recognized
        HTML tags, 260
    resizing screen, 9
    Web site, 9
Prodigy (2.0d), 18
    HTML extensions,
        357-364
    HTML tag attribute
        support, 357-364
    interface, 18-19
    toolbar, 18
    Web site, 19
resources, 372-373
Spry Mosaic
    (CompuServe Spry
    Mosaic .04.10.9.20), 14
    HTML extensions,
        357-364
    HTML tag attribute
        support, 357-364
    interface, 14-15
    Spryhoo page, 14
    Web site, 15
tables, advanced design
    techniques, 269-270
tags, reading, 34

versions, testing new Web pages for old versions, 28

Virtual Place (Ubique Sesame), 26

Web pages, testing, 28

Web sites, resources, 371-372

WebExplorer, 27

BrowserWatch (Web site), 372

BrowserWatch - Plug-In Plaza! (Web site), 373

Business@Web, OpenScape (plug-in), 302

buttons
HotJava interface, 10
Mosaic interface, 12

C

California Internet-Services WWW Servers (Web site), 383

Caligari Home World (Web site), 381

<CAPTION> HTML 3 tag, 141
attributes, 141

Carberry Technology/EBT, FIGleaf Inline (plug-in), 303

Carbon Copy (plug-in), 308

Cascading Style Sheets, Level 1 (Web site), 374

Cello (Web site), 372

CELLPADDING attribute, <TABLE> HTML 3 tag, 141

CELLSPACING attribute, <TABLE> HTML 3 tag, 141

<CENTER> HTML 3 tag, 156

<CERTIFICATE> extension (Netscape Navigator 3), 192

CGI scripts (Common Gateway Interface), 336
defined, 336-338

determining site audience, 345

diagram of scripting process, 337

directories, 338

form scripts, 342-344

image map scripts, 339-341

resources, Web sites, 383-385

service provider options, 322

Web site, 385

CGI Scripts (Web site), 384

Chaco Communications, VR Scout (plug-in), 303

characters
HTML tags, 32
special characters
replacing tags with ASCII equivalent, 34
table of, 367-368

word processors, HTML editing tools, 32-34

Chemscape Chime (plug-in), 308

<CITE> tag, 92

CLEAR attribute, HTML 3 tags
<DIV>, 156
<HR>, 129

client-side image maps, 341

Clip2Gif and GifBuilder (Web site), 378

closing HTML tags, 88
HTML 2, 93

CMX Viewer (plug-in), 303

CMYK color method, 278-280

CNET Browser Review (Web site), 373

CODE attribute, <APPLET> extension (Netscape Navigator), 189

<CODE> tag, 92

CODEBASE attribute, <APPLET> extension (Netscape Navigator), 189

collaborations sessions, Mosaic, 12

Cold Fusion (database conversion program), 51

color
digital color, 278
CMYK color method, 279-280
hexadecimal color method, 128, 279-280
RGB color method, 279-280
palettes, 281
special color names, 282

COLOR attribute
Internet Explorer, <HR> extension, 196
HTML 3 tags, <FONT>, 155

COLS attribute, <FRAMESET> extension, Netscape Navigator, 170

COLSPAN attribute, HTML 3 tags
<TD>, 142
<TH>, 142

Comment statement, JavaScript, 181

Common Gateway Interface, *see* CGI scripts

compression, image files, 286

CompuServe
browsers
HTML 3 embedded table tags, 147
HTML 3 table tags, 153
dial-up service, Wow!, 14

CompuServe Spry Mosaic, *see* Spry Mosaic

Computer Graphics (Web site), 378

Computer Science (Web site), 385

Concurrent Programming in Java (Web site), 376

configuration files, CGI form scripts, 344

conflicts, *see* display conflicts
CONTENT attribute,
<META> HTML 3 tag,
125
Continue statement,
JavaScript, 181
Control Panel, HotJava, 10
CONTROLS attribute,
Internet Explorer HTML
extensions
<IMG>, 198
<NLC>, 215
converters
defined, 30
desktop publishing, 80
*BeyondPress
(QuarkXPress),
80-82*
*Collect HTML
(QuarkXPress), 83*
FrameMaker, 85
*HexWeb XT
(QuarkXPress), 83*
PageMaker, 84
development of, 30
spreadsheets (Excel),
43-44
trial versions, 86
word processors
2 HTML, 40
ANT_HTML, 39
Cyberleaf, 38
HTML Transit, 37
*Internet Assistant for
Microsoft Word, 38*
Web Author, 40
Web Publisher, 39
*WordPerfect Internet
Publisher, 40*
CoolFusion (plug-in), 307
COORDS attribute, <AREA>
HTML 3 tag, 156
copyright symbol (©), HTML
tag, 32
Corel, CMX Viewer (plug-
in), 303
Creating Net Sites (Web site),
373
Crescendo (plug-in), 306

cross-platform issues
style sheet standards, 348
Web site designs, 327
Cross-Platform QuickTime
(Web site), 380
cryptography, public key, 191
CTC Tutorial on Shell Scripts
(Web site), 384
Cyberdog (Beta Release 2),
20
HTML extensions, table,
357-364
HTML tag attribute
support, table, 357-364
icons (Cybericons), 20
interface, 20-21
Web site, 21, 371
CyberGate helper
application, 299
Web site, 372
Cyberleaf (conversion
program), 38

D

databases
editing tools, 45-47
4W Publisher, 52
choosing, 47
Cold Fusion, 51
dbWeb, 49
drivers, 47
*HTMakeL Database
Merge, 52*
Illustra, 48
*Oracle WebServer 2.0,
50*
ODBC (Open Database
Connectivity), 47
DataBlades (Illustra
conversion feature), 48
dbWeb (database conversion
program), 49
DD's Cyberhome (Web site),
380
<DD> tag, 100
definition lists, HTML 2 tag,
100

designing
tables, 154
HTML tags, 140
Web pages for multiple
browsers, 3
*vertical spacing in
Internet Explorer
2.0, 7*
desktop publishing, convert-
ers, 80
BeyondPress
(QuarkXPress), 80-82
Collect HTML
(QuarkXPress), 83
FrameMaker, 85
HexWeb XT
(QuarkXPress), 83
PageMaker, 84
Desktop Video (Web site),
380
DGScripts (Web site), 385
dial-up services, Wow!, 14
digital color, 278
CMYK color method,
279-280
hexadecimal color
method, 279-280
RGB color method,
279-280
Digital Music Zone (Web
site), 380
<DIR> tag, 100
DIRECTION attribute,
<MARQUEE>extension
(Internet Explorer), 195
Directory Buttons, Netscape,
4
directory lists, HTML 2 tag,
100
<DIRECTORY> tag, 100
display conflicts
hardware
incompatibilities, 263
non-recognized HTML
tags, 248
*browser-specific
extensions, 229-237*
defined, 228
HTML 3 tags, 238-247

partially recognized
HTML tags, 262
attributes, 249-252
defined, 228, 249
examples, 254-261
file types, 253
platform
incompatibilities, 263
displaying windows,
PowerBrowser 1.0, 8
distributed applications,
316-317
<DIV> HTML 3 tag, 156
<DL> tag, 100
domain names, registering,
320, 346
<DT> tag, 100
DWG/DXF Plug-in
(plug-in), 310
DYNSRC attribute, <IMG>
extension (Internet
Explorer), 198

E

EarthTime (plug-in), 312
editors, 53
Aardvark Pro V2.0.4,
60-61
features, 365
Arachnid, 65
features, 365
BBEdit, 62-63
features, 365
databases, 45-47
4W Publisher, 52
choosing solutions, 47
Cold Fusion, 51
dbWeb, 49
drivers, 47
HTMakeL Database
Merge, 52
Illustra, 48
Oracle WebServer 2.0,
50
defined, 30
development of, 30
HotDog V2.0, 56-57
features, 365

HTML Easy! Pro, 66
HTML Assistant Pro 2,
54-55
features, 365
HTMLed Pro, 64
features, 365
spreadsheets, 41
application design, 42
converters, 43-44
macros, 42
table of, 365
trial versions, 86
Webber, 66
WebEdit, 66
word processors, 32
mail merge feature, 36
macros, 35
search and replace
feature, 35
special characters,
32-34
spell check, 35
templates, 35
thesaurus, 35
World Wide Web Weaver
V1.1.1, 58-59
features, 365
WYSIWYG editors, 67
FrontPage, 68-69, 366
GNNPress, 76-77
HotMetal Pro, 78-79
Navigator Gold, 74-75,
366
PageMill, 70-71, 366
SiteMill, 72-73, 366
table of, 366
Electric Library, The (Web
site), 388
<EM> tag, 91
<EMBED> extension
Internet Explorer, non-
recognition, 234
Netscape Navigator,
168-169
non-recognition, 229
PowerBrowser, non-
recognition, 229
Emblaze (plug-in), 304

<EMTA> HTML 3 tag, 125
Envoy (plug-in), 313
Eudora (helper application),
300
event handlers (JavaScript),
HTML extensions, 180
Excel, conversion programs,
43-44
Excel to HTML conversion
utility, 44
Excel-to-HTML converter
macro, 43
Explorer 2.0 (Internet
Explorer), 6
display, 6
HTML 2 tags
form tags, 117
listing tags, 103
text formats, 95
HTML 3 attributes to
HTML 2 tags, 136
HTML 3 tags
embedded table tags,
146
non-recognized tags,
245
table tags, 152
HTML extensions,
194-195, 212
<AREA> tag
attributes, 196
<BGSOUND>, 196
<BLINK>, 234
<BODY> tag
attributes, 197
<EMBED>, 234
examples, 200-205
<FONT> tag
attributes, 197
<HR> tag attributes,
196
<IIMG> tag attributes,
198
<MARQUEE>, 195,
230, 234
non-recognized
extensions, 229, 236
partially recognized
extensions, 249, 259

table of, 357-364
<TABLE> tag
    attributes, 199
HTML tag attribute
    support, table, 357-364
interface, 6-7
tables, advanced design
    techniques, 269
Web site, 7, 371
Explorer 3.0 (Internet
Explorer)
HTML extensions,
    206-207
    examples, 208-211
    <FRAME>, 206
    <OBJECT>, 206
    <SCRIPT>, 207
    table of, 357-364
HTML tag attribute
    support, table, 357-364
extensions
    America Online browser,
        357-364
    compressed files, MIME
        types (table), 370
    Cyberdog browser,
        357-364
    HotJava browser, 357-364
    Internet Explorer 2.0/3.0
        browser, 357-364
    Mosaic browser, 357-364
    Netscape Navigator 1.1,
        2.0, or 3.0 browser,
        357-364
    PowerBrowser, 357-364
    Prodigy browser, 357-364
    Spry Mosaic browser,
        357-364
    table of, 369
    see also HTML 2 tags;
        HTML 3 tags

F

FACE attribute, <FONT>
    extension (Internet
    Explorer), 197
Farallon, Timbuktu Plug-In,
    304

Favorites menu, Internet
    Explorer 2.0, 6
Fetch 3.0 (FTP software),
    330-331
FIGleaf Inline (plug-in), 303
files
    animation files, 295
    audio files, 293
        formats, 290-292
        MIME types (table),
            370
        sampling rate, 290
        sound depth, 290
    compressed files, MIME
        types (table), 370
    extensions, table of, 369
    formats, proprietary, 285
    graphics files, MIME
        types (table), 369
    image files
        adjacent images,
            287-288
        color palettes, 281-282
        compression, 286
        design tips, 289
        digital color, 278-280
        GIF (Graphics
            Interchange
            Format), 283-285
        image maps, 287-288
        JPEG (Joint
            Photographic
            Experts Group),
            284-285
        special color names,
            282
    text files, MIME types
        (table), 369
    types, partial recognition,
        253
    video files, 294-295
    VRML files (Virtual
        Reality Modeling
        Language), 296
<FONT> extension, Internet
    Explorer, 249
    attributes, 197, 251
<FONT> HTML 3 tag, 155
For statement, JavaScript, 181

For...in statement, JavaScript,
    181
foreign languages, browsers
    Multilingual Browser
        (Alis), 25
    Multilingual Mosaic, 24
form tags, HTML 2, 111-114
    browser examples,
        116-119
    design considerations,
        120-121
    examples, 115
<FORM> tag, 111
formatting tags
    HTML 2, 91
        browser examples, 95-98
        choosing, 93
        example, 94
    HTML 3, 155
forms, CGI scripts, 342-344
Formula One/Net (plug-in),
    313
Fountain (helper applica-
    tion), 299
Fractal Viewer (plug-in), 307
<FRAME> extension
    Internet Explorer 3, 206
    Netscape Navigator, 171
        non-recognition, 229
    PowerBrowser, non-
        recognition, 229
frame relay connections, 351
frame tags, advanced design
    techniques, 271-275
FrameMaker, conversion
    programs, 85
frames, 4
    Netscape Navigator
        bottom frame, 4
        HTML extensions,
            170-178
        top frame, 4
<FRAMESET> extension
    Internet Explorer,
        non-recognition, 229
    Netscape Navigator, 170
        non-recognition, 229
    PowerBrowser, non-
        recognition, 229

FrontPage (editor), 68-69
    features, 366
FTP (File Transfer Protocol),
    software, 328-329
    Fetch 3.0, 330-331
    Snatcher, 334-335
    WS_FTP, 332-333
FULLSCREEN attribute,
    <NLC> extension
    (Internet Explorer), 215
Function statement,
    JavaScript, 181
functions, JavaScript, 182
FutureSplash (plug-in), 304
FutureTense, Inc. (Web site),
    376

G

Gamelan, Web site, 377
Gamelan's JavaScript (Web
    site), 375
GEO, Emblaze (plug-in), 304
GifBuilder, Clip2Gif (helper
    application), 298
GIF files (Graphics
    Interchange Format),
    283-285
    animated, 295
    compression, 286
    design tips, 289
glorglox Advanced Image
    Mapper (Web site), 386
GNN (Global Network
    Navigator), 26
    Web site, 371
GNNPress (editor), 76-77,
    366
GNNPress, features, 366
GNN Works (browser), 26
Gold Disk, Astound Web
    Player (plug-in), 304
GoldWave Digital Audio
    Editor (Web site), 380
GoldWave (helper
    application), 298
graphics
    files, table of MIME types,
    369

helper applications, 297
resources, Web sites,
    378-379
Graphics File Format Page,
    The (Web site), 378
Graphics Interchange
    Format, *see* GIF files
green support level, 3
GUI Programming Using
    Java (Web site), 377

H

<H1> - <H6> tags, 91
hardware incompatibilities,
    263
head element tags, HTML 3,
    124-126
<HEAD> tag, 88-90
HEIGHT attribute
    HTML 3 tags, <IMG>, 130
    Internet Explorer HTML
        extension
        <MARQUEE>, 195
        <NLC>, 215
    Netscape Navigator
        HTML extensions,
        <APPLET>, 189
helper applications
    audio, 298
    AviLxp AVI Movie
        Viewer, 299
    Cybergate, 299
    defined, 297
    Eudora, 300
    Fountain, 299
    GifBuilder, Clip2Gif, 298
    GoldWave, 298
    graphics, 297
    Imagenation Viewer, 298
    JPEGView, 297
    LView Pro, 297
    media.splash, 351
    MPEG2PLY.EXE, 299
    MPLAYER.EXE, 298
    PhotoSphere Viewer, 299

PKZip, 300
QuickTime VR, 299
RealAudio Player, 298
Sparkle, 298
Stuffit, 300
tips, 315
utilities, 300
video, 298
virtual worlds, 299
WebSpace Navigator, 299
WinZip, 300
see also plug-ins
hexadecimal color coding
    system, 128, 279-280
HexWeb XT (QuarkXPress
    conversion extension), 83
History window,
    PowerBrowser 1.0, 8
HistoryTree (plug-in), 310
horizontal rule tag, HTML 2,
    110
HotDog V2.0 (editor), 56-57
    features, 365
HotJava (Alpha 1.0), 10
    HTML extensions
        *non-recognized 229,
        237*
        table, 357-364
    HTML 2 extensions
        form tags, 118
        listing tags, 105
        text formats, 96
    HTML 3 attributes to
        HTML 2 tags, 138
    HTML 3 extensions
        example, 161
    HTML tag attribute sup-
        port, table, 357-364
    interface, 10-11
    menus, 10
    navigating pages, 10
    Web site, 11, 371
Hotlists, Internet Explorer 2.0
    site, 6
HotMetal Pro (editor), 78-79
<HR> extension, Internet
    Explorer, 110
    attributes, 196, 251

<HR> HTML 3 tag, 129, 249
    attributes, 129
HREF attribute, <AREA>
    HTML 3 tag, 156
HSPACE attribute
    Internet Explorer HTML
        extensions, <NLC>,
        215
    HTML 3 tags, <IMG>, 130
HTMakeL Database Merge
    (database conversion
    program), 52
HTML (HyperText Markup
    Language)
    evolution of, 348-349
        bandwidth
            considerations,
            351-352
        browser considerations,
            351-352
        compression methods,
            352
        HTML design
            strategies, 350-351
    resources, Web sites,
        373-375
    standards, 348-349
        design strategies,
            350-351
    HTML 2 tags
        <!..comment>, 88
        <A>, 109
        <ADDRESS>, 92
        <B>, 91
        <BASE>, 89-90
        <BLOCKQUOTE>, 92
        <BODY>, 88
        body elements, 91-92
            anchor tag, 109
            choosing text formats,
                93
            design considerations,
                120-121
            form tags, 111-114
            form tags HTML
                examples, 115-119
            horizontal rule tag, 110
            image tag, 108

listing tags, 99-101
listing tags; HTML
    examples, 102-106
spacing tags, 107
text formats, 91-92
text formatting HTML
    example, 94-98

, 107
browser-support, table,
    357-364
<CITE>, 92
closing tags, 93
<CODE>, 92
<DD>, 100
<DIR>, 100
<DIRECTORY>, 100
<DL>, 100
document elements, 88
<DT>, 100
<EM>, 91
<FORM>, 111
<H1> - <H6>, 91
<HEAD>, 88-90
head elements, 89-90
<HR>, 110
<HTML>, 88
HTML 3 attributes,
    132-134
<I>, 91
<IMG>, 108
<INPUT>, 111
integrating with HTML 3
    tags, 157
<ISINDEX>, 89-90
<KBD>, 92
<li>, 99
<LINK>, 89-90
<MENU>, 100
<OL>, 99
opening tags, 93
<OPTION>, 114
<P>, 107
<PLAINTEXT>, 92
<PRE>, 91
<S>, 91
<SAMP>, 92
<SELECT>, 113
special characters, 32
<STRIKE>, 92

<STRONG>, 91
<TEXTAREA>, 113
<TITLE>, 89-90
<TT>, 92
<TYPE>, 112
<U>, 91
<UL>, 99
<VAR>, 92
<XMP>, 92
see also HTML 3 tags;
    HTML extensions
HTML 3 browsers, 87
HTML 3 Linking and
    Embedding Model (Web
    site), 374
HTML 3 tags
    <AREA>, 156
    attributes in HTML 2 tags,
        132-134
    <BIG>, 155
    <BODY>, 127
        hexadecimal color
            coding system, 128
    body elements
        body tags, 127-129
        image tag, 130
        listing tag, 131
    <CAPTION>, 141
    <CENTER>, 156
    closing tags, 88
    <DIV>, 156
    <FONT>, 155
    head elements, 124-125
        HTML example, 126
    <HR>, 129
    HTML browser examples,
        158-161
    HTML 2 browsers
        examples, 133-138
        integrating in, 139
    <IMG>, 130
    integrating with HTML 2
        tags, 157
    <LH>, 131
    <li>, 131
    <LINK>, 124
    <MAP>, 156
    <META>, 125

non-recognition, 238, 248
  examples, 240-247
  special characters, 240
  table tags, 239
<OL>, 131
</P>, 129
partial recognition, attributes, 249
<SMALL>, 155
special characters, 32
<SUB>, 155
<SUP>, 155
<TABLE>, 141
table tags, 140-142
  business letter examples, 148-153
  designing tables, 140, 154
  embedded table browser examples, 145-147
  HTML examples, 143-144
<TD>, 142
text formats, 155
<TH>, 142
<TR>, 141
<UL>, 131
version-specific, table, 357-364
see also HTML 2 tags;
  HTML extensions
HTML DTDs (Web site), 374
HTML Easy! Pro (editor), 66
HTML extensions
America Online browser, table of extensions, 357-364
compressed files, MIME types (table), 370
Cyberdog browser, table of extensions, 357-364
HotJava browser, table of extensions, 357-364
Internet Explorer 2.0 extensions, 194-195, 212
  <AREA> tag attributes, 196
  <BGSOUND>, 196

<BODY> tag attributes, 197
<FONT> tag attributes, 197
<HR> tag attributes, 196
HTML examples, 200-205
<IMG> tag attributes, 198
<MARQUEE>, 195
table of, 357-364
<TABLE> tag attributes, 199
Internet Explorer 3 extensions, 206-207
  <FRAME>, 206
  HTML examples, 208-211
  <OBJECT>, 206
  <SCRIPT>, 207
  table of, 357-364
Mosaic browser, table of extensions, 357-364
Netscape Navigator 1.1, table of extensions, 357-364
Netscape Navigator 2.0 extensions, 164-165, 193
  <!..comment>, 179
  <APPLET>, 189
  <BASEFONT>, 165
  <BLINK>, 165
  <BODY>, 166
  <EMBED>, 168-169
  <FRAME>, 171
  frame design considerations, 172-174
  frames, 175-178
  <FRAMESET>, 170
  <IMG>, 165
  Java, 189
  JavaScript, 179-183
  JavaScript HTML examples, 184-188
  <NOBR>, 165

  <NOEMBED>, 168-169
  <NOFRAMES>, 170
  <PARAM>, 189
  <SCRIPT>, 179-182
  <TITLE>, 166
  <WBR>, 165
Netscape 3 extensions, 190
  <CERTIFICATE>, 192
  <PAYORDER>, 192
  public key cryptography, 191
  table of, 357-364
non-recognition
  browser-specific extensions, 229-237
  defined, 228, 248
Oracle Basic extensions, 222
  HTML examples, 223-224
partial-recognition
  attributes, 249-252
  defined, 228, 249, 262
  examples, 254-261
  file types, 253
  table of extensions, 357-364
platform
  incompatibilities, 263
PowerBrowser extensions, 213, 225
  HTML examples, 218-221
  <LAYOUTFRAME>, 217
  <LAYOUTFRAMERESET>, 217
  Network Loadable Objects, 214-215
  <NLO>, 214-215
  table of extensions, 357-364
Prodigy browser, table of extensions, 357-364

special characters, 32
 *replacing with ASCII
   equivalent, 34*
Spry Mosaic browser,
 table of extensions,
 357-364
table of extensions, 369
tables, advanced design
 techniques, 264-270
 see also HTML 2 tags;
 HTML 3 tags
HTML tags
 closing tags, 88
 defined, 87
 frames, advanced design
   techniques, 271-275
 hardware
   incompatibilities, 263
HTML text editors, 53
 Aardvark Pro V2.0.4,
   60-61, 365
 Arachnid, 65, 365
 BBEdit, 62-63, 365
 HotDog V2.0, 56-57, 365
 HTML Easy! Pro, 66, 365
 HTML Assistant Pro 2,
   54-55, 365
 HTMLed Pro, 64, 365
 table, 365
 Webber, 66
 WebEdit, 66
 World Wide Web Weaver
   V1.1.1, 58-59, 365
 WYSIWYG editors, 67
   *FrontPage, 68-69, 366
   GNNPress, 76-77, 366
   HotMetal Pro, 78-79,
     366
   Navigator Gold, 74-75,
     366
   PageMill, 70-71, 366
   SiteMill, 72-73, 366*
HTML Transit (conversion
 program), 37
<HTML> tag, 88
HTML Assistant Pro 2
 (editor), 54-55
 features, 365

HTMLed Pro (editor), 64
 features, 365
HTML Reference Manual
 (Web site), 374
HTTP-EQUIV attribute,
 <META> HTML 3 tag,
 125
HyperText Markup
 Language (HTML):
 Working and Background
 Materials (Web site), 375
HyperText Markup
 Language Specification
 3.0 (Web site), 374

I

<I> tag, 91
ICB, Plug-ins, 304
Ichat Plug-in (plug-in), 305
icons, Cyberdog, 20
If...else statement, JavaScript,
 181
Illustra (database conversion
 program), 48
image files
 color palettes, 281
   *special color names,
     282*
 compression, 286
 design tips, 289
 digital color, 278-280
 formats
   *GIF (Graphics
     Interchange
     Format), 283-285
   JPEG (Joint
     Photographic
     Experts Group),
     284-285*
image maps
 CGI scripts, 339-341
 client-side, 341
 comparisons to adjacent
   images, 287-288
 resources, Web sites, 386
image tag
 HTML 2, 108

HTML 3, 130
Imagenation Viewer (helper
 application), 298
<IMG >extension
 Internet Explorer, 249
   attributes, 198
 Netscape Navigator, 165,
   249
 PowerBrowser, 249
<IMG> HTML 3 tag, 108, 130,
 249
 attributes, 130
Infinet Op, Lightning Strike
 (Plug-In), 305
INFO-MAC HyperArchive
 ROOT (Web site), 378
Inso Corporation, Word
 Viewer Plug-in, 305
Inserting Objects into HTML
 (Web site), 374
Integrated Data Systems,
 VRealm (plug-in), 305
Integrated Digital Services
 Network (ISDN), line
 speed, 351
Intelligence at Large,
 MovieStar Plug-in, 306
InterCAP InLine (plug-in),
 306
Internet Access Providers
 Around the World (Web
 site), 383
Internet Assistant for
 Microsoft Word
 (conversion program), 38
Internet Control Pack (Web
 site), 375
Internet Explorer 2.0, *see*
 Explorer 2.0; Explorer 3.0
Internet Publisher
 (conversion program), 40
Internet Service Providers
 (ISPs), *see* service
 providers
Internet Services (General
 Products and Services),
 Web site, 382
Internet Services Group (Web
 site), 382

Internic domain names, registration fees, 320
InterVU, PreVU (plug-in), 306
Internet Explorer - ActiveX Gallery (Web site), 375
Introduction to CGI Programming (Web site), 384
Introduction to Shell Scripts, An (Web site), 385
ISDN lines (Integrated Digital Services Network), speed, 351
<ISINDEX> tag, 89-90
ISPs (Internet Service Providers), *see* service providers
italic formatting, HTML 2 tag, 91
Iterated Systems, Plug-ins, 307
<ITEXTAREA> tag, 113

J

Java, 316
  applets, defined, 316
  HTML extensions
    Netscape Navigator 2.0, 189
    Netscape Navigator 3.0, 190-192
    non-recognized extensions, 229
  resources, Web sites, 376-377
Java Package Tutorial (Web site), 377
Java: Programming for the Internet (Web site), 376
JavaScript
  HTML tag extensions, Netscape Navigator 2.0, 179
    <APPLET>, 189
    <PARAM>, 189
    event handlers, 180
    examples, 185-188

functions, 182
methods, 184
objects, 183
properties, 183
statements, 181-182
HTML tag extensions, Netscape Navigator 3.0, 190, 192
resources, Web sites, 375-376
Web site, 375
JavaScript Authoring Guide (Web site), 376
JavaScript Index (Web site), 376
JavaWorld (Web site), 377
Java™ Developers Toolkit, The (Web site), 377
JPEG files (Joint Photographic Experts Group), 284-285
  compression, 286
  design tips, 289
JPEGView (helper application), 297

K-L

<KBD> tag, 92
keys, cryptography, 191
Koan Plug-in, 310

languages, browsers
  Multilingual Browser (Alis), 25
  Multilingual Mosaic, 24
<LAYOUTFRAME> extension (PowerBrowser), 217
  non-recognition, 231
<LAYOUTFRAMERESET> extension (PowerBrowser), 217
Learn to Write CGI Forms (Web site), 383
LEFTMARGIN attribute, <BODY> extension (Internet Explorer), 197
<LH> HTML 3 tag, 131

<li> HTML 3 tag , 131, 249
  attributes, 131
Lightning Strike (Plug-in), 305
LINK attribute, <BODY> HTML 3 tag, 127
<LINK> HTML 3 tag, 89-90
  attributes, 124
list header tag, HTML 3, 131
list item tags
  HTML 2, 90
  HTML 3, 131
listing tags
  HTML 2
    browser examples, 103-106
    choosing tags, 101
    definition lists, 100
    directory lists, 100
    examples, 102
    line items, 99
    ordered lists, 99
    unordered lists, 99
  HTML 3, 131
Live Update, Crescendo (Plug-in), 306
Live3D (Plug-in), 309
local links, defined, 325
Location bar, Netscape Navigator, 4
LOOP attribute, Internet Explorer HTML extensions
  <BGSOUND>, 196
  <IMG>, 198
  <MARQUEE>, 195
LView Pro (helper application), 297
Lycos, Inc. (Web site), 387
Lynda's Homegurrl Page (Web site), 378
Lynx, 25
  Web site, 372

M

Mac-ImageMap Home Page (Web site), 386

Macintosh
    conversion programs
        *BeyondPress
            (QuarkXPress),
            81-82*
        spreadsheets, 43-44
        word processing, 38-40
    editors
        Arachnid, 65
        FrontPage, 69
        *World Wide Web
            Weaver V1.1.1, 59*
    helper applications, list
        of, 297-300
    plug-ins, 302, 304-314
    WYSIWYG editors
        FrontPage, 69
        GNNPress, 77
        HotMetal Pro, 79
        Navigator Gold, 75
        PageMill, 71
        SiteMill, 73
Macromedia, Plug-ins, 307
macros
    defined, 35
    HTML editing tools
        spreadsheets, 42
        word processors, 35
Making Sense of Java (Web
    site), 376
<MAP> HTML 3 tag, 156
    non-recognition, 229
Map THIS! Home Page (Web
    site), 386
Mapmaker v1.1 Home Page
    (Web site), 386
MapMarker Home Page
    (Web site), 386
MapServe Home Page (Web
    site), 386
MARGINHEIGHT attribute,
    <FRAME> extension
    (Netscape Navigator), 171
MARGINWIDTH attribute,
    <FRAME> extension
    (Netscape Navigator), 171
<MARQUEE> extension
    (Internet Explorer), 195
    non-recognition, 230, 234

MAZ Sound Tools Page
    (Web site), 379
MBED Software (plug-in), 308
MDL Information Systems,
    Chemscape Chime
    (plug-in), 308
Media.splash, 351
MediaViewer (plug-in), 310
menu bars, Netscape
    Navigator, 4
<MENU> tag, 100
menus
    HotJava (Alpha 1.0), 10
    Internet Explorer 2.0, 6
    PowerBrowser 1.0, 8
    Spry Mosaic, 14
<META> HTML 3 tag,
    attributes, 125
Metasearch (Web site), 387
methods, JavaScript, 184
Microcom, Carbon Copy
    (plug-in), 308
Microsoft ActiveX
    Development Kit (Web
    site), 375
Microsoft Internet Control
    Pack, 317
Microsoft Internet Explorer
    3.0 HTML Support (Web
    site), 375
MIDI files (Musical
    Instrument Digital
    Interface), 290-292
MidiSource QuickHelp (Web
    site), 379
MIME types, table of,
    369-370
modems, bandwidth,
    351-352
Mosaic (NSCA Mosaic 2.0),
    12
    collaboration sessions, 12
    development of, 12
    HTML 2 tags, text
        formats, 97
    HTML 3 tags
        *embedded table tags,
        147*
        table tags, 152

HTML extensions, table,
    357-364
HTML tag attribute
    support, table, 357-364
interface, 12-13
tables, advanced design
    techniques, 270
Web site, 13, 371
see also Multilingual
    Mosaic; Spry Mosaic
movie players, table of
    MIME types, 370
MovieStar Plug-in, 306
Moving Worlds Design - A
    Proposal for VRML 2.0
    (Web site), 382
MPEG2PLY.EXE (helper
    application), 299
MPEGe Lib (Web site), 380
MPEGII, 294
MPLAYER.EXE (helper
    application), 298
MSGTICKER attribute,
    <NLC> extension
    (Internet Explorer), 214
MSG Tutorial: Much Ado
    about Perl (Web site), 384
Multilingual Browser (Alis),
    25
Multilingual Mosaic
    (Accent), 24
    Web site, 24, 372
Musical Instrument Digital
    Interface files (MIDI), 290,
    292
MVP Solutions, Talker 2.0
    (plug-in), 308

N

NAME attribute
    HTML 3 tags
        <MAP>, 156
        <META>, 125
    Netscape Navigator
        HTML extensions
            <CERTIFICATE>, 192
            <FRAME>, 171

<PARAM>, 189
<PAYORDER>, 192
National Center for
    Supercomputing
    Applications (NCSA), 12
Navigator, *see* Netscape
    Navigator 1.1; Netscape
    Navigator 2.0; Netscape
    Navigator 3.0
Navigator Gold (editor),
    74-75
    features, 366
NCompass, OLE Control
    Plug-in, 309
NCSA (National Center for
    Supercomputing
    Applications), 12
NCSA Mosaic 2.0, *see* Mosaic
Netcom, Web site, 372
NetManage Web Surfer (Web
    site), 372
Netscape Navigator 1.1
    HTML extensions, table,
        357-364
    HTML tag attribute
        support, table, 357-364
Netscape Navigator 2.0, 4
    frames, 4
    HTML 2 tags
        form tags, 116
        listing tags, 104
        text formats, 95
    HTML 3 attributes to
        HTML 2 tags, 135
    HTML 3 tags
        embedded table tags,
            146
        example, 159
        non-recognized tags,
            244
        table tags, 152
    HTML extensions,
        164-165, 190-193
        <!..comment>, 179
        <APPLET>, 189
        <BASEFONT>, 165
        <BODY>, 166
        <BLINK>, 165

<CERTIFICATE>, 192
<EMBED>, 168-169
<FRAME>, 171
frame design considera-
    tions, 172-174
frames, 175-178
<FRAMESET>, 170
<IMG>, 165
Java, 189
JavaScript, 179-183
JavaScript HTML
    examples, 184-188
<NOBR>, 165
<NOEMBED>,
    168-169
<NOFRAMES>, 170
non-recognized
    extensions, 229,
    234-235
<PARAM>, 189
partially recognized
    tags, 249
<PAYORDER>, 192
<SCRIPT>, 179-182
table of extensions,
    357-364
<TITLE>, 166
<WBR>, 165
    HTML tag attribute
        support, table, 357-364
    interface, 4-5
    logo, 4
    partially recognized
        HTML tags, 258
    plug-ins
        Live3D, 309
        Web page, 301
    public key cryptography,
        191
    tables, advanced design
        techniques, 269
    Web site, 5, 371
Netscape Navigator 3.0
    HTML extensions, table,
        357-364
    HTML tag attribute
        support, table, 357-364
Netscape Technical Note
    10117 (Web site), 378

<NLO> extension
    (PowerBrowser), 214-215
    non-recognition, 229
NOBORDER attribute,
    <NLC> extension
    (Internet Explorer), 215
<NOBR> extension
    (Netscape Navigator), 165
NOCONTROLS attribute,
    <NLC> extension
    (Internet Explorer), 215
<NOEMBED> extension
    (Netscape Navigator),
    168-169
<NOFRAMES> extension
    (Netscape Navigator), 170
NOHREF attribute, <AREA>
    HTML 3 tag, 156
non-recognized HTML tags,
    238, 248
    browser-specific
        extensions, 229
        examples, 230-233
        HotJava, 237
        Internet Explorer, 236
        Netscape Navigator,
            234-235
    defined, 228
    examples, 240-243
    HTML 3 tags
        America Online
            browser, 247
        Internet Explorer, 245
        Netscape Navigator,
            244
        PowerBrowser, 246
    special characters, 240
    table tags, 239
NORESIZE attribute,
    <FRAME> extension
    (Netscape Navigator), 171
NOSHADE attribute, <HR>
    HTML 3 tag, 129
<NPUT> tag, 111
    TYPE definitions, 112
NSCA Common Gateway
    Interface Specification
    (Web site), 385

O

OAK Repository - SimTel Windows Mirror Index (Web site), 379
Object Oriented Graphics Library, *see* OOGL files
<OBJECT> extension
  HTML 3, non-recognition, 229
  Internet Explorer, 206
  Netscape Navigator, non-recognition, 229
objects, JavaScript, 183
ODBC (Open Database Connectivity), 47
<OL> HTML 3 tag, 99, 131, 249
  attributes, 131
OLE Control Plug-in, 309
OOGL files (Object Oriented Graphics Library), 296
Open Database Connectivity (ODBC), 47
OpenDoc components, 20
opening tags, HTML 2, 93
OpenScape (plug-in), 302
Opera browser, 27
<OPTION> tag, 114
Oracle Basic, HTML
  examples, 223-224
  extensions, 222
Oracle PowerBrowser 1.0, *see* PowerBrowser 1.0
Oracle WebServer 2.0 (database conversion program), 50
ordered lists
  HTML 2 tag, 99
  HTML 3 tag, 131
Overview of CGI (Web site), 385

P

</P> HTML 3 tag, 129
<P> extension, 107
  attributes, 251
<P> HTML 3 tag, 249

PageMaker, conversion programs, 84
PageMill (editor), 70-71
  features, 366
palettes, color palettes, 281-282
<PARAM> extension (Netscape Navigator), 189
partially recognized HTML tags, 262
  America Online browser, 261
  attributes, 249-252
  defined, 228, 249
  examples, 254-257
  file types, 253
  Internet Explorer, 259
  Netscape Navigator, 258
  PowerBrowser, 260
<PAYORDER> extension (Netscape Navigator 3.0), 192
PC Magazine InternetUser - Plug-In Central (Web site), 373
PCN browser, 22-23, 371
Perl, Web site, 384
Perl Reference Materials (Web site), 385
perlWWW (Web site), 384
PHOTOBUBBLE attribute, <NLC> extension (Internet Explorer), 214
PhotoBubbles, 220
PhotoSphere Viewer (helper application), 299
PKZip (helper application), 300
<PLAINTEXT> tag, 92
platform incompatibilities, 263
Play3D (plug-in), 308
plug-ins
  Acrobat Amber Reader, 302
  ASAP WebShow, 311
  Astound Web Player, 304
  Carbon Copy, 308
  Chemscape Chime, 308

CMX Viewer, 303
CoolFusion, 307
Crescendo, 306
defined, 301
DWG/DXF Plug-in, 310
EarthTime, 312
Emblaze, 304
Envoy, 313
FIGleaf Inline, 303
Formula One/Net, 313
Fractal Viewer, 307
FutureSplash, 304
HistoryTree, 310
ichat, 305
InterCAP InLine, 306
Koan Plug-in, 310
Lightning Strike, 305
Live3D, 309
mBED Software, 308
media.splash, 351
MediaViewer, 310
MovieStar Plug-in, 306
Netscape Navigator
  Plug-ins, Web page, 301
OLE Control Plug-in, 309
OpenScape, 302
Play3D, 308
PreVU, 306
QuickTime, 302
RealAudio, 309
Shockwave for Director Plug-in, 307
Shockwave for Freehand, 307
Sizzler, 312
Talker 2.0, 308
Timbuktu Plug-in, 304
tips, 315
ToolVox for the Web, 314
VDOLive, 313
ViewDirector Plug-in, 312
ViewMovie, 304
VRealm, 305
VR Scout, 303
Wavelet Image Plug-in, 312
Wayfarer Plug-in, 314
Web site, 373

WIRL Interactive 3D
Plug-in, 314
Word Viewer Plug-in, 305
see also helper
applications
PM2html (PageMaker
conversion program), 84
PNG (Portable Network
Graphics) Home Page,
Web site, 379
PointCase PCN browser, 22
interface, 22-23
Web site, 23, 371
PowerBrowser (Oracle
PowerBrowser 1.0), 8
Bookmark window, 8
display, resizing, 9
History window, 8
HTML 2 tags
form tags, 119
text formats, 96
HTML 3 tags
non-recognized tags,
246
table tags, 152
HTML extensions, 213,
225
examples, 218-221
<LAYOUTFRAME>,
217, 231
<LAYOUT-
FRAMERESET>,
217
Network Loadable
Objects, 214-215
<NLO>, 214-215
non-recognized
extensions, 229
Oracle Basic, 222-224
partially recognized
tags, 249
table of extensions,
357-364
HTML tag attribute
support, table, 357-364
interface, 8
menus, 8
partially recognized
HTML tags, 260

plug-in support, 301
Web site, 9, 371
<PRE> tag, 91
Presentation Mode, Mosaic,
12
PreVU (plug-in), 306
private key cryptography,
191
Prodigy (2.0d)
browsers, 18
HTML text formatting
tags, 98
interface, 18-19
toolbar, 18
Web site, 19, 371
HTML extensions, table,
357-364
HTML tag attribute
support, table, 357-364
programming languages
Java, 316
Visual Basic, 317
programs, FTP, 328-329
Fetch 3.0, 330-331
Snatcher, 334-335
WS_FTP, 332-333
Progressive Networks,
RealAudio (plug-in), 309
properties, JavaScript, 183
proprietary file formats, 285
Providers of Commercial
Internet Access (POCIA),
Web site, 383
public key cryptography, 191

Q

QT file format (QuickTime),
294
QuarkXPress, conversion
Xtensions
BeyondPress, 29, 80-82
Collect HTML, 83
HexWeb XT, 83
QuarkImmedia, 351
QuickTime (plug-in), 302
QuickTime VR (helper
application), 299
Web site, 381

quotation marks, smart
quotes, 32
HTML tag, 32

R

RadMedia, MediaViewer
(plug-in), 310
RealAudio (plug-in), 309
RealAudio Player (helper
application), 298
recognition conflicts, *see*
non-recognized HTML
tags; partially recognized
HTML tags
red support level, 3
references
absolute
defined, 110
table design, 140
relative
defined, 110
table design, 140
registered trademark symbol
(™), HTML tag, 32
REL attribute, <LINK>
HTML 3 tag, 124
relative links, defined,
325-326
relative references
defined, 110
table design, 140
resources
audio, 379-380
browsers, 371-373
graphics, 378-379
HTML, 373-375
image maps, 386
Java, 376-377
JavaScript, 375-376
search engines, 387-388
server scripts, 383-385
service providers, 382-383
VRML (Virtual Reality
Modeling Language),
381-382
Return statement, JavaScript,
181

RGB color method, 278-280
ROWS attribute,
    <FRAMESET> extension
    (Netscape Navigator), 170
ROWSPAN attribute, HTML
    3 tags, 142
Royal Frazier's
    INTERconNnEcTions
    (Web site), 378

S

<S> tag, 91
<SAMP> tag, 92
sampling rate, 290
<SCRIPT> extension
    Internet Explorer 3.0, 207
        non-recognition, 229
    Netscape Navigator, 179
        event handlers, 180
        functions, 182
        non-recognition, 229
        statements, 181-182
    PowerBrowser, non-
        recognition, 229
scripts, see CGI scripts
Scripts for WWW (Web site),
    384
SCROLLAMOUNT attribute,
    <MARQUEE> extension
    (Internet Explorer), 195
SCROLLDELAY attribute,
    <MARQUEE> extension
    (Internet Explorer), 195
SCROLLING attribute,
    <FRAME> extension
    (Netscape Navigator), 171
Search.com (Web site), 387
search engines, Web sites,
    387-388
Secure WebExplorer, 27
security, service providers,
    323
<SELECT> tag, 113
servers
    CGI scripts
        defined, 336-338
        determining site
            audience, 345

diagram of scripting
    process, 337
directories, 338
form scripts, 342-344
image map scripts,
    339-341
resources, 383-385
commercial service
    providers
    backup systems, 322
    connection speed, 323
    directory setup, 323
    number of Web sites,
        322
    security, 323
    selecting, 324
    software, 323
    technical support, 321
    traffic, 322
domain names, register-
    ing, 320, 346
Web sites
    absolute links, 325
    FTP software, 328-335
    hit statistics, 345
    local links, 325
    mirroring, 324
    organization issues,
        325-327
    putting online, 328
    relative links, 325-326
service providers (Internet
    Service Providers)
backup systems, 322
connection speed, 323
directory setup, 323
domain names, register-
    ing, 320
mirroring Web sites, 324
number of Web sites, 322
resources, Web sites,
    382-383
script options 322
security, 323
selecting, 324
software, 323
technical support, 321
traffic, 322

SGML (Standard
    Generalized Markup
    Language), 24
SHAPE attribute
    Internet Explorer HTML
    extensions, <AREA>,
        196
    HTML 3 tags, <AREA>,
        156
Shareware.com (Web site),
    388
Shockwave for Director
    Plug-in, 307
Shockwave for Freehand
    (plug-in), 307
SHOWBORDER attribute,
    <NLC> extension
    (Internet Explorer), 215
SiteMill (editor), 72-73
    features, 366
SIZE attribute, HTML 3 tags
    <FONT>, 155
    <HR>, 129
Sizzler (plug-in), 312
<SMALL> HTML 3 tag, 155
smart quotes, HTML tag, 32
SmartBrowser, HistoryTree
    (plug-in), 310
Snatcher (FTP software),
    334-335
SoftSource, DWG/DXF Plug-
    in, 310
Software Publishing, ASAP
    WebShow (plug-in), 311
SOUND attribute, <NLC>
    extension (Internet
    Explorer), 214
sound depth, 290
spacing tags, HTML 2, 107
Sparkle (helper application),
    298
special characters
    HTML tags, 32
        replacing with ASCII
            equivalent, 34
    table of, 367-368
    word processors, HTML
        editing tools, 32-34

spell check (word
processors), HTML
editing tools, 35
split-screens, *see* frames
spreadsheets, editing tools
converters, 41-44
application design, 42
macros, 42
Spry Mosaic (CompuServe
Spry Mosaic .04.10.9.20),
14
HTML 2 tags, text
formats, 98
HTML extensions, table,
357-364
HTML tag attribute
support, table, 357-364
interface, 14-15
Spryhoo page, 14
Web site, 15, 371
see also Mosaic
SRC attribute
Internet Explorer HTML
extensions
<BGSOUND>, 196
<NLC>, 215
Netscape Navigator
HTML extensions,
<FRAME>, 171
SSEYO, Koan Plug-in, 310
Standard Generalized
Markup Language
(SGML), 24
Starfish Software, EarthTime
(plug-in), 312
START attribute
Internet Explorer HTML
extensions, <IMG>,
198
HTML 3 tags, <OL>, 131
statements, JavaScript,
181-182
STOCKTIK attribute, <NLC>
extension (Internet
Explorer), 214
<STRIKE> tag, 92
strikethrough, HTML 2 tag,
91
<STRONG> tag, 91

Stuffit (helper application),
300
style sheets, cross-platform
standards, 348
<SUB> HTML 3 tag, 155
Submit It! (Web site), 388
Summus, Wavelet Image
Plug-in, 312
<SUP> HTML 3 tag, 155
Switchboard (Web site), 387
Symantec Java Central (Web
site), 377

T

<TABLE> extension (Internet
Explorer), attributes, 199
TABLE> HTML 3 tag, 141,
249
attributes, 141
table tags
advanced design
techniques, 264-270
HTML 3 tags, 140-142
*business letter
examples, 148-153*
*design considerations,
154*
designing tables, 140
*embedded tables
browser examples,
145-147*
*HTML examples,
143-144*
non-recognition, 239
tags
browsers, reading, 34
closing tags, 88
frames, advanced design
techniques, 271-275
hardware
incompatibilities, 263
HTML 2
<!..comment>, 88
<A>, 109
<ADDRESS>, 92
anchor tag, 109
<B>, 91
<BASE>, 89-90

<BLOCKQUOTE>, 92
<BODY>, 88
body tags, 91-92
*
, 107*
*browser-support (table),
357-364*
<CITE>, 92
<CODE>, 92
closing tags, 93
<DD>, 100
defined, 87
*design considerations,
120-121*
<DIR>, 100
<DIRECTORY>, 100
<DL>, 100
document elements, 88
<DT>, 100
<EM>, 91
<FORM>, 111
form tags, 111-114
*form tags examples,
115-119*
<H1, H6>, 91
<HEAD>, 88-90
head elements, 89-90
horizontal rule tag, 110
<HR>, 110
<HTML>, 88
*HTML 3 attributes,
132-134*
<I>, 91
image tag, 108
<IMG>, 108
<INPUT>, 111-112
*integrating with
HTML 3 tags, 157*
<ISINDEX>, 89-90
<KBD>, 92
<li>, 99
<LINK>, 89-90
listing tags, 99-101
*listing tags examples,
102-106*
<MENU>, 100
<OL>, 99
opening tags, 93
<OPTION>, 114
<P>, 107

<PLAINTEXT>, 92
<PRE>, 91
<S>, 91
<SAMP>, 92
<SELECT>, 113
spacing tags, 107
<STRIKE>, 92
<STRONG>, 91
text formats, 91-93
text formatting tags
    example, 94-98
<TEXTAREA>, 113
<TITLE>, 89-90
<TT>, 92
<U>, 91
<UL>, 99
<VAR>, 92
<XMP>, 92
HTML 3
<AREA>, 156
<BIG>, 155
<BODY>, 127-128
body elements, 127,
    129-131
<CAPTION>, 141
<CENTER>, 156
<DIV>, 156
<FONT>, 155
head elements, 124-126
<HR>, 129
HTML 2 browser
    examples, 133-138
HTML browser
examples, 158-161
image tag, 130
<IMG>, 130
integrating in HTML 2
    browsers, 139, 157
<LH>, 131
<li>, 131
<LINK>, 124
listing tags, 131
<MAP>, 156
<META>, 125
non-recognition,
    238-247
<OL>, 131
</P>, 129
<SMALL>, 155

<SUB>, 155
<SUP>, 155
<TABLE>, 141
table tags, 140-154
<TD>, 142
text formats, 155
<TH>, 142
<TR>, 141
<UL>, 131
version-specific (table),
    357-364
Internet Explorer 2.0
extensions, 194-195,
212
<AREA> tag
    attributes, 196
<BGSOUND>, 196
<BODY> tag
    attributes, 197
<FONT>tag attributes,
    197
<HR> tag attributes,
    196
HTML examples,
    200-205
<IMG> tag attributes,
    198
<MARQUEE>, 195
<TABLE> tag
    attributes, 199
Internet Explorer 3
extensions, 206-207
<FRAME>, 206
HTML examples,
    208-211
<OBJECT>, 206
<SCRIPT>, 207
Netscape Navigator 2.0
extensions, 164-165,
193
<!..comment>, 179
<APPLET>, 189
<BASEFONT>, 165
<BLINK>, 165
<BODY>, 166
<EMBED>, 168-169
<FRAME>, 171

frame design
    considerations,
    172-174
frames, 175-178
<FRAMESET>, 170
<IMG>, 165
Java, 189
JavaScript, 179-183
JavaScript HTML
    examples, 184-188
<NOBR>, 165
<NOEMBED>,
    168-169
<NOFRAMES>, 170
<PARAM>, 189
<SCRIPT>, 179-182
<TITLE>, 166
<WBR>, 165
Netscape Navigator 3.0
extensions, 190
<CERTIFICATE>, 192
<PAYORDER>, 192
public key
    cryptography, 191
Oracle Basic extensions,
222
HTML examples,
    223-224
non-recognition
    browser-specific
    extensions, 229-237
    defined, 228, 248
partial-recognition
    attributes, 249-252
    defined, 228-249, 262
    examples, 254-261
    file types, 253
platform
    incompatibilities, 263
PowerBrowser extensions,
213, 225
HTML examples,
    218-221
<LAYOUTFRAME>,
    217
<LAYOUT-
    FRAMERESET>,
    217

Network Loadable Objects, 214-215
<NLO>, 214-215
special characters, 32
  replacing with ASCII equivalent, 34
tables, advanced design techniques, 264-270
Talker 2.0 (plug-in), 308
TARGET attribute, <FRAME> extension (Netscape Navigator), 174
<TD> HTML 3 tag, 142, 249
  attributes, 142
template files, CGI form scripts, 344
templates (word processors), HTML editing tools, 35
testing Web pages for multiple browsers, 28
text editors, *see* editors
TEXT attribute,
  Internet Explorer HTML extensions, <NLC>, 215
  HTML 3 tags, <BODY>, 127
text files, table of MIME types, 369
text formatting tags
  HTML 2, 91-92
    browser examples, 95-98
    choosing, 93
    example, 94
  HTML 3, 155
<TH> HTML 3 tag, 142
Thesaurus (word processors), HTML editing tools, 35
Timbuktu Plug-in, 304
<TITLE> extension (Netscape Navigator), 89-90, 166
TMS, ViewDirector Plug-in, 312
toolbars
  Internet Explorer 2.0, 6
  Netscape, 4

PowerBrowser 1.0, 8
Prodigy 2.0d, 18
Spry Mosaic (CompuServe Spry Mosaic), 14
ToolVox for the Web (plug-in), 314
TOPMARGIN attribute, <BODY> extension (Internet Explorer), 197
Totally Hip Software, Sizzler (plug-in), 312
<TR> HTML 3 tag, 141, 249
  attributes, 141
Trail Map: The Java Language Tutorial (Web site), 377
<TT> tag, 92
Tumbleweed Software, Envoy (plug-in), 313
Tutorial: Scripts, Forms, and Server-Side Things (Web site), 384
TYPE attribute
  Internet Explorer HTML extensions, <NLC> extension, 214
  HTML 3 tags, 131

U

<U> tag, 91
U.S. Internet Service Providers List (Web site), 383
Ubique, Web site, 372
Ubique Sesame, *see* Virtual Places
UF/NA Perl Archive (Web site), 385
<UL> HTML 3 tag, 99, 131, 249
  attributes, 131
underlining text, HTML 2 tag, 91
UNITS attribute, <IMG> HTML 3 tag, 130

Unix
  conversion programs, Cyberleaf, 38
  helper applications, list of, 298-300
  plug-ins, 309-310
unordered lists
  HTML 2 tag, 99
  HTML 3 tags, 131
Use of CGI Forms and Scripts Tutorial (Web site), 384
USEMAP attribute, <IMG> HTML 3 tag, 130
utilities, helper applications, 300

V

VALIGN attribute, HTML 3 tags
  <TD>, 142
  <TH>, 142
  <TR>, 141
VALUE attribute
  Netscape Navigator HTML extensions, 189
  HTML 3 tags, <li>, 131
Var statement, JavaScript, 181
<VAR> tag, 92
VBA (Visual Basic for Applications), 317
VBScript, defined, 317
VBScript: Working Description (Web site), 375
VDOLive (plug-in), 313
VDOnet, VDOLive (plug-in), 313
video files, 294-295
  helper applications, 298
ViewDirector Plug-in (plug-in), 312
ViewMovie (plug-in), 304
Virtual Places (Ubique Sesame), 26

Virtual Reality Modeling
 Language, *see* VRML
Virtual Reality Modeling
 Language (VRML) Forum
 (Web site), 381
virtual worlds, helper
 applications, 299
Visual Basic, 317
Visual Basic for Applications
 (VBA), 317
Visual Components, Formula
 One/Net (plug-in), 313
VLINK attribute, <BODY>
 HTML 3 tag, 127
Voxware, ToolVox for the
 Web (plug-in), 314
VRealm (plug-in), 305
VREAM, WIRL Interactive
 3D Plug-in, 314
VRML (Virtual Reality
 Modeling Language), 296
 files, 296
 resources, Web sites,
  381-382
VRML Browser Links (Web
 site), 381
VRML Library Archive:
 "History of VRML" (Web
 site), 382
VRML World HotLinks
 Forum (Web site), 381
VRML Repository (Web site),
 382
VR Scout (plug-in), 303
VSPACE attribute
 HTML 3 tags ,<IMG>, 130
 Internet Explorer HTML
  extensions
   <MARQUEE>, 195
   <NLC>, 215

W

W3C (World Wide Web
 Consortium), 87
 HTML standards, 348-349
  design strategies,
   350-351

W3C Tech Reports (Web
 site), 374
Watch Videos (Web site), 381
Waveform File Formats (Web
 site), 379
Wavelet Image Plug-in, 312
Wayfarer Plug-in, 314
<WBR> extension (Netscape
 Navigator), 165
Web browsers, *see* browsers
Web Author (conversion
 program), 40
Web Developer's Virtual
 Library: Providers (Web
 site), 383
Web Hotspots (Web site), 386
Web pages
 browsers, levels of
  support, 3
 designing for multiple
  browsers, 3
Web Publisher (conversion
 program), 39
Web sites
 absolute links, defined,
  325
 browsers, *see* browsers
 conversion programs
  2 HTML, 40
  4W Publisher, 52
  Adobe, 84
  ANT-HTML, 39
  BeyondPress, 82
  Cold Fusion, 51
  Collect HTML
   (QuarkXPress), 83
  dbWeb, 49
  Excel to HTML
   conversion utility,
   44
  Excel-to-HTML
   converter macro, 43
  HexWeb XT
   (QuarkXPress), 83
  HTMakeL Database
   Merge, 52
  HTML Transit, 37
  Illustra, 48

  Oracle WebServer 2.0,
   50
  PM2html, 84
  Web Author, 40
  Web Publisher, 39
  WebMaker 2, 85
  Websucker, 84
  WebWorks Light, 85
  WordPerfect Internet
   Assistant, 40
  XL2HTML.XLS, 43
 editors
  Aardvark Pro V2.0.4,
   61
  Arachnid, 65
  BBEdit, 63
  HTML Assistant Pro 2,
   55-57
  HTMLed Pro, 64
  Interleaf, 38
  Webber, 66
  WebEdit, 66
  World Wide Web
   Weaver V1.1.1, 59
 FTP software, 328-329
  Fetch 3.0, 330-331
  Snatcher, 334-335
  WS_FTP, 332-333
 hit statistics, 345
 HotJava, 11
 local links, 325
 mirroring sites, 324
 moving , 320
 organization issues
  cross-platform issues,
   327
  relative links, 325-326
 putting online, 328
 relative links, 325-326
 resources
  audio, 379-380
  browsers, 371-373
  graphics, 378-379
  HTML, 373-375
  image maps, 386
  Java, 376-377
  JavaScript, 375-376
  search engines, 387-388
  server scripts, 383-385

*service providers,
382-383*
*VRML (Virtual
Reality Modeling
Language), 381-382*
WYSIWYG editors
FrontPage, 69
GNNPress, 77
HotMetal Pro, 79
Navigator Gold, 75
PageMill, 71
SiteMill, 73
WebServer 2.0 conversion
program, 50
Webber (editor), 66
WebEdit (editor), 66
WebExplorer, 27
WebImage Information (Web
site), 379
WebMaker 2 (FrameMaker
conversion program), 85
WebMap for the Macintosh
(Web site), 386
WebPromote™ (Web site),
388
WebSpace Navigator (helper
application), 299
WebSpace™ Availability
(Web site), 381
Websucker (PageMaker
conversion program), 84
WebWorks Light
(FrameMaker conversion
program), 85
While statement, JavaScript,
182
White Paper: Verifying Form
Input with JavaScript
(Web site), 376
Who Is (Web site), 387
WIDTH attribute
Netscape Navigator
HTML extensions,
<APPLET>, 189
Internet Explorer HTML
extensions
<MARQUEE>, 195
<NLC>, 215

HTML 3 tags
<HR>, 129
<IMG>, 130
<TABLE>, 141
<TD>, 142
<TH>, 142
Windows
conversion programs
spreadsheets, 43-44
word processing, 38-40
editors
*Aardvark Pro V2.0.4,
61*
Arachnid, 65
BBEdit, 63
HotDog V2.0, 57
HTML Easy! Pro, 66
*HTML Assistant Pro 2,
55*
HTMLed Pro, 64
Webber, 66
WebEdit, 66
plug-ins, 309, 313
WYSIWYG editors
Arachnid, 69-71
GNNPress, 77
HotMetal Pro, 79
Navigator Gold, 75
Windows 3.1
helper applications, list
of, 297-300
plug-ins, 302-307, 310-314
Windows 95
helper applications, list
of, 297-300
plug-ins, 302-314
Windows NT
conversion programs,
databases, 51-52
helper applications, list
of, 299-300
plug-ins, 302-306, 309-314
WinZip (helper application),
300
WIRL Interactive 3D Plug-in
(plug-in), 314
Wisconsin Web Resources:
Internet Services (Web
site), 383

With statement, JavaScript,
182
Word, conversion programs,
38
word processors, editing
tools, 32
2 HTML, 40
ANT_HTML, 39
converters, 37-40
Cyberleaf, 38
*HTML Transit
program, 37*
*Internet Assistant for
Microsoft Word, 38*
macros, 35
mail merge feature, 36
*search and replace
feature, 35*
*special characters,
32-34*
spell check, 35
templates, 35
thesaurus, 35
Web Author, 40
Web Publisher, 39
*WordPerfect Internet
Publisher, 40*
Word Viewer Plug-in
(plug-in), 305
WordPerfect Internet
Publisher (conversion
program), 40
worksheets, *see* spreadsheets
World Wide Web
Consortium (W3C), 87
HTML standards, 348-349
*design strategies,
350-351*
World Wide Web Servers
(Web site), 383
World Wide Web Weaver
V1.1.1 (editor), 58-59
features, 365
Wow! (CompuServe dial-up
service), 14
WS_FTP (FTP software),
332-333
WWW Browser Plug-Ins!
(Web site), 373

WYSIWYG, HTML editors,
    67
    FrontPage, 68-69
        features, 366
    GNNPress, 76-77
    HotMetal Pro, 78-79
        features, 366
    Navigator Gold, 74-75
        features, 366
    PageMill, 70-71
        features, 366
    SiteMill, 72-73
        features, 366
    table of, 366

X-Y-Z

XL2HTML.XLS (spreadsheet
    conversion program), 43
<XMP> tag, 92

Yahoo (Web site), 387
Yahoo - Browser Usage
    Statistics (Web site), 372
Yahoo - Computers and
    Internet:Multimedia:
    Video:Collections (Web
    site), 380
Yahoo: Web Presence
    Providers (Web site), 382
Yale HTML Style Manual
    (Web site), 374
yellow support level, 3

SOFTWARE LICENSE AGREEMENT

IMPORTANT: IN ORDER TO DOWNLOAD THIS SOFTWARE, YOU MUST FIRST READ THE FOLLOWING TERMS AND CONDITIONS. BY CLICKING ON THE "ACCEPT" BUTTON AT THE END OF THIS DOCUMENT, YOU ARE EXPRESSLY AGREEING TO BE BOUND BY ALL OF THE TERMS AND CONDITIONS OF THIS AGREEMENT. IF YOU DO NOT AGREE TO ALL OF THE TERMS AND CONDITIONS OF THIS AGREEMENT, YOU SHOULD CLICK ON THE "DO NOT ACCEPT" BUTTON AND NOT USE THIS SOFTWARE.

1. **LICENSE GRANT; COPYING.** Harlequin Limited and Harlequin Incorporated ("Harlequin") grant to you ("Licensee"), a non-exclusive, non-transferable license to use one (1) copy of Harlequin's WebMaker™ software in object code form, including documentation (individually and collectively, "the Software"), only for Licensee's internal use. Upon payment of the appropriate license fees to Harlequin and receipt of additional registration numbers from Harlequin, Licensee may use additional copies of the Software, provided that the maximum number of persons using the Software at any point in time does not exceed the number of licenses for which the Licensee has paid. This license does not permit the distribution of the Software, or any part or copy thereof, to any third party. Licensee furthermore agrees not to disclose the location of the file transfer protocol (ftp) site from which the Software is downloaded to any third party. Except as permitted in this Agreement, Licensee shall not copy or permit any party to copy the Software, except to make one (1) single copy of the Software for archival or back-up purposes. If Licensee has paid Harlequin for more than one (1) license, then Licensee may make additional copies of the Software, up to the number of licenses for which Licensee has paid. Licensee shall not modify, reverse compile, disassemble, or otherwise reverse engineer the Software, except that in the European Community, Licensee may reverse engineer only for interoperability purposes and then only if all conditions of Article 6 of Council Directive 91/250/EEC are met.

2. **OWNERSHIP.** This is a license agreement. Consequently, all right, title to, ownership of, and all patent trademark, trade secret, copyright and all other intellectual property or proprietary rights to the Software, or any of its parts, do not transfer to Licensee, but shall remain vested solely in Harlequin or its licenser. Licensee shall reproduce all copyright notices and other proprietary notices of Harlequin and the third party from which Harlequin has acquired license rights, as applicable, on all copies of the software. Licensee shall not remove any product identification, copyright notices, or other legends set forth on the Software. Licensee shall have no right in Harlequin's or its third-party licensers' trademarks in connection with the Software, or with its promotion or publication, without the prior written approval of Harlequin.

3. **CONFIDENTIALITY.** Licensee acknowledges that the Software is owned by Harlequin or its licensers and is protected by copyright law, trade secret law, and as otherwise set forth in this Agreement. Licensee acknowledges and agrees that the Software contains the proprietary information of Harlequin, its subsidiaries, affiliates, and their licensers, and is provided solely under the terms of this Agreement. Licensee agrees not to disclose or make available the Software, or any portion or copy thereof, to any third party without Harlequin's prior written consent. Licensee shall take action by instruction to, or agreement with, its employees who may access the Software to protect the confidentiality of the Software. Licensee shall keep the Software and all related materials secure and shall prevent the unauthorized access, copying, or use thereof.

4. **EXCLUSION OF WARRANTY. LICENSEE ACKNOWLEDGES AND AGREES THAT THE SOFTWARE IS PROVIDED "AS-IS." HARLEQUIN MAKES NO REPRESENTATIONS OR WARRANTIES REGARDING THE SOFTWARE, EXPRESS OR IMPLIED, INCLUDING, BUT NOT LIMITED TO, THE IMPLIED WARRANTIES OF MERCHANTIBILITY AND FITNESS FOR A PARTICULAR PURPOSE.**

5. **LIMITATION OF LIABILITY. IN NO EVENT SHALL HARLEQUIN OR ITS LICENSERS BE LIABLE FOR ANY SPECIAL, INDIRECT, INCIDENTAL, CONSEQUENTIAL OR EXEMPLARY DAMAGES, INCLUDING, BUT NOT LIMITED TO, LOSS OF REVENUES OR LOSS OF PROFITS, HOWEVER CAUSED AND ON ANY THEORY OF LIABILITY ARISING IN ANY WAY FROM THIS AGREEMENT, EVEN IF HARLEQUIN HAS BEEN ADVISED OF THE POSSIBILITY OF SUCH DAMAGES.**

6. **U.S. GOVERNMENT SUPPLY.** The Software is subject to the following Restricted Rights Legend; "Use, duplication, or disclosure by the United States Government is subject to restrictions as set forth in (i) FAR 52.227-14 Alt III, (ii) FAR 52.227-19, (iii) DFAR 252.227-7013(c)(1)(ii), or (iv) the accompanying license Agreement, as applicable. For purposes of the FAR, the Software shall be deemed to be "unpublished" and licensed with disclosure prohibitions, rights reserved under the copyright laws of the United States. Harlequin Incorporated, One Cambridge Center, Cambridge, Massachusetts, 02142, USA."

7. **EXPORT CONTROL.** Licensee may not download or otherwise export or re-export the Software or any underlying information or technology except in full compliance with all United States and other applicable laws and regulations. In particular, but without limitation, none of the Software or underlying information or technology may be downloaded or otherwise exported or re-exported (i) into (or to a national resident of) Cuba, Haiti, Iraq, Libya, Yugoslavia, North Korea, Iran, Syria, or (ii) to anyone on the U.S. Treasury Department's list of Specially Designated Nationals or the U.S. Commerce Department's Table of Deny Orders. By downloading the Software, Licensee agrees to the foregoing and represents and warrants that Licensee is not located in, under control of, or a national or resident of any such country or on any such list.

8. **TERMINATION.** Harlequin may terminate this Agreement at any time in the event that Licensee fails to observe any material term or condition of this Agreement. Upon termination of this Agreement, Licensee shall immediately cease using the Software and shall (i) delete all Software, and other data made available or supplied to Licensee by Harlequin, residing in electronic form; (ii) destroy all tangible copies of the Software; and (iii) certify in writing, upon request, that it has taken such action.

9. **NO ASSIGNMENT**. Licensee shall not sell, assign, sublicense, or otherwise transfer any of its rights or obligations hereunder without Harlequin's prior written consent and any attempted sale, assignment, sublicense, or other transfer shall be void.

10. **GOVERNING LAW.** This Agreement shall be governed by and construed in accordance with the laws of the Commonwealth of Massachusetts, excluding any rule or principle of the conflict of laws that might otherwise refer the interpretation or construction of this Agreement to the law of any other jurisdiction.

11. **ENTIRE AGREEMENT.** The provisions of this Agreement shall constitute the entire agreement between the parties and shall supersede all prior agreements, oral or written, and all other communications between the parties relating to the subject matter hereof. The Agreement may be modified only by a writing signed by an authorized representative of Harlequin.

12. **SURVIVAL.** Sections 2, 3, 4, 5, and 8 of this Agreement shall survive termination of this Agreement.

Check Us Out Online!

New Riders has emerged as a premier publisher of computer books for the professional computer user. Focusing on CAD/graphics/multimedia, communications/internetworking, and networking/operating systems, New Riders continues to provide expert advice on high-end topics and software.

Check out the online version of *New Riders' Official World Wide Yellow Pages, 1996 Edition* for the most engaging, entertaining, and informative sites on the Web! You can even add your own site!

*Hind Fire
Copyright 1995 - John Brooks*

Brave our site for the finest collection of CAD and 3D imagery produced today. Professionals from all over the world contribute to our gallery, which features new designs every month.

From Novell to Microsoft, New Riders publishes the training guides you need to attain your certification. Visit our site and try your hand at the CNE Endeavor, a test engine created by VFX Technologies, Inc. that enables you to measure what you know—and what you don't!

New Riders

http://www.mcp.com/newriders